THE BYZANTINE LEGACY IN EASTERN EUROPE

Edited by
LOWELL CLUCAS

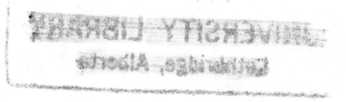

EAST EUROPEAN MONOGRAPHS, BOULDER
DISTRIBUTED BY COLUMBIA UNIVERSITY PRESS, NEW YORK

1988

EAST EUROPEAN MONOGRAPHS, NO. CCXXX

87-80513

CONTENTS

PREFACE

Our subject, The Byzantine Legacy in Eastern Europe, is a subject of perennial interest which has intrigued scholars, politicians and nationalists alike. Despite the inherent importance of the theme scholars, in the past, have had certain difficulties treating it and primarily for two reasons. The first such obstacle arose from the unspoken assumption of the older historiographical tradition of conceptualization always within a narrow political-diplomatic-military framework. Thus, the Byzantine Empire ended on May 29, 1453, when the Ottomans took Constantinople, slew the last emperor, and slew or captured the inhabitants of the imperial city leaving it an uninhabited shambles for a period of time. The Byzantine dynasty, the aristocracies, and the government disappeared. Within this narrower conceptualization of history the most important constituent elements of the history of a people and a civilization had thus vanished. Consequently there was little left worthy of study. Medieval Greek civilization had suffered a complete political truncation, had lost its state form, and so had no political history. In this, Greek civilization contrasted sharply with those of imperial China and Islam, where there was in effect no real caesura in the political history from the later middle ages until the nineteenth century. Hence they could continue to have a political history. The second obstacle to any historian of the Byzantine Legacy in Eastern Europe is the failure of most historians, though not of all, to draw a distinction between the formal and popular components of culture. Up until the 'democratization' of culture, that is until modern society and technology produced mass culture, the culture of a given civilization consisted of two clearly discernible strata: the formal, which was the elements of culture patronized by the dominant stratum, and the popular, consisting of those elements developed by the remainder of society. Since, in this older historiographical tradition, culture was conceived of in a narrower sense as something created by the elite groups of society and as centering primarily on political theory-ideology-law, literature, music, painting and architecture, the aftermath of the fall of Byzantine Constantinople was seen as a cultural wasteland, though even here there was a certain blurring of historical focus.

This methodological blindness in the older historiography was never so pronounced in earlier Balkan and Russian scholarship for the simple reason that the inhabitants of these regions could still feel the Byzantine heritage as a living and vital part of their cultures. Their historical memories never completely faltered, their folk culture was still integrated to the older agricultural, pastoral and maritime economic, social, and religious patterns. Their religious institutions may have suffered alteration but they were still omnipresent. Finally their several languages never ceased to be spoken and written. In this latter category the linguistic heritage was immediately present and accessible to them in a way that their conscious affiliation with the past could never be disrupted by scholarly theories, histories and arguments. Further this Sprachgefühl was something very occasional and rare among western scholars.

The first major scholarly assay of the Byzantine legacy was the provocative work of the fecund Roumanian scholar Nicholas Iorga who attempted to trace the faint lines of continuity in Byzantine formal culture, above all in the circles of the Constantinopolitan Phanariotes and in the courts of the princes of the Danubian Principalities. It was, as were all of Iorga's works, inspired by the breadth of historical vision and knowledge of detail which till this day render him a most insightful author. Nevertheless, Iorga concentrated only on aspects of formal political culture, and the Byzantine legacy was not particularly rich in this realm during the Turkokratia. It was a combination of Byzantinology and modern folklore studies which pointed the way to a more fruitful study of the Byzantine legacy in the four centuries following the Ottoman conquest of Constantinople. The pioneer of this was Phaidon Koukoules, professor of Byzantine civilization at the University of Athens. And though certain scholars have been highly critical of his work, it is the fate of all pioneering works to be subject to such attacks. His multi-volume labor on Byzantine life and culture, published in the period after the second world war, is based on a prodiguous analysis of the vast body of Byzantine texts, with significant inroads on the larger body of ancient Greek and Roman texts. What makes the work particularly relevant here is that his extensive knowledge enabled him to follow the afterlife of much from the Byzantine into the later period. This monumental work has revolutionized both our method for understanding the fate of the Byzantine legacy and also the understanding of this legacy itself. Koukoules did not fundamentally concern himself with the formal structure and content of culture, but rather with the content of popular culture, thus transferring the discussion of continuity and discontinuity to an entirely different level of society, and to a different level of scholarship.

Koukoules was able to proceed to his ambitious scholarly venture not only because classical and Byzantine scholarship had attained a very considerable or critical gravity of scholarly mass, but also because the western discipline of folklore had since the romantic movement evolved into a respectable academic enterprise. For those peoples in particular who had suffered a truncated or impoverished political life folklore provided a compenstatory field for investigation. When Koukoules wrote, Nicholas Polites had long since pioneered the field of Greek folklore; C. Schneeweis had printed the first edition of his synthesis and analysis of the folkloric structure of the Serbs and Croats, the work of the Bulgarian folklorist, C. Vakarleski was to come out a little later. In all these works not only the ancient and Byzantine survivals in the modern cultures of the Balkan peoples emerge clearly, but the interconnection of much in their folklores is evident.

The realms of religion and religious art constituted perhaps those domains in which the continuity of the Byzantine legacy was most apparent. This is particularly salient in liturgy, monasticism, the cult of the icon and the tradition of church decoration with frescoes. The Painter's Manuel of the Greek monk Dionysios from Phourna was translated from the eighteenth century Greek text (itself based on much older tranditions of religious painting) into Roumanian, Bulgarian, and Serbian. Art historians have long acknowledged this common artistic inheritance that Byzantium left to the Balkan peoples and scholarly work is now richly exploring the details and outlines. The domain of the Byzantine legal heritage has in part been explored, and N. Pantazopoulos has given us a bold outline of how the various formal and customary legal systems operated in one and the same Ottoman Empire. Particular attention has been given to the survival of the Byzantine canon law, the legal code of Armenopoulos, and customary law throughout the Balkans, though the picture is still far less clear than in the realm of art. The Ottoman scholar Omer Barkan pioneered the demographic aspect of the Byzantine continuity in the Balkans, for ultimately when we talk of the continuity or discontinuity of the Byzantine legacy we are talking about the demographic continuity of those people in whom this tradition basically resided, and as a result of whom some aspects of this tradition were carried over into Ottoman Muslim society.

Finally, the Byzantine historical past, as well as its legacy, are richly acknowledged in the multivolume histories of the Balkan peoples which have appeared in the post world war two era. Greeks, Roumanians, Serbs, and Bulgarians all acknowledge the importance of the Byzantine tradition in each of their cultural and political lives. It is a tribute to the vigor of this historical remembrance that in the age of fervent nationalism, when these peoples broke away from Ottoman rule, each sought to justify its expansion on the basis of a medieval state and medieval ideology which were spawned under Byzantine influence.

The present volume is a contribution to this complex and fascinating problem. Though it does not pretend to comprehend the whole of this subject, such an undertaking would have necessitated an entire equippe of scholars, unlimited financial resources for publication, and, unlimited time, it makes the effort at "sondages" (soundings) at critical points: The Byzantine legacy in Russia might be said to be a major focus of the volume, since five of the twelve papers are dedicated to some aspect of Russia and the Byzantine legacy. Roumania (both the Principalities and the modern state) are the second focus, with three papers. This emphasis on Roumania and Russia is not entirely disconnected from the traditional fascination of historiography with formal culture and the state. Indeed all save one of the papers, my own, are concerned with formal rather than with popular aspects of surviving Byzantine culture: politics, court life and institutions, diplomacy, political ideology, the church, painting. It is precisely because certain of these problems are so unclear to us that these contributions are of particular interest. The matter of popular culture, though perhaps not as well known as it ought to be in scholarly circles, is nevertheless much more apparent, and the continuities there so much less disputable that the concentration on problems affecting formal culture is especially welcome.

A number of these essays remind us of an important historical fact when dealing with eastern Europe and its relation to the Byzantine legacy. The nationalism of the modern inhabitants of much of the Balkans and Russia resonates strongly against the background of some aspect of the Byzantine legacy. It does so because historical memories in this part of the world are tenacious and "burdened" with a very long and rich historical past. But, the essays will speak much more eloquently to this point and so I leave the contents of the book here.

It remains for me to say something about the genesis of the conference. The Byzantine Legacy in Eastern Europe from which these papers have emerged. The conference, both as to its conception and execution, was the product of the thoughts and activities of the late Lowell Clucas. In stating this fact I enter into the domain of his scholarly formation and life so tragically terminated by death at the moment of the full bloom of his intellectual powers and their scholarly realization. This conference, the fruit of his thoughts, indicates the strength and comprehensiveness of intellect, and shows clearly that the development of his thought and vision was dynamic. Having been trained as a Byzantinist he soon realized that Byzantium did not die in 1453 and so he began to try to reconstruct the historical rhythms of this civilization in Eastern Europe at a time when first the Ottomans and then the Russians appeared on the scene as the heirs to the political testament of the Byzantine state. Thus as a Byzantinist he was forced also to become a Balkanist or East Europeanist. This has been the fate of a restricted number of Byzantinists who have stopped to ask what happened after 1453. This concern sharply differentiates Byzantinists even today, when Russia has become such a given in our world outlook. Lowell Clucas was aware of the profundity of the Byzantine influence and particularly of its longevity. Having arrived at this state of mind, he decided to pursue the matter in a conference which would try to draw a sharper or newer focus on the problem of Byzance après Byzance.

I first came to know Lowell when he matriculated at UCLA and where he took the BA degree in German language and literature in 1966. During the senior year he had enrolled in the survey course on Byzantine history and for reasons which were never clear to me he made the fateful decision to dedicate his life to the study of Byzantine civilization. I can only surmise that the richness, extraordinary variety, and the 'exotic' character of this civilization fascinated him. At that time I suggested to him that he should go away for a period of time and study classical Greek as this would be essential for such a dedication on his part. He quietly agreed, enrolled at San Francisco State where for three years he turned to the study of classical Greek, history (with a special interest in the Islamic World thanks to the presence of the Orientalist Prof. Gerard Salinger). At the end of the three years he had mastered the fundamentals of classical Greek, could read the basic texts, had studied and learned to speak modern Greek, and took the master's degree. In 1969 he returned to UCLA where for the next few years he continued to study classical Greek and had the seminars in Byzantine texts with Professor Milton Anastos and myself. During this period of intense work on Byzantium Lowell had already displayed his great philological dexterity and his intellectual brilliance, particularly in the realm of Ideengeschichte. By 1975 his doctoral dissertation, The Hesychast Controversy in Byzantium in the Fourteenth Century was submitted, accepted, and he received his doctoral degree. The dissertation was a massive work, steeped in the complex texts of the Hesychast and anti-Hesychast circles, some of the texts still accessible only in manuscript form. Unlike much intellectual history this work was based on a simultaneous analysis of the intellectual debate of the times and of the social, economic and political factors which were fast sucking Byzantium into the vortex of political disintegration and destruction. These two features remained characteristic of all Lowell's publications, research, and historical thought, resulting in the book, The Trial of John Italos and the Crisis of Intellectual Values in Byzantium in the Eleventh Century (Munich, 1981). Having begun with the clash of mystical and humanistic strains in Byzantine intellectual life and culture during the Palaeologan era (in his dissertation) he went back in time to this crucial trial of Italos to mark a mile stone in the strenghtening of the mystical or perhaps one should say the "revealed" basis of Byzantine intellectual life. Lowell, throughout his mature life, was exercized by the life of the mind, its freedom, and the history of its release from the historically imposed fetters on the mind, which in the European tradition goes back to the monotheistic revelation and its predominance over the ancient belief in the priority of human reason.

Lowell was also a poet of very considerable merit, and though Plato might have decried the presence of the poet in his ideal society, nevertheless the first historian, Herodotus was greatly affected by the tradition of epic poetry. So also in Lowell we see the union of the historical and poetical tastes and gifts. In the beginning he published his poems individually on single sheets which he then circulated to his friends and of these I am fortunate to have six in my files. He then published in such poetic journals as The Blue Cloud Quarterly, a magazine of Indian themes, and in Hard Pressed. Many of these poems, as well as newer ones, were published in the volume An Indian Triptych and other Poems, The Red Chrysanthemum Press (Berkeley, 1984). He also published a historical drama entitled The Death of Alexander (Oakland, 1982). I have read and reread his poems and have been moved not only by his gift of poetic language but also by his sensitivity to time, to the earth, mountains and streams of California, that is to nature, and by the sensitivity which he shows to the destruction of America's first inhabitants and our great historical innocents, the American Indians. During the final phase of his struggle with death Lowell spoke to me frequently and in our conversations, which in texture, force, velocity and clarity were not unlike the cascading mountain streams of the California mountains which he so dearly loved, his ongoing involvement with poetry received equal attention with this work on Byzantine intellectual history. He was determined to face death bravely, quietly, and to maintain the quality of his intellectual life at the same high level which he had always attained. Thus the conversations interchanged between his two primary concerns: intellectual history and poetry. I can think of no more fitting sample of his poetic and historical mind than to let Lowell's poetry speak for him.

The American River, Sacramento (Sacramento, 1975)

You don't see any more Maidu Indians
down highway 50

beside the American River flowing west
towards Sacramento

Sacramento from *sacramentum*
sacrament

what should be a communion
shared in common

a deep draught of this water
sliding toward dusk

between cottonwoods.

They are gone now, driven out
because we came, because,
as Pizarro growled to Atahualpa
"we suffer from a disease of the heart
that can only be cured
by gold".

In a second poem Lowell contemplates time the eternal.

Palo Colorado Canyon (in Hard Pressed, No 3, Sacramento 1977)

I look up at stars
over towering redwoods

and wonder what ages
layered branches count:

I listen to the far off
murmur of water

and wonder what tales
a man could tell

who held all time
in his hand

like a stone
from a lost creek.

In a third poem we see Lowell's personal feelings.

Winter Passage (Sacramento, 1980)

Bones of trees
wash into the sea
or break into soil.

They scatter seeds
on the forest floor;
new shoots have already
sprung from the ground.

And at your laughter
beside me, as we speak
in a stillness

over the rusing torrent

the little gods of death

regard us quizzically

they fold their feathers,

they fall silent and
sit still at attention.

I stand on the bank
and look up the ravine:

groves of pine, laurel
and taller redwood
rise up green
upon green

in the cold mist.

I close by calling to memory this extraordinary human being, so gifted, intense, and above all creative. We recall his memory fondly and sadly: the wife her husband, the parents their son, the scholars their colleague, the muse her poet, and the teacher his student.

Speros Vryonis, Jr.
Los Angeles 1987

THE EARLY POST-BYZANTINE WORLD

BYZANTIUM, THE ORTHODOX CHURCH AND THE RISE OF MOSCOW

John Meyendorff

The rise of Moscow from the status of a rather insignificant provincial principality in the midst of a fragmented country to that of an imperial capital, was one of the most spectacular developments of East European history in the late Middle Ages. In the middle of the twelfth century, the first mention of Moscow in the Russian Chronicles describes it as a small fortress in the land of Suzdalia. Two centuries later, however, its prince becomes, on a permanent basis, "grand-prince of Vladimir and all Russia", and firmly lays the foundations of what is now the Kremlin – a monumental symbol of wealth and political power.

Quite understandably, all historians of Russia since N. M. Karamzin have been concerned with studying the various factors which caused this extraordinary rise of Moscow. They realized that the khans of the Golden Horde, successors of Chinghis Khan, who had dominated Russia since the first half of the thirteenth century, were instrumental in supporting Muscovite power. Indeed, for several decades the princes of Moscow were the Khan's most faithful vassals and used this Mongol connection against their competitors. Other historians emphasized the position of Moscow as the geographical center of Russia and as the meeting-place of several crucial water-ways. Others still, particularly V. O. Klyuchevsky, saw the economic advantages reaped by Moscow from its fertile lands and wise economic policies. The good relations enjoyed by Muscovite princes with the Tatars prevented Tatar raids and devastations and encouraged immigration. Thus, man-power soon became abundant and relatively secure in the Muscovite realm. Soviet historians also note that the policies of Moscow opposed the tradition of feudal fragmentation of Russia and favored political centralization which they consider an inevitable historical process.

It is not my intention to discuss these various views in detail. They all reflect the different aspects of a development which led Moscow on the way to political leadership, and allowed its princes to overcome their competitors. These were, in the framework of the grand-principality of Vladimir, the prince of Tver; and, within the wider scene of Eastern Europe as a whole, the grand-prince of Lithuania.

In the fourteenth century, several of the historical factors which favored Moscow were also present in the case of Tver. But the grand-principality of Lithuania enjoyed other advantages: it controlled more of the traditional Russian territories than Moscow ever did. Kiev itself – the prestigious former capital – was in Lithuanian hands; and the Lithuanian grand-princes were initially much more active and successful in pushing back the hated Mongol invaders.

My purpose in this essay is to point out one other factor which determined the ultimate triumph of Moscow: the Byzantine connections of medieval Muscovy.

Most of the historians whose views I have just quoted, recognize Moscow's diplomatic success in obtaining the transfer of the ecclesiastical center of Russia from Kiev to Moscow. This event could already be anticipated under Metropolitan Maximus, a Greek prelate who spent most of his tenure as head of the Russian church (1283-1305) in the territory of the North-Eastern principality of Vladimir. His successor, Peter, became the close friend of Ivan I Kalita, prince of Moscow, and was buried in that city in 1326. His tomb is still found in the cathedral of the Dormition today. The significance of these events, however, is not limited to strictly Russian history: they involved a deliberate policy of Metropolitan Peter's ecclesiastical superiors in Constantinople and therefore the interests of what Dimitri Obolensky calls "the Byzantine Commonwealth," based on the acknowledgement of a trans-national religious and cultural unity centered in Constantinople, the "New Rome". It is also my belief that Russian history of that period, and particularly the rise of Moscow, is best understood against the broad background of East-European history as a whole. The Byzantine Empire, in spite of its humiliating political weakness, was still in a position to influence events quite significantly in that region, especially through the persisting and even growing power of the Orthodox Church. The fact that the origin of that power lay outside the limits of Russia itself explains why its impact on contemporary events is often underestimated by nationalistic historians.

Since the tenth century, when, in 988, the principality of Kiev adopted Byzantine Orthodox Christianity as its state religion, the ecclesiastical administration of all the lands depending upon Kiev and known as "the land of the Rus' " *(russkaya zemlya)* or *Rhossia* ('Ρωσία) in Greek, was placed in the hands of a single prelate, who – at least since 1039 – had the title of "metropolitan". Almost invariably, he was a Greek by nationality and was appointed by the civil and ecclesiastical authorities in Constantinople. When Byzantium, in 1204-1261, was conquered by the Crusaders, the appointment was made by the Greek patriarch exiled in Nicea.

Throughout the stormy period of the Mongol occupation, which was marked in 1240 by the sack of Kiev itself, the "land of the Rus", was split between several independent and competing political centers: the Tatar-dominated North-East, the commercial city-republic of Novgorod in the North-West, and the flourishing and Western-oriented principalities of Galicia and Volhynia, which will later be known as the Ukraine. In the fourteenth century, the emerging power of Lithuanian princes, particularly Gedimyn (1316-1341) and Olgerd (1341-1377), succeeded in annexing most of the former Kievan territories, including Kiev itself. Their "grand-principality" now extended from the Baltic to the Black Sea. The Lithuanian rulers began to consider themselves as the true heirs of the Kievan realm, protecting it both from Mongol domination and from intrusions by the Teutonic Knights, who had settled in the Baltic region. However, while ruling a vast population of Orthodox Christians, the Lithuanian grand-princes remained pagan. Gedymin seriously envisaged conversion to Latin Christianity, but never made the final decision. His son, Olgerd, who successively married two Russian Orthodox princesses, received an

Orthodox baptism on his deathbed. The reason why he did not take this step earlier is that he wanted to obtain from Byzantium, as a reward for his conversion, the formal support of the Church against his Muscovite rivals. The fact that he did not obtain that support may well be the reason why Moscow, and not the Lithuanian capital of Vilna (Vilnius), eventually became the center of a "Russian" empire.

Notwithstanding the Mongols and the various conflicts between competing centers of power in Russia, the metropolitan of Kiev, head of the Church, played a role largely independent from local circumstances and pressures. The Mongol rulers were respectful of his power and rights. In general, they practised a policy of relative religious tolerance. The fact that the metropolitan was a Byzantine appointee, allowed him to serve as a diplomatic link between Constantinople and the Golden Horde (the khan's capital on the lower Volga). Indeed, relations between Byzantium and the Mongol khans were generally good, to the point of occasionally allowing a Byzantine princess to join the harem of the khan of Sarai. These diplomatic and political links were also supported by another important participant in the East-European political scene: the Genoese. Their commercial routes from the Orient passed through Sarai, on the lower Volga, through the Genoese Crimean city of Soldaia (in Greek *Sougdaia,* in Slavic *Surozh*), and through Constantinople. The Byzantine emperor Michael VIII Paleologus (1259-1282) had granted to the Genoese a section of the city of Constantinople itself – Galata, from which Italian merchants were able to control the economic and to some degree the political life of the weakened empire of the Paleologans.

Thus, the metropolitan of Russia – who resided in Mongol-dominated Moscow and had even appointed a resident bishop in Sarai itself – represented a powerful element in the political and economic structure uniting Genoa, Constantinople and the Golden Horde. The Byzantine government was interested in maintaining his position and was therefore reluctant to give support to those centers which were situated beyond the limits of Mongol power. On the other hand, and most importantly, the Orthodox Patriarchate of Constantinople was eager to re-affirm bonds of unity which, through the Church, kept alive – against all odds – the Byzantine ideological dream of a single Christian world empire centered in Byzantium. Paradoxically, the religiously tolerant empire of the Mongols and the commercial interests of the Genoese were no real threats to that ideology; whereas the militant spirit of western Crusaders, represented in the fourteenth century by the Teutonic Knights, and also by Poland under Casimir the Great, was basically imcompatible with the Byzantine interests and ideals.

How did the Byzantines understand their ecclesiastical and ideological influence in Russia? The Byzantine historian, Nicephoros Gregoras, writing in the second half of the fourteenth century, in a famous text often quoted by historians of the Russian Church mentions the "very numerous nation" (ἔθνος πολυανθρωπότατον) of Russia, and specifies that, since the beginning, "it has been placed under the rule of a single high-priest," who is himself dependent upon the patriarchate of Constantinople.[1] In an even more explicit and more official document, which is less known to historians, the patriarchal synod of Constantinople proclaims in 1389:

> From the beginning, since the Russians became Christians and submitted themselves to our great, catholic and apostolic church of Christ, the entire province of Russia (ἡ ʽΡωσίας ἐπαρχία) has been placed under the pastorship and administration of a single metropolitan. This did not occur simply, or, as one says, by chance. The divine Fathers of old have determined that the great population of that nation, which numbers thousands, or rather is innumerable (τὸ πολυάν-θρωπον ἔθνος ἐκεῖνο καὶ μυριάριθμον) should have one single leader and catholic teacher. The reason for that determination was that the territory of Russia, being vast, was divided between so many different civil powers and so many states (πολιτείας), that it possessed many authorities, and even more local rulers... Since it was impossible to bring together a single civil rule, [the Fathers established] one spiritual authority, considering rightly that, once placed under one single leader and guide, [the Russians] would find peace with themselves and with each other, honoring the one head [i.e. the metropolitan], which is an image of the perfect, primordial and unique Head, Christ, "on whom," according to the divine Apostle, "the entire body of the Church

depends, bonded and knit together" (Eph. 4: 15-16), and is
brought to the unity of faith.[2]

On the basis of this principle, Byzantium required that the one
"Metropolitan of Kiev and all Russia", while residing in the safe and
loyal principality of Moscow, continue to exercise jurisdiction not only
upon Muscovy and independent-minded Novgorod, but also upon the
dioceses found in the territory controlled by Lithuania, and even the
distant diocese of Galicia, conquered by Poland in 1349.

It is true that political realities did not always allow the Byzantine
authorities to be entirely consistent in their policies, and they
occasionally wavered in their support of Moscow as the only religious
center of Russia. The transfer of the metropolitan's residence away
from its traditional seat in Kiev and his policies of solidarity with
North-Eastern princes, vassals of the Tatars, provoked secessionist
moves in the South-West. Thus, the Galician grand-prince Yuri I
(1301-1308) – who assumed, as did his grandfather Daniel, the title of
"king" *(rex Russiae)* – demanded and obtained from Byzantium the
establishment of a separate metropolitanate of Halich (1303-1305). His
intentions, however, were not actually separatistic: his real ambition
was to have *his* candidate appointed to the see of "Kiev and all
Russia." This opportunity arose almost immediately. In 1305, the
Greek metropolitan of Kiev, Maximus, died; and Yuri solicited from
the patriarchate the appointment of his candidate, the Galician abbot
Peter, to the metropolitanate "of all Russia". It appears that, at this
point, the Byzantines were ready to give the title to a native Russian
rather than a Greek, but Peter's candidacy was challenged by a
compatriot, Geronty, a nominee of Prince Michael of Tver (who also
held the title of grand-prince of Vladimir and thus headed the alliance
of North-Eastern princes).

It is at that historical moment that the Byzantines made the fateful
decision which would determine future events and, ultimately, lead to
the rise of Moscow: Peter, the Galician candidate, was appointed
metropolitan, but also received instructions to choose North-Eastern
Russia as his permanent residence. Furthermore, since the prince of
Tver opposed him because he was not his original candidate for the
metropolitanate, Peter sided with Tver's local political rival, Prince

Ivan Kalita of Moscow. He also initiated the building of a stone cathedral in Moscow, in place of the historic one located in Vladimir-on-the-Klyazma, and was buried in it in 1328.

Thus, Moscow became the religious capital of Russia and, with Byzantine support, withstood all the challenges which it had to face in the latter part of the fourteenth century. A separate metropolitanate of Halich is sometimes mentioned in the sources in the period between 1325 and 1347, but each time it was suppressed again through the efforts of Peter's powerful successor, the Greek Metropolitan Theognostos, who continued the same pro-Muscovite policy, and even obtained a formal patriarchal act transfering the metropolitanate to northern Russia. Only in 1370, after the final occupation of Galicia by Poland, Polish King Casimir the Great, using the full weight of his political power, wrote directly to Philotheos, Patriarch of Constantinople, threatening to "baptize" the Galician Russians into the Latin faith if the patriarch still insisted in having them ecclesiastically dependent upon Moscow. This threat brought immediate results: a separate metropolitan for Galicia, Anthony, was appointed that same year. But even that concession would be only temporary.

In the much larger territories held by Lithuania – the immediate competitor of Moscow for the control of Russia as a whole – the metropolitan Theognostos made frequent visits and asserted his rights in Kiev itself. He never forgot thtat his official title remained "metropolitan of Kiev and all Russia". Even the powerful grand-prince Gedimyn had not enough influence in Constantinople to assure that this Orthodox subjects be exempt from Moscow's jurisdiction. We know, however, that he made attempts in this direction and that a "metropolitanate of Lithuania" made brief appearances in Byzantine episcopal lists in 1317-1329.

Moscow's prestige was further enhanced by a formal *Chrysobull* issued by Byzantine emperor John VI Cantacuzenos in 1347. Rarely do we find documents reflecting better than this text the persistent Byzantine world-view, which affirmed the universal supremacy of the "New Rome" – the Byzantine version of the *pax romana* – an ideology which the grand-princes of Moscow were then learning and which their successors would apply in their own particular way.
The emperor wrote:

Since the time when, by the grace of Christ, the nation of the Russians accepted the knowledge of God, the most holy dioceses found in the region of Little Russia, known as Volhynia – i.e. the dioceses of Galicia, Vladimir, Kholm, Peremyshl, Lutsk and Turov – depended like the most holy dioceses of Great Russia, upon the most holy metropolitanate of Kiev, which is presently held by its most sacred metropolitan Theognostos, *hypertimos* and exarch of all Russia.

However, during the recent times of confusion, those who governed the affairs of the empire and also the man who unworthily presided over the church [i.e. patriarch John XIV Calecas, deposed in 1347], profited from the instability of the times and had no other concern than to fulfil their own appetites. They reversed the normal order of political and ecclesiastical affairs, threw chaos and political confusion everywhere, and caused every possible harm and damage to the souls and bodies of Christians. Among the novelties introduced by them was that they separated the aforementioned dioceses of Little Russia from that most holy metropolitanate of Kiev and placed them in the dependence of the high-priest of Galicia, having promoted him from bishop to metropolitan...

The most noble grand-prince of Russia, Lord Symeon [of Moscow], the very beloved nephew of Our Majesty, presently reported about this to Our Majesty and, in a petition endorsed also by other Russian princes, requested that, by chrysobull of Our Majesty, the said dioceses be restored to the said holy metropolitanate of Kiev...[3]

The "normal order of political and ecclesiastical affairs" which, according to Emperor John VI, implied the unity of the Russian Metropolitanate, with its center in Moscow, was again disturbed in 1352-1353, this time by Olgerd of Lithuania. Rather unexpectedly, the Lithuanian grand-prince could obtain the temporary cooperation of the Tatars and their Genoese allies. The Genoese were unhappy with John VI (who had made an attempt at shaking their domination of

Byzantine economic life); and khan Djanibek of the Golden Horde became suspicious of the growing strenght of Moscow. Olgerd, on the other hand, openly challenged the Byzantine patriarchate by having a "metropolitan of Lithuania", Theodoret, consecrated not in Constantinople, but by the patriarchate of Bulgaria. Finally, in 1354, John VI was himself unseated by his son-in-law, John Paleologos, who was receiving Genoese help.

Under such circumstances, the patriarchate of Constantinople, pressured and blackmailed on all sides, agreed to consecrate Olgerd's candidate, Roman, as metropolitan. For six years, Roman competed with Alexis, the metropolitan who, a few weeks earlier and before the downfall of Emperor John VI Cantacuzenos, had also been consecrated as the successor to Theognostos. The struggle between Roman and Alexis was one of the most scandalous episodes of Russian ecclesiastical history. It ended in 1362 with the death of Roman and the restoration of the old order of things. Travelling to the Golden Horde, Metropolitan Alexis performed the healing of Taidula, the elderly and influential widow of Khan Uzbek, and Tatar and Genoese support swung back from Olgerd to Moscow. Eventually, metropolitan Alexis became regent of Moscow's government during the infancy of grand-prince Dimitri. His influence with the patriarchate of Constantinople was so great that, in June 1370, the patriarch excommunicated several political enemies of Moscow, i.e. the princes who were siding with Olgerd of Lithuania.

However, the year 1370 was the high point of the alliance between Byzantium and Moscow, an alliance based on the ecclesiastical administrative dependence of the Russian metropolitanate upon Constantinople, and also on the mutual interests which held together Byzantium and the Golden Horde. The general political configuration in Eastern Europe began to undergo a drastic change. The decisive element of the change was brought about by dynastic struggles in the Golden Horde which began with the death of Khan Djanibek in 1357 and lasted until 1381. These events themselves reflected dramatic shifts occurring in the huge domain of the former Eurasian empire of Chinghis Khan, such as the end of the Mongol domination of China, the installation of the native Ming dynasty in 1368 and the rise of a new Mongolian empire-builder, Timur or Tamerlane.

As a result, the Mongol grip on Russia weakened; and, gradually, Moscow and Lithuania were left practically alone in their competition for supremacy in Russia: the Tatars were no longer in a position to arbitrate the struggle.

Simultaneously, in Byzantium, the strong personality of Patriarch Philotheos Kokkinos (second patriarchate, 1364-1376) was able to maintain an ecclesiastical policy largely independent of the waverings of the reigning emperor, John V Paleologos. A fried of Cantacuzenos and therefore of Moscow, Philotheos began by giving strong support to Metropolitan Alexis, but, after 1370, he could not afford any more to overlook the violent complaints of Olgerd and, indeed, of his entire Orthodox flock in Lithuania: normal ecclesiastical administration in Lithuania became virtually impossible, as the metropolitan was nothing less than the acting agent of Moscow, an enemy state! Since no Mongol or Genoese pressure could be decisive any longer in defining Byzantine ecclesiastical policies in Russia, these were readjusted to the new situation. Nevertheless, the ideal of unity of all the dioceses, both in Muscovy and in Lithuania, under one metropolitan was firmly maintained.

The new approach, adopted by Philotheos, involved greater ecclesiastical independence and a balanced attitude towards the two competing powers. The patriarchate formally ordered metropolitan Alexis to pay greater respect to the person and interests of Olgerd of Lithuania, and supported the idea of an alliance which would unite all the Russian principalities, including Moscow and Lithuania, against the weakened Tatars. Indeed, the Golden Horde now appeared as unnecessary to the maintainance of Byzantine interests in Russia; whereas a strong Church, uniting the various nations and principalities of the region, could protect the Orthodox faith in Lithuanian ruled areas and maintain the now mainly spiritual and supra-national authority of the ecumenical patriarchate in Eastern Europe.

The principal agent of Philotheos' policies in Russia was the Bulgarian monk Cyprian, whom the patriarchate appointed at first as Metropolitan of Lithuania and then as metropolitan of the whole of Russia.[4] In Russia, Cyprian enjoyed the friendship and support of St. Sergius of Radonezh and other major monastic personalities, who, like Philotheos and Cyprian himself, belonged to the vast movement of religious and monastic revival which had originated at Mt. Athos and spread to the Slavic lands.

Cyprian was appointed metropolitan in 1375, during the lifetime of the aging Metropolitan Alexis, with the right to succeed him after his death. Alexis died three years later (1378). Cyprian's tenure as head of the Russian Church was a stormy one. For several years, he faced stern opposition from the grand-prince of Moscow, Dimitri. The latter hesitated between a pro-Mongol policy, which had helped his predecessors to build up Moscow's strength, and the policy of alliance with Lithuania and resistance to the Mongols which was now promoted by Cyprian. It is noteworthy that Cyprian was the first metropolitan of Russia who *never* visited the Golden Horde, but made several prolonged stays in Lithuania. His political program was a Commonwealth of Orthodox kingdoms and principalities, united by the Orthodox Church and recognizing the symbolic leadership of Byzantium.

To what extent and in what way did this program influence the historical fate of Moscow? In order to answer this question, let us recall four momentous events, which shaped the future:

1) In 1380, the Muscovite armies of grand-prince Dimitri turned against his former Mongol allies and inflicted upon the Tatars their first major defeat on the field of Kulikovo, on the Don River. The grand-prince of Moscow who had, up to this point, the rather justified reputation of being a Mongol "stooge", suddenly became a national hero. The religious leaders of the country, particularly St. Sergius, blessed this reversal. Meanwhile (if we believe some chronicle accounts), Metropolitan Cyprian, who was in Lithuania in 1380, prevented the Lithuanian grand-prince Jagiello – the son of Olgerd and himself an Orthodox Christian – from siding with Moscow's enemies. One should note, however, that an important contingent of Genoese soldiers took part in the battle on the side of the defeated Mongol leader, Mamai. But the victory over the Mongols was not a final one. Khan Tokhtamysh sacked Moscow in 1383, and again obtained Dimitri's obedience to the Horde. However, credit for breaking the myth of Tatar invincibility now belonged to Muscovite armies.

2) The second major event which we must mention occurred in 1386. In that year, the Lithuanian grand-prince Jagiello married the

Polish Queen, Jadwiga, and became king of Poland. The grand-principality of Lithuania eventually went to Jagiello's cousin Vitovt, but henceforth the Polish Crown united Poland and Lithuania in a western-oriented Commonwealth which eventually would become a united Polish Kingdom. Both Jagiello and Vitovt converted to Roman Catholicism. As a result, Moscow could claim to be the only heir to the Byzantine, Orthodox heritage – political, religious and cultural. The vast Orthodox populations found within the Lithuanian and Polish realms would eventually develop their own cultural and national identities, pressured by a nobility which gradually became overwhelmingly Roman Catholic.

3) The third major development involved Moscow's Byzantine patron. In 1438-1439, an imposing Byzantine delegation, including the emperor and the patriarch, travelled to Italy and signed an act of religious Union with Rome at the Council of Florence, hoping to obtain Western help against the Turks. The metropolitan of Kiev and all Russia, Isidore, was one of the leaders of that delegation. He returned to Moscow in 1444 with the title of a Roman cardinal, but found no support there. Indeed, he was first imprisoned and then allowed to escape to the West. In 1448, the Russian bishops elected a metropolitan, Jonas, who assumed power without the sanction of Byzantium. Now Moscow – with some legitimacy – could claim the heritage not only of Orthodox Kiev (which was now in the hands of Roman Catholic Poles), but also of Orthodox Byzantium itself, which had betrayed Orthodoxy at Florence.

4) Divine Providence itself seemed to point in that direction when the fourth major event came about: the fall of Constantinople under the rule of Mohammad the Conqueror in 1453. This event was understandably interpreted as a divine punishment by the Russians.

The later developments are relatively well-known. Ivan III, "the Great", built the huge Muscovite empire. He also married the niece of the last Byzantine emperor and imported to Russia some symbols of Byzantine imperial tradition. Many of the Kremlin monuments we see today were built by him. Some Muscovite ideologists developed the famous theory about Moscow being "the third Rome": true Christianity had been betrayed in the "Old Rome", whereas the "Second Rome" – Constantinople – had fallen under Muslim domination. Moscow alone now remained as the last refuge of Orthodoxy.

However, as many historians have pointed out, the Byzantine religious and political ideology implied in these claims was already an anachronism. Significantly, the Byzantine wife of Ivan III had been educated in Italy and the new Kremlin was built by Italian architects. And when the Muscovite grand-prince finally assumed the title of *tsar* – the Slavic equivalent of *Caesar* or "emperor" – he never pretended to be "emperor of the Romans", as the Byzantine emperors did, but only "*tsar* of all Russia". His real political ambition was to build an empire on national – and largely secular – grounds.

What then was the role of Byzantium in shaping what we know as the Moscovite Russian empire? In many ways, it can be said that Byzantine terminology and ideological concepts were used to cover quite a new and different reality. An example of this can be seen in one of the best-known and most impressive regalias of the Russian tsars: the so-called crown of Monomakh. Tradition associates it with Vladimir Monomakh – a Kievan prince who was probably decended from Constantine IX Monomachos, a Byzantine emperor of the eleventh century. In fact, the crown looks much more like the fur cap of a Mongol ruler, and its real origin has more to do with Russian rule over the territories of the former Golden Horde than the Byzantine inheritance of Russia.

However, whatever political and ideological developments shaped Muscovy once it became an Empire, the Church and Byzantium played a decisive role in the events of the fourteenth century discussed earlier. Without the decisive actions taken by Byzantine ecclesiastical diplomats, Russia could very well have been unified by Olgerd of Lithuania. It would then have become a different country in many ways.

What were the reasons which pushed Byzantium to support Moscow? We have mentioned the practical considerations, involving the economic interests of the Genoese and the alliance between Byzantium and the Golden Horde. We have also referred to the persistent – and undoubtedly justified – defensiveness of the Byzantine religious authorities towards the Latin West. Such events as the capture of Constantinople by the Crusaders in 1204 had shown all too clearly that their Russian daughter-church would be spiritually more secure under the Mongol khans than under Roman Catholic Polish kings.

However, beyond all these political and tactical considerations, I would like to point out to a phenomenon of a different nature which was sweeping the entire area of Byzantine Orthodox civilization in the fourteenth century: this was a movement of religious revival, which attracted the best minds of that period and which served as a compensation for a desperately hopeless political situation. As Turks surrounded the walls of Constantinople, and as Mongols dominated Russia, the contemplative and mystical movement known as hesychasm took over the leadership of the Church in Greek-speaking lands. This movement, however, was not limited ethnically – Mount Athos, Bulgaria, Serbia all witnessed the same revival of monastic spirituality. And in Northern Russia, the fourteenth century was the age of St. Sergius, whose innumerable disciples, like the western Cistercians two centuries earlier, were establishing hundreds of monasteries in the Russian forests. The intellectual and theological aspects of "hesychasm" were mostly inaccessible to Slavic Christians, but they – and particularly the Northern Russians – became excellent pupils of the Byzantines, not only in the field of monastic spirituality, but also art, music and those expressions of the Byzantine civilization which appeal primarily to *religious experience.*

In looking for the Byzantine background of Muscovy, one should not limit one's attention to the heavy grandeur and brutality which reflects Muscovite power and wealth at its zenith, but one should also examine carefully the spiritual legacy of the fourteenth century. Indeed, the remarkable achievements of St. Sergius and his disciples, as well as the frescoes of Theophanes the Greek and of Andrei Rublev, testify to the more eternal and more universal truths which inspired Metropolitan Cyprian in his vision of a broader "land of the Rus," itself a part of the still wider and potentially universal Byzantine Orthodox Commonwealth.

The tradition which they represented never died completely. In the early sixteenth century, the so-called *Non-Possessors,* led by St. Nilus Sorsky, fought against the wealth and wordliness of Russian monasteries, and for a greater independence from the Muscovite state. Even in post-Petrine Russia, the spiritual tradition of hesychasm, with its roots in Byzantium, fascinated Gogol and Dostoyevsky. This tradition is still alive today. But in order to see it, one should learn how to look below the surface, beneath the gold and silver, beneath the outward signs of magnificence and political prestige. It is there that the Byzantine legacy, identified in Russia, almost exclusively, with religious spirituality, has remained as a permanent element in Russian culture and literature.

NOTES

1. Gregoras, *Hist.,* 36: 21-23, Bonn, III, pp. 512-513. The cultural and ecclesiastical relations between Byzantium and Russia in the fourteenth century are discussed in detail in my "*Byzantium and the Rise of Russia*", Cambridge University Press, 1981, where formal documentation for the events described in this paper, can also be found.

2. Miklosich and Müller, *Acta Patriarchatus Constantinopolitani* II, pp. 116-117.

3. K.E. Zachariae a Lingenthal, *Jus graecoromanun,* Leipzig, 1856-1884, III, pp. 700-703.

4. A very compete summary of the evidence concerning the career of Cyprian appears in the recently published *Slovar' knizhnikov i knizhnosti drevnei Rusi* in *Akademiya Nauk, Otdel drevne - russkoi literatury, Trudy, XXXIX,* Leningrad, 1985, pp. 53-71 (article by G. M. Prokhorov).

RUSSIA'S PERCEPTION OF BYZANTIUM
AFTER THE FALL

George P. Majeska

In Russia's perception, the fall of the Byzantine Empire came not with the conquest of Constantinople by the Turks in 1453, but at the Council of Florence in 1439. The Empire's demise was signaled to the Russians in 1441 when the Greek Metropolitan of Kiev, now the "Cardinal" Isidore, proclaimed the Roman Pope's name in the diptychs read at the Moscow Dormition Cathedral and thereby announced the submission of the Greek Church to Roman Catholicism.[1] In other words, the shock felt in Muscovy was religious rather than political, as, in a real way, relations between Russia and Byzantium had been religious more than political. [2] Such a distinction is one made only by modern scholars, of course, and would have been close to impossible for medieval people to make. In the medieval mind, sacred and profane might have been separate, but they were always interrelated, if not actually interlocked.[3] In the case at hand, what is important to realize is that the Byzantine Empire was conceived by most Christian people as the physical shell created by God to protect a spiritual kernal, the Christian Church. Damage to the political shell, thus, was of considerably less import than any harm coming to the precious kernal of God's indwelling in the world, the maintaining of which justified the state's existence. In 1439, at the Council of Florence, the kernal died when the leading officials of the Byzantine Church submitted to the Roman Pontiff and gave up, thereby, their assumed mandate to preserve the special truths of Orthodox Christianity. Without a "true believing" Church in Byzantium to protect, the Byzantine Empire no longer had a transcendental function. It was, like its capital in the second quarter of the fifteenth century, an empty shell. Its physical crushing by the Turks was, thus, of only mundane interest. God, of course, would not let His empire disappear forever; its conquest by the Turks was, thus, assumed to be but a phenomenon meant to punish Christian sins.

Such would seem to be the explanation behind the laconic entry on the fall of Constantinople in the First Sophia Chronicle. This is a comparatively untampered with document of Novgorodian origin that reads like a chronological list mechanically supplemented at regular intervals:

> In the year 1453 [6961], on the ninth day of the month of April, the city of Moscow burned within the walls. In the same year, on the thirteenth of the month of July, the righteous Grand Princess Sophia, called *Sunklitiia* in the monastic order, passed away.
>
> The same year, Prince Dimitry Iurevich Shemiakha passed away in Novgorod the Great and they interred him at the Church of St. George. The same year the Turks took Constantinople [*Tsargrad*], the twenty-ninth of the month of May, and did much evil and shed Christian blood. In the year 1454, Archbishop Ephrem of Rostov and Yaroslav passed away, the twenty-ninth of the month of March...[4]

A shorter version of this chronicle is even more straight forward: "The same year the Turkish tsar Mohammed took Constantinople, May twenty-ninth."[5] The entry is a simple statement of fact, much like the earlier entry, *sub anno* 1437, which noted the event that later Russian material was sure caused the fall: "Metropolitan Isidore came to Moscow from Constantinople in the Spring, after the Great Day [i.e. Easter], and he was in Moscow a short time, and in the Fall he went to Rome, to Pope Eugenius at the Council."[6] The brevity of these entries suggests that the events are not momentous. The same chronicle's treatment of the fall of Constantinople to the Latin crusaders in 1204 must be some fifty times longer, replete with miracle stories and clear moral lessons.[7] The Latin conquest of the Empire was, it would seem, viewed as of more significance at the time it happened than was the Turkish conflict. The realization that the Moslem conquest of the Empire, the Christian Near East, and the Balkans was permanent seems to have come only gradually, and to have slowly amalgamated with growing millenarian feelings focused on the coming of the year 7,000 from the creation [1492 in our reckoning], when it was assumed that the sabbatical millenium would usher in "a new heaven and a new earth" (Rev. 21:1). The coming "end of days" (Acts 2:17 et al.) seemed the only appropriate explanation of the 1453 fall of the "Roman Empire," the empire which God had inspired Caesar Augustus to found as a mechanism for redeeming the world in Christ (the standard medieval explanation of the historical existence of the Roman Empire). If the Empire had genuinely fallen, it must already have served its divine purpose; the Turks were then, logically, the Anti-Christ and there would be no need to prepare calendars beyond the year 7,000 when the eschaton would begin. In fact, calendars were not produced for 1493,[8] and that suggests how seriously, in the end, Muscovy took the disappearance of the empire which much of the world had thought to be eternal.

Coping with "the day the world ended" meant rearranging life and myth, and it is perhaps from studying these adjustments in ways of doing things and in ways of thinking that one can most easily learn how the Russians had viewed Byzantium.

The religious life of Russia, for instance, demanded immediate attention, for its clear disruption had come already in the 1430's. With the Metropolitan of Kiev in the Latin fold, who would administer the hierarchy of the Orthodox Church in Russia? Still apparently unclear on how permanent some of the changes in the Byzantine situation were, the Grand Prince of Moscow, Basil II, in 1441 drafted a letter to the Patriarch of Constantinople, the spiritual leader of Orthodox Christianity, "asking" the freedom to elect a new metropolitan because "travel [to Constantinople] is difficult."[9] For some reason the letter was never sent, although in 1448, as the First Sophia Chronicle puts it, "Grand Prince Vasily Vasilevich [the same Basil II] assembled the hierarchs and appointed for himself a metropolitan in Moscow, Monseigneur Jonah of Riazan."[10] Jonah later described the period from the death of Metropolitan Photius in 1431 to his own appointment as the "widowhood of the Russian Church."[11] Isidore and the pro-unionist Lithuanian metropolitan Gerasimus became "non-persons."[12] In July 1452 the Grand Prince, citing all sorts of reasons (but not imperial apostasy), sought imperial recognition of the Russian churchman's appointment.[13] The request was a simple courtesy; the Russian Church had already effectively declared its independence.

The appointment of Jonah took care of the practical problem of church administration. Creating an appropriate ideological justification for this action of dubious canonicity proved more difficult. The "Tale of the White Cowl," a work which seems to date originally from about the year 1500, was a rather successful attempt to find an acceptable justification for an inconvenient fact of history[14]. According to the "Tale," Emperor Constantine the Great gave a white cowl to Pope Sylvester of Rome when the Emperor moved the capital to "New Rome"; it was "more honorable than the crown of the emperor."[15] Eventually, when the Roman Church fell into heresy, this white cowl came to Constantinople, whence, the Pope Sylvester insisted in a dream, the Byzantine Patriarch had to send it to the Archbishop of Novgorod, for Constantinopolitan Orthodoxy was now also found wanting. The first *translatio imperii* to Russia, thus, was religious. A Russian bishop had inherited the mantle of the first of the patriarchs, the pope of Rome. Certainly so highly regarded a church had the right to choose its own archbishop! While the original moral of the "Tale of the White Cowl" was that the Novgorodian archbishop should not be subordinated to the metropolitan at Moscow, the idea of a *translatio imperii* was now in the cold Russian air, and Moscow appropriated the idea, applying it to the political realm (to the eventual detriment of, among others, Novgorod). In the later form in which we have it, this "Tale" also has Pope Sylvester recounting to the dreaming patriarch of Constantinople that "by the will of Constantine, Emperor of the Earth, the imperial crown of the imperial city is destined to be given to the Russian tsar."[16] Given the close relationship between church and state in the Eastern Christian world, this metamorphosis of what was translated is quite logical. The Russians had obviously listened when, *ca.* 1393, Patriarch Antony of Constantinople lectured Grand Prince Basil I thus: "My son, you say 'we have the Church but do not have the emperor.' It is impossible for Christians to have the Church but not to have an emperor."[17]

Just as Muscovite religious practice and theory had to be "rearranged" after the demise of Orthodox Byzantium, so did Muscovite political practice and theory. The practice part was no great problem. Whatever the Byzantine emperor *thought* his political prerogatives were in Russia, his powers that far north were uniquely moral. We are not talking here of the necessity of the Byzantine emperor's "validating" the position of the Russian prince; Russian princes got their appointments either by genetic seniority, military prowess, Tatar dictation – or a combination of these factors. What we are talking about is a change in the nature of Russian rulership. To have the Church, Patriarch Anthony had reminded Russia, you need an emperor.[18] With no Orthodox emperor after 1439 and no emperor whatsoever after 1453, the existence of the Orthodox Church (which during the continuance of the union existed for the most part only in Russia anyway) was in danger. It needed an emperor to protect it, and emperors were, as Patriarch Anthony had noted earlier, "not like other local princes and sovereigns." They "confirmed and established Orthodoxy in the universe."[19]

Proving that the grand princes of Moscow had the right to the title and role of emperor (*tsar*) took several tacks. We have already seen one: Emperor Constantine the Great had prophesied the future power of the Russian tsar who "will be elevated by God above other nations; under his sway will be many heathen kings."[20] St. Constantine the Emperor (at least as quoted by Pope Sylvester in a dream of Patriarch Philotheus of Constantinople recounted in the "Tale of the White Cowl") would certainly seem a powerful witness to the legitimacy of Russia's accession to imperial status (at least in that simpler time).

Nestor Iskander, that unlikely Russian eyewitness of the actual siege of Constantinople in 1453, seems (at whatever time the text which bears his name was put together) to have sensed the basic lines of the myth that would legitimize Moscow's imperial future. First, the divine protection of the Holy Spirit (in the form of a bright light which visibly quit the dome of St. Sophia) had vacated Constantinople shortly before the city's capture, apparently seeking a new home. Second, a partially misread supposed prophesy by Methodius of Patara and Emperor Leo the Wise, that a "fair people" (which, because of similarlity in pronunciation, became "the Russian people") will triumph over the enemies of Constantinople, suggested whither the Empire's protective power had fled. Finally, Nestor's text notes, Christianity will eventually triumph over Islam (the imperial eagle over the Turkish serpent, in his borrowed metaphor).[21] The inheritor of Byzantine imperial charisma, thus, would be fair/Russian, Christian – and triumphant.

It is interesting that although Muscovy would gradually claim imperial right *qua* defender of the Orthodox Church, it *never claimed* that this imperial status was willed it by the Empire at Constantinople. This is certainly strange, since it is exactly that imperial entity which Muscovy was replacing as protector of the Church. The Muscovite change of status from local principality to realm of an emperor (a "tsardom") evoked a considerable literature of theoretical justification, particularly in the sixteenth century. By way of example, let me just sum up the explanations of why the Muscovite grand prince was a "tsar" according to one of these works, the "Tale of the Princes of Vladimir."[22] According to this work, at the division of the Roman Empire under Augustus, the emperor's (heretofore unknown) brother Prus was assigned the northern climes which had their center around the Vistula and Nieman rivers, the area thereafter called "Prussia" after him. Riurik, the traditional founder of the Russian state and progenitor of the grand princes of Moscow, was a descendant of the Roman imperial prince Prus. The Muscovite prince, then, descended from the great imperial family of Rome. The Muscovite prince was also tsar, it is claimed in this work, by descent from Vladimir the Saint who converted Russia to Christianity in the tenth century. Finally, and most intriguingly, he is tsar by descent also from the Russian Grand Prince and "Tsar" Vladimir Monomach. This prince, the reader is informed in the "Tale of the Princes of Vladimir," got his Byzantine imperial name not from his mother, a relative of the Byzantine emperor Constantine Monomach, as others had thought previously, but from the fact that the Emperor Constantine Monomach (died 1055) sent the Russian prince (ruled 1113-1125) his own imperial crown and regalia together with an embassy to crown Monomach's "free and autocratic empire."[23] The imperial regalia which the embassy brought included all sorts of wonderous treasures with which later Russian grand princes were endowed; they came from the Byzantine emperor, however, only after the Russian prince had attacked imperial territory. The gifts, the embassy reported to the Russian ruler in this tendentious document, were in recognition of the prince's imperial status "since the immemorial beginnings" of his lineage and descent.[24] In practical terms, they are depicted as a bribe from a Byzantine Empire terrorized by Russia's power.

The "Tale of the Princes of Vladimir" is a good example of the essentially anti-Byzantine (rather than just "post-Byzantine") flavor of much of the early-modern Russian political literature.[25] Note to what lengths the myth-making pamphleteers go to avoid connecting Russia with the Byzantine Empire in a "direct" line. Moscow the "Third Rome" is utterly separated from Constantinople, the "Second Rome."

Byzantium does not willingly "pass on the torch" to the successor it has chosen, rather it is forced to deliver the regalia under military threat. Indeed, it turns out, the imperial regalia handed over to the Russian prince and his line were not even genuinely Byzantine – they were the imperial trappings of "Nebuchadnezzar the Tsar of Babylon" which the Greeks had appropriated (with the necessary aid of a Russian!). This is the explanation of the provenance of Russia's coronation regalia offered by the "Tale of the Babylonian Empire," a late-fifteenth century Russian work.[26] Byzantium, in the cases noted, is tainted; the taint comes from having "sold out" the Orthodox Christian faith with which it had been entrusted. Moscow's claim to an imperial inheritance stems not from close connection with Byzantium, but rather from distancing itself from its Byzantine competitor.

Understanding this fact will explain why, unlike later non-Russian scholars, no Muscovite source claims the imperial title for Russia on the basis of Ivan III's marriage to Sophia Palaeologos, an erstwhile heiress of the Byzantine throne. If the Muscovite court had wanted to connect itself to the historical Byzantine Empire rather than to the abstract concept of empire, Ivan's marriage to this scion of the last Byzantine ruling family would have been the way to do it.

A good example of the Muscovite tendency to distance the new
tsars of Moscow from their Byzantine counterparts is the sixteenth-century Muscovite reediting of the chronicle compilations to replace the
rather simple and straight forward story of Metropolitan Isidore and
the unionist Council of Florence which was quoted earlier. We hear
about the Greek Emperor John [VIII], "covered with the darkness of
faithlessness... caught in nets of gold... perishing through the lies of
Isidore."[27] How different from the "faithless" emperor of the Greeks is
the young Muscovite Grand Prince Basil II, who

> when he had seen the edict with the enactments of their
> false-minded council and heard from [Isodore's] lips the name
> of the pope mentioned, was the first to recognize the heresy of
> the rapacious wolf Isidore, did not accept the blessing from
> his hand, and called him a heretical Latin deceiver. Quickly
> accusing him, he covered him with shame and called him a
> wolf rather than a shepherd and teacher. He soon ordered
> that he be removed from his throne as metropolitan as a mad
> deceiver and apostate from the faith.[28]

As one of the reworked Russian sources on the Council of
Florence, that by Simeon of Suzdal, notes, "burning with the flame of
piety" the young Grand Prince Basil could be likened to the
"Equal-of-the-Apostles" Emperor Constantine, and his own ancestor
St. Vladimir who had first baptized Russia.[29] The Russian Prince Basil
II is seen as the true Orthodox emperor already in 1441 (by our
functional definition, viz., as protector of the true Church) in
contradistinction to the "traitorous Emperor of the Greeks."

The Russian ruler eventually sees the need to seek a legitimizing
symbol of his imperial status, a ritual coronation in what modern
scholars insist on calling the "Byzantine fashion," but which should
more correctly be called the "Orthodox ritual." But here we have come
to the crux of the dilemma of Russia's perception of Byzantium after
the fall, namely, that the Muscovites have to accept as normative the
empire from which they are trying so hard to distance themselves, for
the Orthodox Christianity which justifies the existence of the
Muscovite tsars is defined precisely by the Byzantine experience which
formed it.

The importance of the "rejected" Byzantium as the norm of correct policy was nowhere better demonstrated in early-modern Russian history than in the well known and long-lived argument between the pro-Hesychast followers of the hermit Nil Sorsky (the "Non-Possessor" or "Trans-Volga Elders" party) and the more legalist coteries of Joseph Volotsky of Volokolamsk (the "Josephites"). In general the dispute was over the treatment of heretics and over monastic ownership of peasant-settled villages.[30] The ammunition in this war of words was Byzantine precedent, almost completely as found in written materials. To the Josephites there seemed to be little difference in value between the Holy Scripture, canon law, writings of the fathers of the Church, and Byzantine civil law and practice. "From the first honorable and holy Emperor Constantine, Equal-of-the-Apostles, and also after him under the honorable emperors ruling in Constantinople," religious institutions have owned land.[31] That, suggests Volotsky, settles that. "Righteous tsars" always punished heretics; Justin and Tiberian did this. The Empress Theodora and her son Michael even wanted to have a patriarch blinded for heresy. Heraclius had ordered the Jews to be baptized or killed.[32] All of these actions, because they were performed by imperial rulers of Byzantium, should serve as models for the Russian tsar, Joseph thinks. In one letter, to prove his position, Joseph cites a rule of St. Gregory of Agrigentum, a decree of the Seventh Ecumenical Council, a law of the Emperor Justinian, a rule of the local Council of Carthage, and sayings of Pseudo-Dionysius the Aereopagite, St. Basil the Great and St. Athanasius of Sinai;[33] all, it would seem, of equal weight, for all witness to the practice of the Byzantine Empire, which is the touchstone of correct theory and practice. "It is written in the *typica* and in the *Lives* of the Holy Fathers that monks may drink wine at the proper times, sometimes one cup and sometimes two or three... As many noble men and monks who have been in Constantinople and on holy Mount Athos and other places there bear witness, not only monks, but also all Orthodox Christians hate and loathe drunkenness."[34] Note that the appeal is not to reason or experience, it is to the Byzantine practice.

Joseph's ideological enemies, the Trans-Volga elders (and Maksim Grek who doubtless knew the Greek reality far better than the Josephites) preferred to cite the Bible, particularly the New Testament, and draw inferences; they lost out.

The proof-texting in Byzantine sources by the Josephite faction within the Russian Church became the dominant mode in sixteenth-century Russia, not just in thought, but also in behavior. The triumphant Josephites attempted to recreate in Moscow their paper vision of the divinely constituted Byzantine Empire. The Russian Church Council "of the Hundred Chapters" in 1551 suggests that monasteries follow Constantinopolitan schedules for mealtimes. It rails against the celebration of pagan Greek festivals which are completely unknown in Russia, and searches for Byzantine imperial precedents for how to behave when the tsar's birthday falls on Sunday.[35] In a decree of Tsar Ivan IV, the Terrible, who, playing the role the emperor had played in Byzantium, convoked the council, it is announced that "our Orthodox religion is guided by the laws of Greece."[36] The decree is included in the acts of the council, in which is also included the address of the Tsar wherein he asks rhetorically, "Why did the Lord deliver Tsargrad [Constantinople] to people of another race, the impious Turks?"[37] The irony of Russia trying so hard to model itself on the Byzantium that fell leaving Russia as its heir seems not to have been recognized in Moscow.

When the Russian Prince Andrei Kurbsky defected from Moscow and charged Ivan the Terrible with not sharing power with his boyars, Ivan answered that he was "Orthodox."[38] He drew parallels to his reign from Byzantine history: emperors who shared power were not successful and that is why the godless Mohammed extinguished the Greek people.[39] "Recall to memory Constantine, mighty even among the saints, how he killed his son, begotten by him, for the sake of his kingdom."[40] He also draws biblical parallels, but always as an amplifications of the Byzantine "moral." Correct equals Byzantine, and Byzantine means an artificial Russian creation based on what written materials happened to have been translated into Slavic, happened to have come to the attention of Russian writers, and happened to fit their needs of the moment. It is on the basis of such a construct that Ivan answers the charges of Kurbsky, one of Russia's first political thinkers.

The first person who seems to have realized clearly that the Byzantium held up for imitation in Muscovy was but an artifice of Muscovite bookmen was Ivan Peresvetov, a pamphleteer contemporary with Ivan the Terrible. Indeed, Peresvetov appropriated the symbol of Byzantium for his own purposes. In a short work called the "Tale of the Books, of Sultan Mohammed, and of Emperor Constantine," he depicts the Byzantine Empire not as an "icon of the kingdom of heaven," but as a purely human entity, a decentralized feudal state of corrupt and uncontrollable nobles that fell because of the weakness of the central government and the power of the magnates.[41] Indeed, in Peresvetov's analysis, Byzantium stands as a new kind of symbol, a would-be prototype of pre-autocratic Russia which, his metaphor intimated, was also destined to fall if noble power prevailed. What is startling here and seems to hereld the advent of a modern (*sc.* secular) world in Russia is that the parable attributes to the Turkish conqueror of Byzantium the solution to Byzantium's [i.e. to Russia's] political problems, namely, that to be successful an autocratic monarch must work through his freely chosen appointees rather than through a hereditary nobility. The new model of political behavior proposed to Ivan the Terrible is not the sacred figure of the Christian emperor of Byzantium, but the "Anti-Christ" Moslem sultan who defeated him.

NOTES

1. See M. Cherniavsky, "The Reception of the Council of Florence in Moscow," *Church History* 24 (1955), 347-59; G. Alef, "Muscovy and the Council of Florence," *Slavic Review* 20 (1961), 389-401.

2. Russia's religious ties with the Byzantine Empire are treated in standard histories of the Russian Church; see E.E. Golubinskii, *Istoriia russkoi tserkvi.* 3 vols. in 4+ atlas (Moscow, 1901-11); A. V. Kartashev, *Ocherki po istorii russkoi tserkvi.* 2 vols. (Paris, 1959); and, at least tangentially, in works dealing with "Moscow the Third Rome"; see, for example, the material cited in G. Majeska, "The Muscovite Coronation of 1498 Reconsidered," *Jahrbücher für Geschichte Osteuropas* 26 (1978), 353, n. Purely political relations are chronicled in M.V. Levchenko, *Ocherki po istorii russko-vizantiiskikh otnoshenii* (Moscow, 1956).

3. Ecclesiastical and political relations have been treated in an integrated fashion recently in D. Obolensky, *The Byzantine Commonwealth. Eastern Europe, 500-1453* (London, 1971) and J. Meyendorff, *Byzantium and the Rise of Russia* (Cambridge, 1981).

4. *Sofiiskaia pervaia letopis,* Polnoe Sobranie Russkikh Letopisei (hereafter: PSRL) 5 (St. Petersburg, 1851), 271. On this chronicle see D.S. Likhachev, *Russkie letopisi i ikh kul'turno-istoricheskoe znachenie* (Moscow, 1947), 451-57.

5. *Sofiiskaia pervaia letopis',* 271.

6. Ibid., 267.
7. See ibid., 171-72 and the material cited there.
8. Golubinskii, *Istoriia russkoi tserkvi* II/1, 608-09.
9. *Russkaia Istoricheskaia Biblioteka* (hereafter: *RIB*) 6 (St. Petersburg, 1908), cols 525-36.
10. *Sofiiskaia pervaia letopis',* 269.
11. Letter to Prince Alexander Vladimirovich of Kiev, 31 January 1451, *RIB* 6, col. 557.
12. Bishop Gerasimus of Smolensk was appointed metropolitan by the Byzantine authorities after the death of Metropolitan Photius. Probably because of his assumed pro-Lithuanian sentiments, Gerasimus' jurisdiction was never acknowledged in Muscovy, and thus Constantinople appointed Isidore in his stead; see Golubinskii, *Istoriia russkoi tserkvi,* II/1, 416-18.
13. *RIB* 6, cols. 576-86.
14. See "Povest' o novgorodskom belom klobuke," ed. N.N. Rozov, *Pamiatniki literatury drevnei Rusi: Seredina XVI veka,* ed. D.S. Likhachev (Moscow, 1985), 198-233.
15. Ibid., 225.
16. Ibid.
17. *Acta et Diplomata graeca medii aevi* 2, ed. F. Mikosich and I. Müller (Vienna, 1862), 191.
18. Ibid.
19. Ibid.
20. "Povest' o novgorodskom belom klobuke," 225.
21. "Povest' o vziatii Tsar'grada Turkami v 1453 godu," ed. O.V. Tvorogov, *Pamiatniki literatury drevnei Rusi: Vtoraia polovina XV veka,* ed. D.S. Likhachev (Moscow, 1982), 216-67.
22. *Skazanie o kniaziakh vladimirskikh,* ed. R.P. Dmitrieva (Moscow, 1955).
23. Ibid., 164-65.
24. Ibid., 164.
25. On the "anti-Byzantine" strain in other areas of Russia's religious and intellectual life, see G. Florovsky, *Puti russkogo bogosloviia* (Paris, 1937) and G.P. Fedotov, *The Russian Religious Mind. Kievan Christianity, the Tenth to the Thirteenth Centuries* (Cambridge, Mass., 1946). Older works treating the image of Byzantium in Russia include V. Ikonnikov, *Opyt' issledovaniia o kul'turnom znachenii Vizantii v russkoi istorii* (Kiev, 1869) and F. Ternovskii, *Izuchenie vizantiiskoi istorii i ee tendentsioznoe prilozhenie v drevnei Rusi.* 2 vols. (Kiev, 1875-76).
26. "Skazanie o Vavilonskom tsarstve," ed. N.F. Droblenkova, *Pamiatniki literatury drevnei Rusi: Vtoraia polovina XV veka,* 182-87. 182-87.
27. *Voskresenskaia letopis',* PSRL 8 (St. Petersburg, 1859), 105. On this compilation, see Likhachev, *Russkie letopisi,* 472-74.

28. Ibid., 109; cf. *Nikonovskaia letopis'*, PSRL 12 (St. Petersburg, 1901), 25-61 *passim;* cf. Likhachev, *Russkie letopisi,* 475-79.

29. V. Malinin, *Starets Eleazarova Monastyria Filofei i ego poslaniia.Istoriko-literaturnoe issledovanie* (Kiev, 1901), Appendix, p. 99.

30. On the conflict between these two ecclesiastical parties see N.A. Kazakova and Ia.S. Lur'e, *Antifeodal'nye ereticheskie dvizheniia na Rusi XIV-nachala XVI veka* (Moscow, 1955) and A.I. Klibanov, *Reformatsionnye dvizheniia v Rossii* (Moscow, 1960).

31. *Poslaniia Iosifa Volotskogo,* ed. A.A. Zimin and Ia.S. Lur'e (Moscow, 1959), 322.

32. Ibid., 164; cf. 177.

33. Ibid., 188-89.

34. *The Monastic Rule of Iosif Volotsky,* ed. and trans. D. Goldfrank (Kalamazoo, Michigan, 1983), 126. The "Discourse" continues, "O Russia! Another custom, another law..."!

35. *Stoglav,* ed. D.E. Kozhanchikov (St. Petersburg, 1863), 62-63, 261-67, 268-69.

36. Ibid., 239.

37. Ibid., 53.

38. *The Correspondence between Prince A.M. Kurbsky and Tsar Ivan IV of Russia,* ed. and trans. J.L.I. Fennell (Cambridge, 1963), 12-14 and *passim.*

39. Ibid., 48-56.

40. Ibid., 38.

41. *Sochineniia I. Peresvetova,* ed. A.A. Zimin (Moscow, 1956), 221-34; cf. also 123-84. On Ivan Peresvetov see A.A. Zimin, *I.S. Peresvetov i ego sovremenniki* (Moscow, 1958).

BYZANTINE GREEKS IN LATE FIFTEENTH - AND EARLY SIXTEENTH CENTURY RUSSIA*

Robert Croskey

I

"And from the princes, [her brothers] came with her an ambassador, Dmitrii by name, with many Greeks and many Greeks came with her [own suite], attending her." So wrote the Russian chronicler of the entourage which accompanied Zoë Palaeologus on her journey to Moscow to marry Grand Prince Ivan III in 1472[1]. Some of these people stayed on at the Russian court, and they were later joined by other Greek immigrants who came to Russia to enter the service of Ivan III. Greek immigrants were not making their first appearance in Russia in the second half of the fifteenth century; Greeks had journeyed north since the earliest period of Russian history, but most of the earlier immigrants were clerics or artists. What was new in Ivan III's reign was his frequent appointment of Greeks to important government posts.

The purpose of this paper is to explore both the background of these people before they came to Russia and their careers in Russia. This topic is part of the larger question of the role of foreign influence in Russia, and a clearer understanding of the Greeks in Ivan III's service should tell us something about the nature of their influence on Russian developments.

Others have examined the topic of Greeks in fifteenth-century Russia. Tikhomirov, for example, has looked at Morean Greeks important in the Russian Church earlier in the fifteenth century,

Skryzhinskaia has looked specifically at the Ralev clan, and Alef has given a survey of the whole question of Greeks in Ivan III's reign. Khoreshkevich has assembled much useful information on the subject.[2] In this paper, I will concentrate on those Greeks who were important in state service, and at the court, rather than in the church. I am able in some cases to present new information, to definitely indentify some individuals and to postulate cultural links between fifteenth-century Russia and the Mediterranean world.

II

The most important of the Greeks in Ivan's employ, his treasurer, Dmitrii Vladimirovich Ovtsa-Khovrin, did not arrive in the entourage of Zoë Palaeologus, but was a member of a family which had been resident in Moscow since 1403.[3] The treasurer was among the most important officials of the Russian prince. He was in charge of the Grand Prince's valuable personal possessions, responsible for the collection of certain taxes, and conduct of the Grand Prince's merchant enterprises; he participated in the reception of foreign emissaries and was responsible for keeping important records.

According to Russian sources, the Khovrins were Greek princes from the Crimea. Vasiliev has identified them as descended from the Gabras family, the ruling family of the Greek principality of Theodoro-Mangup in the Crimea.[4] The standard phonetic changes in Russianizing the name Gabras could produce something close to Khovrin. Veselovskii, who appears to be unaware of Vasiliev's interpretation, has questioned the princely status of the Khovrins and suggested instead that the name derives from a Russian nickname, "Khovra" meaning daydreamer, or talkative old woman. Veselovskii believes the Khovrins were originally Greek merchants. Alef, citing the later concoction of titles by the Russian nobility in the sixteenth-century, agrees with Veselovskii. Vasiliev's view has recently been accepted by Anthony Bryer.[5]

Obviously the truth here is a matter of conjecture, but in favor of the Vasiliev thesis, it might be pointed out that the Russianized form of Gabras could have been identified with the existing Russian word "khovra."

Greeks in this period would probably have a family name which descended in some branch of the family, but Russian family names tended to be created anew in each generation from the father's given name or nickname. In the case of the Khovrins, the name was associated with the family for several generations, indicating an established family name on the Greek, rather than the Russian pattern. The Greeks who came to Russia later in the fifteenth-century also carried stable last names which derived from Greek family names. Byzantine noble status did not preclude involvement in merchantile activities, so the Khovrins could descend from a princely family and be merchants as well.[6] In Russia, the Khovrins were not accorded the title of prince, but a member of the family reached boyar status under Vasilii II and four members of the Golovin branch of the family served as treasurers in the sixteenth-century. The family's Greek origins were remembered as late as the second half of the sixteenth-century.[7]

III

The Greeks who came to Russia in Ivan III's reign and who served in important government posts were members of four families: the Rhallis, the Tarchaniot, the Lascaris and the Angelos-Doukas families. The first problem in studying these people as members of families, and trying to trace their antecedents and descendents, is the transmission and stability of family names in Byzantium. A man usually took his father's surname, but not necessarily. The mother's maiden name or even the maternal grandmother's maiden name could also be used, if this name carried more prestige.[8] Multiple family names compiled from various branches of the family also appear. It is tempting to think that an individual's choice of family name could reveal that he wished to ally himself with the traditions associated with the name, in this case some connection with Russia, but it is not clear that this is the case.

Another characteristic of Greek personal nomenclature, use of the paternal grandfather's, or in some cases, maternal grandfather's first name for a child, is of some use in suggesting possible family connections, but some names, such as Dimitry and George are so common, that this characteristic is not too useful.[9] Spelling has not been stabilized in this period either, and the problem is further complicated by transmission from one language to another. The name Rhalles, for example, also appears in Greek as Raoul, and Rales, and in Russian as Ralev, and by metathesis, Larëv.[10] The Trachaniotes family appears as Tarcognota, bizarrely as Percognota, and in Russian as Trakhaniot.[11] The Russian patronymic form, Trakhaniotov does not seem to have been used until the sixteenth-century. The Angelov family in Russian appears to derive from the Angelos-Doukas family in Greece.[12] The name Laskaris remains in an easily recognizable form in Russian, Laskarev.[13]

What do we know about these four families in Byzantium? Of the Trakhaniot family, one genealogist says, "The Trachaniotai were a noble and wealthy house, attested since the eleventh century, and during the period of the Palaiologoi they repeatedly intermarried with members of the ruling family."[14] The Rhallis family in the late empire was most important in the Morea, that part of the Peloponnese ruled by the cadet branch of the Palaeologi from which Zoë came. There members of the Rhallis family were civil and military officials, diplomats and courtiers. Many of them were notable for their strong resistance to the Turks.[15] In fifteenth-century Constantinople, the family was considered to be among the primary nobles of the capital.[16] Two members of the family with imperial connections were sent as ambassadors to Spain, France and Russia at the beginning of the fifteenth-century.[17] The Angelos family was an imperial one, but all male members died out in the twelfth-century, and the later families with the name all took it from the female line.[18] The Lascaris family was an imperial family, and at the capture of Constantinople, in 1453, the Lascaris family was considered to be among the first rank of noble families in the city.[19] Noble families of the highest rank were involved in trade in Constantinople, including the Palaeologus family. Of these four families, the Lascaris and the Ralles families had merchant members.[20]

To sum up the general information about these families before they appear in Russia, they were closely interrelated; they were, if not imperial families themselves, intermarried with imperial families, they were considered to be among the leading noble families of Constantinople and the Morea. Members of these families held important court, government, and military posts both in the Morea and in Constantinople.[21] Some of them were important in trade. These are the traditions they brought to Russia.

IV

Of the four families, the Rhallis clan had the longest tie with Russia. Dimitri Obolensky has discovered that a Rhallis probably connencted to the ruling Palaeologus dynasty was sent as ambassador to Russia in 1400. Obolensky believes this is probably Constantine Rhales Palaiologos. If Obolensky is right, this man was later sent on embassies to Spain and France to raise money for the empire. This was probably his mission in Russia as well, Obolensky concludes.[22] One wonders if there was not some connection here with trading activities and the arrival of the Khovrin family in Russia at about the same time.

There are other scattered notices of the name in late Byzantine sources. In 1436, Michel Rallis Isses was major-domo for Thomas Palaeologue.[23] After the capture of Constantinople by the Turks in 1453, a George Rhali remained in the city, while others with this name were scattered throughout the Mediterranean world.[24] A Manuel Raul was persuaded to return to Constantinople in 1453 by the Sultan.[25] In 1461, a Nicholas Rali appears in Milan as emissary from the Russian ruler. There is no account of this episode in Russian sources, and one wonders if there is not some connection, or confusion with the embassy of Nicolas Ralli Isses, sent from Thomas Paleologue, father of Zoë, to the Duke of Milan in the late 1450's.[26]

The most interesting and, in Europe, the most important historically of the Ralevs associated with Russia is the Dimitrii Kavakes Ralles sent as representative of Zöe Palaeologus's brothers in the wedding party which went to Moscow in 1472. In the past there has been some confusion over the identity of the ambassador from Zöe's brothers. Pierling in his first study of Zoë's marriage identifies the ambassador as Dimitrii Trakhaniot. Possibly this was done on the evidence of the sixteenth-century Nikon Chronicle, which probably uses genealogical material as its basis here. Later Pierling identified him as Dimitrii Ralles. In the most nearly contemporary Russian chronicle, the ambassador is identified only as Dmitrii the Greek. Consultation of Papal archives clearly identifies this individual as

Demetrius Cavathis Rales. This information is confirmed by marginal notes made by Demetrius Rales in his manuscript copy of Strabo.[27]

Demetrius Rales was a noble and wealthy man in the Morea who turned to literary activities after his arrival in Rome in 1466. He took the name Rales from his mother's family. In Greece, he had been a pupil of Georgios Gemistos Plethon, the Platonist and philosopher at the court of the Morean despots. Plethon attended the council of Ferrara-Florence, where he was a strong opponent of the union of the Churches. The visit to Florence made Plethon known to the western European world, where his influence was very great: he was the inspiration for Cosimo de Medici's Platonic Academy and according to Platina, Plethon was esteemed second only to Plato himself. A later scholar says Plethon was a "daring social and political reformer" and the "first figure in the revival of Platonism." Demetrius Cavathis Rales devoted much of his life in exile to preserving and developing the teachings of Plethon.[28] Rales' early knowledge of Russia may have come from Plethon's *Excerpts* and *Corrections* to Strabo, which were apparently compiled shortly after 1439. According to Anastos, this was, for its time, the most accurate account of Russia, and Rales is known to have had a copy of it, though it does seem this copy dates to the period of his life after his trip to Russia.[29]

In Rome, Rales was associated with Cardinal Bessarion, the major sponsor of Zoë's Russian marriage. This, and his importance in the Morea before the conquest probably accounts for Rales' appointment as ambassador. After his return from Russia, Rales lived on to the age of ninety or more, dying before 1520. Rales seemingly embraced paganism, particularly a form of sun worship which he derived from Plethon and from the writing of Julian the Apostate, whose works he helped diseminate along with those of Plethon. In spite of Rales' beliefs, he was buried in the Church of the Holy Apostles, Cardinal Bessarion's church in Rome. Rales left a son, Manilius, a minor Latin poet and friend of the more important poet, Michele Marulio Tarcognota, about whom, more below.

Rales was in Russia only briefly, from May 1472 to January 1473. He appears to have returned to Russia on a second embassy in 1474.[30] His son Manilius may have accompanied him on one of his journeys, and remained for a time in Russia, although he is clearly not the

Manuil Ralev who served on numerous Russian embassies.

The next representative of the Rales family associated with Russia appears in 1485. In that year, according to the Russian chronicle, Ivan Ral' Paleolog arrived in Moscow from Constantinople with his two sons, Dmitrii and Manuil. Western European sources indicate that Johannes Ralli Paleologus was accompanied by his wife and daughters as well, and that he passed through Germany in 1482, on his way to Russia, so apparently he and his family were in residence in western Europe and did not come to Russia directly from Constantinople.[31] For the next twenty years, Dmitrii and Manuil Ralev were active in the government service of Ivan III. They were sent a number of times as ambassadors to western Europe, often with the task of recruiting craftsmen and specialists to work in Russia.[32]

This family of Ralevs seem to disappear from Russia early in the sixteenth-century. Skrzhinskaia associates this family with the Ioannes Ralles sent as ambassador of Thomas Paleolog to the Pope in 1460. Some sources indicate that this individual had a family connection with the Palaeologi, as had the Russian Ralevs. However, according to the Russian Chronicle, the Russian Ralevs came from Constantinople, and Ioannes is not known to have lived there. Before the Turkish conquest, he was in the Morea, whence he fled in the 1460's; afterwards, until possibly 1472, he was in Italy. The Russian Ralevs more probably descend from the Manuel Raul who was persuaded to return to Constantinople by the Sultan in 1454. This form of the family name is closer to that first associated with the Ralevs in Russia, and the same given name of Manuel indicates that the returnee of 1454 and the Russian diplomat may be grandfather and grandson.[33]

In the early part of the sixteenth-century, one of the Ralevs remaining in Constantinople, a nobleman, is known to have moved to Russia. He left Constantinople about 1518 and died before 1578. Fairly clearly this Ralles was engaged in the trade between Constantinople and Moscow.[34] Possibly this is the Ivan, son of Thomas Larёv, mentioned in a *Razriadnaia kniga* for 1530.[35] This seems to be the last mention of the family in connection with Russia. Presumably Dimitrii and Manuel had left to find their fortunes elsewhere.

Clearly the Rhalles family was part of the Byzantine ruling class; in Russia, they were valued for their knowledge of Western Europe and apparently their commercial acumen. Trading activities were not scorned by the Byzantine civil aristocracy and all Greek noble families after the Turkish conquest increasingly turned to trade as a means of livelihood.[36] The Rhalles family was known to have been engaged in trade even before the Turkish conquest. It is not possible to trace specific family ties among all the Rhalleses associated with Russia, but there does seem to be an association between the family name and Russia. There seems to be some evidence that the Russians preferred to deal with those who already had some family tie to Russia, so those who could claim descent from the Rhalleses, may have used this family name to ease their acceptance in Russia.[37]

V

The Trachaniotes family, like the Ralev family, was involved in government and particularly diplomatic service. Manuel Tarchaniotes Boullotes held the rank of Senator and was sent as an emissary to the Council of Florence, where he supported the Union of the Churches. This appears to be the origin of notion that the Trakhaniot family in Russia was Uniate. Some of Herberstein's remarks could also support this view, but it seems to me that the strong anti-Catholic hostility in Russia, and role this played in Polish-Russian relations would make it impossible for anyone to enter the service of Ivan III and openly accept either Papal supremacy or the Latin rite. Since the given name of Boullotes is Manuel, as is that of the father of those Trachaniotes who came to Russia, some have assumed them to be one and the same person. However, Manuel Tarchaniotes Boullotes does not seem to have been associated with the Morea, as were the Trachaniotes who came to Russia.[38]

According to Pierling, George Trakhaniote, in Italian exile, was the major-domo of Thomas Paleologue, Zoë's father. Pierling also says that George helped negotiate the marriage and was part of the wedding party which went to Moscow in 1472. There is some confirmation of this in Russian sources. The fifteenth-century grand-princely chronicle mentions that the Greek Iurii, the Russian version of George, was sent to Moscow in 1471 by Cardinal Bessarion to arrange the marriage, and a Russian genealogy says that Dmitrii and Iurii Trakhaniot came to serve in Russia in 1472. According to Herberstein, George the younger, in Russian, Iurii or Iushka Malyi, the son of Dmitrii, also came to Russia in Sofia's suite.[39] Sofia was the name Zoë Palaeologus took in Russia. If the family did come to Russia in the early 1470's, there is no mention of it in Russian documents for the next 10 years, until 1485-6, when Iurii Trakhaniot is noted in the service books. His brother Dmitrii is described as a boyar in the service of Grand Princess Sofia. On other occasions we find Dmitrii Grek acting in diplomatic ceremonies on behalf of Sofia. In a wedding ceremony of 1500, we find all three members of the Trakhaniot family attending the sleigh of Sofia, as her boyars.[40]

While Dmitrii Trakhaniot seems to have remained in the service of Sofia, Iurii Trakhaniot and Dmitrii's son, Iurii the Younger were active in diplomacy. Iurii Trakhaniot was sent on three trips as ambassador to several western rulers, including Maximilian, the King of Rome, who acted for his father, the Holy Roman Emperor, and to various Italian rulers. He was also ambassador to Denmark and took part in diplomatic receptions in Moscow. Khoroshkevich has noted a gap in the diplomatic activity of Iurii Trakhaniot from 1494 to 1500, when Sofia Palaeologus and the Greek party seem to have been out Ivan's favor. The elder Trakhaniots disappear from the documents in the last years before Ivan III's death in 1505. The period of disgrace in the 1490's does not seem to have harmed the career of Iurii the Younger, who took part in a formal reception for an emissary from Maximilian in 1493. In 1495, Iurii the Younger was a chamberlain *(postel'nik)* for Ivan, and from 1503-1510 he was keeper of the seal *(pechatnik)*. Actually we find him performing tasks which fall under this last category as early as 1490. In 1509, under Vasilii III, Iurii the Younger became treasurer and in this capacity played a major role in the reception of emissaries from the Teutonic Order and the Holy Roman and Ottoman Empires.[41] Herberstein, the Imperial ambassador to Russia in 1517 and 1526 gives some information about Iurii the Younger, in the English version of Herberstein called George the Little. Herberstein refers to Iurii the Younger as the "treasurer and Chief councillor" of Vasilii. Herberstein further says that Iurii the Younger was a man "of remarkable learning and extreme experience". Beyond that, it is difficult to sort out the incidents Herberstein relates about Iurii the Younger. Some of Herberstein's information is clearly mistaken, but nevertheless, has been used as a basis for considerable speculation, particularly concerning the relationship between Iurii the Younger and Maxim the Greek.[42]

Maxim the Greek (c. 1470-1556, born Michael Trivolis) was an Orthodox monk who came to Moscow from Mt. Athos in 1518 to prepare translations from the Greek for the Russians. Most of his early life had been spent in Italian exile, where he was associated with John Lascaris, Ficino and Aldus Manutius, In Florence, he fell under the influence of Savonarola. In 1525 after seven years in Russia, Maxim was convicted of a number of charges, including heresy, treasonous relations with the Turks, and so on. He seems to have been actually guilty of refusal to recognize the independence of the Russian church from Constantinople and of refusal to accept extensive land ownership by the Russian church. After his conviction, Maxim spent most of the rest of his life in prison. He was the most prolific writer in medieval Russia, and he was a means by which some of the intellectual currents of western Europe made themselves felt in Russia.[43]

In Herberstein's account of the affair of Maxim the Greek, he says that Maxim stated in the presence of Vasilii III that "he who did not follow the Roman or Greek ritual was evidently a schismatic," implying that the Russians were schismatic.[44] Herberstein then says that Maxim was reported drowned, apparently as punishment for his comments. Herberstein further states that a Greek merchant, Marcus was seized and "put out of the way." Herberstein does not make it clear whether Marcus was seized for implying that the Russians were schismatic or for repeating stories about Maxim's fate.

More to the point for our purposes, Herberstein says that Iurii the Younger lost "all his posts" because "he encouraged and defended the same cause." Again it is not entirely clear that Iurii the Younger was disgraced for implying the Russians were schismatic, for repeating stories about Maxim's fate, or for interceding on behalf of Marcus. In any event, according to Herberstein, Vasilii III found Iurii the Younger too valuable to dismiss, and he was "restored to favor and placed in a different office." Herberstein goes on to mention that Iurii's wife was beaten for concealing that Solomea, Vasilii III's first wife, divorced as barren in 1525, had said that she was pregnant at the time of the divorce.[45] There is Russian information of uncertain date tying Iurii the Younger to this issue, but since no children had been produced in the marriage for over twenty years, and since Iurii the Younger was the chief advisor of Vasilii III, it is not surprising that he was in some way and at some point involved in this matter.[46]

If Herberstein's account is correct, then we can conclude that Iurii the Younger was alive and in favor in late 1526, when Herberstein left Russia for the last time. Following Herberstein, Zimin assumes that Iurii Trakhaniot fell into disgrace in 1522, since after that time, there is almost no information about him in Russian records.[47] Indeed, were it not for Herberstein's remarks, one could assume that Iurii the Younger died in 1522. We know for certain only that he was dead in 1527.[48]

Herberstein drew up his account of Russia in the late 1540's. He did not rely on memory alone, but used notes he had made at the time of his trips to Russia, over twenty years before.[49] In spite of this use of contemporary notes, Herberstein's remarks about Maxim the Greek's disgrace and Iurii the Younger's involvement in it are at least in part erroneous. According to Russian diplomatic documents, written probably a very short time after the events, the "Greek" merchant Mark was in fact a "friazin" – probably an Italian – and a doctor in Russian service. One passage does describe him as a merchant, but his primary occupation seems to have been that of physician. According to Russian documents, the issue concerning him was his departure from Russia, requested by the Sultan. This request was based on the initiative of Mark's wife's brother, and it is not clear that Mark himself even wanted to leave Russia. Vasilii III's response to the Sultan's request was that Mark had entered Russian service, and Vasilii III asked instead that Mark's wife and children be sent to him, in Russia. The imprisoned merchant was not Mark, but a Turk, Adrakhman, and he was imprisoned and threatened with execution for creating a disturbance in Vasilii III's treasury. He was released at the instance of the Sultan's ambassador, Iskendr. These events took place in late 1522 or early 1523 – before March of 1523.[50]

It does seem that Iurii Trakhaniot passed from the scene before the issue of Mark the physician arose in December 1522. The last mention of Iurii Trakhaniot's participation in diplomatic affairs dates to May of 1522. Another bit of information indicates that Iurii the Younger did not fall in disgrace in 1522. Skindr or Iskindr, the Greek merchant who converted to Islam and made several trips to Moscow as merchant and emissary from the Sultan, came to Russia in the spring of 1524. He had last left Russia in March of the preceding year, when the affairs of Mark and Adrakhman were issues of discussion between himself and Russian officials. When Iskindr returned to Russia in 1524, a merchant Fĕdor, described as the brother of Iurii the Younger, came with him.[51] It seems to me unlikely that Iskindr would return with Iurii the Younger's brother, if he knew that Iurii the Younger was in disgrace when he left Russia in 1523.

It seems to me unlikely as well that Iurii the Younger would have suggested that the Russians were schismatic. He had been raised at the Russian court, and had, by 1522, held responsible posts in Russian service for thirty years. He had witnessed the suppression of the Judaizer heresy in the 1490's, a process in which his father and uncle had played some role. He was certainly aware that the long-standing conflict with Poland/Lithuania had an important and sensitive religious component which set Russian Orthodoxy against Catholicism. The importance of the religious question in Russia, and his own long service at the Russian court would seem to indicate that Iurii the Younger's religious views were acceptable in Russian eyes.

If Iurii the Younger did not die in 1522, the explanation for the silence of the Russian records regarding him may lie in further information supplied by Herberstein. Herberstein mentions that Iurii the Younger was so ill that he had to be carried to the palace.[52] Possibly after 1522, Iurii could not carry out his judicial and diplomatic responsibilities because of illness. These are the tasks which ordinarily find reflection in the Russian records. He may have continued to advise Vasilii III until his death, sometime before 1527, but this kind of activity is rarely mentioned in Russian documents.

Iurii the Younger seems to have been close to the royal family. He had a house in the Kremlin, near the grand prince's quarters; this was characteristic of the treasurer.[53] As keeper of the seal, during Ivan III's reign, he held the keys to Ivan's jewel chests.[54] In 1503, Elena, Vasilii III's sister, Queen of Poland by marriage, wrote to Iurii the Younger asking him to send her black sables for making a hat.[55] Herberstein mentions that Iurii the Younger hoped to marry his daughter to Vasilii

III, presumably in 1505, when Vasilii III first married. In the event, Vasilii did not marry the daughter, but chose his bride from a concourse of the daughters of the Muscovite boyars.[56]

In comparison to the Ralevs, who stayed longer in Western Europe, and who seem to have been employed in tasks which took advantage of their commercial ties to Western Europe – hiring craftsmen and selling furs – the Trakhaniot family was more important at court and in diplomatic relations with Western Europe and the Ottoman empire. The Greeks were less frequently employed as emissaries to Poland/Lithuania and the Crimea.

We know that the Trakhaniots seem to have been valued for their intellectual ties, and their ideological skills as well. In 1486, Iurii Trakhaniot the Elder dictated a lengthy memorandum on Russia at the Duke of Milan's court.[57] In the struggle against the Judaizers, an heretical sect, the Trakhaniots supported the champion of orthodoxy, Archbishop Gennadii of Novgorod and advised him on questions of the calendar and numerology.[58] Iurii Trakhaniot the Elder was the agent by which Gennadii learned of the operation of the Spanish Inquisition from the German Imperial ambassador. Gennadii hoped to use this method against his own religious non-conformers. At court, we see the Trakhaniots opposed to the Kuritsyns, who were part of the heretical party.[59] The Trakhaniots were also important in receptions of Imperial ambassadors, where Russian pretensions to equal importance had to be upheld. Some of the earliest uses of the title *tsar'* for Ivan III appear in documents sent by Iurii Trakhaniot the Elder.[60]

Herberstein gives an interesting example of Iurii the Younger attempting to buttress the prestige of Vasilii III by claiming that the people of Iugra, a region in the Urals under Russian rule, were in fact Hungarians. Iugra had been conquered by the Russians, and therefore Russian subjects, these pseudo-Hungarians, had at one time "devastated a great part of Europe." Although Herberstein does not mention it, this may have been part of a Russian claim to the Hungarian throne, which was then a subject of contention. Herberstein does say that Iurii the Younger wrote "treatises" developing Russian claims to "the grand duchy of Lithuania, the Kingdom of Poland, etc." In some of these writings Iurii the Younger used characteristically Greek etymological arguments.[61]

We know that the Trakhaniots were connected with the seal, Iurii the Younger as early as 1490, and he was officially keeper of the seal from 1504 to 1509.[62] We may assume that they played some role in developing a new, more pretentious seal and title and that they played some role in the decision to build a new palace and new ambassadoral reception chambers. Probably they also played some role in the decision to keep more thorough diplomatic records. In all of this, they could draw upon the family's experience at the court of the Palaeologi, both in the Morea and in exile in Italy, where they probably became familiar with West European customs as well.

In addition to the brother Fëdor mentioned above, there is further evidence that Iurii Trakhaniot the Younger maintained ties with Greeks in the Black Sea region. In 1514, we find a Greek converted to Islam, "Kamal kniaz' Feodorit" (Prince Kamal of Theodorit, another Gabras connection?) sending his nephew Manuel to Iurii the Younger to make his fortune.[63]

Unlike the Ralevs, the Trakhaniot family remained in Russia. One of Iurii the Younger's sons, Vasilii, held the rank of boyar, and others held court and government positions. Members of the family are recorded to the end of the seventeenth century.[64]

An apparently unrelated member of the Tarchaniot family appears to have been in Russia as well, probably coming as a member of Zoë's wedding party. This is the Latin poet Michele Marullo Tarcaniota, who lived from about 1453 to 1500. Michele Marullo Tarcaniota's visit to Russia has been noted by only one other scholar, Denis Zakythinos, writing in modern Greek, and it has escaped the attention of Russian historians.[65] His presumed Russian adventures are known from references in his poetry to serving a "barbarian master" in "Scythia". Other references are to the Rhiphaen chill and the cold Tanais – the Don. On learning of the death of his brother, he returned to Italy through "Scythia," from the Rhiphaen cold. In another passage, he compares those without honor to those who cultivate chill Scythia's thickets. He makes reference to "fleeing proud Scythia." Possibly most interesting is his clear indication that he wrote poetry in "Scythian": he says he used the Latin plectrum and the "Scythian" plectrum. This would seem to indicate he wrote in "Scythian." This is not as unlikely as it may seem, as Tarcaniota was raised in Ragusa, and he may have known a Slavic language.[66]

Others, however, have felt Tarcaniota's foreign service was in Hungary, and as evidence of this, they point to a laudatory poem to Mateus Corvinus, King of Hungary. This poem is in contrast to Tarcaniota's clear unhappiness elsewhere with his "barbarian master" and the poem to Corvinus could have been written in an attempt to enter Corvinus' service. Possibly Tarcaniota served in both Hungary and Russia, as did the Lascaris family who came to Russia later.[67]

Tarcaniota's term "Scythia" is not helpful in determining where he served, since in classical times, Scythia was used to refer to almost any territory north of Italy. But in favor of the Russian identification it is worth noting that by the late fifteen-century Scythia is located on maps to the north and east of Russia, quite far from Hungary. The Rhiphaen mountains are in the very far north and Tanais seems always to have been the Don. The thickets or brush of Tarcaniota's Scythia would seem more applicable to Russia than Hungary.

Both the time of Tarcaniota's foreign service, the early 1470's, and his personal associations strengthen the argument that Tarcaniota was in Russia. We know he was a friend of Manilio Rhallo, the son of Demetrius Ralles, the ambassador to Russia in 1472 and 1474. The poet Tarcaniota is known to have served under a Rhalles, this may refer to his presence in the wedding party. Manilio Rallo also served a "harse tyrant" as well, so he may have been in Russia service too.[68] With these points in mind we cannot regard Tarcaniota's Russian service as certainly proven, but it is probable.

Zakythinos assumes that Tarcaniota was related to the Trakhaniotes family in Russia. There is no evidence of a close connection. He took the name Tarcaniota from his mother's father, his own father's surname was Marullus. Tarcaniota was for a time married to the daughter of the secretary of Lorenzo d'Medici, and there is a web of personal ties which connect both him and Manilio Rhallus with Maxim the Greek. Janus Lascaris, the teacher of Maxim the Greek was married to the daughter of Manilio Rhallus. Tarcaniota wrote an ode to Janus Lascaris and Lascaris in turn wrote an epitaph for Tarcaniota.[69]

Precisely why Tarcaniota may have left Russia is uncertain. From his poetry, it is clear that he disliked the cold and political conditions in

"Scythia". Certainly his neo-pagan outlook, his enthusiasm for Hellenic culture and a revived Greek nation could have found little support in Russia either.[70]

VI

The other two Greek families who came to Russia were of considerably less importance than the Rhalles and Trachaniotes families. The Angelov family had few representatives in Russia. The name presumably derives from the Angelos-Doukas family. A Manuil Angelov was sent as ambassador from Russia to Venice in the 1490's, and a Mikhail Ivanovich Angelov held a number of posts at court and in government service in the 1490's and early in the sixteenth centuries. In 1509, he was appointed keeper of the seal, to succeed Iurii the Younger Trakhaniot who became Treasurer at that time.

Khoreshkevich lists three members of this family: Manuil, Mikhail – nicknamed Mikula or Nikula – and Nikita. She notes Zimin's suggestion that Nikita is simply an error for Nikula. It seems to me likely that Manuil and Mikhail are the same person as well and we have only one Angelov in Russian service. There is however evidence of an appointment for Mikhail in Moscow at a time when Manuil was supposedly still in Europe.[71]

Mikula was employed on particularly sensitive missions to Elena, Queen of Poland and daughter of Ivan III, to find out if in Poland she was allowed to follow the Orthodox rite, and if she was pregnant.[72] The family does not seem to have survived in Russia.

VII

The Lascaris family, in Russian, Laskarëv, came to Russia in 1496. The first Laskarëv in Russia was Fëdor, son of Dmitrii, who is described as a *tysiatsskii tsaregorodskii,* which in literal translation would be *chiliarch* of Constantinople. I think actually the position in Constantinople must have been *strategos,* for in Russian, the *tysiatsskii,* like the *strategos* was the main military official of a region. The Greek *chiliarch* was a low-ranking official. Fëdor Laskarëv had served in Hungary before coming to Russia. Fëdor's son, a second

Dmitrii, was ambassador to the Danish king and the German emperor.[73] The family survived in Russia, and its most important representative was Fëdor's great-grandson, Fëdor Mikhailovich, a noted general in the sixteenth-century.[74]

An interesting sixteenth-century Russian genealogy for the Lascaris family traces the family back to one of four brothers brought to Constantinople by Constantine in the fourth-century. Supposedly Constantine directed that the emperor should be chosen from among these four families by the "whole land" *(vsia zemlia)*, if the existing imperial line failed. The genealogy provides an interesting example of the sixteenth-century Russian understanding of Byzantine history and possibly is intended to suggest that a member of the Laskaris family be chosen Russian tsar, if the Rurikid dynasty died out, as it eventually did.[75] In the event, of course, a member of the Laskarëv family was not chosen, but the new dynasty was formally elected by the "whole land" as the genealogy indicates the Russians understood Byzantine practive to have been.

Again, there is no clear tie between the Russian Laskarëvs and other members of this family. A possible ancestor for the Russian Laskarëvs is the Theodore Lascaris who fled Constantinople on the eve of the Turkish conquest.[76]

VIII

The Greeks in Russia in the fifteenth and early sixteenth centuries were important for a number of reasons. Most obviously, they occupied important posts at court, specifically the post of treasurer, who was responsible for diplomatic matters and conduct of the grand prince's trading activities. The Greeks seemed to have been prized for this post as they had extensive connections throughout the world of the Mediterranean and the Black Sea. In so far as court procedures are concerned, the Greeks came from families with long traditions of service at Byzantine courts. They were familiar with the etiquette and symbolism of the more sophisticated Greek setting and probably for this reason were employed in such tasks as keeper of the seal, where they probably helped develop a more impressive seal and title for Ivan III and his son. They were probably responsible for developing a more sophisticated court ceremony. They were important in developing the image the Russian ruler wished to present to the outside world. They also acted as conduits for intellectual currents from the outside world to Russia. In this practice of employing immigrant Greeks, the Russians were not alone; Greek émigré scholars and diplomats found a place at many European courts of the time.

The most important representatives of the Renaissance, Demetrius Ralles and Michele Marullo Tarcaniota did not stay in Russia, but their presence there does indicate that Russian contacts with the world of the Renaissance were more significant than was hitherto known. These contacts also demonstrate that Maxim the Greek's arrival in Russia was not unprecedented. Maxim, Ralles, and Tarcognota were all three part of the Italian Renaissance, Maxim being of considerably less importance in Italy than the other two. The varying fates of the three men indicate that Russia was ready to welcome representatives of foreign intellectual currents only if they came in the service of Russian Orthodoxy. Even then, as the story of Maxim the Greek indicates, the experience of such men could be difficult.

The most successful Greeks in Russia were the Trakhaniots, a family which seems to have thrived by demonstrating its loyalty to the ruling dynasty. The intellectual interests of this family were limited to assistance to staunchly orthodox Russian clergymen and to providing intellectual and symbolic justification for the rule of the Russian grand prince.

From these Greeks, about whom we know something, we can tentatively conclude that the many others whose identities have not survived were of similar background. Contarini writes of meeting in Moscow, in 1476, many Greeks from Constantinople who came in Sofia's suite.[77] They must have constituted a sizeable group at the Russian court. They were familiar with Greek and Italian court and administrative practice, and they had extensive commercial and intellectual connections. While it is difficult to tie specific developments to even those individuals who are known, it is clear the Greeks as a group must have played a role in the transplant of "Byzantine" customs and ideology to Russia. Somewhat paradoxically, they clearly played a role in the development of ties with Western Europe as well.

NOTES

* Part of the work on this paper was done during an NEH summer workshop at Dumbarton Oaks. Peter Topping and Alexander Kazhdan have made helpful suggestions and Eyvind Ronquist, Lowell Clucas and John D' Amico translated Greek and Latin for me.

1. *Polnoe sobranie russkikh letopisei* (hereafter PSRL), vol. 25 (Moscow, 1949), p. 296.

2. M.N. Tikhomirov, "Greki iz Morei v srednevekovoi Rossii," *Srednye veka,* vol 25 (1964), pp. 166-175; E. Ch. Skrzhinskaia, "Kto byli Ralevy, posly Ivana III v Italiiu (k istorii italo-russkikh sviazei v XV veke," in *Problemy istorii mezhdunarodnykh otnoshenii: sbornik statei pamiati Akademika E.V. Tarle* (Leningrad, 1972), pp. 267-281; Gustave Alef, "Diaspora Greeks in Moscow," in *Rulers and Nobles in Fifteenth-Century Muscovy* (London, 1983), section XI; A.L. Khoroshkevich, Russkoe gosudarstvo v sisteme mezhdunarodnykh otnoshenii kontsa XV-nachala XVI v. (Moscow, 1980).

3. S.B. Veselovskii, *Issledovaniia po istorii klassa sluzhilykh zemlevladel'tsev* (Moscow, 1969), pp. 442-8.

4. Alexander Alexandrovich Vasiliev, *The Goths in the Crimea* (Cambridge, Mass., 1936), pp. 198-201.

5. Alef, op. cit., n. 2, p. 29. Anthony A.M. Bryer, *The Empire of Trebizond and the Pontos* (London, 1980), section IIIa "A Byzantine Family: The Gabrades, c. 979-1653," p. 172 and section IIIb "A Byzantine Family: The Gabrades, an Additional Note," written with Sterios Fassoulakis and D.M. Nicol.

6. Angeliki Laiou-Thomadakis, "The Byzantine Economy in the Mediterranean Trade System; Thirteenth-Fifteenth Centuries," *Dumbarton Oaks Papers* nos. 34 §-35 (1980-81), pp. 177-222; Nicolas Oikonomides, *Hommes d'affaires Grecs et Latins à Constantinople (XIIe-XVe siècles)* (Montreal, 1979).

7. Veselovskii, op. cit., n. 3, pp. 442-8. If the Gabras-Khovrin connection is correct, this places the proposed marriage of 1475 between Ivan Ivanovich, the son and then heir of Ivan III and Maria, daughter of Isaac, Prince of Mangup, in a new light; *Sbornik Imperatorskogo Russkogo istoricheskogo Obshchestva* (hereafter SIRIO) vol. 41, pp. 12-13. The marriage would have been between a distant relation of Ivan III's treasurer, Dmitrii Vladimirovich Ovtsa-Khovrin, and the heir presumptive of Muscovy. This marriage did not take place, apparently because the Gabras dynasty in the Crimea was conquered by the Turks in that same year; N. Banescu, "Contribution à l'histoire de la Seignurie de Théodoro-Mangoup en Crimée, *"Byzantinische Zeitschrift,* vol. 35 (1935), p. 21. Breyer, op. cit., n. 5, IIIa, p. 173 gives the name of the last ruler of Theodoro-Mangup as Alexander, Banescu has Alexis, op. cit., p. 22. Banescu says Isaac was the brother of Alexis. Their sister, another Maria was the second wife (1472-77) of Stephan of Moldavia. In the event, young Ivan married the daughter of Stephan of Moldavia by his first marriage. Also see A.V. Boldur,

"Slaviano-moldavskaia khronika v sostave voskresenskoi letopisi, *"Arkheografi-cheskii ezhegodnik za 1963 god* (Moscow, 1964), p. 82. The proposed marriage between Ivan Ivanovich and Maria calls to mind the account in Herberstein about a proposed marriage between the daughter of another Greek treasurer at the Russian court, Iurii the Younger Trakhaniot and Vasilii Ivanovich, who ultimately became the heir of Ivan III. This proposed marriage would date to 1505, but some of Herberstein's details are wrong: Iurii the Younger was not, in 1505, Treasurer, as Herberstein indicates, nor was Vasilii Ivanovich then Grand Prince of Muscovy as Herberstein implies; Sigismond van Herberstein *Notes upon Russia,* vol. I, vol. 10 of the Publications of the Hakluyt Society (London, 1851), p. 50. One wonders if Herberstein, who first came to Muscovy in 1526, has not in some way confused accounts of the proposed marriage of 1475 with that of 1505. As a final note on the relations of the Mangup dynasty to Russia, we should mention that a Prince Constantine of Mangup was present at Sofia's betrothal ceremony in Rome, accompanied her to Moscow and eventually became a Russian saint, under the name of Kassian. Paul Pierling, *La Russie et le Saint-Siège* — *études diplomatiques* (Paris, 1896), vol. I, p. 161; Ia. S. Lur'e, *Ideologicheskaia bor'ba v Russkoi publitsistike kontsa XV-nachala XVI veka* (Moscow, 1960), pp. 314-5.

8. Demetrios I. Polemis, *The Doukai: A Contribution to Byzantine Prosopography* (London, 1968), pp. 2-3.

9. Steven Runciman, *Mistra: Byzantine Capital of the Peloponnese* (London, 1980) p. 51.

10. S. Fassoulakis, *The Byzantine Family of Raoul-Ral(l)es* (Athens, 1973); Skrzhin-skaia, op. cit., n. 2, pp. 275-6.

11. V.I. Rutenburg, "Ital'ianskie istochniki o sviaziakh Rossii i Italii v XV v., *"Issledovaniia po otechestvennomu istochnikovedeniiu* (Leningrad, 1964), pp. 460-1.

12. Polemis, op. cit., n. 8, p. 85.

13. In the face of this diversity of usage, it seems to me that it would be false to attempt to impose uniformity. It may in fact be useful to others to preserve the differences in spelling found in the various sources, so names have been spelled as they are found. In those cases where the discussion is not tied to specific sources, the standard usage for the particular context will be used, e.g. Trakhaniot for the Russian, Tarchaniotes for the Greek. The Palaeologus family is sometimes referred to by the French form, Paleologue, again in reflection of the source in which the passage is based.

14. Polemis, op. cit., n. 8, p. 183.

15. Fassoulakis, op. cit., n. 10, pp. 3-4.

16. Nicolas Iorga, *Notes et extraits pour servir à l'histoire des Croisades au XVe siècle* vol. 4 (Bucharest, 1915), p. 196.

17. D. Obolensky, "A Byzantine Grand Embassy to Russia in 1400," *Byzantine and Modern Greek Studies,* vol. 4 (1978), pp. 127-30.

18. Polemis, op. cit., n. 8, pp. 11-2.
19. Iorga, op. cit., n. 16, p. 196.
20. Oikonomides, op. cit., n. 6, pp. 121-2.
21. On intermarriage, see Fassoulakis, op. cit., n. 10, p. 89, Polemis, op. cit., n. 8, pp. 85, 139, 152, 172, 183; and Angeliki E. Laiou, "The Byzantine Aristocracy in the Palaeologan Period: A Story of Arrested Development, "*Viator, Medieval and Renaissance Studies* vol. 4 (1973), pp. 131-152.
22. Obolensky, op. cit., n. 17.
23. Denis A. Zakythinos, *Le Despotat de Morée: Histoire politique* (London, 1975), vol. II, p. 92.
24. N. Iorga, *Byzance après Byzance* (Bucharest, 1935), p. 17.
25. Apostolos E. Vacalopoulos, *Origins of the Greek Nation 1204-1461)* (New Brunswick, N.J. 1976), p. 208.
26. Skrzhinskaia, op. cit., n. 2, p. 277; Zakythinos, op. cit., n. 23, vol. I, p. 283.
27. Paul Pierling, *La Russie et l'Orient: marriage d'un tsar* (Paris, 1891), p. 195; PSRL, vol. 12, p. 147; Pierling, op. cit., n. 7, vol. I, p. 161; PSRL, vol. 25, pp. 296, 299, 300; Vat. Reg. no. 681 f. 273 (old n. 276); Aubrey Diller, *The Textual Tradition of Strabo's Geography* (Amsterdam, 1975), pp. 144-5.
28. On Demetrius Rales: Fassoulakis, op. cit., n. 10, pp. 83-5, § A. Keller, "Two Byzantine Scholars and their Reception in Italy, "*Journal of the Warburg and Courtauld Institutes,* vol. XX, nos. 3-4 (July-Dec., 1957), pp. 366-70. On Plethon: François Masai, *Pléthon et le Platonisme de Mistra* (Paris, 1956). Quotations from John Wilson Taylor, *Georgius Gemistus Pletho's Criticism of Plato and Aristotle,* Dissertation, University of Chicago, 1921. Also Milton V. Anastos, "Pletho's Calendar and Liturgy, *Dumbarton Oaks Papers* no 4. (1948), p. 186.
29. Milton V. Anastos, "Studies in Pletho," Unpublished Harvard dissertation, 1940, pp. 117-8, 150-3.
30. PSRL, vol. 25, pp. 300, 305.
31. Skrzhinskaia, op. cit., n. 2, pp. 279-80; Khoreshkevich, op. cit., n. 2, p. 211; Iorga, *Notes,* n. 16, vol. V (Bucharest 1915), p. 126.
32. Khoreshkevich, op. cit., n. 2, pp. 188-92. It would seem that the Manuilo Grek, found in the diplomatic documents for 1484, which Khoreshkevich cites, must be another person.
33. Skrzhinskaia, op. cit., n. 2, p. 280; Fassoulakis, op. cit., n. 10, pp. 81-2; Vacalopoulos, op. cit., n. 25, p. 208. One of Skrzhinskaia's points, that the Russian Ralevs could not be related to the Palaeologus family, is evidently incorrect.
34. Stephan Gerlach, *Dess aeltern Tage-büch etc.* (Frankfort, 1674), p. 456.
35. *Razriadnaia kniga, 1475-1605* vol. I (Moscow, 1977), ed. V. I Buganov, comp. N.G. Savich, p. 220.
36. Apostolos E. Vacalopoulos, *The Greek Nation, 1453-1669* (New Brunswick, N.J., 1976), pp. 238-41.
37. Ambrogio Contarini, *Travels to Tana and Persia,* vol. 49 of the Publications of the

Hakluyt Society (London, 1873), p. 149.

38. Miroslav Labunka, "The Legend of the Novgorodian White Cowl: The Study of its 'Prologue' and 'Epilogue'," Unpublished Dissertation, Columbia University, 1978, pp. 75-6; Sigismond von Herberstein, op. cit., n. 7, vol. I, pp. 83-4. In this connection it should be mentioned that Iurii Trakhaniot the Younger did carry on negotiations with the ambassador of the Prussian order about the union of the Churches. This was done with the knowledge of Vasilii III and there is no indication that Iurii the Younger supported the Union. The Prussian account of these negotiations, which took place in 1517-18, is notable for the evidence that the theory of Moscow as the "Third Rome" was always more popular outside Russia than it was inside the country. Erich Joachim, ed., *Die Politik des ersten hochmeisters in Preussen, Albrecht von Brandenburg* vol. II (Leipzip, 1894), pp. 175-77.

39. Pierling, op. cit., n. 7, pp. 112, 162. PSRL, vol. 25, p. 281; *Rodoslovnaia kniga Kniazei dvorian Rossiiskikh... kotoraia izvestna pod nazvaniem Barkhatnoi knigi* (Moscow, 1787), vol. 2, pp. 276-7.

40. Khoreshkevich, op. cit., n. 2, pp. 229-30; SIRIO vol. 35, p. 117; *Pamiatniki diplomaticheskikh snoshenii* (hereafter PDS), vol. I (St. Petersburg, 1851), c. 34; *Razriadnaia kniga 1475-1598*, ed. V.I. Buganov (Moscow, 1966), pp. 16, 44.

41. Khoreshkevich, op. cit., n. 2, pp. 229-30; PDS vol. I, c. 50.

42. Herberstein, op. cit., n. 7 vol. I, p. 50; B.I. Dunaev, *Prep. Maksim Grek i grecheskaia ideia na Rusi v XVI v.* (Moscow, 1916), pp. 13-15.

43. A short but authoritative recent account of Maksim, with citations to the relevant literature is Dimitri Obolensky "Italy, Mount Athos, and Muscovy: The Three Worlds of Maximos the Greek (c. 1470-1556)," *Proceedings of the British Academy*, vol. 67 (1981), pp. 143-161.

44. Herberstein, op. cit., n. 7, vol. I, pp. 83-4.

45. Herberstein, op. cit., n. 7, vol. I, p. 51.

46. A.A. Zimin, *Rossiia na poroge novogo vremeni* (Moscow, 1972), p. 293.

47. Zimin, op. cit., n. 44, p. 275.

48. A.A. Zimin, "O sostave dvortsovykh uchrezhdenii russkogo gosudarstva kontsa XV i XVI v.," *Istoricheskie zapiski*, no. 63 (1958), p. 187, n. 45.

49. Herberstein, op. cit., n. 36, vol. I, p. clxi.

50. Dunaev, op. cit., n. 42, pp. 52-3. The second part of Dunaev's book, pp. 33-92, consists of documents relating to foreign affairs which are not published elsewhere.

51. Dunaev, op. cit., n. 42, pp. 34, 39, 60, 65.

52. Herberstein, op. cit., n. 7, p. 84.

53. Khoreshkevich, op. cit., n. 2, p. 230.

54. Robert Craig Howes, trans. § ed., *The Testaments of the Grand Princes of Moscow* (Ithaca, N.Y. 1967), pp. 296-7.

55. SIRIO, vol. 35, p. 415.

56. Herberstein, op. cit., n. 7, vol. I, p. 50. This same method was used to find a bride

for the emperor in eighth-century Byzantium. Romilly Jenkins, *Byzantium, the Imperial Centuries, A.D. 610-1071* (New York, 1966), p. 98. Also Warren Treadgold, "The Bride Shows of the Byzantine Emperors," *Byzantion*, vol. 49 (1979), pp. 395-413. Also note speculation above, n. 7. on this topic.

57. M.A. Glukovskii, "Soobshchenie o Rossii Moskovskogo posla v Milan (1486 g.), *"Voprosy istoriografii i istochnikovedeniia istorii SSSR* (Moscow, 1963), pp. 648-55. Glukovskii is certainly wrong in his belief that the Georgius Percaneotes of the Milanese document is not Iurii Trakhaniot the Elder. See also V.I. Rutenburg, "Ital'ianskie istochniki o sviaziakh Rossii i Italii v XV v., *"Issledovaniia po otechestvennomy istochnikovedeniiu* (Leningrad, 1964), pp. 455-462.

58. I.S. Lur'e, op. cit., n. 7, pp. 144, 135, 393.

59. It is interesting that Afanasii Kuritsyn, son of the heretic Fëdor Kuritsyn emerges as an official at about the time that Iurii Trakhaniot the Younger disappears. Afanasii appears as a clerk in 1520, and as a participant in diplomatic receptions in 1522. A.A. Zimin, D'iacheskii apparat v Rossii v XV-XVI vv, *"Istoricheskie zapiski* no. 87 (1971), p. 245.

60. PDS, cc. 64, 105.

61. Herberstein, op. cit., n. 7, vol. II, pp. 46-7.

62. Khoreskevich, op. cit., n. 2, p. 230; PDS, c. 650.

63. SIRIO, vol. 95, (St. Petersburg 1895), pp. 90-2.

64. *Barkhatnaia kniga*, n. 39, vol. II, pp. 276-7. The Barkhatnaia kniga errs in saying that Dmitrii Trakhaniot had no children; it is Iurii the Elder who was childless. Khoreskevich, op. cit., n. 2, p. 230 lists two other members of the family, Nil Bishop of Tver' and Andrei Trakhaniotov. As Alef, op. cit., n. 2, p. 32 indicates, the evidence that Nil was a member of the family is unclear, and the Andrei Trakhaniotov – the patronymic form is unusual at this time (1506)– seems to have been sent to Russia by a western ruler.

65. Denis Zakythinos, "Mikhail Maroullos Tarkhaniotes hellen poietes ton chronon tes Anagenneseos, *"Epeteris Hetaireias Byzantionon Spoudon* vol. 5 (1928), pp. 200-42, and especially pp. 204-5. Zakythinos also says that Theodore Lascaris went to Russia in the wedding party.

66. Michele Marullo Tarcaniota, *Carmina* ed. Alessandro Perosa (Turici, 1951), pp. 73-4, 10, 180, 44, 155, 133.

67. Rosario Tosto, "Per la biografia di Michele Marullo Tarcaniota," *Medioeve e Rinascimento veneto con altre studi in onore di Lino Lazzarini* (Padua, 1979), pp. 557-70. Also Benedetto Croce, *Michele Marullo Tarcaniota, le elegie per la patria perduta ed altri suoi carmi* (Bari, 1938), introduction.

68. Croce, op. cit., n. 67, p. 18.

69. Mario Emilio Cosenza, *Biographical and Bibliographical Dictionary of the Italian Humanists and of the World of Classical Scholarship in Italy, 1300-1800* (Boston, 1962-67), vol. 3, pp. 2219-204, 1936-8, vol. 4, p. 3029.

70. Vacalopoulos, *Origins*, n. 25, pp. 260-3.

71. Khoreshkevich, op. cit., n. 2, pp. 231-2.
72. SIRIO, vol. 35, pp. 239-40, 489-90.
73. Khoreshkevich, op. cit., n. 2, p. 231.
74. *Razriadnaia kniga, 1475-1598,* ed. V.I. Buganov (Moscow, 1966), pp. 272, 284, 312, 320, 348, 359, 377, 381, 415.
75. "Rodoslovnaia kniga..." *Vremennik Imperatorskogo Moskovskogo Obshchestva istorii i Drevnostei Rossiiskikh,* book 10 (1851), pp. 176-81.
76. Vacalopoulos, *Origins,* n. 25, p. 201.
77. Contarini, op. cit., n. 37, p. 160.

THE BYZANTINE LEGACY
IN THE BALKANS
UNDER OTTOMAN RULE

BYZANTINE LEGACY IN ECCLESIASTICAL ARCHITECTURE OF THE BALKANS AFTER 1453*

Slobodan Ćurčić

The half a century following the fall of Constantinople to the Turks in 1453 saw a gradual, but inevitable crumbling of the remaining Christian states in the Balkans. The Turks took Athens in 1456. Serbia fell in 1459, the Despotate of Morea in 1460, and the Kingdom of Bosnia in 1463. By the end of the century the Turks had reached the shores of the Adriatic. In the following three decades they made a deep penetration into central Europe.

Having defeated the Hungarians in 1526, their 'Drang nach Westen' was stopped only after their unsuccessful seige of Vienna in 1529. Inasmuch as the Turkish conquests in Central Europe proved to be untenable, their conquest of the Balkans was a more durable achievement. Notwithstanding the temporary losses of territory to the Austrians in the course of the later seventeenth and eighteenth centuries, the Turks maintained a stronghold in the Balkans until the nineteenth century. Starting only with the First Serbian uprising of 1804, followed by the more successful Second Serbian uprising in 1815, and by the Greek uprising of 1821, the slow process of liberation of the Balkan people from the Turkish rule was set into motion. This process was brought to a successful completion only a century later, at the end of the Balkan war of 1912.

Culturally speaking, the situation in the Balkans was somewhat different. The fall of Byzantium, and in its wake of several other

Balkan Christian states, did not spell an imminent end of Byzantine culture. Owing to the relative religious tollerance of the Turks, particularly during the period of their military strenght and economic prosperity, the creative arts of the Orthodox Christians were permitted to continue, and even flourish at times. Ultimately, following the end of the Turkish rule, this natural process of artistic *survival* was to a large extent surplanted by an artificial and generally sterile process of artistic *revival* of the Medieval tradition.

The artistic legacy of Byzantium in the Balkan lands under the Turkish occupation was recognized as an important phenomenon long ago. Dubbed "Byzance après Byzance", this material has not been adequately studied.[1] Of little interest to the hard-core Byzantinists, and of no consequence to the Renaissance art historians, this vast artistic heritage has been relegated to the regional specialists. Recent years have witnessed a fair number of studies dealing with the art of this period. Published in Albania, Bulgaria, Greece, and Yugoslavia, these studies refleet modern scholarly parochialism, and fail to convey a larger picture of Christian artistic production in the Balkans under Turkish domination.[2] The study of the architectural heritage of this period has generally lagged behind the study of other arts, and particularly that of painting. Within the last few years, however, there has been a sudden surge of publications dealing with regional architectural developments within Albania, Bulgaria, Greece, and Yugoslavia.[3] These pioneering endeavors are invaluable in their own right, but they, too, generally fall short of illuminating the larger framework with which each of these regional developments is associated. It would be more than presumptious to claim that shortcomings of this kind can be rectified in a short article such as this one. Instead, I will merely point out some ways of looking at general issues pertaining to architecture, and suggest some means by which current research and results already achieved could be meaningfully integrated into a broader general framework.

My first area of concern will focus on problems of architectural scale. Christian church architecture under the Turkish rule, as one might expect, did not enjoy official status and, therefore, held a place second to Islamic mosques. In contrast to earlier popularly held views, however, Christian church architecture was *not* systematically eradicated.

Notwithstanding the fact that churches *were* occasionally converted into mosques, and that some *were* destroyed, the vast majority were allowed to stand and continue to serve their original function.[4] What is more, the Turkish law was favorably disposed toward restoration and reconstruction of old buildings fallen into disrepair, Christian churches included.[5] Under certain circumstances, even construction of new Christian churches was permitted. To be sure, the vast majority of churches built under the Turkish rule were of relatively modest scale. The physical smallness of these churches is a correct gauge of the general status enjoyed by Christianity within the Ottoman empire.[6] It is also a correct gauge of the economic power of its patrons: a modest Christian middle class and generally small monastic communities. The number of such churches still preserved to this day throughout the Balkans is vast. To engage in their listing, however, would be counterproductive at this point. For our purposes, suffice it to refer to two churches which we may think of as 'typical' in the given category. The church of the Hagioi Anargyroi Kolokynthe of the north slope of the Acropolis in Athens, built ca. 1600 (Fig. 1), and the church of St. George in the village of Banjani, near Skopje, built in 1543 (Fig. 2), are both simple, single-aisled structures, lacking external articulation.[7] Such churches are found in towns as well as in the countryside; they were built as monastic, as well as parish churches. They simply constitute the bulk of ecclesiastical construction in the Balkans during the Turkish rule.

Although small-scale churches were predominant, they were by no means the only churches built. In certain instances, under particularly suitable political and economic circumstances, large churches which matched or even exceeded the scale of medieval buildings were built.[8] Invariably, such churches were monastic, and were removed from urban areas. The largest concentration of such churches is found on Mount Athos, where numerous new churches were built in the course of the sixteenth and later centuries.[9] In central Greece one also finds a considerable amount of architectural activity in the course of the sixteenth, seventeenth, and eighteenth centuries with a good number of large-scale churches resulting. The most prominent among these are: the Katholikon of the Great Meteoron Monastery, built in 1544; The Katholikon of Flamouri Monastery near Magnesia on Mount Pylion, built in 1595, the Katholikon of Petra Monastery, near Kataphygi on Mount Pindus, begun ca. 1550 (?), the main part of the superstucture built ca. 1625 (Figs. 3 and 4), the Katholika of the Monastery of Hagia Triada near Drakotrypa (ca. 1742), and the Monastery of Hagia Triada near Zoupani, built before the end of the eighteenth century.[10] A comparable phenomenon may be noted on the territory of Bulgaria where, in 1603, the Katholikon of the medieval Bachkovo monastery underwent a complete rebuilding (Figs. 5 and 6).[11] Sizeable churches were also built in parts of Serbia and Bosnia.[12]

Following the liberation of the Balkan states from the Turkish rule, one witnesses an entirely new phenomenon with regard to the scale of church building. Nurtured by the Romantic spirit and buoyed by national pride, the new patrons and architects created many new churches whose scale emulated not the architecture of the medieval period, but the sixth-century Hagia Sophia in Constantinople. This process which began in the nineteenth, was intensified in the first half of this century and, to an extent, is still going on.[13]

The capital cities of the new Balkan states –Athens, Sofia, and Belgrade– boast huge cathedrals and churches which illustrate this phenomenon best. In Athens, the new Orthodox Cathedral, dwarfing the late twelfth-century Metropolis, was built between 1840 and 1850 (Fig. 7).[14] In Sofia, the city's skyline is dominated by the Cathedral of Alexander Nevski, begun in 1882, and dedicated only in 1924 (Fig. 8). Its 170 ft. - high main dome falls only ten feet short of the height of the dome of Hagia Sophia in Constantinople.[15] The church of St. Mark in Belgrade, built between 1932 and 1936, is alledged to be the tallest of all Balkan Orthodox churches, its dome rising to a height of approximately 195 ft. (Fig. 9). The church of St. Mark is interesting from yet another viewpoint. Its design was based on the early-fourteenth century church of Gračanica, but its size was literally tripled.[16] The result of this 'scale-explosion' is the elephantine quality of such component parts as the supporting piers (Fig. 10). Executed in reinforced concrete, they resemble true columns, but in terms of their scale they exceed anything encountered in medieval practice. The severe interior surfaces which remain undecorated, dramatize the problems related to the mechanical process of scale magnification.

In concluding this discussion dealing with questions of architectural scale, it should be noted that ecclesiastical architecture built under the Turkish rule –both large-scale and small– was essentially compatible with medieval achievements. There was a true sense of survival in what has come to be known as 'post-Byzantine' architecture. The nineteenth and twentieth-century neo-Byzantine architecture, by contrast, broke with that tradition. The sense of continuity with the past became a matter of a deliberate, highly self-conscious revival. The change in architectural scale is one of the clearest manifestations of this important shift.

I shall turn next to the problems pertaining to the form of church buildings. Orthodox churches built during the period of Turkish rule display a surprisingly wide range of formal solutions: from the most readily recognizable emulations of medieval concepts, to churches of drastically modified designs. The former category is conditioned by the survival of strong local traditions, or by the dissemination of concepts from an important center (e.g. Mount Athos). The latter category is conditioned by a variety of factors, among them the creative powers of individual builders and patrons, and the 'active' Turkish impact being the most prominent.

Outright emulation of medieval prototypes is one of the better known, if not the most common, among the formal phenomena. This conservative development closely paralleled a similar trend in painting, and with similar results. It was marked by a certain 'frozen' quality of design, and by execution which was competent as best, but never brilliant. Examples of this kind of architecture may be found in all parts of the Balkans. The seventeenth-century church of St. Nicholas of Mistra illustrates the perserverance of a local tradition during the period of Turkish rule. (Figs. 11 and 12).[17] The church is marked by its large size, its generally Byzantine, and specifically local appearance. Its cross-in-square plan is characterized by the central location of the main dome, and by four lesser domes between the arms of the cross (Fig. 13). The general building form and the disposition of its plan find close parallels among the surviving monuments of medieval Mistra. The church of the Pantanassa Monastery, founded in 1428, may be referred to as the closest relevant example, similar in overall disposition and in the characteristics of external articulation (Figs. 14 and 15)[18].

Dissemination of planning and formal concepts from an important center, such as Mount Athos, accounts for another important category of post-Byzantine monuments which display strong affinities with medieval achievements. Mount Athos has already been mentioned as an area where a considerable number of large-scale churches were built in the sixteenth and later centuries.[19] What is of even greater significance is that most of these churches share common planning features which were preserved from medieval times. The outstanding features of what is generally referred to as a typical "athonite church plan" are: a cross-in-square naos, expanded laterally by an apsed bay to the north and to the south of the main cross arms, and preceded by a spatious narthex (or exonarthex), called the *liti*.[20] The Katholikon of Koutloumousiou Monastery, built in 1540, illustrates all of these points (Figs. 16 and 17).[21] Popularity of this church type in different parts of the Balkans in the course of the sixteenth and later centuries is remarkable. Among the Greek examples we may refer again to the Katholikon of Petra Monastery, begun ca. 1550 (?) (Figs. 3 and 4), and the related group of monuments.[22] The outstanding Bulgarian example is the large Katholikon of Bachkovo Monastery, as rebuilt in 1603 (Figs. 5 and 6).[23] Monuments in Yugoslavia which show affinities with athonite churches, do so in plan only, whereas their general architectural character deviates from the athonite prototypes. The best examples are the church of St. Nicholas at Novo Hopovo Monastery built in 1576, (Figs. 18 and 19), and the church of Papraća Monastery, from the second half of the fifteenth century.[24] Links with the medieval Serbian development known as the "Morava School" have frequently been cited as an explanation for the plan of Novo Hopovo.[25] The fact of the matter is that the "Morava School" churches, without exception, lack the massive pair of piers which separates the sanctuary from the naos. Such a pair of piers, on the other hand, is found in all athonite churches. Considering the differences in the external appearance of Katholikon of Koutloumousiou and the Novo Hopovo (Figs. 17 and 19), one is apt to conclude that a local building crew had at its disposal a drawing of an athonite church plan.

In the category of modified church designs from the period of Turkish rule several different phenomena stand out. At the one end of the scale we find creative outbursts, while at the other we find what may be referred to as 'muted' solutions – familiar medieval types, but deprived of certain crucial formal components (e.g. the dome). This wide range of modified church designs was effected by an equally wide range of determining factors. These vary from particularly suitable economic circumstances, enterprising skills and imagination of patrons and builders, on the one hand, to official Turkish regulations and restrictions effecting church designs, on the other.

In the first group of churches, distinguished by their creative design, we are confronted with a relatively small number of monuments. The singularly most spectacular example of creative design modification preserved anywhere in the Balkans in the church of the Monastery of Doliana (or Krania) on Mount Pindus (Figs. 20 and 21).[26] This curious church is based on the cross-in-square plan elaborated by the addition of not one, but three apses on each of the lateral facades. In its original form, built during the second half of the eighteenth century, the building had only three domes over the main bays of the naos. At a later time, between 1840 and 1848, nine more domes were added resulting in a fantastic building silhouette for which no precedents in Byzantine architecture are known. It is worth mentioning that a similar, though almost certainly unrelated phenomenon of dome multiplication, occurred in eighteenth-century Russia. The wooden church of the Transfiguration on the Island of Khizhi, built in 1714, is one of the best Russian examples.[27] Its tall, picturesque silhouette is studded with as many as twenty-one domes. Here, as with nine of the twelve domes at Doliana, there is no physical link between the domes and the interior space – domes have truly become decorative features of the exterior. One must be reminded, however, that the imaginative solution of the Doliana church constitutes an exception in every respect.

Elaboration upon known Byzantine architectural types occurred but rarely in post-Byzantine architecture. Far more common was a conservative approach which generally yielded buildings readily equateable with medieval achievements. Such an approach was governed, among other factors, by technical practicalities. Maintaining active building workshops that would have been involved in building Christian churches must have been a difficult proposition for any given area under the Turkish rule. Emulation of past practices would thus have come as the easiest way of "conforming", even for not so accomplished a building crew. What intrigues an architectural historian is that there appears to have been virtually no professional interaction between builders of Christian churches and builders of Islamic mosques.[28] This is all the more surprising if one recalls that residential architecture of Christian and Islamic communities showed no appreciable differences. In the realm of what we might refer to as "passive" Turkish influence on Christian church architecture, one is limited to very few examples. The church of unknown dedication, built ca. 1455 for the Bosnian ruler Herceg Stjepan, near the fortress Soko, is one of the best examples of this phenomenon.[29] In plan, the church is a simple, single-aisled structure, with a single dome occupying the central of the three bays. (Fig. 22-B). It is in the structural and formal articulation of this bay, that we perceive the degree of Turkish influence. (Fig. 22-A). The principal arches supporting the dome are all pointed, while squinches, instead of pendentives, occupy the four corners transforming the square bay into an octagon. A shallow octagonal drum is further transformed into a sixteen-sided polygon by means of lesser squinches. It is only from this base that the actual curvature of the dome itself begins. The lowest portion of the stone dome is further articulated by means of fourteen ogival arches forming a decorative frieze at the base of the dome. The use of squinches, pointed and ogival arches are all Turkish architectural elements and, as such, illustrate the extent of borrowing from the Turkish tradition.[30]

Another example of obvious dependence on Turkish architecture is seen in the church of the Monastery Sv. Jovan Bigorski in western Macedonia. (Fig. 23).[31] The church was completely rebuilt in 1796 on the site of a much older church of which nothing survives. The present church features an unusual plan in which the entire naos is covered by a relatively large dome (9.02m in diameter). The dome is enveloped externally in a two-tiered octagonal false drum, and capped by a low conical roof. The narthex of the church is crowned by a secondary, smaller dome supported internally by squinches and encased externally in a low octagonal drum. The architectural character of the church leaves no doubt as to its links with Turkish mosque architecture.

Far more subtle is the example of 'passive' Turkish influence in the church of St. George at Mlado Nagoričino.[32] (Figs. 24 and 25). In many ways – in its plan, manner of construction, articulation of facades, and its dedication – this church was modelled closely on the nearby fourteenth-century church of St. George at Staro Nagoričino (Fig. 26). In some of its details, however, the Mlado Nagoričino church departs from its predecessor, and reveals Islamic models.[33] This is true of the pointed main arches on its facades with their stone voussoirs of alternating colors, as well as of the ogee-shaped tympana above principal windows (Fig. 24). The church at Mlado Nagoričino shares all of these characteristics, along with high quality ashlar construction, with the Tatar Sinan Bey Mosque (built 1520-30) at Kumanovo, some twelve kilometers to the east (Fig. 27).[34] Mlado Nagoričino is not securely dated, but the probability of the same builders being responsible for their execution is great.

The church of St. George at Mlado Nagoričino displays yet another important architectural characteristic which points to another form of Turkish influence, one we refer to as 'active' influence. The feature in question is the low, blind dome, concealed under a low pyramidal roof (Fig. 25). This form of a dome is in sharp contrast with the highly visible domes of Staro Nagoričino, elevated on tall drums perforated by slender windows (Fig. 26). The change in design may reflect modifications induced by Turkish regulations. Although domed church architecture was by no means unknown during the Turkish times, it was generally uncommon in urban centers. A cursory examination of churches built during the Turkish period in such cities as, for example, Thessaloniki, reveals the predominance of domeless, mostly basilican churches. The church of Hagios Athanasios, in its present form built in 1818, is a case in point.[35] The reappearance of the basilica in Greece in the course of the eighteenth and nineteenth centuries has been explained as resulting from a number of factors.[36] There is no doubt that the growing economic power of the Christian middle class exerted a major impact on this development. At the same time, as in the very beginnings of Early Christian architecture, the basilica would have been the most expedient answer to increased demands, with the shortage of time and the lack of skilled craftsmen as the major constraints. Indeed, basilican churches also appear in other parts of the Balkans during the Ottoman period.[37] The church of the Archangels Gabriel and Michael in Sarajevo illustrates the type which, in this case, may go as far back as the fifteenth century (Fig. 28).[38] In its

present form the church is a result of a thorough reconstruction dating
from 1793. There is no reason to suspect, however, that the older
versions of the church were not basically of the same character. A
general observation may be made that basilican churches predominate
in urban centers, while domed churches are more frequent in
extra-urban monastic centers. Although this must not be mistaken for
a fast rule, it *is* a general indicator. Short of being able to point to
specific Turkish regulations restricting the construction of domed
Christian churches, the general pattern with which we are confronted
suggests that Turkish regulations did play some role in the formation
of Orthodox church architecture from the fifteenth to the nineteenth
centuries. This notion would seem to be substantiated by the wholesale
return to domed church architecture in all Orthodox areas of the
Balkans following the liberation from the Turkish rule.

We are in a much better position to make judgements regarding
church belfries under the Ottoman regime. Here, the evidence shows
plainly that the use of bells was officially prohibited, and that such
regulations were rigorously enforced, particularly in urban areas.[39]
Only in certain peripheral regions of the Turkish empire was the use of
bells condoned.[40] According to Leo Allatios, "the Turks feared that the
sound (of bells, *sic.*) might strike fear into wandering souls and destroy
peace which they enjoy".[41] According to other, popular Islamic beliefs,
bells were thought to attract evil spirits, or to keep angels away.[42] Not
only was there a strict policy forbidding their use, but there were
evidently continuous efforts at complete eradication of bells.[43] The few
surviving examples of medieval bells have been preserved, it would
seem, because they were buried to protect them from the Turkish
purges.[44]

The general Turskish attitude toward bells, and the resulting policy
prohibited their use, left an imprint on Orthodox church architecture.
Turkish wrath was directed not solely against bells, but also against
architectural features associated with them – belfries. Their highly
visible presence on a city's skyline must have been perceived by the
Moslems as an unwanted competition with their minarets. Dismantling
of belfries, therefore, became a norm. Archaeological work on
churches throughout the territory once held by the Byzantine empire
suggests that many more once had belfries than is now apparent.[45]

Indeed, the few preserved examples of belfries, particularly among urban churches, did survive only because they were adapted for minarets by the Turks. The case of the cathedral church of medieval Prizren – Bogorodica Ljeviška – is the best known example. (Fig. 29).[46] The church of St. Peter at Bijelo Polje, on the other hand, illustrates a case where one of a pair of towers was maintained by the Turks, while the other one was completely dismantled (Fig. 30).[47]

Even the liberal Turkish policies governing restoration of old churches were evidently modified when it came to belfries.[48] During the veritable church building boom following the re-establishment of the Serbian patriarchate in 1557, a number of important medieval churches underwent extensive necessary restorations, but none of them regained their lost belfries.[49] Among these, the most telling examples are those of the patriarchal complex of churches at Peć, and that of Gračanica. At Peć, the original open exonarthex built in front of the three main churches by the Archbishop Danilo II around 1330 was seriously damaged before 1557, requiring extensive repairs.[50] The resulting structure, which we see today, differs substantially from the originally open, light and airy exonarthex (Fig. 31). A similar change, and for similar reasons, occurred at Gračanica, where the remodelling took place in the late 1560's (Fig. 32).[51] The present appearance of the Gračanica exonarthex constitutes a recent restoration attempt at returning it to its original appearance (Fig. 33).[52] In both cases – at Peć and at Gračanica – the original exonarthexes included axially placed belfries, but these were suppressed in the sixteenth-century restorations. We are fortunate, however, that visual documents recording the appearance of both of these belfries have been preserved. In the case of Peć, the document is a fresco painted before 1337, depicting the donor, Archbishop Danilo II with the model of the church complex (Fig. 34). The model shows clearly not only the form of the lost belfry, but also the fact that it had at least two bells hanging within it. In the case of Gračanica, the visual document is a woodcut in an Octoechos printed in 1539 at Gračanica (Fig. 35). It also shows two bells hanging within the open superstructure of the belfry. The actual raison d'être for the reconstrucion of the two monuments may have been the damage inflicted by the Turks during earlier efforts to eradicate belfries. Our evidence, unfortunately, is only circumstantial. A cursory examination of Serbian medieval churches damaged during the Ottoman rule reveals a curious recurring pattern of damage concentrated in the area of narthexes.[53] Through the destruction of extant belfries, and regulations prohibiting the reconstruction of old or the construction of new ones, the Turks exercised a major "active" role in the shapping of Orthodox church architecture from the fifteenth through the eighteenth centuries.

That the suppression of belfries was an unpopular Turkish policy imposed on the Orthodox church is best gleaned by considering contemporaneous Orthodox church construction in areas of the Balkans not under the Turkish rule. Thus, for example, Orthodox churches in the area around the Bay of Kotor built in the eighteenth century during the Venetian control, invariably display prominent, axially placed belfries. The church of the Dormition of the Virgin at Savina Monastery, built between 1777 and 1799 is the largest, and the most important example (Fig. 36).[54] Similar proliferation of belfries may be noted on the Mani Peninsula, and in certain restricted areas under nominal Turkish control, but enjoying some degree of autonomy, as was the case with Mount Athos.[55] An even more emphatic demonstration of the significance of belfries in the Orthodox church is found in the region of Fruška Gora. A large number of churches were built here before and during the period of Turkish control. Then, within a few decades following the final expulsion of the Turks in 1716, every major monastic church acquired a huge axially placed Baroque belfry.[56]

Construction of makeshift belfries and installation of bells was paramount on the minds of priests and monks in areas newly liberated from the Turks. An episode from the history of Gračanica Monastery illustrates this phenomenon. In 1903, with the Turkish control in the central Balkans waning, a bell was smuggled into the monastery and rung for the first time since the sixteenth century.[57]

In areas of Serbia liberated from the Turks in the course of the eighteenth and nineteenth centuries, churches with integrally built belfries became commonplace. In fact, in the later eighteenth and the first half of the nineteenth century, belfries became far more common an aspect of Serbian Orthodox churches than the familiar Byzantine domes. The new Orthodox cathedral of Sremska Mitrovica, built between 1781 and 1794 (Fig. 37), and the new cathedral of Belgrade, built between 1837 and 1845 (Fig. 38), are among the largest and the best known examples.[58] The obvious absence of rapport with the medieval tradition has generally been regarded as the result of a wave of western influence which swept in following the departure of the Turks. In particular, the proliferation of belfries, was seen as but one of the many manifestations of this westernizing wave. Their Baroque style, needless to say, seemed to readily confirm such notions. On the basis of our analysis, however, this interpretation has to be revised. Only the style of such buildings as the cathedrals of Sremska Mitrovica and Belgrade is genuinely western. The presence of axial belfries fronting these, churches, on the other hand, should be viewed as a survival of the medieval tradition. It would thus seem that the Turkish efforts to suppress the use of bells and construction of belfries, achieved the opposite result. In the final analysis, then, the belfry inadvertently became the paramount symbolic feature of Serbian Orthodox church architecture displacing, if only temporarily, the dome in that role. With the Neo-Byzantine revival of medieval architectural types, in the second half of the nineteenth and twentieth centuries, the belfry retained its place, now alongside with the more familiar medieval church forms.[59] The churches of Alexander Nevski in Sofia, and St. Mark in Belgrade may be referred to again to illustrate this point (Figs. 8 and 9). The church of St. Mark which, as we have already seen, was designed as a deliberate emulation of the fourteenth-century church of Gračanica, was an archaeologically 'correct' copy, as far as its belfry is concerned. Its design includes an axial belfry precisely in the same location as that shown on the 1539 woodcut of Gračanica (Fig. 34), although that belfry was destroyed shortly thereafter, and never rebuilt.[60]

Questions raised with regard to belfries in post-Byzantine church architecture call for a brief re-assessment of the role of bells and belfries in Byzantine church architecture. This subject has not attracted much attention in the past.[61] The prevalent viewpoint in scholarship has been that belfries did not appear in the Byzantine world before the thirteenth century and that they were imported from the West.[62] Our growing knowledge of individual monuments in recent years has begun to alter this simplified perception of the problem. It is now clear that many churches in the principal urban centers of the Byzantine empire once had belfries, although very few of these have actually been preserved. The churches of Hagia Sophia, the Virgin Pammakaristos, the Chora, the so-called Kilise Camii, and possibly also the Kalenderhane Camii, are all known cases in the Capital.[63] New research suggests that the cathedral of Saint Sophia in Ohrid, and the church of the Holy Apostles in Thessaloniki also once had belfries.[64] Various written sources clearly indicate that bells were used in Byzantium long before 1204.[65] Thus, the emerging notion is that bells and belfries, if not indigenous to Byzantium, were certainly known earlier than previously postulated, while their number must have been appreciably greater than once thought.

This matter is of importance for our discussion because it illustrates that belfries had an established place within Orthodox Christian church architecture in the Balkans prior to the Turkish conquest. The subsequent development which saw the general Turkish opposition to the use of bells and the ensuing policies suppressing bells and belfries resulted, it would seem, in a dormant passion for bells among the Orthodox Christians. This passion which manifested itself on rare occasions during the period of Ottoman rule, exploded in a wave of belfry construction following the liberation from the Turks. Belfries were being built either as integral components of new churches, or as additions to the existing ones. This, decidely conservative wave, was a reflection of western impact only insofar as the Baroque style of the belfries is concerned. Conceptually, however, these belfries constitute a direct link with an interrupted and suppressed Byzantine tradition. As such they illustrate, more clearly than any other aspect of Orthodox churches, the degree of the Turkish role in the shaping of Orthodox church architecture in the Balkans after 1453.

Orthodox church architecture in the Balkans from ca. 1450 to the twentieth century reveals a continued strong presence of the Byzantine legacy. The preservation of this legacy took place under the auspices of the Orthodox church, and in particular of its monastic institutions. The pronounced architectural conservatism, which we have noted, manifested itself in two principal ways: first, as a *survival* of the medieval-Byzantine tradition, from ca. 1450 through the eighteenth century, superseded by a *revival* of the same tradition, but on a grander scale, in the nineteenth and twentieth centuries, following the termination of the Turkish rule. These trends have been recognized and studied in part within the individual national contexts, be it Greek, Serbian, or Bulgarian. Transcending these national constraints, however, we were able to discern a number of common architectural developments:

1. Changes in architectural scale – from small, or moderately large, under the Turkish domination, to gargantuan, following the liberation from the Turkish rule.

2. Changes in building forms and methods of constructions – initially dependent on medieval practice, these were gradually modified by the intrusion of western, mostly stylistic elements, only to be superseded by a deliberate, academic revival of medieval forms.

3. The impact of Turkish culture on Orthodox Christian church architecture manifesting itself in two different modes – the "passive" and the "active" – the latter being far more significant than the former.

In sum, we may conclude that the study of ecclesiastical architecture in the Balkans after 1453 offers invaluable insights about itself, but also on a much broader plane. A continued broadening of interpretations, alongside with the essential ground work which must go on, will, no doubt, shed new light not only on the Orthodox Christian cultural life in the Balkans under the Turkish domination, but on the ultimate source of this rich legacy – Byzantium itself.

NOTES

* The author is grateful to the late Professor Lowell Clucas whose original invitation for participation in this symposium inspired the following study.   wing study.

1. The pioneering stury by N. Iorga, *Byzance après Byzance* (Buchurest, 1935), chartered the field.

2. For Albania see: T. Popa, *Piktorët mesjetarë shqiptare* (Tirana, 1961), a survey of documented works and known painters and workshops. More accessible is a short essay by Dhorka Dhamo, "Le Moyen Age (X^e - XIXe siècles)," in anexhibition cataloque *L'art albanais à travers les siècles* (Paris, n.d.), not paginated. Dhamo discusses, among others, the work of three major post-Byzantine "Albanian" painters – Onofrios (16th cent.), Konstantin Shpataraku (18th cent.), and Konstantin Zograph (18th cent.). Additional literature on Onofrios, in particular, is numerous; T. Popa, "Onufre, une figure éminente de la peinture médiévale

8877144

albanaise," "*Studia Albanica,* 3, no. 1 (1966), 291-309, is the most comprehensive study. Its title illuminates an obsessive preoccupation of all Albanian scholars with the question of ethnic origins of medieval and post-medieval artists who are invariably portrayed as Albanians. For Bulgaria see: Magdalina Stancheva, "Postizheniia i problemi na arkheologicheskoto prouchvane na kŭsnoto srednove-kovie (XV-XVII v.)" [Fr. Sum.: "Réalisations et problèmes des études archéologi-ques du bas moyen age (XVᵉ - XVIIᵉ s.)"], *Arkheologiia,* 16, no. 3 (1974), 73-81; Atanas Boschkov, *Le peinture bulgare des origines au XIXᵉ siècle* (Recklinghausen, 1974). Both of these general discussions show similar preoccupations with the questions of ethnic origins of most-often unknown artists. Less stooped in nationalist issues is the work of Assen Tschilingirov, *Die Kunst des Christlichen Mittelalters in Bulgarien 4, bis 18. Jahrhudert* (Berlin, 1978), though it, too, isolates the Bulgarian material from that of the other areas of the Balkans. For Greece see: Manolis Chatzidakis, "Considérations sur la peinture postbyzantine en Grèce," *Actes du Premier congrès internationale des études Balkanique et Sud-Est Européennes,* 2 (Sofia, 1969), 705-714, and a series of collected essays by the same author in idem. *Études sur la peinture postbyzantine* (London, 1976). For Yugoslavia see: Sreten Petković, *Zidno slikarstvo na području Pećke patrijaršije 1557-1614* [English sum.: "Wall Painting on the Territory of the Patriarchate of Peć (1557-1614)"] (Novi Sad, 1965), a truly pioneering work noted for its unusually objective approach to the material: Zdravko Kajmaković, *Zidno slikarstvo u Bosni i Hercegovini* (Sarajevo, 1971). A helpful overview of the main issues in the context of the Balkan Peninsula as a whole is given by André Grabar, *Die Mittelalterliche Kunst Osteuropas* (Baden-Baden, 1968), chapter VI. The most important work to appear in recent years, without a question, is Machiel Kiel, *Art and Society of Bulgaria in the Turkish Period* (Assen, 1985). Though focusing on Bulgaria, Kiel is concerned with much broader issues pertaining to the historiography and ideology of modern scholarship in the Balkans. Critical of much of the older literature, Kiel provides a well-documented and objective assessment of the society and art in Bulgaria (and occasionally in other parts of the Balkans, as well) during the Turkish rule. His approach is bilateral, insofar that it also takes into account Turkish documents which most often provide a clearer and more accurate picture than could be gleaned from non-Turkish sources. Though cumbersome and difficult to read, Kiel's work will nevertheless, serve as a guide for future scholarship dealing with this material.

3. In addition to a host of monographic studies of individual monuments, a number of syntheses dealing with regional architectural developments have also appeared within the last decade. For Albania see: Aleksandër Meksi and P. Thomo, "Arkitektura pasbizantine në Shqiperi "(French sum.: "L'architecture postbyzan-tine en Albanie"), *Monumentet,* 11 (1976), 127-145; also: idem., *Monumentet,* 20 (1980), 45-68; and idem., *Monumentet* 21 (1981), 99-143. For Bulgaria see: Magdalena Koeva, *Pametnitsi na kulturata prez bŭlgarskoto vŭzrazhdane* (Sofia, 1977), and M. Kiel, op.cit. For Greece see: Charalambos Bouras, ed., *Ekklēsies stēn*

Hellada meta tēn Alosē ("Churches in Greece 1453-1850"), vol. 1 (Athens, 1979), vol. 2 (Athens, 1982), two collections of essays written by different authors on individual monuments; hereafler; *Ekklēsies*, 1 and *Ekklēsies*, 2. For Yugoslavia (Serbia) see: Vojislav Matić, *Arhitektura fruškogorskih manastira* (Novi Sad, 1984), a study of a cluster of post-byzantine monasteries on Fruška Gora; Marica Šuput, *Srpska arhitektura u doba turske vlasti, 1459-1690* ("L'architecture serbe pendant la domination ottomane, 1459-1690") (Belgrade, 1984).

4. On the general questions pertaining to the conversion and destruction of churches under the Ottoman rule see the very useful discussion by M. Kiel, op.cit., pp. 167-184; and also: Olga Zirojević, *Crkve i manastiri na području Pećke partijaršije do 1683. godine* (Belgrade, 1984), pp. 17-26. On some specific examples of church conversion see Andrej Andrejević, "Pretvaranje crkava u džamije" (Engl. sum.: "On the Transformation of Churches into Mosques"), *Zbornik za likovne umetnosti*, 12 (1976), 99-117.

5. On the Turkish official policy toward the restoration of churches see M. Kiel, op.cit., pp. 184-191; and Zirojević, op. cit., pp. 27-31.

6. Here we must disagree with M. Kiel, op.cit., pp. 256f, who attempts to show that church architecture built in Bulgaria (and implicitly in the Balkans, in general) was on a comparable scale, if not more monumental than medieval church architecture. Efforts to quantify such an assertion are risky. For one, the number of medieval monuments lost is certainly greater than the number of vanished post-Byzantine monuments. Furthermore, the proportion of the small-scale churches to the large-scale ones would seem to be much greater for the post--Byzantine period. This is true of many regions of the Balkans. As a good example of a regional development see Charalambos Bouras, A. Kaloyeropoulou, and R. Andreadi, *Churches of Attica* (Athens, 1970). Differences between the town and the countryside must also be born in mind. Effects of various Turkish regulations were always felt more keenly in urbanized areas than in the country. We must agree with M. Kiel, however, that much of the older scholarship would hardly admit that church construction of any consequence actually took place during the Turkish times.

7. For Hagioi Anargyroi Kolokynthe see Anastasios Tanoulas, "Oi Anargyroi Kolokynthe sten Athena, *"Ekklesies*, 2, pp. 179-190; for St. George at Banjani see Go jko Subotić, "Sveti Djordje u Banjanima. Istori ja i arhitektura" (French sum.: "Saint-Georges de Ban jani. Histoire et architecture"), *Zbornik za likovne umetnosti, 21 (1985), 135-160.

8. Kiel, op.cit., pp. 256f., as well as note 6, *supra*.

9. A monumental corpus of Athonite monasteries is under preparation by Paul Mylonas. For a preliminary report see P. Mylonas. "L'architecture du Mont Athos," *Thesaurismata*, 2 (1963), supplement, 18-48; also idem., "Research on Athos. Memorandum on Works Accomplished and Projected," *Actes du XVe Congres internationalle*. Of all the major Athonite churches only five are actually medieval (Protaton at Karyes, and the Katholika of the Great Lavra, Vatopedi,

Iviron, and Chilandari monasteries). Alla of the other principal churches are post-Byzantine. Two major periods of construction stand out - during the fifteenth and during the nineteeth centuries.

10. For the Katholikon of the Great Meteoron see G. Sotiriou, "Ai Monai ton Meteōrōn," *Epetēris Hetaireias Byzantinōn Spoudōn,* 9 (1932), pp. 383-415. For the remaining churches referred to see: Yannis Kizis, "Hē Monē Flamouriou sto Pēlio, *Ekklēsies,* 2, pp. 151-166; Paul M. Mylonas, "Hē Monē Petras stēn Notia Pindo," *Ekklēsies,* 2, pp. 121-138; Yannis Karatzoglou, "Hē Monē Hagias Triados Drakotrypas (Sklatainas)," *Ekklesies,* 2, pp. 139-150; Rea Leonidopoulou-Stylianou, "To katholiko tēs Monēs tes Hagias Triadas sto Zoupani," *Ekklēsies,* 1, pp. 67-82.

11. For the Katholikon of Bachkovo see Stefan Boiadzhiev, "Kŭm vŭprosa za datirovkata na dvete tsŭrkvi v Bachkovskiia manastir," *"Rodopski zbornik,*3 (1972), 79-103.

12. Groupings of larger churches are found in the region of Fruška Gora (see Matić, op.cit., note 3, *supra),* in the Ovčar-Kablar Gorge and in north-eastern Bosnia (see Šuput, op.cit., note 3, *supra,* pp. 68-86, passim, who cites relevant literature for individual monuments).

13. Neo-Byzantine architecture is a totally unstudied field. Isolated studies of individual buildings, or architects do exist, but they are random, and provide no coherent understanding of the problems at hand. For an attempt at illuminating aspects of recent Greek-Orthodox church architecture in the U.S. see Anthony Cutler, "The Tyrany of Hagia Sophia: Notes on Greek Orthodox Church Design in the United States," *Journal of the Society of Architectural Historians,* 31, no. 1 (March 1972), 38-50.

14. The new Orthodox Cathedral of Athens was planned as early as 1840, and its designer may have been the Danish architect Theophilus Hansen. The construction of the church began in 1843, and Hansen may have been relieved of his responsibility shortly after that time. In any case, the church was finished by others. See V. Villadsen's entry on Theophilus Hansen in Adolf K. Placzek, ed., *Macmillan Encyclopedia of Architects* (New York and London, 1982), v. 2, 305-306.

15. For the church of Alexander Nevski see Liuben Tonev, et al., eds., *Kratka istoriia na bŭlgarskata arkhitektura* (Sofia, 1965), p. 556, according to whom the church was a work of the architect Pomerantsev (Russian?, *sic.*), and was based on a Russian church plan which evolved in the course of the second half of the nineteenth century.

16. Djurdje Bošković, "Crkva Sv. Marka u Beogradu kao karikatura Gračanice," *Srpski književni glasnik,* N.s., 36, no. 4 (June 16, 1932), 302-304, is a sharply worded architectural critique of the building. The church was built by the architects Petar and Branko Krstić. Its interior was left unfinished at the outbreak of W.W.II, and remains unfinished to this day. I am most grateful to Mr. Robert van Nice who has kindly put at my disposal his photographs of the church of St. Mark, taken at the time when the building had just been completed.

17. The building is essentially unpublished. The main dome, as shown on Fig. 11, is a result of modern reconstruction. The church lay in ruins at the beginning of this century; see Gabriel Millet, *Monuments byzantins de Mistra* (Paris, 1910), pls. 6, fig. 2 (plan); 11, figs. 3 and 5 (gen. views); 15, fig. 6 (interior).

18. For the Pantanassa and the related group of medieval churches of Mistra see Horst Hallensleben, "Untersuchungen zur Genesis und Typologie des 'Mistratypus'," *Marburger Jahrbuch für Kunstwissenschaft*, 18 (1969), 105-118.

19. See note 9, *supra*. On the circumstance on Mount Athos after the Turkish conquest see Nicholas Oikonomidès, "Monastères et Moines lors la conquête ottomane," *Südost-Forschungen*, 35 (1976), 1-10; also Georgije Ostrogorski, "Sveta Gora posle Maričke bitke," *Zbornik Filosofskog fakulteta*, XI-1 (1970), 277-282.

20. Mylonas, "L'architecture du Mont Athos,"

21. A brief note in Adriano Alpago Novello, *Crecia Bizantina* (Milano, 1969), 97-99.

22. For the Katholikon of Petra Monastery and the related churches see note 10, *supra*.

23. See note, 11, *supra*.

24. For the church of St. Nicolas at Novo Hopovo see Matić, op.cit., pp. 105-118; for Papraća see Šuput, op.cit., pp. 80-83, figs. 34-1 and 35, and pls. 42-44.

25. Matić, op.cit., pp. 39-48, passim.; Kiel, op.cit., pp. 139-142. Šuput, op.cit. p. 56 is ambivalent about the sources of Novo Hopovo, but correctly associates Papraća with Hilandar (Chilandari) Monastery on Mount Athos, ibid., pp. 80-83, passim.

26. Paul M. Mylonas, "Hē Monē Dolianōn e Kranias stēn Pindo," *Ekklēsies*, 1, pp. 93-110.

27. David Buxton, *The Wooden Churches of Eastern Europe: An Introductory Survey* (Cambridge, 1981), pp. 64-69, figs. 96-98.

28. Petković, *Zidno slikarstvo*, p. 51, and n. 133, points out cases of minor borrowings of architectural elements.

29. Mirko Kovačević, "Crkva pod srednjovekovnim gradom Sokolom," *Starinar*, N.s., 18 (1968), 221-224.

30. On the links with Turkish architecture see Vojislav J. Djurić, in M. Djurović, et al. eds., *Istorija Crne Gore*, 2, part 2 (Titograd, 1970), 448-452, esp. 449, and 452.

31. Vladimir R. Petković, *Pregled crkvenih spomenika kroz povesnicu srpskog naroda*, Srpska akademija nauka, Posebna izdanja, 157 (Belgrade, 1950), pp. 24-25, and p. 548, fig. 73 (plan, dome section, and church elevation).

32. Šuput, op.cit., pp. 87-88.

33. Machiel Kiel, "Armenian and Ottoman Influences on a Group of Village Churches in the Kumanovo District," *Zbornik za likovne umetnosti*, 7 (1971), 247-255.

34. Ibid., 255. To my knowledge, the Tatar Sinan Bey Mosque is an unpublished building. Passing remarks in Andrej Andrejević, *Islamska monumentalna umetnost: kupolne džamije* (Engl. sum.: "Sixteenth-Century Islamic Monumental Art in Yugoslavia: Domed Mosques") (Belgrade, 1984), pp. 48, 63, and 64, suggest several unique aspects of this building, thereby supporting Kiel's notion that it, along with a group of churches in the area, may have been built by a team of masons from elsewhere (Asia Minor?).

35. Maria Ch. Cambouris-Vamvoukou, "Ho Hagios Athanasios Thessalonikes," *Ekklesies,* 1, pp. 33-46.

36. Charalambos, Th. Bouras, "Ho architektonikos typos tēs vasilikēs kata tēn Tourkokratia kai ho Patriarchēs Kallinikos," *Ekklesiēs,* 1, pp. 159-168.

37. The largest number of post-Byzantine basilicas, outside of Greece, is found in Albania; see Aleksandër Meksi and P. Thomo, "Arkitektura pasbizantine në Shqipëri (Basilikat)", *Monumentet,* 21 (1981), 99-148.

38. Djoko Mazalić, "Stara crkva u Sarajevu: razmartranja o njezinoj arhitekturi i prošlosti, *"Glasnik hrvatskih zemaljskih muzeja u Sarajevu* (also: *Glasnik zemaljskog muzeja u Sarajevu),* 54 (1942), 221-269.

39. Leo Allatios, *The Newer Temples of the Greeks,* transl. by Anthony Cutler (University Park and London, 1969), pp. 5-6. Allatios (1586 or 87-1669), a native Greek converted to Catholicism, writes: "When Byzantium was taken, the empire plundered, and the remaining sovereignty of the Greeks seized, the use of bells in the cities in which they lived was interrupted" (p. 5); and further on: "Bells of brass or copper are very rare in Greece unless the town in which the Christians live is far removed from traffic with the Turks" (p. 6).

40. "In no parts of Turkie, or Dominions of the G. Signor, unless in Moldavia, Valachia, and Mount Athos are Bells permitted." See Sir Paul Rycaut, *The Present State of the Greek and Armenian Churches, Anno Christi 1678* (London, 1679), p. 209.

41. Allatios, op. cit., p. 5.

42. Henry Harris Jessup, *The Women of the Arabs* (New York, 1873), p. 304: "The Moslems abhor bells. They say bells draw together evil spirits." F.W. Hasluck, *Christianity and Islam under the Sultans,* vol. 1 (Oxford, 1929), p. 189, f.n. 1, regarding the supposed effect of bells on angels.

43. Malcom Letts, transl. and ed., *The Pilgrimage of Arnold von Harff Knight from Cologne... which He Accomplished in the Years 1496 to 1499,* The Hakluyt Society, 2nd Ser., No. 94 (London, 1946), p. 247, writing about Adrianople (Edirne): "We went further into another house close by, which was full of whole and broken Christian bells which had been captured in Christian countries and carried there, from which cannon are cast. It was told me that each Turk, when he crosses a mountain or the sea to conquer a country, must bring back a piece of a bell."

44. Pera Popović, "Nekoliko zvona iz XV veka, *"Starinar,* 3rd Ser., 4 (1926-27), 105-110. Burying of bells as a result of Turkish threat was practiced also in the Catholic areas of the Balkans" Pavao Andjelić, *Bobovac i Kraljeva Sutjeska* (Sarajevo, 1973), pp. 78-81.

45. A brief check list provided by Horst Hallensleben, "Byzantinische Kirchtürme," *Kunst-Chronik,* vol. 19, no. 10 (October 1966), 309-311, who enumerates twenty-seven churches with ascertained, and twelve churches with questionable belfries. This number has grown since 1966.

46. Andrejević, "Pretvaranje crkava," p. 111, and fig. 6.

47. Ibid., p. 111, and drawing no. 2.

48. On Turkish policies governing restoration of old churches see Note 5, *supra*. Unfortunately, and surprisingly, M. Kiel does not discuss the use of bells or belfries at all.

49. Regarding the restoration of Serbian monasteries following the re-establishment of the Serbian Patriarchate in 1557 see a brief historical account in: S. Petković, *Zidno slikarstvo*, pp. 49-50. Among the reconstructed monasteries were: Peć (after 1557), Gračanica (1560's), Žiča (1562), Morača (ca. 1570), Studenica (before 1568), Nikola Dabarski (Banja), Mileševa, Gradac. Of these, only Žiča retains its medieval belfry, evidently not damaged prior to the reconstruction. Peć and Gračanica are known to have had belfries, but these were not restored (see below). The same may have been the case also with Mileševa and Gradac, where recent excavations have turned up foundations of twin-towers fronting church exonarthexes.

50. Marica Šuput, "Architektura pećke priprate" (Fr. sum." "L'architecture de l'exonarthex de Peć"), *Zbornik za likovne umetnosti*, 13 (1977), 45-69.

51. S. Ćurčić, *Gračanica: King Milutin's Church and Its Place in Late Byzantine Architecture* (University Park and London, 1979), pp. 15-17, and pp. 21-22.

52. Branislav Vulović, "Nova istraživanja arhitekture Gračanice" (Fr. sum: "Nouvelles recherches sur l'architecture de Gračanica"), *Vizantijska umetnost početkom XIV veka* ("L'art byzantin au debut du XIVe siècle"), S. Petković, ed. (Belgrade, 1978), pp. 155-72, esp. 168-170.

53. Churches of St. Nicholas at Kuršumlija and St. George at Staro Nagoričino as well as the monastery churches of Djurdjevi stupovi, Žiča, Gradac, Sopoćani, Banja, Banjska, Mileševa, Ravanica and Manasija, to name but the best known ones, suffered extensive damage precisely in their western parts, i.e. in the areas of their narthexes and exonarthexes.

54. Dejan Medaković, *Manastir Savina: velika crkva, riznica, rukopisi* (Ger. sum.: "Kloster Savina: Hauptkirche, Schatzkammer, Handschriftensammlung") (Belgrade, 1981), esp. pp. 39-52.

55. Several churches with prominent belfries were built on the Mani Peninsula during the second period of Venetian rule (1685-1715); see M. Michaelides and A. Christophilou, "Hagios Spyridonas Kardamilēs" (Engl. sum." "Aghios Spyridon at Kardamyli) and V. Palantzes, "Ho naos tou Hagiou Nikolaou sto Prasteio tēs Dytikēs Manēs" (Engl. sum." "The Church of Aghios Nikolaos in Prasteion, Western Mani"), both in *Ekklēsies*, 2, pp. 299-310, and 311-326, respectively. A large number of athonite churches had medieval belfries or acquired new ones during the period of active construction in the sixteenth century; see Gabriel Millet, *L'école grecque dans l'architecture byzantine* (Paris, 1916), pp. 136-138.

56. The most important examples are: Šišatovac (belfry, 1742), Novo Hopovo (belfry, 1750-51 and 1753-60), Rakovac (belfry 1735), Bešenovo (belfry, 1771), Velika Remeta (belfry, 1733-35), and Divša (belfry, 1762-66); see Matić, op. cit., pp. 99 (Šišatovac), 114 (Novo Hopovo), 122 (Rakovac), 140 (Bešenovo), 152 (Velika Remeta) and 201 (Divša).

57. Janićije Popović, *Manastir Gračanica* (Belgrade, 1927), pp. 47-48. The bell was acquired a year or so earlier, but was hidden because the local priest feared a Turkish reprisal. It was hung initially within the exonarthex, and moved in 1908 to the first provisional belfry on the north side of the church. That belfry was replaced by the second wooden one, on the south side of the church, in 1926.

58. For Sremska Mitrovica see Gordana Prica and Branko Vasilić, "Arhitektura u XVIII i XIX veku," in Radomir Prica, ed., *Sremska Mitrovica* (Sremska Mitrovica, 1969), p. 153. For Belgrade see Milorad Panić-Surep, *Cultural Monuments of Serbia* (Belgrade, 1965), p. 47.

59. Scores of large Neo-Byzantine churches with single, axial belfries, or pairs of belfries were built in many towns in Orthodox parts of Yugoslavia (Belgrade, Smederevo, Sarajevo, Mostar, Uroševac, etc.), in Greece (Athens, Thessaloniki, etc.), and Bulgaria (Sofia, Svishtov, Turnovo, etc.). Unfortunately, most of this material remains totally unpublished.

60. For the church of St. Mark see p., and n. 16, *supra;* for Gračanica see p. and notes 50 and 51, *supra.*

61. The principal study, Ch. Barla, *Morphē kai exelixis tōn byzantinōn kōdōnostasiōn* (Athens, 1959), is now generally out of date. Other general works includes the useful overview of the material: H. Hallensleben, "Byzantinische Kirchtürme," op.cit., see note 45, *supra.,* and most recently, Edmund V. Williams, *The Bells of Russia: History and Technology* (Princeton, 1985), esp. pp. 21-24 ("Bells of Byzantium"). For the Serbian material see S. Stanojević, "Bila, klepala i zvona kod nas," *Glas Srpske kraljevske akademije,* 153 (Belgrade, 1933), 81-90, and Olivera M. Kandić, "Kule-zvonici uz srpske crkve XII-XIV veka" (Fr. sum.: "Les tours de clocher aupres des églises serbes du XIIe au XIVe siècle"), *Zbornik za likovne umetnosti,* 14 (1978), 3-75.

62. This viewpoint was formulated early; see Gabriel Millet, op.cit., pp. 135-140, who states unequivocally: "Le clocher est latine" (p. 135). This somewhat oversimplified point of view has been shared by the majority of scholars ever since. For example, Cyril Mango, *Byzantine Architecture* (New York, 1976), p. 254, states: "Gothic architecture was thus transplanted to Byzantine lands and left a noticeable, if not a major, imprint in features such as the pointed arch, the rib vault, the belfry..." Williams, op.cit., pp. 21-24, accepts that bells were used in Byzantium before 1204, but considers them a western import. In recent literature, to my knowledge, only Charalambos Bouras, *Nea Moni on Chios: History and Architecture* (Athens, 1982), p. 186, considers axial belfries in front of churches a "purely Byzantine tradition."

63. For the belfry which once stood above the exonarthex of Hagia Sophia, see Williams, op.cit., p. 23, who cites the relevant literature. For the Virgin Pammakaristos see Horst Hallensleben, "Untersuchungen zur Baugeschichte der ehemaligen Pammakaristoskirche, der heutigen Fethiye camii in Istanbul, *"Istanbuler Mitteilungen,* 13-14 (1963-64) esp. pp. 183-188. For the Chora (Kariye Camii) see Robert G. Ousterhout, "The Architecture of the Kariye Camii in Istanbul," Ph.D. diss, University of Illinois, Urbana-Champaign, 1982, pp.

144-149, and figs. 13-14 (hypothetical reconstruction), also gives a thorough discussion of other belfries in Late Byzantine architecture. For the Kilise Camii see Horst Hallensleben, "Zu Annexbauten der Kilise camii in Istanbul," *Istanbuler Mitteilungen,* 15 (1965), esp. pp. 215-217. For the suggestion of a possible existance of a tower at Kalenderhane see Cecil L. Striker and Y. Dogan Kuban, "Work at Kalenderhane Camii in Istanbul: Fifth Preliminary Report (1970-74), "*Dumbarton Oaks Papers,* (1975), 309-310.

64. For Saint Sophia at Ohrid see Dj. Bošković and K. Tomovski, "L'architecture médiévale d'Ohrid, "*Recueil de travaux. Musée national d'Ohrid* (Ohrid, 1961), esp. pp. 77-81. For the Holy Apostels in Thessaloniki see G. Velenis, "Oi Hagioi Apostoloi Thessalonikēs kai hē scholē tēs Kōnstantinoupolēs, "*Akten XVI Internationale Byzantinistenkongress,* II Teil, 4 Teilband, *Jahrbuch der österreichischen Byzantinistik,* 32/4 (1982), pp. 457-467.

65. For the discussion of the main relevant sources see Williams, op.cit., pp. 21-24. Additional sources could be cited, but this will remain a part of a future study.

1. Athens, Hagioi Anargyroi Kolokynthē (author)

2. Banjani, St. George (author)

3. Petra Monastery, Katholikon, from South (Cecil Striker)

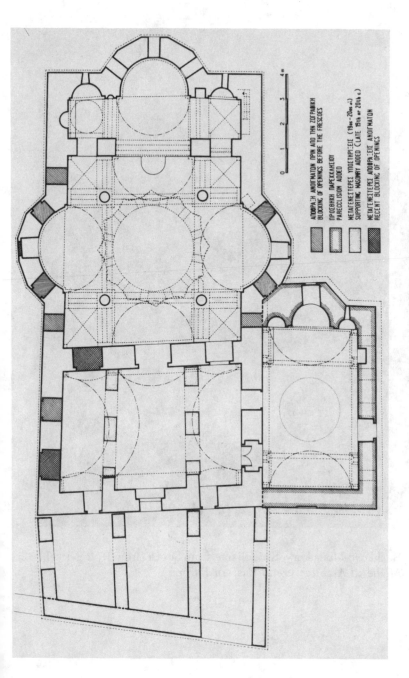

ΑΠΟΦΡΑΞΗ ΑΝΟΙΓΜΑΤΩΝ ΠΡΙΝ ΑΠΟ ΤΗΝ ΖΩΓΡΑΦΙΚΗ
BLOCKING OF OPENINGS BEFORE THE FRESCOES

ΠΡΟΣΘΗΚΗ ΠΑΡΕΚΚΛΗΣΙΟΥ
PARECCLISION ADDED

ΜΕΤΑΓΕΝΕΣΤΕΡΕΣ ΥΠΟΣΤΗΡΙΞΕΙΣ (19ou-20ou α.)
SUPPORTING MASONRY ADDED (LATE 19th or 20th c.)

ΜΕΤΑΓΕΝΕΣΤΕΡΕΣ ΑΠΟΦΡΑΞΕΙΣ ΑΝΟΙΓΜΑΤΩΝ
RECENT BLOCKING OF OPENINGS

4. Petra Monastery, Katholikon, Plan (Paul M. Mylonas)

5. Bachkovo Monastery, Katholikon, from South (from H. L. Nickel,
Medieval Architecture in Eastern Europe

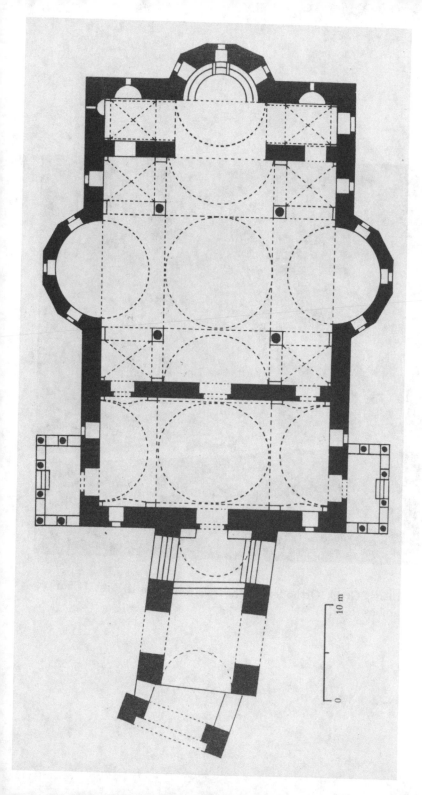

10 m

6. Bachkovo Monastery, Katholikon, Plan (Assen Tschilingirov)

7. Athens, Greek Orthodox Cathedral, from South–West (Charalambos Bouras)

8. Sofia, Cathedral of Alexander Nevski, from South (Elka Bakalova)

9. Belgrade, St. Mark's (Robert van Nice)

10. Belgrade, St. Mark's, Interior, Looking East (Robert van Nice)

11. Mistra, St. Nicholas, from East (author)

12. Mistra, St. Nicholas, Main Apse, Detail (author)

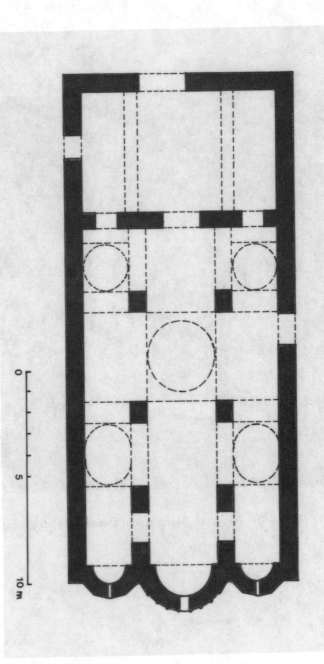

13. Mistra, St. Nicholas, Plan (delin. by Nora Laos, after Gabriel Millet)

0 5 10 m

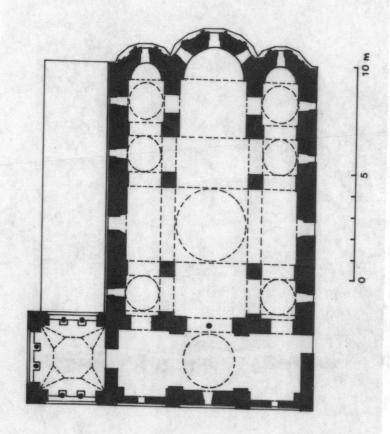

14. Mistra, Pantanassa, Plan (delin. by Nora Laos, after Gabriel Millet)

15. Mistra, Pantanassa, East End (author)

16. Koutloumousiou Monastery, Katholikon, from North–West (author)

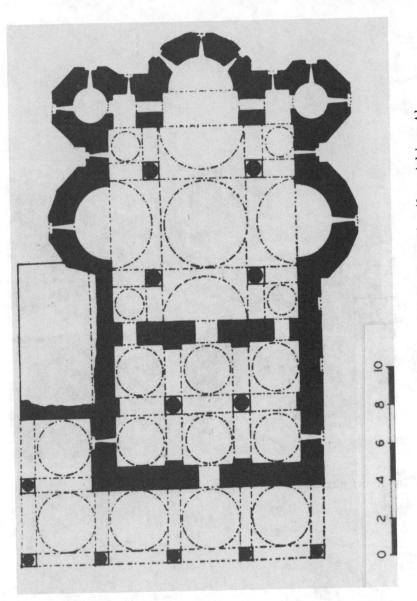

17. Koutloumousiou Monastery, Katholikon, Plan (from Adriano Alpago Novello, Grecia Bizantina)

0 2 4 6 8 10

18. Novo Hopovo Monastery, St. Nicholas, from East (author)

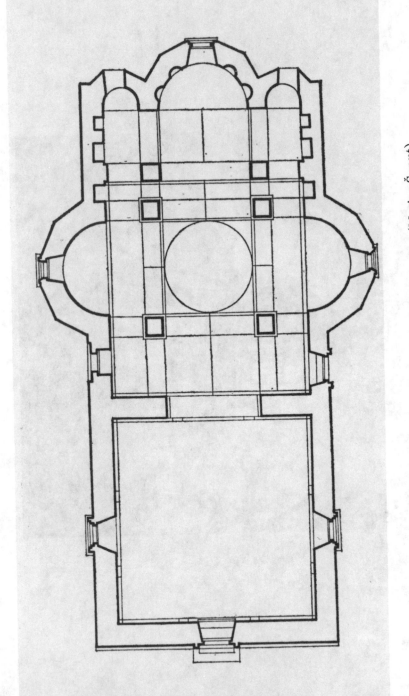

19. Novo Hopovo Monastery, St. Nicholas, Plan (Marica Šuput)

20. Doliana Monastery, Katholikon, East Elevation (Paul M. Mylonas)

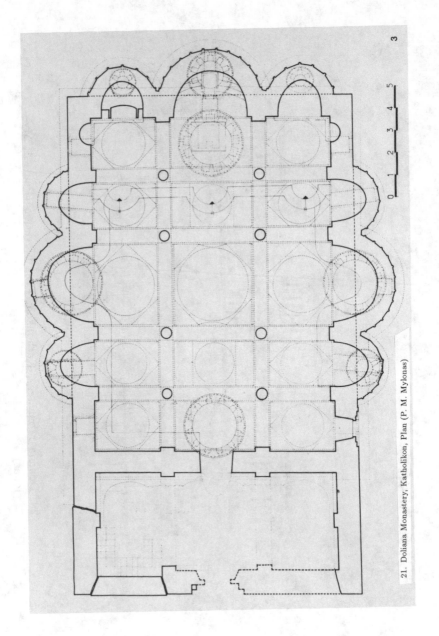

21. Doliana Monastery, Katholikon, Plan (P. M. Mylonas)

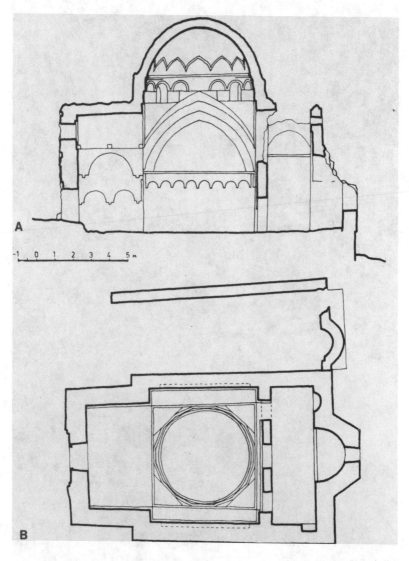

A

-1 0 1 2 3 4 5 м

B

22. Soko, Church of Herceg Stjepan, (A) Section, (B) Plan (Mirko Kovačević)

23. Sv. Jovan Bigorski Monastery, Church, from South (author)

24. Mlado Nagoričino, St. George from West (author)

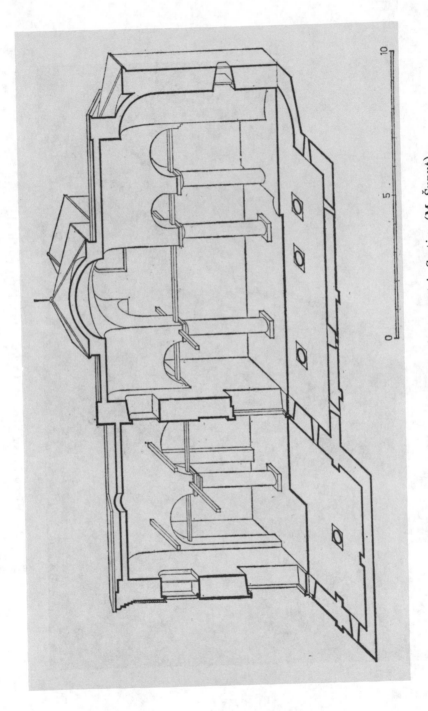

25. Mlado Nagoričino, St. George, Axonometric Section (M. Šuput)

26. Staro Nagoričino, St. George, from West (author)

27. Kumanovo, Tatar Sinan Bey Mosque, from South (author)

28. Sarajevo, Church of Archangels Gabriel and Michael (author)

29. Prizren, Bogorodica Ljeviška, from West (author)

30. Bijelo Polje, St. Peter, from South (author)

31. Peć, Patriarchal Complex of Churches, from North–West (author)

32. Gračanica Monastery, Church before Restoration, from North–West (author)

33. Gračanica Monastery, Church after Restoration, from North–
West (author)

34. Péc, Church of the Virgin, Fresco Portrait of Archbishop Danilo
II, Detail, Model of the Church Complex (author)

35. Octoechos printed in 1539, Gračanica (from Dejan Medaković,
Stari srpski drvorez

36. Savina Monastery, Church of the Dormition, from North–West (from Lazar Seferović, *Umetničko blago Herceg–Novog*

37. Sremska Mitrovica, Serbian Orthodox Cathedral, from West (author)

38. Belgrade, Serbian Orthodox Cathedral, from South–West (Carol Krinsky)

SACRED MUSIC IN THE POST-BYZANTINE ERA*

Dimitri E. Conomos

Modern scholarship in Eastern chant has largely concentrated on the musical genius of medieval Byzantium and its neighbours and many problems concerning the correct interpretation of the Greek and Slavonic traditions and their function in Orthodox divine services have been clarified and, perhaps, partly resolved. The year 1453, or thereabouts, has been considered terminal by most writers and while none would flatly deny that traditional musical elements, both practical and theoretical, were preserved at least until the middle of the sixteenth century, most would uphold the view that the hymnodic productions of the Ottoman era represent a disintegration of the authentic, Byzantine forms of artistic expression and were the results of a growth of new and innovative impulses that were alien to the spirit and evolutionary pattern of the medieval past. It should be emphasized that our present concepts of the performance pratice, the theoretical advances, the manuscript tradition, the stylistic traits and, indeed, the origins of the music of this era are gained from several studies that carefully analyze a few picked examples but do not review the extant documentation as a whole and there has been a constant danger of making general statements which, being based on isolated instances, have given rise to false notions. Occasionally, chants with some peculiar historical or stylistic feature have been taken as normal while the standard repertory has been entirely ignored. The fact that evidence needs to be draw from a diversity of data illustrates several important aspects that should be used to control an interpretation of sacred music in the post-Byzantine era, namely, that every new fact brought to light opens up a wide area of previously hidden historical relationships and the possibility of renewed speculation; that the search for such facts must continue unremittingly, for the information that has been gleaned, even from the primary sources, has by no means been exhausted; and that we must beware of making hasty judgments, as a new discovery may at any time compel us radically to change, or at least to modify, our previous concepts.[1] As we look closer into the history of Christian art in Ottoman times, we may detect in the literature a curious duality: a mixture of conservatism and elasticity, of traditional compositional methods and personal self-aggrandizement, of laconic control and specious exoticisms. This duality is particularly apparent in the musical repertory where both old and new are seen to exist side by side. It is perhaps difficult to determine, at least for the duration of the Ottoman empire, which was the normal, and which the abberant, tendency; possibly both were always in existence. But it is worth reminding ourselves that a policy of artistic liberalism and reverence for the past was the hallmark of the epoch. For while resemblances to past practices stand out as both familiar and apparent, it is also the differences manifested within the familiar procedures that grant the absorbing attention and appeal experienced in the music, and this becomes increasingly obvious the more we discover the historical and technical processes and the origins and transmissions of the compositions. Ultimately, each chant is unique in some particular way and even a passing familiarity with the musical conventions of the time, makes it possible for us to appreciate many of the individual features. Collectively, these elements create a new musical vocabulary, one which characterizes and eventually epitomizes an emerging neo-Hellenic style. From an accumulated experience of these individual traits, our knowledge of this style is more certain and we can begin to move with more assurance to its proper interpretation and evaluation. Otherwise, we shall forever be unable to fathom fully the sophisticated craft that those diligent scribes from Constantinople, Mount Athos, Cyprus, Crete, Serbia and Moldavia enshrined in collections which until today have been undeservedly ignored.

* * *

A strong case can surely be made to classify the period of musical composition from around 1500 to 1820 (when musical print replaced the handwritten codex) neither as "post-Byzantine" nor "neo-Byzantine", nor even as "Byzantine", but rather as neo-Hellenic, since the musical aspect of artistic creation, particularly after the seventeenth century, participated with other art forms in establishing a widely-acknowledged modern Greek renaissance. Understood in this manner, it is less likely that one will view the artistic and technical productions of the Ottoman years merely as an extension of Byzantium or as its decadent and aesthetically-inadequate off-spring.

At the forefront of this renaissance is sacred chant, the recorded history of which is preserved in an imposing bulk of musical manuscripts (most of them dated) that are located in widely-dispersed and often inaccessible collections: public, private and monastic. Despite the fact that it may take a great many years to acquire a thorough familiarity with all of the sources that are known today, it is yet possible for us to divide the history of the evolution of church music from the fall of Constantinople until the Greek revolution into five periods:

(a) 1453-1580 – a time of renewed interest in traditional forms, the growth of important scribal workshops beyond the capital, and a new interest in theoretical discussions;

(b) 1580-1650 – a period of innovation and experimentation, the influence of foreign musical traditions, the emergence of the kalophonic (or embellished) chants as a dominant genre, and the conception of sacred chants as independently-composed art-objects;

(c) 1650-1720 – when extensive musical training was available in many centres and when elegantly written music books appear as artistic monuments in their own right. Musicians of this age were subjecting older chants to highly sophisticated embellishments and their performance demanded virtuosic skills on the part of the singers. In addition, the first attempts at simplifying the increasingly complex neumatic notation were being made;

(d) 1720-1770 – a period of further experimentation in notational forms, a renewed interest in older, Byzantine hymn settings, the systematic production of music manuscripts and of voluminous Anthologies that incorporated several centuries of musical settings;

(e) 1770-1820 – a time of great flowering in church music composition and the supremacy of Constantinople's Hagia Sophia as a centre where professional musicians controlled initiatives in the spheres of composition, theory and performance. Among these initiatives were: further notational reforms, new genres of chant, the reordering of the old music books, the more prominent intrusion of external or foreign musical elements, and, finally, by 1820, the termination of the hand-copied manuscript tradition.

* * *

(a) 1453-1580

The fifteenth and sixteenth centuries in Byzantium witnessed a remarkable flowering of musical activity and the products of this age were to have far-reaching consequences for the future of sacred musical composition in Eastern Europe. Important names from this period are Manuel Vlatyros (with an autograph dated 1425), the hieromonk Markos from the monastery of Xanthopoulon and later metropolitan of Corinth (with an autograph dated 1434), David Raidestinos (with autographs dated 1431 to 1436), Grigorios Bounes Alyates (with musical and non-musical autographs dated between 1433 and 1447) and the most celebrated of all, Manuel Chrysaphes, the lampadarios (flourished around 1440-1463). Music scribes of this period were content to copy the old music books as they had received them: the Heirmologion, for the musical settings of the model verses for the kanons; the Sticherarion, for the proper troparia of the Offices; and the Papadike or Akolouthia, a comprehensive volume incorporating the most widely-used chants in all of the Orthodox services.

With Manuel Chrysaphes, the great musical tradition of Byzantium finds its belated consummation. Although very little is known about his life and growth as a musician, he was clearly the most impressive, prolific and distinguished Byzantine composer, singer, scribe and theoretician at the time of Constantinople's political decline. Chrysaphes held the position of lampadarios (leader of the left hand choir) in the capital and a number of documents indicate that certain of his compositions were commissioned by the two last Byzantine emperors, John VIII Palaeologos (1428-1448) and Constantine XI Palaeologos (1449-1453). Furthermore, it is known that he spent some time in Crete, that he wrote music in Sparta after the fall of Constantinople, and that he even travelled as far as Serbia where he was involved in musical composition. Chrysaphes is the scribe of a musical anthology now held in the library of the Iviron Monastery on Mount Athos, MS 1120, which bears the date July, 1458, and in the same volume also appears his widely-known treatise on music entitled Περὶ τῶν ἐνθεωρουμένων τῇ ψαλτικῇ τέχνῃ καὶ ὧν φρονοῦσι κακῶς τινες περὶ αὐτῶν ("On the theory of the art of chanting and on certain erroneous views that some hold about it") which is rich in significance both for exposing hitherto unexplained aspects of modal theory and musical practice and for providing a great deal of important information about the development of the tradition of East Christian singing in the fourteenth and fifteenth centuries.[2] Chrysaphes's treatise is the last statement on music to be written in the Byzantine period proper, and as such it at once reflects the thoughts of one man about the true nature of musical performance and reveals the general condition of Byzantine chant at the end of a powerful and fascinating evolution. His musical compositions, too, were held in high esteem and most can be found in musical sources well into the late seventeenth century.

After Chrysaphes, the output of original compositions declines in the capital and the main thrust of musical activity is confined to manuscript copying (especially on Mount Athos) and to teaching. Few new personalities arise at this time and it would seem that church music relied heavily on the precious heritage of the past. For obvious reasons, Constantinople ceased to be the epicentre of musical endeavours, while in certain peripheral areas, particularly those that were not under Turkish rule, significant steps were being taken. Notably in Serbia, Moldavia, Cyprus and Crete, artists from Constantinople sought refuge and, by combining their tradition with local musical elements, they produced a new style of music that possessed innovative and remarkably original qualities. Important regional composers in the Serbian Orthodox sphere, such as Stefan,

Isaiah and Nikola wrote hymns in both Slavonic and Greek and their works are found in several bilingual manuscripts of the fifteenth and sixteenth centuries.[3] In Moldavia, also, a major scriptorium at the monastery of Putna produced a handsome collection of bilingual songbooks under the influence of the talented fifteenth-century scribe, singer, and composer, Evstatie, the monk and protopsaltes (leader of the right choir).[4] In both regions, the extant compositions bear witness to a rich heritage, embracing foreign and local elements and they identify the existence of major centres of church music in the non Greek-speaking regions.

A similar situation can be noted in Cyprus, where musical activity had developed and matured even before Constantinople's decline and where the musical compositions were stamped with an individual and identifiable quality (certain works are labelled "as sung by the Cypriots"). Two significant contributors to the Cypriot repertory in this period were Ioannes Kordatos and Ieronymos Tragodistes. Church music in Crete also flowered both before and after 1453. Under the direct influence of fleeing Constantinopolitan musicians, composition, music copying and singing reached a powerful acme which came to an abrupt end around 1669 when the island became subject to Turkish occupation. One important and highly-controversial figure in this movement was the Cretan poet, theologian, calligrapher, singer, diplomat, scribe and priest Ioannes Plousiadenos (born around 1429) who later became Joseph, Bishop of Methone.[5] After 1454, he was one of twelve Byzantine priests who officially supported the union of the Eastern and Western Churches ratified by the Ferrara-Florence Council of 1438 and 1439. He even wrote the texts for two parahymnographical kanons, one entitled Κανὼν εἰς τὸν ἅγιον Θωμᾶν τὸν Ἀγχίνουν ("Kanon to Saint Thomas Aquinas"), which glorifies the great Catholic theologian, and the other, Κανὼν τῆς ὀγδόης συνόδου τῆς ἐν Φλωρεντίᾳ γενομένης ("Kanon for the Eighth Ecumenical Council which assembled in Florence"). The latter is modelled on the metrical and rhythmical patterns of one of the Resurrection kanons in mode IV plagal by Saint John of Damascus, but it was hardly likely to have been used in the Greek church because of its pro-henotic sentiments, triumphantly celebrating the outcome of the Council of Florence at which

Orthodox acceptance of the "filioque" phrase in the Nicene Creed was allegedly secured.

ᾮδή III

Εὐσεβείας οἱ πύργοι, ἐκκλησιῶν πρόμαχοι
καὶ τῆς οἰκουμένης ποιμένες [τε] καὶ δάσκαλοι,
οἱ θεολόγοι λαμπρῶς ἐκ το[ῦ] πατρὸς καὶ υἱοῦ τε
εὐσεβῶς ἐκήρυξαν τὸ π[νεῦμα] σήμερον.

ᾮδή V

[Τὴν σεβάσμιον τ]αύτην [καὶ ἁγίαν σύνοδον]
πιστῶς γεραίρομεν, τὴν ἐν [Φλωρεντί]ᾳ
ἱερῶς συναχθεῖσαν ἐν πν[εύματι
καὶ τὰς] ἐκκλησίας διερρηγμένας ἀν[ιάτως]
ἐν ἑνώσει αὐτὰς κατευθύνασαν.

Ode III

Towers of piety, defenders of Churches, shepherds and teachers of the universe, today the theologians proclaimed in piety that the Spirit clearly proceeds from both Father and Son.

Ode V

We loyally honour this venerable and holy Council devoutly assembled in Florence by the Spirit, who has guided the irremediably sundered Churches to unity.

Very recently, evidence has been discovered of Plousiadenos's involvement in musical composition to serve the same end. In an attempt to introduce Western polyphony into the Greek Church, Plousiadenos wrote at least one, or possibly two, communion verses (koinonika) in a primitive kind of two-voice discant. Both pieces are preserved in a late sixteenth-century anthology from the monastery of Docheiariou on Mount Athos.[6] The first, a setting in mode IV plagal of Psalm 148:1, Αἰνεῖτε τὸν κύριον ἐκ τῶν οὐρανῶν ("Praise the Lord from the heavens"), the communion for Sundays, is preceded by the remark, Διπλοῦν μέλος κατὰ τὴν τῶν ἐλατίνων [sic]

ψαλτικὴν ("A double melody according to the chant of the Latins").
It is written in close score, with both lines of notation – the upper
voice in black ink and the lower in red – inscribed above the text. The
second is a setting of Saint John 14:9 with 6:56. Ὁ ἑωρακὼς ἐμὲ
ἑώρακε τὸν πατέρα καὶ ὁ τρώγων μου τὴν σάρκα καὶ πίνων μου τὸ
αἷμα ἐν ἐμοὶ μένει κἀγὼ ἐν αὐτῷ [εἶπεν ὁ κύριος] ("He who has seen
me has seen the Father and he who eats my flesh and drinks my blood
dwells in me and I in him [saith the Lord"), the communion antiphon
for Mid-Pentecost. (See Examples 1 and 2).

Example 1. Ioannes Plousiadenos, Psalm 148:1; Mount Athos,
Monastery of Docheiariou, MS-315, fol 66ᵛ

Rubric: Διπλοῦν μέλος κατὰ τὴν τῶν ἐλατίνων ψαλτικήν. ('A
double melody according to the chant of the Latins.').

Example 2. Ioannes Plousiadenos, St. John 14:9, 6:56; Mount Athos, Monastery of Docheiariou, MS.315, fol 67 г.

Rubric: ῾Ο αὐτὸς στίχος ψάλλεται ὑπὸ δύο δομεστίκων ὁμοῦ· καὶ λέγει ὁ εἰς τὸ κείμενον καὶ ὁ ἄλλος τὸ τενόρει. ('This verse is chanted by two domestikoi together; one sings the keimenon and the other the tenori.')

Apart from these isolated examples[7], the experiment with Latin polyphony in the East had run its course, and inevitably so. It was not until several decades later that the choral *ison* or drone-singing was introduced into Greek church music,[8] marking a fundamental change from the centuries-old monophonic tradition.

A less well-known composer, but one whose work is, perhaps, of much greater significance for the musical history of Crete, was Akakios Chalkeopoulos (flourished around 1490 to 1530). His only surviving autograph preserves new musical settings for the Anastasimatarion[9] as well as his interesting and highly original theoretical treatise. The latter, largely unknown to scholars, contains many new ideas and may be extremely valuable in helping to piece together Crete's musical character in this period.

(b) 1580-1650

From the late sixteenth to the middle of the seventeenth centuries there were manifestations of certain signs of revival and widespread activity in the spheres of music composing, singing, manuscript copying and musical pedagogy. Monastic and urban scriptoria produced large numbers of systematically-copied codices, many of which were elegantly wrought. Crete, in particular, continued to provide exceptional musicians, such as the protopsaltes, Antonios Episkopopoulos, his son, the priest, Venediktos Episkopopoulos, Dimitrios Damias, "the protopsaltes of Crete", and many others. Damias must have had a very wide reputation since his compositions appear in many anthologies of chant, frequently with the indication "as written and sung by Dimitrios Damias".

In Constantinople, too, there was a resurgence of musical activity. The traditional music books continued to be reproduced faithfully (the Sticherarion, the Heirmologion, the Kratematarion and the Papadike) but, at the same time, the repertory of chants was expanded not only by new settings of new composers but also by the abundant embellishments of older works. A major musical personality was the Athenian, Theophanes Karykes, at first protopsaltes at Hagia Sophia (1578) and later Ecumenical Patriarch (1597). Much of his work remains unknown, but it is certain that his edition of the

Heirmologion occupied a crucial position in the history of this musical literature for it provided a pattern that would be imitated by seventeenth– and eighteenth-century composers, such as Joasaph "the New Koukouzeles", Balasios, Petros Peloponnesios and Petros Byzantios. This edition included new musical settings and, by way of innovation, it also incorporated the so-called "foreign" (ἐξωτερικὰ) melodies, such as the Kratema entitled ἰσμαηλίτικον [10].

During the same period, certain Athonite monks also contributed to this musical revival. One notable composer and scribe, the monk Clement (ca. 1600), also spent a part of his life at the monastery of Leimonos on Lesbos and, consequently, he is as frequently called Mytilenaios as he is ἁγιορίτης. Clement is known to have copied at least three musical manuscripts[11] but there also exist several others which very likely are his work. His original compositions are encountered in the manuscript tradition throughout the seventeenth and eighteenth centuries and were known both for their artistry and difficulty. From Vatopedi Monastery appear two important composers and teachers, the monk Joasaph, known as the New Koukouzeles, and the hieromonk Arsenios the Younger (both flourished at the beginning of the seventeenth century). Both were prolific writers and both exercised a considerable influence on the contemporary and later tradition. It is unfortunate that no autograph of the former survives, for he is frequently cited as the "unrivalled calligrapher of music". The latter continued the practice of using foreign (ἐκ τῶν ἔξω) instrumental and national melodies as a basis for his vocal kratemata; for example, the one labelled τὸ λεγόμενον σύριγξ, παρὰ δὲ τῶν ἰσμαηλιτῶν μουσχάλι ("the so-called pipe, known to the Ishmaelites as mouschali"),[12] and the other called δὶς διαπασῶν ("double diapason").[13]

(c) 1650-1720

The diverse directions that musical activity took in the years before 1650 were both formative and pregnant. Certain significant steps had been taken with respect to the opening up of new styles, the development of larger forms, and the evolution of new theories. The seventy years between 1650 and 1720 may be seen as a kind of focal point on to which the several trends merged and flowered into a highly individual and thoroughly genuine musical idiom. Many new and important composers came to the forefront, and each individual contributed something unique and personal to the art. Side by side with the innovative stood the traditional repertory, now more than ever subject to a process of modernization or "interpretation" (ἐξήγησις) in order to make it more compatible with the aesthetic of the times. Even the notation itself became the target for drastic simplification and adaptation. Manuscripts of exceptional artistic merit were produced in abundance and scribes went to great pains in order to provide as much descriptive and historical information about the chants which they had chosen to copy.

The first and most important of the great composers in this period was Chrysaphes, protopsaltes of the Great Church (flourished around 1650 to 1685), known as 'the New" (not to be confused with the older Manuel Chrysaphes, the lampadarios), whose major contribution to the repertory of sacred chant was a new musical setting of the old Sticherarion originally edited by Manuel Chrysaphes. Chrysaphes himself states in an extant autograph of 1625... ἐκ τοῦ παλαιοῦ Στιχηραρίου καὶ ἰδιοχείρου γράμματος τοῦ παλαιοῦ κὺρ Χρυσάφου τοῦ Ἐμμανουὴλ ἐκτονισθεῖσα, ἀλλ᾽ ἐν καινῷ τινι καλλωπισμῷ καὶ μελιρρυτοφθόγγοις νεοφανέσι θέσεσι, καθάπερ τανῦν ἀσματολογεῖται τοῖς μελῳδοῦσιν ἐν Κωνσταντινουπόλει... κατὰ τὴν ἣν παρέλαβον εἰσήγησιν παρὰ τοῦ ἐμοῦ διδασκάλου κὺρ Γεωργίου τοῦ Ραιδεστινοῦ ("... from the old Sticherarion and from the musical handwriting of Emmanuel Chrysaphes himself, but with certain new embellishments and with novel notated theseis, as are now chanted by the singers in Constantinople... to which I was introduced by my teacher, Georgios Raidestinos"). Little time passed before this Sticherarion replaced the former and together with the Sticherarion of Chrysaphes's student, Germanos, metropolitan of New Patras, (see below), it occupied a dominating position for the remainder of the seventeenth century and for virtually all of the eighteenth. In a similar manner, Chrysaphes made a new setting of the Anastasimatarion, preserved in another autograph dated 1671 (MS Xenophontos 128), which he described as a "new embellishment and composed with novel theseis, such as are now chanted by the singers in

Constantinople". The new "theseis" were vocal ornamentations which had entered the oral tradition in the capital and which now were brought into the written tradition by Chrysaphes and his followers. Aside from these two editions, Chrysaphes wrote a host of other musical compositions for all of the genres of chant and these were copied and sung for many decades.

A second major musical personality was Metropolitan Germanos of New Patras (flourished aroung 1660 to 1685). A prolific composer, he wrote original pieces and subjected many well-known, older works to artistic embellishment. Of significance is the fact that he was the chief exponent of the new idiom of kalophonic heirmos, which received subsequent cultivation both by Balasios and especially by Petros Bereketes. It is precisely this style that expresses most definitively the new musical tendencies and the emancipation from the restrictions of standard, traditional forms.

After Chrysaphes and Germanos there followed Balasios the priest and nomophylax (flourished around 1670 to 1700), a musician of considerable eminence, not only because of his great work – great both in bulk and in importance – but even more because of his diligence at transcribing, for the first attempts at a simplified, analytical interpretation of the old notation, and finally, because of his general focus of activity within the revivalist climate of the two former masters. Particular mention should be made of his embellishment of the old Heirmologion for, with its appearance, was completed the work of modernization that had begun with Chrysaphes the New (Sticherarion-Anastasimatarion) and Germanos of New Patras (Sticherarion). By integrating the current practices of singers in the capital, Balasios, too, shares in the credit for transmitting to distant regions the musical tradition of Hagia Sophia. In effect, his Heirmologion was very widely circulated and for about a century it held a place of virtually unchallenged supremacy. Of further interest is Balasios's application of a new species of kalophonic heirmos, one which involved even greater amplification and beautification of the traditional melody. Finally, at the theoretical level, Balasios was one of the first to attempt a reform of the complex notational system – an issue that became more and more urgent by the turn of the century and that substantially affected the musical climate of the time.

Of equal significance was Petros Bereketes (flourished circa 1680 to 1710/15), a figure well-attested by his oeuvre but with very few details known about his life and activity. In spite of the fact that he lived, sang and worked in Constantinople, it appears that he had no connections with the musical life of the Great Church. Chiefly, his compositional activity was in the Papadike idiom; that is to say, he was not preoccupied in writing exclusively for the more popular Anastasimatarion, Heirmologion or Sticherarion. Moreover, he was readily open to a wide range of influences, including foreign musical practices. Bereketes's music, which usually displays an incomparable degree of charm and artistry, gained very wide recognition and his Complete Works, assembled quite early into a Collection, quickly became an independent music book with its own particular position in the manuscript tradition. Indeed, it is well worth noting that his compositions were transcribed independently into the New Method of 1814 by two of its leading protagonists, Grigorios the protopsaltes and Chourmouzios the archivist. Specifically, Bereketes composed two settings of the Polyeleos, music for Lauds, oktoech arrangements of the Magnificat and the Doxology, a Polychronion for Peter the Great of Russia, as well as many other chants.

But the genre in which Bereketes succeeded preeminently, to an even greater degree than Balasios and his contemporaries, was that of the new species of kalophonic heirmos which he wrote in a style totally different from that of his Complete Works. Great in number, set in all of the modes, and frequently appended with the description "most artistic and sweet", they are usually found in anthologies of the Papadike after his time. Furthermore, it should be noted that Bereketes's kalophonic heirmoi provided the foundation for the subsequent shape of the Kalophonic Heirmologion, especially the form that it took towards the end of the eighteenth and beginning of the nineteenth century. Thus, Petros Bereketes, with his voluminous number of compositions and his equally extensive teaching activity, must be viewed as the foremost musician of his time. In his capacity as a composer, he was one of the most popular and influential throughout the entire eighteenth century.

(d) 1720-1770

The next period in the history of neo-Hellenic sacred chant was one of transition and preparation. Alongside the production of the new works, there was also a revival of interest in the compositions of the great masters of the past. For a time the old musical manuscripts were brought back into current usage – they were either copied identically or scribes created their own compilations of the traditional material.

Panagiotes Chalatzoglou (d. 1748) is a representative case for this period. A student of music on Mount Athos, he later became primikerios (around 1703), teacher (1708), lampadarios (1721-1726) and, finally, protopsaltes (1735-1736) of the Great Church. He was the first of an impressive line of lampadarioi and protopsaltai in Constantinople's cathedral who, for more than a century, determined the course and evolution of sacred music's theory and practice. For example, in Chalatzoglou's works one can trace the beginnings of what was to become a unique style and utterance of Hagia Sophia, as opposed to the more familiar, vague and older description, "politikon". This new style constituted a summary of compositional practices that had developed in the musical repertory of the Great Church and that were subjected to a fuller and more definitive expression in the works of later musicians. Chalatzoglou was also interested in the musical relationships between sacred and foreign secular songs and in this connection he wrote a fascinating monograph entitled *A Comparison of Arabopersian Music with our Sacred Chant* which reveals his wide knowledge of the richness and diversity of both of these musical traditions.

Nevertheless, the dominating musical personality of this period was Chalatzoglou's student, Ioannes Trapezoundios, domestikos (around 1727), lampadarios (1728-1734/36), and finally protopsaltes (1734/36-1770) at Hagia Sophia. A versatile composer and an important theorist, he continued in the compositional tradition of his teacher and was an industrious scribe. To date, six autographs, covering the years 1728-1769 are known. Ioannes's most important work was related to the perennial problem of notational revision. He contributed decisively to the formation of an analytical graphic system and he established certain procedures which led to the final resolutions of the 1814 reform. Another significant musician of this school was Kyrillos Marmarinos, bishop of Tinos (flourished around 1730-1760), also a student of Chalatzoglou. In addition to composing liturgical music, Kyrillos also wrote a short theoretical treatise entitled *Introduction to music in dialogue form* which, like the aforementioned document of his teacher, makes reference to Arabopersian music. He also compiled an alphabetical list of old and new music teachers and composers and this forms the catalogue which was published in the second part of Chrysanthos's Μέγα Θεωρητικὸν of 1832 (see below).

(e) 1770-1820

This great and final period of church music composing, as represented in the manuscript tradition, was inaugurated by the highly renowned chanter, composer and teacher, Petros Peloponnesios (ca. 1730-1778). He received his first music lessons in the monastic communities of Smyrna and in 1764 he travelled to Constantinople where he became associated with Ioannes Trapezoundios, with whom he chanted as second domestikos in the right choir at Hagia Sophia. He held this office until his promotion to lampadarios between 1769 and 1773. Petros was made an instructor of chant in the second patriarchal school of music which was founded in 1776, and from this time his reputation as an important teacher and composer was established. It is known that he was also a specialist in Armenian and Turkish music and that he composed melodies based on the oriental *maqamat.*[14]

The creative activity of Petros falls into two categories. The first comprises his original musical compositions which include his contributions to the Offices and liturgies of the Church. He wrote complete sets of cherubika and communion chants arranged in all eight modes as well as music for funerals, ordinations, baptisms, weddings, etc. In addition, he composed exercises and lessons for students of chant. Although his life as a composer was short (his musical career was prematurely terminated when he died in a plague which swept Constantinople in 1778), Petros proved to be the most prolific writer of the entire post-Byzantine era and his works are available in many musical anthologies from the eighteenth and nineteenth centuries.

Apart from his original compositions, Petros wrote many interpretations of older chants. His system of interpreting melodies was further developed by Petros Byzantios, his pupil, and was subsequently employed by the three nineteenth-century reformers, Chrysanthos of Madytos, Grigorios the protopsaltes and Chourmouzios the archivist (see below). One manuscript in particular, Lavra E. 103 (late eighteenth century) contains Petros' interpretations of works by the fourteenth-century Byzantine musicians Ioannes Glykys and Ioannes Koukouzeles. Petros was one of the first to cultivate the σύντομον ("quick") melodies into the liturgical anthologies. These were designed for ordinary services which required simple, unembellished chants.

An indefatiguable worker, Petros rewrote virtually all of the old music books: the Anastasimatarion, the Heirmologion and the Doxastarion, all within the decade 1765-1775. These quickly gained a wide reputation and gradually replaced the older editions and settings of Chrysaphes the New, Balasios and Germanos. Even today, these music books retain a dominant position in liturgical practice. Continuing the work of Ioannes Trapezountios, Petros developed an even simpler and more analytical system of musical writing which contributed directly to the formulation that transpired in 1814. His successors, Petros Byzantios (d. 1808) and the protopsaltes, Iakovos Peloponnesios (d. 1800), preserved the same tradition: the former specializing in new interpretations following the analytical notation of Petros Peloponnesios, and the latter, by way of retrospection, avoiding modern innovations and preferring to derive his inspiration from the older, simpler chants. Most of the musical settings of these composers were assembled in an updated version of the Papadike, known as the Anthology of the New Papadike, which contained their realizations of the old melodies as well as many original works.

Taking an independent path was the important composer, interpreter, scribe and theoretician, Apostolos Konstas (flourished around 1790 to 1835) who was active in Constantinople but did not hold an official ecclesiastical office. An extremely competent and artistic scribe, his autographs to date number around sixty and they contributed enormously to expanding the circulation of the music of Petros Peloponnesios, Petros Byzantios and Iakovos Protopsaltes. Around 1800, he wrote a theoretical manual entitled, Μουσικὴ τέχνη τῆς κοινῆς παραδόσεως καὶ τεχνολογίας.

Written with clarity and precision, the treatise demonstrates Konstas's total familiarity with the old, traditional, notational system. For modern scholarship this is a useful tract for it provides much information about the state of music theory less than two decades before the definitive instigation of the New Method. The urgency for notational reform was by that time most apparent and although Konstas was conservative in his thinking, he was certainly not unfamiliar with the progressive musical trends of the time. Using his own system, he made interpretations of many traditional chants and of the works of his senior contemporaries.

The following decade, 1810-1820, was, for the history of Greek chant, both turbulent and decisive. Two major goals were finally achieved; first, the implementation and universal acceptance of an entirely new notational system (1814) which had evolved from the interpretative experiments of Balasios at the end of the seventeeth century through the formulations of the protopsaltes, Ioannes Trapezoundios (1756), of Petros Peloponnesios, of Petros Byzantios and of Georgios of Crete; and second, as a consequence to the former, the invention of musical print and the simultaneous publication of the first music book (1820).

Chrysanthos of Madytos (ca. 1770- ca. 1840), an uncommonly well-educated and highly-cultured hierarch, was primarily responsible for the reform and his system survives until this day. He had an excellent knowledge of Latin and French, and was familiar with European as well as with Arabic music, being proficient in playing the western flute and the eastern "nay". Chrysanthos had learned the art of chanting from Petros Byzantios and himself taught singing. As a composer and educator, he became acutely aware of the need for more clarity in the process of studying and understanding of Greek church music. The medieval neumatic notation had now become so complex and technical that only highly-skilled chanters were able to interpret the symbols accurately. To facilitate that end and to simplify the teaching of this difficult art, he invented a set of monosyllabic sounds for the musical scale based on the European sol-fa system but using the first seven letters of the Greek alphabet. Each degree corresponded to one note in the scale:

Π<u>Α</u>-<u>Β</u>ΟΥ-<u>Γ</u>Α-<u>Δ</u>Ι-Κ<u>Ε</u>-<u>Ζ</u>Ω-Ν<u>Η</u> = RE-MI-FA-SOL-LA-SI-DO.

In addition, he systematized the ordering of the eight modes into the three species: diatonic, chromatic and enharmonic. Within each of these three categories, the intervallic progression of the degrees was fixed according to elaborate mathematical calculations. Chrysanthos also introduced new processes of modulation and chromatic alteration and abolished some of the notational symbols. As a result of these efforts, a large repertory of hymnody was made available to chanters who were ignorant of the melodic and dynamic content of the old signs.

Owing to this breach with the traditional methods of teaching, Chrysanthos is said to have been exiled to Madytos by order of the Constantinopolitan patriarch. Yet, apparently this did not stop him from pursuing his highly original approach to the teaching of ecclesiastical music. In Madytos, he found that his pupils were able to learn in ten months what had formerly taken ten years. The crucial device speeding up the process of learning appears to have been his use of the aforementioned newly-invented solmization syllables. Finally exonerated by the Holy Synod, Chrysanthos was then given a free hand to teach music as he saw fit. It was at this point that he joined forces with the protopsaltes, Grigorios and the archivist, Chourmouzios, both of whom seem to have had less formal education than Chrysanthos, yet according to their biographies possessed a great natural ability for music. All three taught at the Third Patriarchal School of Music (opened 1815) and this ensured the success and propagation of the new system. The results of Chrysanthos's research and teaching methods appeared in print for the first time in a treatise entitled Εἰσαγωγὴ εἰς τὸ θεωρητικὸν καὶ πρακτικὸν τῆς ἐκκλησιαστικῆς μουσικῆς συνταχθεῖσα πρὸς χρῆσιν τῶν σπουδαζόντων αὐτὴν κατὰ τὴν νέαν μέθοδον ("Introduction to the theory and practice of ecclesiastical music written for the use of those studying according to the new method") published in Paris in 1821. Eleven years later there appeared in Trieste the more exhaustive and highly influential Θεωρητικὸν μέγα τῆς μουσικῆς ("Great Theory of Music") which, in its first part, expounded the new theories and notational principles of the three reformers.

The second part of the *Great Theory* is purely historical. Chrysanthos made an ambitious but unsuccessful attempt to present, in the form of a chronicle, a general history of music from the time before the Great Flood to his own day. It is recorded that he wrote many other works, including transcriptions of Greek church music to European staff notation and European music to the notation of the new method, but none survives. Despite its numerous shortcomings, the oeuvre of Chrysanthos is a landmark in the history of Greek church music since it introduced the system upon which are based the present-day chants of the Greek Orthodox Church.

Grigorios the protopsaltes (1777-1821), the second of the three teachers, was essentially self-taught but gained some musical experience in an Armenian Church of Constantinople. Because of his natural ability for singing, he was apprenticed first to Iakovos the protopsaltes, then to Petros Byzantios and finally to Georgios of Crete. Grigorios was also trained in Turkish music and played a local lute-like instrument known as the pandoura. His chief contribution is in the transcription of very many melodies from the old to the new graphic system of notation. Among these are a four-volume Anthology of the New Papadike, the Kalophonic Heirmologion, the Complete Works of Bereketes in two volumes, the Sticherarion of Germanos and the major compositions of Petros Peloponnesios, Petros Byzantios and Chrysaphes the New. He was also a fine composer, both of sacred and of secular music, and in the latter category many of his non-Greek songs have survived.

According to Chourmouzios's (ca. 1770-1840) biography, he managed to fill some seventy volumes with his own musical interpretations of the works of the great figures of Greek Church music, including that of Koukouzeles, Kladas, Germanos, Chrysaphes the New, Bereketes, Petros Byzantios, Petros Peloponnesios, and others. A student of Iakovos the protopsaltes and Georgios of Crete, his manifold activities included the researching and publishing of music books, teaching and composing. He is credited as being the author of two manuals on the theory and practice of music and one bulky notebook in which he outlines all of the merits and defects of the old and new methods. Chourmouzios also established the rules of musical orthography, that is, the correct writing of the musical characters according to the revised system of the notation.

* * *

The invention of musical type marked the end of the long and fascinating tradition of the music manuscript. In 1820, Peter Ephesios, a student of the three teachers, published in Bucarest the editions of the Anastasimatarion and Syntomon Doxastarion by Petros Peloponnesios. And, of the older pieces, those that entered the printed repertory were randomly selected by subsequent editors. After 1830, the official musical tradition of the Greek Orthodox Church was represented by the following books: the Anastasimatarion, the Heirmologion and the Syntomon Doxastarion of Petros Peloponnesios, the Syntomon Heirmologion of Petros Byzantios, the Doxastarion of Iakovos the protopsaltes, and the New Anthology of the Papadike – all re-written according to the interpretations of Grigorios protopsaltes and Chourmouzios in the new, simplified notation of Chrysanthos.

NOTES

* I am very grateful to the Social Sciences and Humanities Research Council of Canada for providing generous support for this study, making it possible for me to visit libraries in Greece, Jugoslavia and Romania.

1. See, for example, Egon Wellesz, *A History of Byzantine Music and Hymnography* (Oxford, 1961), p. 238.
2. A critical edition of Chrysaphes's treatise, accompanied by an English translation, has been published by this writer, *The Treatise of Manuel Chrysaphes, the Lampadarios: On the Theory of the Art of Chanting and on certain erroneous views that some hold about it* (Vienna, 1985).
3. On the Serbian tradition, see D.I. Stefanović, "Two Bilingual Manuscripts from the Fourteenth and Fifteenth Centuries," *Communications du XIVᵉ Congrès International des Études Byzantines* (Bucarest, 1971), 308-309; idem, *Stara Srpska Muzika* (Belgrade, 1975); A.E. Pennington, "Stefan the Serb in Moldavian Manuscripts," *Slavonic and East European Review* 51 (1973), 107-112; D.E. Conomos, "The Monastery of Putna and the Musical Tradition of Moldavia in the Sixteenth Century," *Dumbarton Oaks Papers* 36 (1982), 15-28.

4. On the Moldavian tradition, see A.E. Pennington, "Evstatie's Song Book of 1511: Some Observations," *Revue des études sud-est européennes* 9 (1971), 565-585; *idem,* "The Composition of Evstatie's Song Book," *Oxford Slavonic Papers,* New Series 6 (1973), 92-112; *idem,* "Music in Sixteenth-Century Moldavia: New Evidence", *Oxford Slavonic Papers* New Series 11 (1978), 64-83; *idem,* "Seven Akolouthiai from Putna," *Studies in Eastern Chant* 4, eds. E. Wellesz and M. Velimirović (New York, 1979), 112-133; D.E. Conomos, "The Monastery of Putna and the Musical Tradition of Moldavia in the Sixteenth Century," *op. cit.*

5. For information on Ioannes (Joseph) Plousiadenos, see L. Petit, "Joseph de Méthone," *Dictionnaire de théologie catholique,* ed. A. Vacant and E. Magenot, 8 (Paris, 1925), cols. 1526-1529; G. Hofmann, "Wie stand es mit der Frage der Kircheneinheit auf Kreta im XV. Jahrhundert?", *Orientalia Christiana Periodica* 10 (1944), pp. 106-111; N. Tomadakis, Μιχαὴλ Καλοφρενᾶς Κρής, Μητροφάνης Β΄ καὶ ἡ πρὸς τὴν ἕνωσιν τῆς Φλωρεντίας ἀντίθεσις τῶν Κρητῶν, 'Επετηρὶς 'Εταιρείας Βυζαντινῶν Σπουδῶν 21 (1951), pp. 110-139, esp. 136-139; M. Candal, "La 'Apologia' del Plusiadeno a favor del Concilio de Florencia," *Orientalia Christiana Periodica* 21 (1955), 36-57; M. Manoussakas, "Recherches sur la vie de Jean Plousiadenos (Joseph de Methone) (1429?-1500), *Revue des Etudes Byzantines* 17 (1959), 28-51; S.G. Papadopoulos, 'Ιωσήφ, Θρησκευτικὴ καὶ ἠθικὴ ἐγκυκλοπαιδεία 7 (Athens, 1965), 117-119.

6. MS Docheiariou 315, fols. 66v-67r. These unusual items are noted in G. Stathis, Τὰ χειρόγραφα βυζαντινῆς μουσικῆς. "Αγιον "Ορος, 1 (Athens, 1975), p. 352; Stathis also provides excellent colour facsimiles on pp. 350-351. Although only the Mid-Pentecost communion is directly attributed to Plousiadenos, Stathis is obviously correct in assuming that the Sunday chant, immediately preceding and in the same unique style, is the work of the same hand. Plousiadenos's musical compositions are preserved in many liturgical anthologies (for example, Mount Sinai, Saint Katherine's Monastery, MSS 311, 312; Lesbos, Leimonos Monastery, MSS 238, 243, 249, 255; Athens, National Library of Greece, MSS 886, 893, etc.) but these are the only known examples of polyphony by him. See V. Beneshevich, *Catalogus codicum manuscriptorum graecorum qui in monasterio S.l Catharinae in Monte Sina asservantur* 1 (Saint Petersburg, 1911), pp. 165-632; A. Papadopoulos-Kerameus, Μαυρογορδάτειος Βιβλιοθήκη (Constantinople, 1884), pp. 115, 116, 118, 119; I. Sakkelion, Κατάλογος τῶν χειρογράφων τῆς ἐθνικῆς βιβλιοθήκης (Athens, 1892), pp. 160-161.

7. For two others, see D.E. Conomos, "Experimental Polyphony 'according to the ... Latins,' in late Byzantine psalmody", *Early Music History* 2 (1982), 7-16.

8. The earliest notification of the custom appears to have been made in 1584 by the German traveller, Martin Crusius; see K. Levy, "Byzantine Rite, Music of the", *The New Grove Dictionary of Music and Musicians,* ed. S. Sadie, 20 vols. (London, 1980), 2, p. 561.

9. This is a volume containing, in the order of the eight modes, the proper chants for the Offices on Sunday.

10. A kratema is a musical unit of nonsense syllables known as *teretismata* which is often appended to or inserted in Byzantine hymns in order to lengthen their duration. Some are given descriptive titles, such as 'bell', 'viola", or 'trumpet'. Kratemata are frequently collected and arranged according to the eight modes in a volume called the Kratematarion. Karykes' ἰσμαηλίτικον kratema is transmitted in MS. Ecumenical Patriarchate Library, fonds K. Ananiadou 6, fols 111v-112r.For further information on Karykes, see E. Voulisma, Θεοφάνης Καρύκης ὁ πατριάρχης, 'Εκκλησιαστικὴ 'Αλήθεια IV (1883-84), 336-38· M.I. Gedeon, Γράμμα τῷ Καρύκῃ, 'Εκκλησιαστικὴ 'Αλήθεια XXXII (1912), 203-04; A. Theologitou, Θεοφάνης Καρύκης ὁ ἐξ 'Αθηνῶν, 'Εφημέριος VII (1958), 565-69.
11. MSS Leimonos 212, 288 and Athens 2796.
12. MS. Ecumenical Patriarchate Library, fonds K. Ananiadou 6, fols. 113r-113v.
13. MS. Leimonos 8, fols 315v-316r.
14: The eastern scale or modal system.

THE BYZANTINE LEGACY IN FOLK LIFE AND TRADITION IN THE BALKANS

Speros Vryonis, Jr.

The general theme which our symposiarch has set for us has two
very broad characteristics which I should wish to underline at the
onset. It is, first, of epic proportions. Geographically it stretches from
the Mediterranean Sea to the Sea of Archangel, from Belgrade to
Vladivostok. The second characteristic is that our ideas about this
period and world are vague, diffuse at best, almost non-existent at
worst. In contrast to the Islamic and Western medieval traditions,
which suffered no truncation of political institutional life and
development, the Byzantine tradition was politically decapitated by the
victorious armies of the sultan Mehmed II, that military and political
genius who replaced the Byzantine imperial tradition with that of the
Islamic world. Given the fact that history and historians, until
relatively recently, had as their almost exclusive concern the study of
political history with its dates, significant battles, institutional and
legal forms, it was natural, historiographically, that the very idea of an
afterlife in the history of Byzantine civilization should be only vaguely
understood. This is of course an oversimplification. Two older scholars
from the past generation of nationalist Balkan historians-philologists
had charted two paths into the ongoing rhythms and lives of the
Byzantine tradition during the period that is the focal center of our
conference. Nicholas Iorga, in his imaginatively titled book, *Byzance
après Byzance*, had seized upon the pale political and ideological

survival of Byzantine political theory and institutions in the Phanariots and in the milieu of the princes of the Roumanian principalities. Phaedon Koukoules, in his monumental *Vyzantinon vios kai politismos,* in six volumes of accumulated data, the variety and chronological spread of which remains prodigious, focussed upon the popular life and culture of the Byzantine empire and in so doing traced the origins of these popular cultural institutions and practices in the period of Graeco-Roman antiquity and then into the post Byzantine period, i.e. during the Turkokratia and modern times.[1] It is the task of some of the papers in the present conference to follow the path of Iorga, that is to say, to map out what, if any, are the evidences for the nachleben of the Byzantine political tradition. My task, as assigned to me by the symposiarch, is to follow in the second path and to attempt to say something meaningful about the Byzantine after – life on the level of the popular culture of the Balkan peoples.

I have written, in the past, in rather great detail as to the effect of the Ottoman conquest and rule on the institutions and life of the Balkan and Anatolian peoples and so I shall not go into any great detail as to these effects.[2] It will, however, be necessary to remark on three aspects of this subject, aspects which will serve as the broader background for my specific remarks as regards the Byzantine legacy in the popular traditions of the various Balkan peoples. I wish, first, to underline the generally conservative character of the Ottoman conquests in the Balkans. They were, by comparison with the centuries of long warfare and conquests in Anatolia, relatively quick, with destruction it is true but of a limited and controlled character, with no massive nomadic settlements on the scale that Anatolia saw. Finally they were carried out by one, well-organized political entity which enjoyed a considerable centralization of political and military authority. Second, these conquests destroyed the political dynasties and aristocratic structures of the Greeks, Bulgars, Serbs, and Albanians, and took control of the economic, demographic, and fiscal resources of this vast area. Thus the kingpins, i.e. the patrons and artistic executors of the formal culture of the various Balkan peoples disappeared and this formal culture atrophied. But the peasant masses remained in place, in their centuries old economic occupations as farmers and shepherds, with their old religious and cultural institutions.

These cultural institutions, which survived, and which I characterize as popular culture, had both elements that were common to the various Balkan peoples as well as local and ethnic variety.

Many folklorists who have studied the various folk cultures of Greeks, Bulgars, Roumanians, Serbs, and Albanians, and to a lesser degree of Turks, have assumed a dynamic theory of culture, thats is they see popular culture as a phenomenon which has a vertical and horizontal structure. The horizontal structure constists of well defined layers of popular culture, often chronologically and politically separable the one from the other. The vertical structure consists of the historical processes which posit one layer atop another and during which processes the new and the old interact, producing elements of both continuity and change. This approach has been very useful and has led to a significant gain in our understanding of the history, cultures and ethnogenesis of the various peoples that inhabit the present day Balkans. It allows for the maximum number of possibilities in explaining cultural phenomena and historical developments in an area as complex as that of the Balkans. It also represents a shift of historical and scholarly interests from the narrowly prescribed and circumscribed circles of diplomatic, political history and so represents a vast enrichment of our historical understanding of the Balkan peoples, their past and present.

Further, at almost all times, at least since the fourth century B.C. the various peoples inhabiting the Balkan peninsula have been subject not only to the internal dynamic or genius of their own immediate cultures, but also to the interaction of these latter with the unifying cultures and political forces of imperial peoples and structures: first, those of Philip and Alexander the Great, then those of the Roman and Byzantine Empires, and finally by the forces of the Ottoman Empire. Also, to this latter category of outside unifying imperial forces one should add the impact of the West. In each era of imperial rule one sees an internal adjustment of the local cultural traditions to the unifying forces of these centralizing political institutions. In the Graeco-Roman, early Byzantine period it was reflected in the massive-Romanization and Hellenization of the local Balkan tongues, as well as by the spread of an urban and rural economic system which imposed uniform institutions on large areas and masses of people. At the same time, however, there is every reason to suspect that local varieties survived these unifying forces, though it is very difficult to trace them for this early period. Under Byzantine influence Christianity spread and added a most important layer, a significant horizontal layer, in the cultural life of the Balkan peoples. The local varieties in the popular cultures had once more to accommodate themselves, this time to Christianity, and Christianity, conversely, had to accommodate itself to the local cultures. The same can be said of Ottoman rule, though its effect was more limited to the negative aspects of political effects. Thus, in the specific remarks that are to follow I wish to make observations about particular cultural phenomena which can best be understood against the background of this crude and rapidly sketched theoretical structure. For, when we talk about the Byzantine legacy we are talking about a legacy with a complex and long historical past. The Byzantine legacy is not only those elements which in the popular culture of the Balkan peoples can be pointed to as a purely Byzantine creation, i.e. the monastic and hagiolatric aspect of religious life. It also includes those cultural legacies which were absorbed into the popular culture of the Byzantine period from pre-Christian times and cultural life, such as incubation, animal sacrifice, and the seasonal calendar. These latter were absorbed by Christianity because they were a vital force in the life of the inhabitants of the peninsula, and were functional. Thus, when speaking of the Byzantine legacy we include not only those things which were purely and originally Byzantine in creation, such as formal Christianity, but also all the pagan elements which Christianity absorbed as it evolved into a universal religion and as it penetrated the life of the rural areas. We come back again to the theory of cultural evolution as consisting of chronological layers of culture related to one another and interacting with one another through the process of time and under the impact of political, demographic, and technological movements.

In surveying the Byzantine legacy in the folk life and tradition of the Balkans, I shall attempt to illustrate the nature of this phenomenon by touching, very briefly, for I can do no more than that, on six separate topics: Constantinople-Istanbul; religion; man's relation to human life and to the unknown; the agricultural and pastoral cycles and calendars; the panegyris; and finally, the legend of Alexander the

Great. By looking, ever so briefly it is true, at each one of these disparate topics we shall begin to understand the nature and complexity of the popular culture of the Balkan peoples during the long period of Turkish rule, and in part thereafter.

Constantinople-Istanbul

That the Ottoman conquest of Constantinople on May 29, 1453 constitutes a major landmark in the history of the eastern Mediterranean is of course such a well known commonality of history that its mention occasions no surprise. Yet, that which is of interest to us here is whether or not its long pre-existence as the center of Greek and Christian culture and politics had any effect on the nature of the new city, Ottoman Istanbul, which replaced the Greek Christian city of Constantinople.[3]

The Ottoman conquest of the city was a brutal and bloody event in which the Ottoman sultan turned the city over, by sultanic decree, to a three day pillaging and sack (yagma) by his victorious troops. The destruction was most extensive and when, after the three days of sacking, it terminated and Mehmed inspected the ravished city, he found it completely uninhabited.[4] The 60,000 Byzantines who had survived the killing were all taken out of the city as the slaves of the victorious troops. Many, though not all, of the buildings, particularly churches, were sacked and abandoned. Mehmed immediately turned to the rebuilding and settling of the city with sürgüns after deciding to make of it the capital city of the Ottoman empire and his official residence. The new city which was built, over the next century, soon reached splendid and magnificent proportions, both in terms of the numbers of the population and of the newly built mosques, bazaars, palaces and other official buildings.[5]

Was there, then, anything of the past that survived in Ottoman Istanbul and which would preserve memories and the culture of the past?

First, it would seem that the sultan's policy of repeopling the city included provision for the return of a portion of the original population: those who had fled the city prior to the siege, as well as those who had gone into hiding in Galatia, and finally, those of the Constantinopolitans who had been taken prisoner in the final capture but who had been allowed to return either as a result of ransoming themselves or of being allowed to work toward the paying off of the ransom. These constituted the original Greek population that was allowed to return to Constantinople. They were given houses in the city and along with Muslim and other Christian immigrants whom the sultan brought from all over the empire, constituted the original population of Ottoman Istanbul.[6] Thus there was en element of demographic continuity, though its proportion to the total population of the new city was of course considerably diminished. The sultan also provided for the re-erection of the patriarchal institution around which the life of the Greek population of the city was to center, and he temporarily assigned the Church of the Holy Apostles as the Patriarchal church and residence. Thus at the level of living institutions, i.e. demographic and religious, there is this thread of continuity from the past, and with these two institutions, elements of both the popular and formal culture of Byzantium survived in a functioning form. We do not know a great deal about the popular and formal culture of the Greek Christians of the Ottoman Istanbul during the first century of their existence. The history of the patriarchate at this time unfolded at a much reduced level in terms of the prestige, glory and economic resources which it had once known. Nevertheless it presided over what little was left of the formal aspects of the culture of the Greek Christians... we know that one century after the conquest Theodore Zygomalas was ordered to draw up a catalogue of the manuscripts still in the patriarchal library, but only a portion of this catalogue, listing some 174 ms. has survived so that we do not know what its extent was.[7] The patriarchate eventually lost control of all Byzantine churches save one, the churches having passed into the hands of Muslims, were either converted into religious establishments, or into residences, or stables for animals.[8] As for the historical memories of the Greek Christians, it is difficult to know what they preserved during this early Ottoman period, what they recalled of the glorious Byzantine past of the city of Constantinople. Daily they saw the mining of the old Byzantine monuments, which were used as stone quarries for the building of the palaces, mosques and medresses of the new city, and is seems that with the disappearance of the monuments many Greeks gradually lost the memory of these monuments from the past. It is this which we seem to imply from the complaints of the European student of the Byzantine monuments of the city in the early sixteenth century, Pierre Gyllius. In this important archaeological survey of what remained of Byzantine Constantinople, Gyllius relates that he went about the city in search of these monuments, but when he asked the Greeks of a given neighborhood as to the identity of this or that ruined structure often they did not know. On other occasions they seemed to knov the identity.[9]

Nevertheless a folklore of legends and vague historical remembrances did survive and evidently came to constitute a very definite body of popular lore that survived over the centuries of Ottoman rule and into the twentieth century. The final siege and destruction of the city by the Turks was firmly fixed in the popular memory of the Greeks of Istanbul as in the memory of a large part of the Greek nation, and gave rise to a body of popular literature and lore that are well known to all students of Greek folklore. One such legend has as its subject the last liturgy performed in the great church of St. Sophia, and according to which legend the Turks' sudden entrance into the church prevented the termination of the liturgy, the priest having disappeared into the walls of the church during the celebration of the liturgy. The great altar of St. Sophia also disappeared. According to another legend the last emperor Constantine Palaeologus did not perish in the fighting but disappeared, went into underground hiding and went into a deep sleep and/or was turned to marble, the marmaromenos vasilias. In all these tales the resolution of each individual story, i.e. the return of the priest to finish the liturgy in St. Sophia, the return of the great altar, the awakening of the last Emperor will occur at that time when God has decided that Constantinople, the empire, and St. Sophia shall all be returned to the Greeks. This will occur when God's angel will awaken the emperor, arm him with the sword and he will remove the Turks. This is of course the folklore basis for the historical construction of the most powerful Greek ideology in the late eighteenth, throughout the nineteenth and into the twentieth centuries: the Megale Idhea, the reconstitution of Greek political power in Constantinople and Asia Minor.[10]

I have not studied this particular body of popular legend and belief in terms of its knowledge among Muslim Turks in the early Ottoman period. But as for the Greeks, the fall of Constantinople was a momentuous tragedy, so for the Muslim Turks it was the most felicitous occasion in their long history of conquests. The conquest is celebrated in the chronicles, in poetry, and in prose because of its glory and because of the extension of the domain of Islam. No less was it comemmorated or remembered as the occasion of great enrichment. The chronicler Neshri records the popular Turkish memory of the great wealth that fell into the hands of the conquerors in 1453. He writes of the booty taken on that occasion:

"Since that time was the proverb that they say to one who is wealthy, 'Did you participate in the pillaging of Istanbul'?"[11]

(Neshri, II, 705-707)

Before entering into a discussion of the passage of Byzantine folklore into Turkish we need to pause and to say a word about the fate of the Byzantine buildings of Constantinople and also of the attitude of the sultan Mehmed II to this Byzantine patrimony.

The studies on the period of Mehmed II are sufficiently detailed so that scholars have now begum to focus rather sharply on his personality and his historical actions. The Ottoman chronicles record that though he gave over the city and its inhabitants to the pillaging of his troops he retained the claim and title to all of the buildings and the walls. His first official act upon entering the city was to enter the great church of St. Sophia, to smash the altar, and to have the Friday prayer of the Islamic faith recited.[12] He thus picked it to be the central and official mosque in his empire and bestowed upon it great wealth through the waqf foundation, including, 1,428 Byzantine houses.[13] Second, he ordered the repair of the great land walls which had been breached by his cannon. Third, he eventually ordered the demolition of the Church of the Holy Apostles, for centuries the official burial place of the Byzantine emperors, and built there his own kulliyet, complete with his own turbe. Thus he appropriated buildings and sites with Byzantine traditions and functions and adapted them to his own desires and needs. Within his new palace on the Saray Burnu he brought together an important collection of Greek, Latin, Armenian, Syriac and Slavonic manuscripts. These included manuscripts of Homer, Arrian's account of the exploits of Alexander the Great, Polybios, Ptolemy's Geography, Xenophon, Hesiod, Pindar, Diogenes Laertius, to mention the more important of the classical authors.[14]

Among the Byzantine Greek texts were to be found John Cantacuzenos' history, the Geoponica, the Old Testament, the New Testament,
Zonaras, the nomocanon, hymnal and psalters, and the texts known as
the Diegesis (building of St. Sophia) and the Patria Constantinoupole-
os (an account of the history and monuments of Byzantine
Constantinople).[15] Further, is has been established that Mehmed was
an avid collector of Christian relics, to which he attributed religious
efficacy.[16]

In his reign he had Persian and Turkish translations made of a
popular reworked Greek version of the Diegesis, the Byzantine text
that describes the history of the building of the great church of St.
Sophia. The Persian text was executed 28 years after the capture of
Constantinople by the devish Shemseddin. Indeed, not only do we
know from the catalogue of the Greek and other non-Muslim
manuscripts of the palace library of Muhammed that he had in his
library the Greek texts on the history of St. Sophia and of the
monuments and the city of Byzantine Constantinople. We are told,
further, that he had a great interest in the history of the city which he
was transforming into an Islamic world capital. The texts and
knowledge which were recorded in or rather translated into Turkish
and Persian in his reign were based on popular Greek lore that had
been written down in Byzantine times. Their passage into Persian and
Ottoman Turkish constitute an interesting phenomenon. They testify
not only to the survival of Greek popular lore about the great city and
its monuments and thus its passage into Islamic knowledge. They
represent also the transformation of what was a popular body of
folklore in the Greek milieu, into a formal and learned tradition in the
Islamic milieu. Thus the Greek legends and lore were transformed
from something appertaining to popular culture in one society into
something appertaining to formal literary culture in the second society.

But this passage occured also at the level of popular Turkish culture
and folklore. And here we come back to both the Byzantine
monuments that the Ottomans found still standing at the time of the
conquest, but also to the body of Greek folklore which survived among
the Ottoman Greek population of Istanbul, and which had as its
unifying theme the reversal of political fortunes which would once
more bring Constantinople into the hands of the Greeks. This has to

do with the lore, in Turkish, of the kizil elma, the red or the golden apple. In Turkish lore it became associated with supreme political power and sovereignty, and the kizil elma (this symbol of power) changed its location, moving from one city to another. This Turkish legend of the kizil elma, seems, so far as I have been able to ascertain, to go back to an old and rich Byzantine legend that was associated with the famous equestrian statue of Justinian the Great in the Augusteum just near the entrance to the great palace. This statue is described by Procopius as presenting Justinian seated on the horse, with the globus crucifix in his left hand and his right hand directed toward Asia. Procopius gives us the earliest, in a long series, interpretation of this monument. The globe signifies his world dominion, and his outstretched hand is intended to halt the nations of the east (Persia at that time) from advancing. The globus, which symbolized world dominion, eventually fell from the hands of Justinian's statue in the fourteenth century and its fall was interpreted as signifying that political dominion would pass from the hands of the Greeks to the hands of the Turks. The globus came to be called the golden apple and eventually it passed into the hands of the Turks. Thus for the Turks the golden apple, kizil elma, was the symbol of political sovereignty. In modern Greek folklore the golden apple tree, kokine melia, came to be associated with the origins of the Turks, and with the tradition of chasing the Turks back to their place or origin.[17]

In all of this lore centering about the golden apple it is of interest to look at one of the Persian versions-translation of the Diegesis on the construction of St. Sophia. It records elements that are missing from the extant Greek text. It attributes to Justinian a conversation purportedly addressed to his successor Justin prior to his death, instructing him to erect a bronze equestrian statue to himself.

> "...When you have consigned my body to the earth you shall erect an equestrian statue of myself, gilded in copper. In my hand I shall hold an *apple* (according to version B; a ball according to the other version) and I shall hold the other hand open so that those who gaze on me shall realize that I ruled over a quarter of the inhabited world in the very same manner that I hold the *apple* (ball) in my palm".[18]

What is of further interest to note is that this great statue of Justinian was one of the relatively small number of classical and Byzantine statues to have survived into the fifteenth century and beyond into the period of Ottoman rule. It was, for some years, a prominent landmark in the landscape of early Ottoman Istanbul, and thus the Ottomans had not only the Turkish and Persian translations from the Greek recording the meaning of the "golden apple" held in the hand of Justinian, but they had a view of the statue itself until it was toppled from atop its column by lightning in the latter part of the fifteenth century. It was finally melted down for the casting of cannon in the Ottoman ordinance where the European observer Pierre Gyllius saw it and measured its leg, nose, and the horse's legs and hoofs, all that remained of this Byzantine wonder.[19]

Coming back to the city of Constantinople and Istanbul we thus see the Byzantine legacy in the folklore of both Turks and Greeks during the Ottoman period. This folklore, in the hands of the Muslim Turks, was often given a twist which would allow its incorporation more readily into the body of Islamic folklore. Such an example emerges again from the Persian translation of the Greek text on the building of St. Sophia and on the wonders of Byzantine Constantinople.

> "It is related that during the night when Muhammad was born, several churches and statues of idols crumbled... At that same time half of the dome of Saint Sophia fell..."[20]

Religion in the life of the Balkan peoples

This history of the formal religious structures and of popular religious practices among the inhabitants of the Balkan peninsula is a very long and complex one, stretching from the second millenium B.C. until modern times, with elements both of continuity and change. At the earliest level are the well studied structures and practices of Graeco-Roman antiquity which include not only the beliefs, ceremonies and institutions of the Greeks and Romans but also those of the non-Greek, non-Roman populations such as the Dacians, Illyrians, and Thracians. Much less is known about the religious life of the latter than of the former. Graeco-Roman paganism itself was the result of the fusion of many elements and practices, some sanctioned and especially sponsored by the state, others enjoying popularity in the non-sponsored, popular realm of culture and society. The god Dionysus and his worship enjoyed both a formal worship, as elaborated and controlled by state festivals of Dionysiaca, and a popular worship, as evidenced by popular ceremonies associated with religious practices in rural society which stood well out of the monitoring powers of the city-state or the empire. Further, Greek religion, according to Nilsson and other students, was the result of a fusion, at times imperfect, of pre-Greek chthonic elements and the religious beliefs and practices of Greek newcomers to the peninsula, a religiosity often symbolized by the duodecadic pantheon of the gods. As this religion came into contact with religious practices of Thracians (the cult of the rider hero, etc.) and other Balkan peoples there was further accommodation of Graeco-Roman and local gods and religious practices, to which were added the cults of the Near Eastern Mystery religions, especially in the period of the Roman Empire.

When Christianity began to spread into the peninsula in the period of the Roman Empire, the bases were laid for the next great strategraphic overlay on the religious life of the Balkan inhabitants: the official adoption of Christianity as the religion of the state, and the attempts of the emperors from the time of Constantius II, the son of Constantine the Great, through Justinian in particular to enforce conversion to Christianity by legislation and severe legal penalties for those who were recalcitrant. This resulted in mass conversions throughout the empire. Now it is precisely the phenomenon of mass conversions which results, most effectively, in the survival of prior religious cults, practices, and beliefs. In this, mass conversion serves as a protection or insulation for the earlier religious life of the converts. In contrast individual conversion can and often is a more thorough process in that the individual is isolated from the body of his former co-religionists and is persuaded to make a true change and conversion. Thus during the period of mass conversions of paganism and pagans to Christianity the converts, especially in the rural areas, but in the towns, often, as well, preserved their former religious beliefs, associations and practices within the framework of the church. Conversely, the church, in asserting its dogmas and cultic practices had, nevertheless, to accommodate also much that was not Christian and that was indeed out and out pagan. This basic process of the accommodation of Christianity and pagan religiosity occurred thus from the very time of the first appearance of Christianity in the Balkans, in an ever intensifying manner, right into the reign of Justinian. It was, therefore, a process which had run a full cycle by the time of the appearance of the Slavs in the Balkan peninsula.

When the Slavs came, from the little that we know of their religious life (the earliest and most detailed description of their religious beliefs and institutions occurs in the Byzantine historian Procopius) it was a type of polytheism-polydaemonism in which they believed in a supreme sky and weather god (not unlike Zeus and Jupiter), and in spirits that inhabited the waters, the mountains and the forests (like the Greek nereids, dryads, oreads).[21] We know very little about the contact of the Slavs with the older Balkan peoples prior to the Christianization of the Slavs in the ninth and tenth centuries but their entrance, formally, into Christianity in the ninth and tenth centuries brought them into intimate contact with the formal, religious life, beliefs, and ceremony of Greek Christianity. But from the study of the popular religious practices and beliefs of Roumanians, Bulgarians,[22], Serbs,[23] and Greeks, it would seem that the Slavs also came into contact with the popular religiosity of the pre-Slavic peoples and it would be difficult to suppose that this occurred exclusively as a result of their formal Christianization. Thus in the religious life of the newcomers we might reasonably expect to see a fusion of Christian religiosity (itself already a fusion of Christianity with Graeco-Roman paganism in its evolved state of late antiquity) with Slavic popular religion. And indeed when we look at the religious life of this newer demographic-ethnographic element in the Balkans, we see a formal religious life which is formally completely Christian, but which at the popular level is very heavily influenced by the earlier Graeco-Roman and Slavic pagan practices, rites, and beliefs. Even aspects of their formal Christianity and Christian life had long ago been formed from a fusion of pagan and Christian elements.

Thus, returning, briefly, to the earlier theoretical statement and structure of the consideration of the popular culture of the Balkan peoples and the survival of the Byzantine legacy therein, we see once more that the concept of a series of cultural layers dynamically connected in cultural evolution is a concept of considerable utility in getting at the heart of the subject under consideration. In the area of religion we see the following strata:

> Chthonic pre-Greek
> Greek and Roman
> Indigenous-Thracian, Dacian, Illyrian
> Oriental Mystery religions
> Christianity
> Slavic paganism-Slavic Christianity and popular religion in the Christian era

Let us return to the subject, more strictly speaking, of the Byzantine tradition in the realm of religion. With Christianization the Balkan Slavs entered a formal religious world of highly developed metaphysical speculative dogma, of formalization of dogma, belief, cultic practice through the mechanics of centralized church councils, and of a legalistic church structure buttressed by the centralized promulgation of a church law known as canon law. Indeed the medieval Serbian and Bulgarian states adopted Byzantine Christian dogma and the seven ecumenical councils, the hierarchical administrative structure of the Byzantine church, eventually creating for themselves patriarchates also, and of course they adopted the same system of canon law. But all these are elements of formal religious life and do not form the subject proper of our present discourse... nevertheless, formal religious life was important for popular religious life inasmuch as it formed or constituted one of the basic forces in the overall synthesis and character of popular religious life. And to this extent the influence of the Byzantine legacy in Balkan religious life was decisive, both in the pre-Turkish era as well as in the era of Ottoman rule.

The most striking elements of the Byzantine legacy in the popular religious life of the Balkan populations are to be seen in monasticism, hagiolatry, iconolatry, the appearance of neomartyrdom as a result of clashes with Islam, the survival of pagan animal sacrifices, the beliefs surrounding the Christian mystery of baptism, and indeed the existence of a religious calendar which is closely modeled on and adopted from the calendar and cycle of practices and beliefs associated with ancient paganism.

In the period following the Ottoman conquests and into the sixteenth century the number of Slavic monks on Mount Athos seems to have been substantial, and monasticism remained a vital institution in the popular religious life of all the Balkan Christians throughout the period of Ottoman rule. The tradition of martyrdom for the faith, so prominent in the earliest spread of Christianity during the reigns of Decius and Diocletian, had with the triumph of Christianity subsided. Then with the appearance of the new Muslim conquerors in the Balkans during the fourteenth century, and throughout their five hundred years of political sovereignty there was an apposition of Christianity and Islam. The latter, enjoying the prestige of political superiority and economic affluence, followed a double policy toward Christianity. On the one hand there was formal institutionalized tolerance of Judaism and Christianity so that the masses of Christians survived the five hundred years of Ottoman rule without surrendering their religion. On the other hand the missionizing spirit was inbuilt into the teaching and the spirit of Islam so that there was substantial conversion of Christians in the Balkans, though not on the same massive scale as in Asia Minor, and very often these conversions took place in stressful times.[24] Within this domain of restricted conversion there were individuals who underwent death and martyrdom for their Christian faith. The neo-martyrs, as a cult, appear early in the Ottoman conquests of the Balkans, as is evidenced by the martyrdom of St. George of Sofia, a Christian soldier in the Ottoman armies, and continued into the very late period of Ottoman rule, as witness the martyrdom of the neo-martyrs St. George of Jannina who was martyred in an Ottoman military camp, and Constantine the Neomartyr who underwent his tribulation in the early nineteenth century Izmir. As a phenomenon, neomartyrdom was a continuation of the phenomenon which first arose among Christians in the Turkish domains of Seljuk Anatolia.[25]

Certainly the most important of all the aspects of popular religious life of the Balkan peoples was hagiolatry, the cult and worship of the saints. One should note the following important characteristics of hagiolatry: the worship of the saint is localized and personalized; the local patron saint is the single most important religious figure in the life of the inhabitants of the Balkan village and town during the Ottoman period, as also the Byzantine period.

For he, or she, is the most efficacious supernatural force in the life cycle of the Balkan Christian, more powerful than Christ, the Virgin, and God. He is the most important because he is present in the village or town. The Byzantines and modern Greeks called him sympolites, co-citizen. Very often they have in the village reliquary or in the church's foundations a relic of that saint, which means that the magic of his presence resides in his actual presence, his physical presence, pars pro toto. A great deal of scholarly attention has been given to the cults of individual saints, as indeed to the entire phenomenon.

At one stage of scholarship there were attempts to point to connections of individual saints with individual Graeco-Roman pagan deities: Poseidon, St. Nicholas; Athena, the Virgin, etc., because there was a strong suspicion that the cult of the saints grew out of the polytheistic cults of antiquity. It is perhaps simplistic to look for direct continuity between pagan deities and a given saint. But one should examine, and indeed this has been done successfully, the continuity of functions and attributes between pagan deities and Christian saints, as a more promising sector of research. And then finally, one should examine the function of the entirety of the structure of hagiolatry as a religious phenomenon and should do so comparatively with the polytheistic nature of Graeco–Roman religion. Given the undoubted importance of each individual saint in the local life of various villages and towns, and the elaborate cult attendant upon the worship of each, one cannot but be struck by the emphasis on the many rather than on the one in Orthodox Christianity in the Balkans. This emphasis on the varied rather than on the unified one in popular religiosity of course recalls the lack of a rigidly enforced unity in pagan religion. In effect, hagiolatry is a partial replacement of and a partial continuity of the ancient polytheistic and polydaemonistic concept of religion. So in this respect hagiolatry is polytheistic. Further, there is no doubt that the attributes and functions of ancient deities have been taken over by various saints.[26]

In this respect, it is instructive to look for a moment at the cult of the Prophet Elijah, first among the Byzantines and modern Greeks, and then among the Bulgars and Serbs. In the Byzantine and modern Greek tradition, Elijah (in Greek he is called Elias) is the saint of rain, thunder, lightning, and the wind. According to Greek folklore lightning and thunder are his weapons and he unleashes them as he chases the devil, or variously, the dragon, across the heavens in his chariot. His chapels are most conspicuously placed on mountain tops and heights... he has an almost exclusive monopoly of these, man's highest landscapes, those points of the earth's surface which are closest to the heavens. It had been pointed out by the Greek folklorist Nikolas Polites, with a high degree of probability, that these attributes of Elijah represented an appropriation of the principal characteristics of the pagan Greek god Zeus, who was also the Indo-european god of thunder, rain, and the skies, and to whom heights were sacred. Both by the philological proximity of the names Elias-Helios, and by further appropriation, it has been indicated, again with a high degree of probability, that the cult of the Prophet Elijah expropriated the functions of the sun god Helios, also close in position and function to Zeus.

Scholars who have studied this particular Byzantine cult have, further, examined the cultic practices attendant upon the worship of the Prophet Elijah and these too are instructive as to the composite character of his attributes and prehistory. It has been observed that on the highest landmark of Mt. Taygetus, dominating the Spartan plain, the Greek peasants used to ascend the mountain on his feast day, July 20, to light fires in his honor and to throw incense into the fire as an offering to the prophet-saint. Down below on the plains, the peasants lighted their own fires, dancing around them and jumping over the flames. Further, it was the practice to sacrifice a rooster to him, a practise closely associated with the worship of the pagan god of the sun Helios. As a symbol of the sun, whose rays first fell on the mountain tops, the cock sacrifice was adopted into the cult of Elijah who also inherited some of the traits-attributes of Helios, as well as of Zeus. Thus the farmers used to believe that they could foretell the weather from the crowing of the rooster. As an Old Testament Prophet, Elijah, it was believed, could foretell the future, and so on his feast day the peasants consulted him from the colors of the burning incense which the faithful offered to him in the fires on the mountain heights. In eastern Rumelia peasants sacrificed bullocks to him in an effort to ward off contagious diseases.[27]

In short, we have a picture of a composite Byzantine-neohellenic saint, the Prophet Elijah. From Hebraic Old Testament prophet, he became a «Greek-speaking» heir to Zeus-Helios, and was finally consecrated a saint. Thus there are at least three layers, historically speaking, three overlays, which went into the composite picture of this important figure in the Byzantine hagiolatric calendar.

What do we find in the popular religious calendar, beliefs, and practices of the Serbs and Bulgars? On July 20 the Serbs and Bulgars worship Sv. Ilija Gromovnik... his Serbian epithet Gromovnik is indicative, for it means the thunderer. His fellow saints hide from him on his feastday proper for fear that he might unleash terrible storms. At that time people are forbidden to work lest they be struck by lightning, a belief that prevails even among South Slavs converted to Islam. In eastern Serbia and Bulgaria the patriarch of the household must sacrifice a rooster on his feast day lest he himself perish. In parts of Bulgaria the rooster is broiled and devoured at a common meal held atop a nearby mountain dedicated to Saint Ilija[28]. Thus, from this brief description we see that the cult of the Prophet Elijah passed to the South Slavs in its Byzantine form; that is a composite saint with elements from the Old Testament Elijah, the pagan Zeus and Helios, and the Byzantine saint's cult.

This example can be multiplied by a very large number of similar and parallel cases of Byzantine saints who represent Christianized attributes of pagan deities and deamons.

Moving from the category of hagiolatry to cult practice, I should like to mention, en passant, certain pagan cultic practices which were absorbed by the religious practices of the Byzantines and then passed on into the practices of the Balkan peoples: animal sacrifice and offerings of boiled wheat-panspermia-kollyva.

Blood sacrifice is one of the most striking aspects of classical Graeco-Roman paganism, as it is of the other early religious traditions elsewhere. Doubtlessly it was also practiced by the Slavs when they first entered the Balkan peninsula, though we have no early direct sources in this matter. Though sacrifice was combatted as a distinctly pagan practice by the early church, its persistence was such that its prohibition is to be seen in the canons of the church as well as in survivals into modern times. The canons forbade the roasting of animals on skewers following the church service and in the church courtyard, a prohibition which indicates that this pagan remnant continued into the Christian era. Other survivals in modern Greek folklore of the sacrifice of oxen, sheep, and roosters are well known and indicate a popular survival into modern times of pagan sacrificial practices.[29] Similarly, Serbian folklore studies record the practice of sacrificing a rooster at the plowing season in the presence of a priest who performed a special litany[30], and Bulgars traditionally performed a sacrifice (a kurban) for the dead.[31] But such practices of performing a sacrifice may have arisen independently in each of these three traditions: Greek, Bulgar, Serb. Are there any indications of a common thread or origin of such practices within the realm of pagan sacrifice?

If one looks into the seasonal and Christian calendars of all three of these peoples, he will see a startling similarity in the realm of sacrificial practices in a sufficient number of cases to point to common origins or at least to common results. On July 20, the feast day of the Prophet Elijah, Greeks, Serbs, and Bulgars sacrificed roosters to Elijah and lit fires on heights in his honor[32].

On April 23 all three peoples celebrated the feast of St. George by the sacrifice of a young lamb, a ritual meal, and by all sorts of magical practices associated with the spring cycle in the life of the pastoral sector of Balkan society and in the movement of the flocks[33].

Three observations are in order in regard to these common sacrificial practices of a major portion of the Balkan peoples in medieval and modern times. First, there is the identity of sacrificial and other rites; second there is the fact that they occur at specific times in the rural-economic cycle of life which is as ancient as those occupations; third, they are ancient pre-Christian practices which, because of their importance in the economic and seasonal cycles, persisted. The church, in early Buzantine times, simply incorporated these pagan-seasonal practices in the rural areas and it was natural that they should be absorbed in the hagiolatric calendar which so prevailed in the rural areas. Here, old pagan practices were regularized under the mantle of the church and they passed into the worship of the saints. Obviously animal sacrifice, fires, and popular-magical practices attendant on pastoralism were anything but Christian. When the Slavs entered the Balkans they found these practices in effect, and when they came into contact with Christianity and with the pre-Slavic Balkan peoples they absorbed these practices. Thus we have here, in animal sacrifice, a legacy of Byzantium in the popular culture of the Balkan peoples.

The persistence of these ancient pre-Christian, and then Christianized, practices are also to be observed among Muslims, probably converts, during Ottoman times. Thus, the lamb sacrifice and sacrificial meal attendant upon the celebration of St. George on April 23 has been observed, in modern times, among the Muslims of Bosnia, themselves largely and ultimately composed of Bosnian Slavs converted to Islam in Ottoman times[34].

Many aspects of this pagan form of sacrifice, sanctified later by popular Christianity, survived among muslims on a largely scale, as the sixteenth century Croatian observer Bartholomaeus Georgiewitz in – forms us. In a paragraph entitled «The manner of their sacrifice (Turks)» he states that at a time of danger or of illness they sacrifice an ox or a sheep. After the sacrifice, they apportion the dead animal in such a manner that the «priest» receives the skin, head, feet, and a fourth part of the flesh. Another part is given to the poor, and the rest they and their friends devour. He notes that in this respect they do exactly as do the Greeks and Armenians in Asia Minor. What is of interest here is the «priest's» share. It is precisely the same share which a sacrificing priest was given in many parts of the ancient Greek world in the fourth century B.C., and this share was then called «dermatikon» after the skin of the slain animal[35].

If there be any doubt left as to the continuity of this type of sacrifice among Balkan Muslims one need only look at the practices of Balkan Muslims on the feast days of the Prophet Elijah and of St. George. On April 23-4 the Bosnian Muslims sacrifice a lamb to St. George, and on the feast day of the Prophet Elijah they sacrifice a lamb (not a rooster).

Next I wish to look at a widespread practice among the Balkan peoples at certain religious celebrations. This has to do with the preparation of kollyva: the word is common to Greeks, Bulgars, Slavs, as is the practice assosiated with kollyva. What is kollyva? In Byzantine times it indicated the boiled wheat usually distributed to the faithful on certain religious feasts, particularly however, it was associated with the commemoration and/ or propitiation of the souls of the departed. The word is copiously attested to in the medieval Greek authors (see Ducange) and is also known in the ancient lexica. Thus the word goes back to Byzantine and to classical Greek times. What of the practices associated with this boiled wheat?

Among modern Greeks boiled wheat, usually interspersed with raisins, almonds, sugar, and sometimes pomegranate, is most frequently given to the faithful at religious ceremonies that are concerned with the dead: funerals, commemorations of the soul of the departed at three months, six months, one year, etc. But they are also distributed to the faithful on New Year's day, in commemoration of souls, on the feast days of St. Tryphon (an agricultural festival dedicated to the fields and to the vines) and on December 4, the feast day of St. Barbara.

Among Serbs, kollyva are prepared and eaten on Christmas Eve to commemorate the souls of the dead, as well as on the occasion of the Slava, a feast which celebrates the ancestor of the household and also the patron saint of the household[36]. The Serbs, like the Greeks[37], offer kollyva to St. Barbara on her feast day. For the Serbs, St. Tryphon is the patron saint of vegetation and of vineyards, as in the case of the Greeks, but Schneeweis does not inform us whether or not the Serbs offer him kollyva on the occasion of his feast[38].

The Bulgars, much like the Greeks and Serbs, prepare kollyva as a part of the rituals attendant upon funerals and upon the commemoration of the souls of the dead. Further for them, as for the Greeks and Serbs, St. Tryphon is associated with the vegetation cycle and specifically with their cultivation of the grapevine. On this day the Bulgar peasant went to the vineyards and pruned the grape vines. The peasant took to the fields with him, on this occasion, wine, brandy, and kollyva[39].

It is of interest to note that among many Yugoslav Muhammedans St. Barbara's day continued to be celebrated by the preparation of kollyva.[40]

We see, then, that the practice of preparing, offering, and eating kollyva among Greeks, Serbs, and Bulgars are associated with the commemoration of the souls of the dead, and also with agricultural-vegetative celebrations. Further we see that these celebrations, at least in terms of the few examples presented, are synchronized chronologically in the year's calendar and around the personalities of specific saints in some cases. What is, then, the origin of the similarity of religious practice in the case of kollyva?

We have already noted the Greek origin of the word, that it is copiously noted in Byzantine times, from the fourth century on. In Byzantine times, without going into any great detail, kollyva were prepared, and eaten, on religious occasions in which the souls of the dead were commemorated, and also were offered up to certain saints. Specifically they refer to prayers over the kollyva for the dead, and also to prayers over the kollyva on behalf of the memory of the saints. Byzantine hagiographical and religious authors tended to attribute the origins of the practice of kollyva to the cult of St. Theodore. Thus we see that in early Byzantine times the preparation of the wheat in honor of the dead and of the saints was early incorporated into the church and was a universal phenomenon.

In effect the statement that the practice originated in conjunction with a Christian cult, that of St. Theodore, is a pious fib intended to give this practice Christian origin. In effect it is pagan and very ancient. The great historian of ancient Greek religion, Martin Nilsson, had already made the association between the modern Greek kollyva and their ancient progenitor, the panspermion.

«The Panspermia, a mixture of all kinds of fruits, was often found in the ancient Greek cult, either in the cult of the dead at the general Feast of Souls, or at festivals held for the protection of the standing crops and growing fruit. In modern Greece it is just as common and makes its appearance in the same occasions. It has different names; in some cases the old term is preserved, but most frequently it is called kollyva, from the boiled grains of wheat which form one of its principal ingredients. It has its established place in the cult of the dead... just as in classical times. It is also found at the general feast of Souls from which the Saturday before Whitsun takes its name of the Sabbath of Souls. At the festival of harvest all kinds of fruits are brought to the church, are blessed by the priest, and part of them are strewn before the altar and the rest distributed... At Arachova, near ancient Delphi... the panspermia has kept its old name»[41].

Once more, with the kollyva and its ceremonial attachments, we find a practice in the popular culture of the Balkan peoples which is a

Byzantinized version, i.e. a Christianized form, of an ancient pagan practice.

Having discussed, and given brief illustrative examples of the hagiolatric and cultic practices common to the Balkan peoples, I wish to turn briefly to that other salient feature of popular religiosity among the Balkan peoples, iconolatry, that is, reverence or even worship of the holy icons. The cult of the images was so widespread, in modern times, among Greeks, Bulgars, Roumanians, and Serbs that it is not necessary to dwell upon this fact at any length. The painted image plays a central role in the domain of both the church and the house; particular icons are endowed with mystical qualities and powers to heal, to protect, to fulfill aspirations, etc. Obviously the cult of the religious images is a Byzantine inheritance pure and simple in the popular, as well as in the formal, religious life of the Balkan peoples. Both their technological and liturgical function are Byzantine on the one hand, and also their artistic production is the direct legacy of Byzantium, though western influence also intruded in the Renaissance and Baroque periods. Nevertheless their iconography, if not always their style, is a Byzantine legacy.

But what of their more general cultural function? How far can this be traced?

As is well known the principle object of cult worship in Graeco-Roman paganism seems to have been the statue, though painted forms were also known. Each deity had his or her iconographic sculpted type, and each god-godess had its own attributes and miraculous powers and specialization. Further, the statues, if prayed to and propitiated, could cure illness, thwart foes, fulfill desires, etc.

Because the statues were so intimately associated with paganism the Greek church fought them relentlessly and finally forbade sculpture in the round. But pagan customs and habits persisted and so the painted image replaced the statue. It assumed, however, all the same religious and social functions. Just as in the case of statues so there were icons which were palladia of towns and armies, there were icons which cured, icons which assured economic enterprises, etc. Just as there had been statues said to have been made by other than human hands (diopeteis) and which had come from the heavens, so there were magical icons which also were not painted by humans (acheiropoietoi).

Thus the function of the icon was identical to the function of the statue in most of its attributes.

The art of the painting of the icon came to the Balkan peoples from Byzantium. Then, in the eighteenth century Dionysios o ek Phourna, the Greek monk and painter from Mount Athos, composed his manual Ermeniea tes Zographikes, which going back to older texts and traditions about painting reformulated the various techniques for painting (Byzantine and western), and prescribed the iconographies, proportions of subjects in all scenes depicted in icons. This text intended as a manual for painters, was then translated into Roumanian and Serbian. The transmission of this text which is at the same time a religious and artistic text, gave the possibility for the renewal of the unification of both the art and cult of the icon among the Balkan peoples, and originates, as in Byzantine times, from a Greek source and tradition[42].

The relation of man to the World and to the World beyond

In all societies man has associated a complex unity of beliefs and ritual practices with the major rites of passage through life, from birth to death. For all these crucial points in the passage are fraught with danger, with mystical meaning, and with apprehension. Thus the rites and beliefs are intended to protect and to assure case of passage through these stages. Religious beliefs and practices in particular cluster about these crucial points or stages.

Life begins with wondrous mystery of birth, as awesome today despite all our scientific discoveries as it was for primitive man. Into the mystery of birth is locked the future of the newborn.

Among modern Greeks there prevailed the belief that the fate of the newborn infant was determined by the Three Fates who came on the third night after the birth in order to determine its fate. On that evening it was customary for the relatives of the child to gather and to prepare a reception for the Fates, setting the table for them with food and drink and with proclamation of the phrase: «O Fates, Fates, of the Fates! Come to determine the fate of the child of so and so»[43].

The Serbs also believed that in the period of the first three nights after the birth the orisnici (women fates) come, invisibly, into the house, sit near the child and determine the fate of the child: length of life, marriage, wealth.

The family prepares a rich meal and sets it for the three fates; with clean napkins and with a silver brocaded dress of the mother. All of these are offered to the three fates in order to please them[44].

The belief of the modern Bulgarians was largely identical with that of the Greeks and Serbs. Bulgarians believed that on the third night after the birth, the orisnici (women fates) come, invisibly, into the house, sit near the child and determine the fate of the child: length of life, marriage, wealth. The family prepares a rich meal and sets it for the three fates; with clean napkins and a silver brocaded dress of the mother. All of these are offered to the three fates in order to please them.[45]

The similarity of belief in this aspect of birth, i.e. the third night, and the similarity of practice are clearly indicative that we are dealing with one and the same practice among modern Greeks, Bulgars, and Serbs.

This belief, among the Balkan peoples, suggests strongly a common origin and we are left to choose between independent common practice among early indo-european peoples, or else an ancient Graeco-Roman origin in the classical belief that it was the three fates, the moirai, who determine the fate of the newborn child. The identity of the belief and even the common word from Greek, orisnici, would strongly suggest that whatever the early pagan Slavs had believed in regard to the determination of the infant's fate, there is either a direct influence from antiquity via Byzantium, or at least a strong Greek overlay[46].

Common to all three peoples also are the practices of bathing the infant on the third day, sprinkling his body with salt, and finally of giving him silver money. The salting and bathing of the infant have survived among rural Anatolian Turks as sulamak and tuzlamak[47].

These practices attendant upon the newborn child are attested in Byzantine times, and the second century Greek physician Galen had already recommended the salting of infants as beneficial[48].

A final observation having to do with the period immediately following birth is of course baptism. This is the fundamental rite of passage for the new human being as his basic entry into Christianity. It is a religious practice which came to Serbs, Bulgars, and Roumanians from Byzantine, Greek Christianity, and the relationship between godfather and godson is very special in all three cultures. Baptism remained a very important ceremony even among many converts to Islam, taking on, usually, certain less Christian connotations. In the twelfth century the canon lawyer Balsamon remarked that already:

«...it is the custom that all the infants of the Muslims be baptized by Orthodox priests... for the Agarenes suppose that their children will be possessed of demons and will smell like dogs if they do not receive Christian baptism»[49].

As late as the seventeenth century[50] the Constantinopolitan patriarch threatened to defrock all Christian priests who continued to administer baptism to the children of Ottoman Muslims[51].

Thus we see a number of beliefs and customs attendant upon the birth and first two months in the life of a child which are very prominent not only in the life of the Christian Serbs, Roumanians, Bulgars, and Greeks, but also in the life of the Muslim converts. And this complex of beliefs and practices entered the lives of these peoples in the Byzantine stratum of cultural influence which in turn was the result of a fusion of classical pagan and Christian beliefs and practices. One could continue to illustrate this condition by pointing to numerous similarities in customs and beliefs attendant upon marriage and death,[52] but this would not alter basically the point and conclusion of our analysis. It would only enrich the examples and strengthen the proof of this more general proposition as to the origins and evolution of the popular culture of the Balkan peoples in this realm.

I wish now to turn to the domain of man's relation to the world beyond, to examine certain particulars which will again give us some notion as to the manner by which Byzantine elements influenced the popular culture of the Balkan peoples.

Though the world of the Balkan Serbs, Greeks, and Bulgars was a Christian world and so the relations of man to the world beyond were dominated by the basic Christian suppositions, yet there were important exceptions. First we see the popular belief in spirits and demons that have nothing to do with the formal Christian world. When Christianity preempted the religious domain of the Mediterranean, and specifically of the Balkans, it swept aside the great duodecadic pantheon of the Graeco-Roman, the oriental mystery religions, and the various local gods and godesses. These were replaced with the triune Trinity and with the panoply of saints. So much for formal religion and the principal deity. But the horizon of ancient paganism was dominated by a whole host of lesser spirits and demons. These Christianity was not able to remove from the religious consciousness of the Christian masses. Among Bulgars, Serbs, and Greeks we see the popular belief in an evil sky spirit, usually dragonlike in form, known in all three languages as the Lamia[53]. When these spirits struggle in the heavens or when they are chased through the heavens by Elijah the blows result in the hail storms which lash the earth. The term Lamia points to its Greek origin (ancient) where it is a female spirit that is hostile to man.

Of greater interest is the belief among Greeks, Bulgars, and Serbs in nymphs who inhabit the water, the mountains, and the forests. Known variously in Slavic as gorska majka, vili, samovili, and in Greek as neraides, oreades, dryades, they have a curious relation to mankind and are particularly prominent in water[54]. Here there seems to be a strict philological division in the terms used to designate them between Greek speakers and Slavs, so that there is no evidence, at least that is known to me, showing a borrowing of Greek terms. Further, from the earliest passage that we have describing Slavic religion in Procopius he refers to an early Slavic belief in and reverence of rivers and nymphs[55]. Thus we have here a concrete example of parallel beliefs which could have separate immediate origins, all going back to a common indo-european religious life. Schneeweis is of the opinion, on the basis of the study of the typology, that this early Slavic belief in the vili, which originally had the character more of house and death spirits, underwent transformation when the South Slavs came into contact with Graeco-Roman antiquity and took on the characteristics of the ancient oreades, neraides, and dryades[56].

The seasonal and religious calendar of the Balkan peoples

The seasonal and religious calendar of the Balkan Orthodox peoples is remarkably similar and though it has many local variations it nevertheless displays a clear structuring that has incorporated pagan Graeco-Roman, pagan Slavic, and Byzantine Christian strata, so that all coexist in one and the same seasonal and religious calendar, and the various elements have been integrated into a harmonious whole. It would seems that the pagan Slavic calendar was intergrated into the combined Graeco-Roman pagan and the Byzantine Christian caledar so that it is the latter elements which have given whatever unity there is in this aspect of the popular calendar of the Balkan peoples of the Orthodox persuasion.

One can begin with the celebration of Christmas and the period of the Duodecameron that follows thereafter until the day of Epiphany. In the very beginning Christmas was adopted by the early church and by Byzantine society from the pagan calendar, it having been the day of Sol Invictus. Common elements among Greeks, Bulgars, and Serbs in the celebration of this period are the following: offerings to the dead, that is, there is a cult of souls attached to this celebration; sumptuous Christmas dinner, pyromancy, and the bands of young children that go from door to door singing the news of the birth of Christ in the famous calends (in Greek, kalanda, in Slavic, koleda, also in Roumanian), derived from the celebration of the Roman calends. The period between Christmas and Epiphany is an «impure period» during which impure spirits known in Greek as Kalikantzaroi, and in Serbian and Bulgarian as Karakandzolu, roam the streets and houses[57]. It has generally been held that all these elements are of a pre-Slavic and pre-Christian origin, and that the early Slavs had only mid-winter and new month observance. Thus, according to Schneeweis and others, the basic foundations of Serbo-Croatian Christmas customs are the Calends celebration of Graeco-Roman antiquity[58]. The adoption or rather the creation of Christmas by Christianity provided another layer in which all these practices and beliefs were given Christian meaning.

St. Tryphon's, February 1, as has been mentioned earlier, was a common feast day in which Greeks, Bulgars, and Serbs, celebrated not only the patron of viticulture, but in which they carried out celebrations that had little to do with Christianity in the more formal sense. Pruning of the vines was carried out; the Serbs referred to St. Tryphon as pijanica, the drinker, and also both Serbs and Bulgars, referred to him as zarezan, the pruner. In Epirus, St. Tryphon is invited by the villagers to «come and drink»[59].

Carneval is centainly one of the most richly celebrated of all the festivals of the Balkan peoples, occurring as it does just before the great Lent. It lasts for a period of three weeks, begins with eating and drinking which is then, over the three weeks, gradually diminished. Among Greeks, Serbs, and Bulgars the Carneval is marked by a number of very strong resemblances, some of which go beyond the Balkans, others of which are Balkan in geographical extent. First there is the feasting, drinking, and visiting. There are in addition masquerades as well as the presentation of plays of individuals attired in specific costumes. These plays often have as their subject marriage, but also other themes as well. There are mummers, dances, and representations of more solemn subjects which have to do with the mysteries of fertility and agricultural life. There are scenes of actual ceremonial plowing and phallic representations enjoy a considerable prominence in a cycle of celebrations which obviously have to do with inductive magic and the fertility of the soil. These events are often accompanied by scenes of symbolic sowing as well as of plowing.[60]

Lent is uniformly a religious period among the peoples in question, but in the first week after Easter Greeks, Serbs, and Bulgars celebrate a holiday in which flowers are carried variously from house to house and to the graves, a celebration which in South Slavic is called Rusalia, and is a direct descendant of the Roman cult of the dead known by the same name, the Latin dies rosationis.[61]

Finally I shall refer to the feasts of St. George, April 23, 24, St. John the Baptist, and of the Prophet Elijah, all of which are celebrated with many similarities by Greeks, Bulgars, and Serbs. St. George, as was mentioned earlier, is celebrated in conjunction with the cycle of pastoralism in a process involving sacrifice and rites that have nothing to do with Christianity but which are the ancient heritage of livestock raising in the Balkans.[62] Serbs, Greeks, and Bulgars commemmorate the birthdate of St. John the Baptist on June 24 by the lighting of fires and, in the case of Serbs and Greeks, by jumping through and over the fires. Divination is commonly practiced at this time. As for the Prophet Elijah, July 20, we have already noted the burning of fires on the mountain tops, sacrifice of the rooster and the association of Elijah with the heavens and thunder, a striking recollection of the attributes of Zeus and of the ancient Slavic god of the skies.[63]

From this brief and superficial survey of the calendar of the Balkan Orthodox Christians we clearly see the strength of the Byzantine influence in this domain of life, which in preindustrial society dominated the agricultural and pastoral lives and practices of the majority of the population. Most of the actual practices are pre-Christian, most of these, though not all, are Graeco-Roman, and Byzantine Christianity incorporated them all into one uniform religious and seasonal calendar. This calendar gave a color, tone, and essence to the popular life of Balkan culture which were dominant.

The panegyris

One of the most astute observers of the life and culture of the inhabitants of the Balkan peninsula in the late eighteenth and early nineteenth century was the Frenchman de Pouqueville, whose numerous writings have greatly enlightened us as to the ethnic, social, cultural, and political situation of the region. In chapter ninety-four of his *Voyage en Grèce* he gives a table of the principal commercial fairs (which he calls panegyreis) of Rumelia.

place of panegyris	dates of opening	time of duration	names of provinces
Stroungia	Feb. 29	15 days	Illyria, Macedonia
Preloub	April 30	25	Macedonia Cisaxeni
Moscoulouri	May 20	15	Thessaly
Nicopolis	Ascension	3	Epirus
Mavronoros	July 30	15	Macedonia Cisaxeni
Zeitoun	Aug. 1	8	Thessaly
Pogoniani	Aug. 15	15	Epirus
Vrachori	Sept. 8	8	Aetolia
Pharsala	Sept. 15	8	Thessaly
Mavrovo	Nov. 29	20	Macedonia Cisaxeni.[64]

De Pouqueville mentions that Greeks, Albanians, Slavs, Vlachs, and other peoples came to these fairs to buy and sell. In effect he tells us specifically that these fairs are the descendants of older religio-commercial fairs, also called panygereis in Byzantine and classical times, in which the religious, coultural, and economic life of the inhabitants was combined. These panegyreis in our period were held on the days of the celebration of the local patron saint. Though it is difficult to say how extensive the panegyris was in early modern times, certainly it was a live and vital religious - commercial institution in the south and central Balkans, if not beyond, as well as in parts of Asia Minor.

In a detailed study on its origin, development and afterlife in this area, I showed the following:

In origins it is a pagan institution first mentioned and described in the Homeric Hymns, and that it was highly developed as a religious, commercial and cultural event throughout the classical period; that it was continued in Byzantine times under the aegis of the cults of the saint and in partnership with the Byzantine state; that it survived the Turkish invasions of Anatolia and the expansion of the Serbs and Bulgars toward the south Balkans with the adoption and incorporation of the panegyris by the Bulgars, Serbs, and of course the Greeks, as well as by the Ottoman Turks. The panegyris is thus a very ancient institution and its commercial and religious character passed into the lives of the Balkan and Anatolian peoples from Byzantium, whereas its form in Byzantine times represents a Christianization of an already pre-existing commercial and religious institution of Greek antiquity.[65]

The figure and legend of Alexander the Great

The importance of the figure and legend of Alexander the Great in the popular literature and lore of the Balkan peoples has only recently been examined in a systematic and scholarly fashion. The subject is not only «glamorous» because it deals with one of the world"s most «glamorous» heroes, but also because it is an important aspect of both Balkan literature and of world literature, given the fact that aspects of the Alexander legend have been adopted in over 35 languages. As far as the Balkan peoples during the Ottoman period are concerned, there are manuscripts and printed books in Greek, Serbian, Bulgarian, and Roumanian, as well as manuscripts in Persian and Ottoman Turkish.

There are ultimately three basic groups of sources for the Alexander myth, legend, and history available during this period.

a) First there are the ancient historians themselves, particularly Arrian, Plutarch, Quintus Curtius, and others. It may be argued that they are insignificant prior to the rise of modern historical scholarship, and particularly for this part of the world. Yet this is an oversimplification as now emerges from the fundamental study of G. Veloudes, who points to the use of these sources by the learned Greek historians of the Ottoman period. As an example he quotes the historian Kontaris of Kozani, c. 1675, who not only knew these sources but used them for purposes which Veloudes terms the cultivation of national consciousness.[66]

b) Second there is the popular legendary tradition of the Pseudo-Callisthenes text-texts, which transform Alexander's real world into an illusionary one and the hero himself is transformed into a mould for all heroes. It was this version of Alexander which captivated the mind of the Byzantines and as a result of which they not only took over the text but reworked it frequently, variegated it, producing versions in both prose and poetry.[67]

c) Third there is the oriental version of the Pseudo-Callisthenes much reworked by Firdausi, and later in the second half of the twelfth century by the Persian poet Nizami in the Iskandarname, a masnavi of over 10,000 verses.[68]

As is obvious, the first of these sources is a learned scholarly tradition, whereas the other two are legendary and literary.

We see, from this very brief introduction, that the figure and legends of Alexander are spread from the eastern to the northwestern boundaries of the Ottoman Empire, as indeed far beyond both of these borders. We must now ask two questions. (1) What were the origins of the Alexander figure and legends in the Ottoman period? (2) How widespread were these legends about Alexander: was it a popular phenomenon, or was it restricted to literary circles? or was it both?

What Were the Origins of the Alexander Figure and Legends in the Ottoman Period

1. *The Tradition in Greek* - An anonymous author composed a poem of 6,120 unrhymed «political» verses on Alexander in 1388, which is preserved in a manuscript written down in 1391-1404. The author utilized the Pseudo-Callisthenes material, from the Byzantine chroniclers George Monachus and Zonaras, and he wrote in a language close to the late Greek vernacular but also with a command of the learned language. The oldest prose composition on Alexander at this late date is in Vindob. Theol. gr. 244, probably composed between 1435-43.[69]

Thus we have extant prose and poetic compositions on Alexander, in Greek, at the onset of the Ottoman period, all of them obviously tied to the Pseudo-Callisthenes but reworked.

2. *The Tradition in Serbian* - At the end of the fourteenth century a work entitled Alexandrida was translated into Serbian/Slavonic, based on the Pseudo-Callisthenes and which deals of course with the legends of Alexander the Great, but does so in a peculiar fashion, reflecting feudal society and Christianity.[70]

3. *The Bulgarian Tradition* - There is a version of the Serbian/Slavonic of the Alexandrida, written in the language of west Bulgaria.[71]

4. *The Tradition in Roumanian* - There is the manuscript of Neamtzul (F) of the sixteenth century, written in the so-called Bulgaro-Vlach used in Roumania at this period. By the end of the sixteenth or the early seventeenth century, the Slavic text of the Alexandrida was translated into Roumanian.[72]

5. *The Tradition in Ottoman Turkish* - At the time of the conquest of Constantinople and during the period of the reign of Mehmed II he himself had access to at least a double tradition on the figure of Alexander: first, there was the learned Greek tradition, as his library possessed copies of the Greek text of Arrian. Further, his biographer Critobulus and other Greek learned men at his court constantly compared him to Alexander and discussed Alexander with him. In addition there was the long mesenvi of Ahmedi (early fifteenth century), the Iskandarname, a poem on the deeds of Alexander the Great that goes back to the Persian model of Nizami (second half of the twelfth century) in over 10,000 verses.[73]

Thus we see from this rapid survey that Greeks, Serbs, Bulgars, Roumanians, and Ottomans had produced versions of the Alexander legend or romance in their own languages in the period between the late fourteenth and the sixteenth or early seventeenth century.

The ultimate source for these versions was the Pseudo - Callisthenes in one or another, or more, of its different versions. Further, there is no reason to assume that the Christian and Muslim versions of the fifteenth-sixteenth century had any affiliation or that one influenced the other. They simply came together on the domains of the Ottoman sultans, and indeed to some degree in the person of the Ottoman sultan himself, Mehmed 11.

Inasmuch as the fifteenth and sixteenth century versions of the Alexandrida among Roumanians and Bulgars came from the Serbian version, one need not seek further for the immediate origin of the Bulgarian and Roumanian Alexandrida, in Turkish times. Though the first of the Slavs to translate a version of the Preudo-Callisthenes were the Bulgars, the translation which they made from a Byzantine Greek text of the Pseudo-Callisthenes probably in the tenth-eleventh century, it is agreed that this earlier version «subsided» and it was the later

Serbian version which replaces it through new «translations».[74] The problem which has not yet been satisfactorily addressed is the relation of the fourteenth century Greek and Serbian texts. Murko and Georgiev suggest that the Serbian has been translated from a Greek text influenced by the western romance, whereas Marinković, in leaving the question open, indirectly suggests the priority of the Serbian over the Greek late Byzantine text. Thus the question of whether the Alexander legend among the Christian Balkan populations is a Byzantine legacy or not remains in part still open. Ultimately, however, the origin seems to be the Byzantine version of the Pseudo-Callisthenes.

Was the Alexander Legend Widespread ? Was It a Learned or a Popular Tradition or Both?

1. *The Greek Tradition during Turkokratia* - Veloudes in his remarkable book has stated that the modern Greek Alexander romance is the only one which stands at the end of a 2,000 year development. Its development phases are not interrupted by translations from foreign languages and it is marked by an unbroken series of reworkings within the same language. He concludes, from the oldest Pseudo-Callisthenes text to the last edition of the modern Greek popular book in 1926 that there is no decisive break.[75] Naturally the question of the priority of the late Byzantine romance or the Serbian Alexandrida remains unsolved, but even if the priority of the Serbian should later be demonstrated, it would not substantially take away from the case which Veloudes has made. It would be well to pause for a moment and to consider his conclusions as they bear upon the question as to how widespread this material was among Greeks during the Ottoman period. Veloudes found and catalogues 46 separate editions of the printed form of the prose Alexander romance in Greek, the editions dating from 1680 to 1926.[76] Thirteen, or a little over a third, date from the period before the outbreak of the Greek Revolution. In the form of what he calls and defines as a Volksbuch the romance circulated among Greeks via public readings and recitations by wandering reciters, was very popular, and was heard throughout the Greek-speaking world. But beyond popular consumption, the figure of Alexander was the subject in one form or another of Greek historians

during the Turkokratia, who often went back to the original sources, and of literary figures who utilized the example of Alexander only for moral, rhetorical, comparative reasons, but also as an expression of national aspirations. The uniqueness of the Greek Alexander tradition is further illustrated, Veloudes quite properly asserts, by the vast proliferation of the legend in oral materials: lore, tales, folk songs, magical imprecations. His figure early penetrated that spectacular borrowing from Turkish popular culture, the shadow plays of Karagöz. For the Greeks, the Alexander legend was extremely widely diffused in many of its literary and oral manifestations. And, as Veloudes has asserted, this was a survival and further development of the Byzantine version of the Pseudo - Callisthenes.

2. *The Serbian Tradition during Ottoman Rule* - The Serbian version of the Pseudo-Callisthenes Alexander seems also to have been widely diffused, influential and popular among the Serbs of the Ottoman period. This is particularly demonstrable for the literary Serbian world of that period, as some 350 manuscripts of the romance are known. Marinković states that generations of Serbs formed their tastes, style, and literary language on the basis of this change, which in time underwent changes of language, content and tone. But though the Byzantine origin of the original Serbian is neither proven nor disproven, nevertheless, the contets go back to the Pseudo-Callisthenes.[77]

3. *The Bulgarian Tradition* - At this moment it has been studied even less than the Serbian, so the degree of its diffusion into Bulgarian society cannot be discussed, although the conditions of the Turkish period were particularly infelicitous for the Bulgarians and so it would be surprising to see this legend as developed and as diffused as it was first among the Greeks and second among the Serbs.[78]

4. *The Roumanian Tradition* - Here it seems to have been at first an import from Serbia, and once translated into Roumanian it still must have been restricted to the learned circles of the courts of Moldavia and Wallachia.[79]

Conclusion: The figure of Alexander the Great, primarily in his legendary Pseudo-Callisthenes form, was a Byzantine legacy among Greeks, Serbs, Bulgars, Roumanians, and Turks. Among the Turks it came through the oriental version that split off early from the Greek or

Byzantine Pseudo-Callisthenes version, and once it came to the Turks it remained largely and hermetically sealed off from the Balkan traditions. The Byzantine tradition remained strongest, most diffused, and variegated among the Greeks, secondarily among the Serbs. Among the Roumanians and Bulgars it probably remained restricted due to social and political conditions in both regions.

. . . .

From the bried analysis of Constantinople-Istanbul, religion, man's relation to human life and to the unknown, the agricultural and pastoral cycles and calenders, the panegyris, and the legend of Alexander the Great we see that the Byzantine experience of the Balkan peoples was a profound one with enduring influences on their popular culture. In effect, Iorga's concept of Byzance après Byzance is more nearly applicable to the layer of popular culture in the Balkans than it is the political domain where Iorga had sought to find it.

NOTES

1. N. Iorga, *Byzance après Byzance* (Bucharest, 1935; reprind Bucharest, 1971).
   P. Koukoules, *Byzantion vios kai politismos* (Athens, 1948-1952), I-IV.

2. S. Vryonis, *The Decline of Medieval Hellenism in Asia Minor and the Process of Islamization from the Eleventh through the Fifteenth Century* (Berkeley, 1971). Also in Studies on Byzantium, *Seljuks and Ottomans*. Reprinted Studies (Malibu, 1981), see the following studies: *"Religious Changes and Patterns in the Balkans, 14th-16th Centuries;" "The Byzantine Legacy and Ottoman Forms;" "The Greeks under Turkish Rule".*

3. See the forthcoming, Vryonis *"Byzantine Constantinople and Ottoman Istanbul: Evolution in a Millenial Imperial Iconography".*

4. For a martialing and detailed analysis of the copious evidence, Vryonis, *"S.J. Shaw, History of the Ottoman Empire and Modern Turkey... A Critical Analysis"* (Thessaloniki, 1983), 215-238.

5. H. Inalcik, *"Istanbul",* EI.2

6. Inalcik, op. cit., 224-225.

7. K. Manaphes, *Ai en Konstaninoupolei vivliothekai autokratorikai kai patriarchikai kai peri ton en autais cheirographon mechre tes aloseos 1453* (Athens, 1972), 148. This catalogue was published by S.R. Förster, *De antiquitatibus et libris manuscriptis Constantinupoleos* (1877), 10-23.

8. R. Janin, *Constantinople byzantine,* 2nd ed. (Paris, 1964) S. Runciman, *The Great Church in Captivity* (Cambridge, 1968).

9. P. Gilles, *The Antiquities of Constantinople, with a Description of its Situation, the*

Conveniences of its Port, its public Buildings, the Statuary, Sculpture, Architecture and other curiosities of that City, tr. J. Ball (London, 1729),127-130, passim.

10. Vryonis, *The Decline of Medieval Hellenism,* 437-438.

11. *Neshri tarihi,* ed. F. Unat and M. Köymen (Ankara, 1957), II, 705-707.

12. Ducas, *Istoria Turco-bizantina* (1341-1462), ed. V. Grecu (Bucharest, 1958), 375.

13. Inalcik, op. city., 224-225.

14. A. Deissman, *Forchungen und Funde im Serai mit einem Verzeichnis der nichtislamischen Handschriften im Topkapu Serai zu Istanbul*(Berlin-Leipzig, 1933).

15. F. Tauer, *"Notice sur les versions persanes de la légende de l' édification d' Aya Sofya,"* Fuad Köprülü Armağani (Istanbul 1953), 487-494; *"Les versions persanes de la construction d' Aya Sofya",* Byzantinoslavica, XV (1954), 1-20.

16. J. Raby, *"Mehmed the Conqueror's Greek Scriptorium",* Dumbarton Oaks Papers, XXXVII (1983), 15-34.

17. Vryonis, *The Decline of Medieval Hellenism,* 436-438.

18. Tauer, *"Les versions persanes..."* 17.

19. P. Gilles, op. cit., 127-130.

20. Tauer, op. cit., 19.

21. Procopius, *De bello gothico,*

22. See my forthcoming, Prior Tempore, Fortior Iure, the chapter entitled *"The Theory of a Tripartite Ethnogenesis of the Bulgarian People and the Rise of Thracology in Contemporary Bulgarian Scholarship".*

23. Runciman, op. cit., passim. B. Djurdjev, *Ulova tsrkva u starijoj srpskog naroda* (Sarajevo, 1964). *Srpska pravoslvna tsrkva 1219-1969* (Belgrade, 1969).

24. Vryonis, *"Religious Changes and Patterns in the Balkans...",* passim.

25. Vryonis, *Decline of Medieval Hellenism,* 360-362. C. Patrinellis, *"Mia anekdote pege yia ton agnosto neo-martyra Georgio (1437)",* Orthodoxos Parousia, I (1964), 65-74. I. Delehaye, *"Greek Neo-Martyrs",* The Constructive Quarterly, IX (1921), 701-712.

26. M. Nilsson, *Greek Popular Religion* (New York, 1940). J.C. Lawson, *Modern Greek Folklore and Ancient Greek Religion. A Study in Survivals* (New York, 1964). For many of the details of pagan survivals see especially the work of D. Constantelos, *"Paganism and the State in the Age of Justinian",* Catholic Historical Review, XXIII (1978), 217-234. *"Cannon 62 of the Synod in Trullo and the Slavic Problem",* BYZANTINA, II (1970), 23-35.

27. G. Megas, *Greek Calendar Customs* (Athens, 1958), 142-144.

28. E. Schneeweis, *Serbokroatische Volkskunde* (Berlin, 1961), 142. For suvivals of Christian hagiolatry among Balkan converts to islam, C. Vakarelski, *"Altertümliche Elemente in Lebensweise und Kultur der bulgarischen Mohammedaner",* Zeitschrift für Balkanologie, IV (1966), 149-172.

29. Megas, *Zetemata ellenikes laographias,* pt. III (1950), 20-21; Greek Calendar Customs, passim.

30. Schneeweis, op. cit., 116.

31. Vakarelski, *Bulgarische Volkskunde* (Berlin, 1969), 308.

32. Schneeweis op. cit., 142; Megas *Greek Calendar Customs,* 142-144; Vakarelski, op. cit., 221-222.

33. Megas, op. cit., 115; Schneeweis, op. cit., 136; Vakarelski, op. cit., 321-322.

34. Schneeweis, op. cit., 146.

35. Vryonis, *"Religious Changes and Patterns in the Balkans...",* 174-175, and notes ≠47, ≠48.

36. Schneeweis, op. cit.,146.

37. Megas, op. cit., 24, 44, 55.

38. Schneeweis, op. cit., 110, 111, 117, 120.

39. Vakarelski, op. cit., 308, 313, 319.

40. Schneeweis, op. cit., 146.

41. Nilsson, op. cit., 300-301.

42. On the function of the icon, E. Kitzinger, *"The Cult of Images in the Ate before Iconoclasm",* Dumbarton Oaks Papers, VIII (1954), 83-150. For the text and commentary on Dionysios of Phourna, Papadopoulos-Kermaeus, *Denys de Phourna Manuel d' iconographie chrétienne accompagné de ses sources principales inédites avec préface, pour la premier fois en entier d' après son texte original* (St. Petersburg, 1909). For the Roumanian translation and diffusion in the non-Greek Balkan world, V. Grecu, *"Byzantinische Handbucher der Kirchenmalerei",* Byzantion, IX (1934), 675-701. It also had a great inflnence on Bulgarians, A. Vasiliev. Erminii, Tehnologiia i ikonografiia (Sofia, 1976).

43. Megas, Zetemata, I, 35.

44. Schneeweis, op. cit., 45-46.

45. Vakarelski, op. cit., 234-235, 286.

46. H. J. Rose, *A Handbook of Greek Mythology* (New York, 1959), 24-25, 38-39. Oxford Classical Dictionary, "Fates".

47. Megas, *Zetemata,* I, 29; Vakarelski, op. cit., 284-285; Schneeweis op. cit., 44.

48. Vryonis, *The Decline of Medieval Hellenism,* 494.

49. Idem, 487.

50. Vryonis, *"Religious Changes and Patterns...",* 174.

51. Koukoules, op. cit., IV, 54-55.

52. For death: Schneeweis, op. cit., 106-109; Vakarelski, op. cit., 301-311; Megas, Zetemata, I, 102-114; D. Loukatos, *"Laographikai peri teleutes endeixeis para Ioannou tou Chrysostomou",* Epeteris tou Laographikou Archeiou (1940), 30-117, for the Byzantine period. M. Alexiou, *The Ritual Lament in Greek Tradition* (Cambridge, 1964).

53. Schneeweis, op. cit., 12; Vakarelski, op. cit., 232-233.

54. On these spirits see Schneeweis, op. cit., 14-15; Vakarelski, op. cit., 230-232; Megas, op. cit., passim.

55. Procopius, *De bello gothico,* VII, xiv, 22-30. Vryonis, *"The Evolution of Slavic Society and the Slavic Invasions in Greece. The First Major Slavic Attack on Thessaloniki A.D. 597",* Hesperia, L (1981), 385.

56. *Schneeweis,* op. cit., 33.

57. Megas, *Greek Calendar Customs,* 27-33, ff; Schneeweis, op. cit., 117-122, 125;

Vakarelski, op. cit., 313-314, 318-319.

58. Schneeweis, op. cit., 122.

59. Megas, op. cit., 55; Schneeweis, op. cit., 125; Vakarelski, op. cit., 319.

60. Megas, op. cit., 59-67; Schneeweis, op. cit., 126-128; Vakarelski, op. cit., 324, 380-388.

61. Megas, op. cit., 128; Schneeweis, op. cit., 139, Vakarelski, op. cit., 326; Oxford Classical Dictionary, "Rosalia".

62. Megas, op. cit., 113-116; Schneeweis, op. cit., 136-137; Vakarelski, op. cit., 320-322.

63. Megas, op. cit., 142-144; Schneeweis, op. cit., 142.

64. De Pouqueville, *Voyage en Grèce* (Paris, 1820), III, 456-459.

65. Vryonis, *"The Panegyris of the Byzantine Saint. A Study in the Nature of a Medieval Institution, its Origins and Fate"*, in The Byzantine Saint, Sobornost (1981), 196-227. For the panegyris in the Ottoman period see S. Faroqi, *(The Earl History of the Balkan Fairs"*, Südost-Forschungen, XXXVIII (1978), 59-68.

66. G. Veloudis, *Der neugriechische Alexander Tradition in Bewahrung und Wandel* (Munich, 1938), 167.

67. H-G. Beck, *Geschichte der byzantinischen Volksliteratur* (Munich, 1971).

68. R. Levy, An Introduction to Persian literature (New York, 1969), 88-91.

69. Beck, op. cit., 31-32, 125.

70. R. Marinković, Srpska Alexandrida. Istorija osnovnog teksta (Belgrade, 1969), 337 ff.

71. Marinković, op. cit., 343.

72. Marinković, op. cit., 343. *Istoria Rominiei*, ed. A. Otetea et al (Bucharest, 1974), III, 278.

73. *"Ahmedi"*, Islam Ansiklopedisi, 218. F. Babinger, Die Geschichtsschreiber der Osmanen und ihre Werke (Leipzig, 1927), 11-12. Levy, op. cit., 89-91.

74. V. Velcev, E. Georgiev, P. Dinekov, *Istoriia na bylgarskata literatura* I. Starobylgarski literatura (Sofia, 1962), 166-167. M. Murko, *Geschichte der alteren südslawischen Litteraturen* (Leipzig, 1908) 95-96, 182-183. Marinković, op. cit., 337-346.

75. Veloudis, op. cit., 5.

76. Veloudis, op. cit., passim.

77. Marinković, op. cit., 337 ff.

78. I. Köhler, *Der neubulgarische Alexanderroman. Untersuchungen zur Textgeschichte und Verbreitung* (Amsterdam, 1973), pp. v, 1, 4-10, 74-75, 131-144, 149, 210. Köhler gives a clear analysis of the origins of the modern Bulgarian Alexander Romance, primarily from the Roumanian and secondarily from the Neo-Hellenic versions, the Roumanian going back to the late medieval Serbian version.

79. Nevertheless the Alexander Romance was more widespread and more popular among eighteenth century Roumanians than among contemporary Bulgarians, Köhler, op. cit., passim. G. Dancev, *"Traduceri ale Alexandriei din limba romana in limba bulgara moderna"*, Romanoslavica, XV (1967), 109-116.

THE BYZANTINE LEGACY IN RUSSIA
AND ROMANIA

CICERO AND THE ICON PAINTERS:
THE TRANSFORMATION OF BYZANTINE IMAGE
THEORY IN MEDIEVAL MUSCOVY

Declan C. Murphy

The subject addressed in this essay is complex and susceptible to a variety of methodological approaches. One could build a case, for example, that the transformation of Byzantine image theory in old Russia began with the selection of pertinent texts the Byzantines dispatched to the Russians. Indeed, a recent empirical investigation I conducted of the Byzantine image theory available to Old Russia suggests that the legacy was highly fragmented. One is fully justified in speaking of a "Slavonic recension" of this theory.

One could also expand upon the transformational consequences of this fragmented legacy. One such consequence was a phenomenon I shall call perceptual asymmetry. More specifically, the relatively circumscribed number of image theory texts Byzantium transmitted to Old Russia occasionally led the Russian to take concepts that were quite peripheral to the major agendas of Byzantine image theory and place them at the center of their own thinking about images.

To illustrate, the central tenet of Muscovite image theory was the demand that the icon painter imitate "ancient models". Whereas in the medieval West the practice of depicting objects from an *exemplum* was only an artistic convention, in Muscovy it was a canonically prescribed requirement. The 43rd Canon of the Council of the Hundred Chapters (Stoglav), for example, states:

> And on this point let great care and caution be taken that
> skillful icon painters and their pupils paint from ancient
> models, but let them not depict the divinity from their own
> fancy, by their own conjectures, as it were.[1]

To reiterate, this notion is the most crucial tenet of old Russian image theory. It recurs, with increasing frequency, in the 15th, 16th, and 17th centuries and, unlike most of the theoretical concepts available to Muscovy from Byzantine image theory, there is clear proof that it penetrated down to the level of the artists themselves.[2] Indeed, one could even argue that the entire history of Old Russian image theory in the 17th century effectively reduces to a history of the decline of this one construct.

The requirement that artists imitate ancient models was an idea of unimpeacheable Byzantine pedigree. The Byzantines had always believed that the icon was first and foremost a cult image and as such it was expected to exhibit a high degree of historical veracity. Festal icons, for example, were believed to be precise reproductions of historical events, while images of Christ and the saints were considered sacred portraits that faithfully reproduced the countenances of the holy ones.[3]

The perception of the icon as a sacred portrait is unquestionably responsible for the way the *Acta* of the Seventh Ecumenical Council defined the relationship of the artist to his material.

> The conception and the tradition (of an image) belong (to the
> church fathers) and not to the artist. Skill alone is the
> property of the artist, but the arrangement (of an image) is
> manifestly the property of the Holy Fathers.[4]

Within the corpus of Byzantine image theory, however, the issue of adherence to traditional iconographic models is of marginal significance compared, for example, with the relationship of the image concept to the dual natures of Christ. In Byzantium, the question of reliance upon conventional iconographic types never achieved the central thematic significance for image theory that it did in Old Russia.

This essay, however, will not dwell any further on perceptual asymmetries between Byzantine and Old Russian image theory. It will instead address why the notion of imitating ancient models declined in seventeenth-century Muscovy. For I shall contend that if we can understand how and why this idea lost its sway, we shall also have explained much about how the Muscovites transformed Byzantine image theory and ultimately supplanted it with a very different sort of art theory, more appropriate, perhaps, for a more secular age.

During the sixteenth century, the major changes that occurred in Russian art were all iconographic. By the 1650's, however, the internal development of Russian painting had forced a change in this pattern. The single most controversial innovation of the seventeenth century was the rise of a new, naturalistic style of painting. Its exponents began to depict landscapes, architectural backgrounds, and the faces of Christ and the saints with an increased fidelity to nature quite unknown, in the art of previous centuries. The new naturalism did not, of course, immediately supplant the traditional stylized manner of painting. Indeed, the advocates of the two styles engaged in polemics throughout most of the second half of the seventeenth century.

This antagonism derived in part from the increasingly visible Western presence in the artistic life of Muscovy during this period. Western artists like the Dutch painter Daniel Wuchters and Hans Deters were then teaching in the Tsar's "Academy of Arts" in the Kremlin Armoury,[5] while Western engravings circulating throughout Muscovy made Baroque art directly accessible even to those outside the capital.[6] There was thus some justification for the Old Believers' view of the new naturalism as yet another example of Muscovy's failure to maintain its cultural purity. The archpriest Avvakum denounced this innovation with his customary vehemence:

> Icon painters of an unfitting kind have multiplied in our Russian land... they paint the image of the Savior Emmanuel with a pudgy face, red lips, curly hair, fat fingers, and legs, with fat hips, in all, completely like a German, only the sword is lacking at his hip... Rus', why do you desire the customs and habits of the Germans...? Do not bow down... to unsuitable images painted in the German tradition.[7]

Avvakum directs his strictures against what he considers to be unacceptable stylistic innovations and thereby reverses the customary terms of debate. As I indicated above, the Byzantine church fathers reserved for the church the right to regulate the iconographic content of sacred images but left style as the prerogative of the artist. The motivation for Avvakum's shift in emphasis is clear. In his view, the degenerate naturalism copied from the "Germans" detracts from the validity of the image, which no longer resembles its prototype and therefore can no longer fulfill its sacred functions. Even if a Christ painted in the "German" manner had all the proper iconographic attributes, it would still not be worthy of veneration.

Avvakum's views illustrate a recurrent contradiction within the Old Believer movement. Had the Old Believers been willing to abide by the principles of Byzantine image theory, they would have been forced to accept the naturalistic icons. By rejecting these images, they in effect abandoned the image doctrine that formed part of the very tradition they were trying to preserve. The position of Byzantine image doctrine on stylistic matters had placed the Old Believers in an impossible position.

While conservatives like Avvakum saw the stylistic decline of the Russian icon as the direct result of the imitation of Western models, there were others who looked to the imitation of nature as the only available means to save Russian art from ossification. Iosif Vladimirov, the theoretician of the naturalistic style, offered the following explanation for the ills affecting traditional icon painting:

> Many Russian paintings do not agree with good Greek models; the new with the old and the old with the new are much at variance, for the ancient images... have grown old and dirty. Others have been besmirched and soiled with many [coats of] oil by stupid icon peddlers.[8]

The problem to which he refers was a very practical one. It stemmed from the role of the icon in the ritual life of the Russian Church. Over the centuries, the candles which were kept burning before the icons as signs of reverence and the incense released during the daily celebration of the liturgy had blackened and soiled Vladimirov's "good Greek models" to a deplorable extent. In the absence of modern restorative techniques, ordinary icon painters looked upon these darkened boards as authentic ancient models to be imitated. Hence, they intentionally painted icons with a monotonous, gloomy coloration. Furthermore, as Vladimirov points out, unscrupulous peddlers deliberately blackened more recent icons in order to pass them off as authentic "ancient" specimens. We can sense his frustration as he exlaims:

> Simpletons and ignorant people do not understand correctly... what has happened in icon painting; whatever has grown old, that they adhere to. And if something long ago grew dark or decrepit, this they especially take as a reason to praise its age and dinginess.[9]

Vladimirov, then, atrributes the decline of the Muscovite icon to the ignorance of the painters who mechanically imitated corrupt models in the mistaken belief that they were thus reproducing "ancient models". To resurrect icon painting from its moribund condition, he introduces two highly innovative concepts into the Muscovite art theoretical vocabulary: "zhivopodie" (lifelikeness) and "zhivopisanie" (painting of life).[10]

"Zhivopodie" represented a fundamental break with the Byzantine theory of images. The church fathers did not attempt to provide any criteria for assessing the aesthetic worth of a picture, for the definition of beauty was not their concern. An icon was simply adequate insofar as it conformed to "ancient models". Vladimirov, by contrast, was a practicing painter who took a professional interest in the assessment of artistic skill. His concern with skill is mirrored in his concept of "zhivopodie" which provided a purely aesthetic standard for the evaluation of icons. Moreover, Vladimirov's demand that the artist imitate nature implied a belief in the progressive stylistic perfectability of sacred art: the more closely an icon conformed to nature, the "better" it would be. The belief that "artistic progress" could be achieved only through an increasingly sophisticated naturalism thus supplanted the more static, but also more tolerant, patristic image doctrine.

As Ernst Gombrich has written, the concept of progress is every bit as divisive in the arts as it is in politics.[11] Once it has been formulated, one can only come out for it or against it, and those against it invariably fall by the wayside. The notion of artistic progress based on an ever more successful imitation of nature first arose in Renaissance Florence and soon gained acceptance throughout most of Italy. Those local schools like the Sienese that refused to subscribe to this idea were soon reduced to "charming backwaters".[12] In Muscovy, the refusal of most icon painters to take up Vladimirov's call for naturalism was closely followed by the decline of icon painting to the status of a peasant handicraft. It is difficult to escape the conclusion that the subsequent triumph of Western art forms in Russia was closely related to the inability to the icon to ally itself with the forces of "artistic progress".

"Zhivopisanie", on the other hand, did not simply summarize Vladimirov's program for the stylistic reform of icon painting. Much of the admittedly fragmentary evidence at our disposal suggests that the social history of the artist in Muscovy was not the happy success story it was in the West. It is by now a convention among social historians to draw attention to the rise in the status of artists during the Renaissance.[13] Whereas in the medieval West, the artist was only considered a manual laborer and hence unworthy of a high social ranking, in the Renaissance a much higher value was placed on the skill of the individual artist, whose status rose accordingly. In Russia, icon painters during the early middle ages were clerics, who *ipso facto* possessed a somewhat higher social status than ordinary craftsmen.[14] By the early sixteenth century, however, lay icon painters were increasingly common and by the 1550's, they constituted a sizeable majority.[15] The laicization of the icon painters' craft did non result in an immediate decline in their social status. In fact, the middle decades of the sixteenth century were the palmy days of the Muscovite icon painter.

This happy situation was largely the work of the Metropolitan Makarii. By a fortunate coincidence, Makarii was himself a practicing icon painter and restorer, and being well disposed toward icon painters as a group, he even had them legally endowed with a special status.[16] In the *Stoglav* it is specifically stated that if an artistically gifted icon painter lives a moral life appropriate to his sacred calling, the tsar and the bishops should honor him "more than other men".[17]

Unfortunately for the icon painters, however, their new status was only founded upon an administrative fiat; it had no basis in any broad change in social attitudes towards artists. Hence, with the death of their patron, the status of the icon painters suffered a precipitous decline. In the seventeenth century, most of them apparently lived in utter squalor. For example, systematic study of the social and economic status of the icon painters in the northern city of Tikhvin has revealed that they were among the poorest of all the town's craftsmen.[18] Even in Moscow their position was scarcely better. Some of the most gifted icon painters active there during the reign of Alexis Mikhailovich received a state salary insufficient to cover their daily expenses. One such unfortunate, Fedor Zubov, was at one point close to starvation.[19]

Vladimirov was well aware of the disjunction between what the *Stoglav* had to say about the status of icon painters and the actual living conditions of his fellow artists in Moscow.[20] In fact, he manifested his concern with the status of his craft throughout his lengthy treatise. He was at pains, for example, to speak about the art of painting only in the most laudatory of terms. It is "most wise", "honorable", and "elevated".[21] At the same time, the vitriolic tone of his attacks on mediocre painters suggests that he blamed their inferior craftsmanship for the low esteem enjoyed by icon painting:

> And where have such disorders been seen as here today?
> Insult and humiliation have been done to the most wise art of icon painting by ignoramuses...[22]

Vladimirov had the good sense to realize that the status of painters would only rise when the ruling circles of society began to attach value to their skill. His desire to assimilate the art of the icon to the tastes of the court has been frequently noted by scholars.[23] "Zhivopisanie" thus acquires a further programmatic significance: it could ameliorate the position of the icon painter by allowing him to demonstrate his skill in producing beautiful objects for aristocratic delectation.

The aesthetic changes and social tensions reflected in Vladimirov's treatise provided the indispensible background for the even more radical innovations contained in the anonymous treatise, *A Discourse to a Lover of Icon Painting.*[24] Scholars have differed sharply over the question of its authorship. G.D. Filimonov, the original publisher of the treatise, cautiously observed that it "was written not without the participation of Simon Ushakov", the most renowned artist of the Russian seventeenth century.[25] In 1911, A. Nikol'skii stated flatly that Ushakov was the author, and proposed 1668 as the date of its composition.[26] Two decades later, N. P. Kondakov, the doyen of Muscovite art historians, made a more novel suggestion: "Judging by the heavy, bookish language, Simon Ushakov left his views and his knowledge for explication to an unknown scribe..."[27] In 1953, Iu. N. Dmitriev again insisted that Ushakov was the anonymous author.[28] Four years later, however, a Belorussian scholar, V.I. Puzikov, discovered that two passages in the treatise were to be found in an almost identical form in an unpublished manuscript written by Simeon Polotskii,[29] the erudite, Jesuit-educated, Belorussian émigré and court poet of Alexis Mikhailovich. Accordingly, he divided the treatise into a longish theoretical section he ascribed to Simeon, and a brief practical section he attributed to Ushakov. Surprisingly, Soviet art historians have consistently ignored Puzikov's revelations and have continued to assign the entire treatise to Ushakov.[30]

In what follows, I shall argue on the basis of new evidence that Simeon did indeed write the theoretical portion of the treatise and that in doing so he made crucial innovations in Muscovite art theory. These innovations, in turn, consisted above all in the attempt to draw ideas from Roman writers and Baroque scholars and by so doing to reorient Russia's theory of the visual arts in a decidedly Western direction.

Simeon had almost certainly read Vladimirov's work and in any case they were in complete agreement about the reasons for the decline of the Muscovite icon. Like Vladimirov, Simeon criticized the ignorance of the painters who "had not learned their ABC's".[31] He also reiterated Vladimirov's condemnation of the dark, forbidding coloration employed by most icon painters, saying that they did not understand "the distinction of colors" (razlichie sharov).[32] But whereas Vladimirov hoped to revitalize icon painting by turning the attention of the artist away from corrupt "ancient models" and toward the more congenial model of nature, Simeon took the final radical step and banished the concept of "ancient models" from the Muscovite art theoretical vocabulary. The artist's own imagination ("fantazia") now becomes the ultimate criterion for what is proper in a painting:

The most wise Artificer of all abstract and material creation
who created man in His own image and likeness, has given
him the mental capability, which is imagination ["fantazia"],
to draw images of all creation...[33]

Simeon's invocation of "fantazia", like Vladimirov's call for the
imitation of nature, is meant to be taken in opposition to the imitation
of "ancient models". "Fantazia" represents Simeon's own prescription
for the stylistic rejuvenation of icon painting. At the same time, by
extolling the God-given creative power of the artist, whom he views as
a fully autonomous creative entity, Simeon, like Vladimirov, hoped to
inspire a new respect for painters as a social group.

The importance of "fantazia" as a breakthrough in Muscovite art
theory is self-evident. But what justifies our ascription of his concept to
Simeon rather than to Simon Ushakov, who is traditionally held to be
the author of the tract? On the one hand, there is no evidence that
Ushakov ever employed "fantazia" as an artistic *modus operandi,* for
his paintings, despite their incipient naturalism, are all quite traditional
in their iconography.[34] On the other hand, there are excellent reasons
for supposing that Simeon knew and valued the concept of "fantazia".
In an unpublished and virtually unknown Polish-Slavonic lexicon that
he compiled while in Muscovy, "fantazia" appears in its Polish form
"fantazya". It is defined in Slavonic as "opinion" (*mnenie*), "misunder-
standing" *(izherazumnenie),* and "imagination" *(mechtanie).*[35] The
unfinished lexicon was conceived on a rather small scale and,
consequently, Simeon must have chosen his entries with some care. It
provides clear proof that he was well acquainted with the term
"fantazia" in a variety of its semantic reflexes.

Difficulties arise, however, when one tries to establish the definitive
source for Simeon's application of "fantazia" to painting. Renaissance
art theorists had designated "fantazia" as the means by which the artist
might transcend the mere imitation of nature.[36] Simeon, by contrast,
had defined it as the "mental capability to draw... images of all
creation". The highly idiosyncratic use of the term is without parallel
(as far as I am aware) in Renaissance or Baroque art theory.[37]

Like Vladimirov, Simeon also wished to raise the status of painting
in Muscovite society. Yet in gathering its praises he drew on very
different sources:

> Although there are many different arts in the world, only seven among them are liberal; the Greeks of old held image making to be the... first step [*nachalo*] in this group (according to the testimony of Pliny).[38]

By introducing the popular Renaissance notion of painting as a liberal art, Simeon was able to formulate a theory of art that was very close to those popular in the seventeenth century West- and very far indeed from the Byzantine theory of the icon.[39] Furthermore, by invoking Pliny, he created a whole new notion of the authoritative sources for art theory. The secular writers of antiquity could now be used in the same way that traditional Russian writers on art had used the Greek Fathers.

By far the most striking innovation in the treatise, however, is Simeon's attempt to provide a secular definition of art. Traditional Byzantine and Muscovite attempts to define the essence of the icon had centered upon its mystical relationship to a divine prototype. Simeon, by contrast, supplied a definition that had nothing to do with mystical referents:

> For images are the life of the memory, the propagation of those who have lived, a witness of times gone by, a proclamation of the virtues, a demonstration of courage, a restoration of the dead to life, an immortality of praise and glory, an incitement of the living to imitation, a recollection of past deeds; images make things standing at a distance [seem] to be present and things in different places [seem] to be represented at one time.[40]

Although it is couched in the perfervid language of epideictic rhetoric, the central point of this definition is clear: art is a kind of history-made-visible. Similar ideas were present in the Byzantine tradition. St. John Damascene, for example, had written:

> The sixth kind of image serves to record events, be it a miracle or a virtuous deed, for the glorification... of men who have excelled and distinguished themselves in virtue... So even now we eagerly delineate images of virtuous men of the past for the sake of love and remembrance.[41]

But whereas St. John Damascene had only endeavored to describe the commemorative potential inherent in sacred images, Simeon interpreted Art as the analogue of History. In so doing, he made available another theoretical insight of the Renaissance: if painting was a "liberal" art, it could be analyzed by analogy to other "liberal" arts.[31] The extent to which Simeon believed that Art and History were somehow parallel is evident in the very phraseology of his definition. For its source is none other than Cicero's famous definition of history in *De Oratore*:

> SIMEON POLOTSKII:
> For images are *the life of the memory,* a propagation of those who have lived, *a witness of times gone by...*

> CICERO:
> History is truly *a witness of times gone by,* the light of truth, *the life of the memory....*[43]

We are thus confronted with a strange and unexpected situation: the first attempt on Russian soil to provide an original definition of art is suffused with the elegance of Ciceronian rhetoric. Like the Renaissance humanists, Simeon had turned to the rhetorical writings of Cicero to find new concepts for the analysis of art.

Or had he? Further research suggests it would be wrong to assume that Simeon derived this definition directly from primary sources. Although he was unquestionably familiar with *De Oratore* from his rhetorical studies in Kiev and Vilnius, the body of his definition is lifted from an intermediate source.[44] It was no doubt at the Jesuit college in Vilnius that Simeon first became acquainted with the treatise on ancient art by the Jesuit antiquarian Julius Caesar Bulengerus (Boulenger) entitled, *De Pictura, Statuaria, Plastice, Libri Duo.* Compare Bulengerus' definition of painting with Simeon's definition cited above:

> It [painting] is the life of the memory, the light of life, the witness of times gone by, a proclamation of virtue, a restoring of the dead from death, an immortality of praise and glory, a propagation of those who have lived; a painting is that which makes things standing at a distance [seem] to be present and

things which are in different and distant places [seem] to be represented at one time.[45]

The discovery of this source reconfirms Simeon's authorship of the theoretical part of the treatise; there is simply no evidence whatever that Ushakov was familiar with Bulengerus or that he could even read Latin. Simeon's use of Jesuit models marked the final step in the Westernization of Muscovite art theory. The patristic view of art as a sacred nexus through which the prayers of the faithful might pass from this world to the next was now formally supplanted by a Counterreformation theory of *"ut historia pictura"*.

★ ★ ★

In summation, it may be observed that the indirect impact of Cicero's *De Oratore* on the transformation of Muscovite image theory provides a graphic example of the fate of the classics in Muscovite civilization; they came late and they came secondhand. Although Muscovy undoubtedly possessed a clearer vision of ancient culture by the end of the seventeenth century, there is still very little evidence during that period of any direct source study by the Russians themselves. Russia still had to address herself "... a quella che è dopo tutto la tradizione dell' Umanesimo...: confrontare i testi".[46]

NOTES

1. *Stoglav* (St. Petersburg, 1863), p. 153.
2. The relevant *Stoglav* canons are reproduced in an icon painter's manual from the seventeenth century. See A. I. Uspenskii, ed., *Podlinnik Ikonopisnyi* (Moscow, 1901), pp. 18 ff.
3. On this point, see M. Chatzidakis, "L' Icone Byzantin", *Saggi e Memorie di Storia dell'Arte,* 2 (1959), pp. 14-15 and especially G. Ostrogorskij, "Les Decisions du Stoglav concernant la Peinture d' Images et les Principes de l' Iconographie Byzantine", in *L' Art Byzantin chez les Slaves. Premier Receuil dédié à la Mémoire du Théodore Uspenskii,* Vol. 1, Pt. 2 (Paris, 1930), pp. 394-398; reprinted in his collected essays *Byzanz und die Welt der Slawen: Beitraege zur Geschichte der Byzantinisch-Slawischen Beziehungen* (Darmstadt, 1974), pp. 122-40.
4. J.D. Mansi (ed.) *Sacrorum Conciliorum Nova et Amplissima Collectio,* Vol. 13 (Florence, 1767), col. 252 C.
5. On Daniel Wuchters, see A.I. Uspenskii, *Tsarskie Ikonopistsy i Zhivopistsy XVII v.*

Vol. 2 (Moscow, 1910), p. 55; Alexandrine Miller, "Daniel Wuchters", *Oud Holland,* 57 (1940), pp. 40-48 (English summary, p. 48). Wuchter's painting "An Episode from the Life of Alexander the Great" is unfortunately now lost. It was commissioned by B.M. Khitrovo, the director of the Tsar's Armoury in which the "Academy of Art" was located. The commissioning of such a picture again illustrates the interest in antiquity of the Russian court during this period (*ibid.,* pp. 46,47. On Hans Deters, see A.I. Uspenskii, *Tsarskie Ikonopistsy i Zhivopistsy XVII v.* vol. 2, p. 69.

6. Johannes Piscator's *Theatrum Biblicum,* an illistrated Dutch Bible of the early seventeenth century, provided the iconographic source material for some of the most interesting church frescos executed in Iaroslavl' during the second half of that century. See E. Sachavets-Fedorovich, "Iaroslavskie Stenopisi i Bibliia Piskatora", in *Russkoe Iskusstvo XVII veka* (Leningrad, 1929), pp. 85-108.

7. N.K. Gudzii, ed., *Zhitie Protopopa Avvakuma Im Samim Napisannoe i Drugie ego Sochineniia* (Moscow, 1960), pp. 135, 137.

8. Iosif Vladimirov's treatise, *Poslanie nekoego Iosifa k tsarevu Izugrafu i mudreishemu zhivopistsu Simonu Fedorovichu,* has been edited and published by E.S. Ovchinnikova in *Drevnerusskoe Iskusstvo. XVII vek* (Moscow, 1964), pp. 24-61. The excerpt quoted in the text appears on p. 25.

9. *Ibid.*

10. *Ibid.,* pp. 24,55; ZE. Saltykov, "Esteticheskie Vzgliady Iosifa Vladimirova (po "Poslaniiu k Simonu Fedorovichu"), "*Trudy Otdela Drevnerusskoi Literatury,* 28 (1974) p. 271-288. Both terms "zhivopisanie" and "zhivopisets" ("one who paints life") had been in use in Muscovy for a very long time. The earliest use of the term "zhivopisets" that I have been able to discover is, in fact, from the Kievan period where the word occurs in a festal Menaion from the year 1097 (*Slovar' Russkogo Iazyka XI-XVII vv.,*vyp., 5 [Moscow, 1978], p. 102, cf. I.I. Sreznevskii, *Materialy dlia Slovaria Drevnerusskago Iazyka,* Vol. 1 [St. Petersburg, 1893], p. 866). The term "zhivopisanie" does not appear to be as old. The earliest use of it I have found is in Joseph Volotskii's *Epistle to an Icon Painter* (N.A. Kazakova and Ia. S. Lur'e, *Antifeodal'nye Ereticheskie Dvizheniia na Rusi XIV-nachala XVI veka* [Moscow-Leningrad, 1955] p. 323), an example apparently unknown to the Soviet lexicographers who compiled the most recent dictionary of the Old Russian language (*Slovar' Russkogo Iazyka XI-XVII vv.* vyp. 5, p.102). They date the first appearance of this word to the seventeenth century. In any case, by the seventeenth century "zhivopisets" and "zhivopisanie" had come to mean simply "painter" and "painting", respectively. Vladimirov, however, revived their pristine meanings and harnessed them in defense of the new naturalistic style he sought to defend. "Zhivopisets" and "Zhivopisanie" are, of course, calques of "Zographos" and "Zographia".

11. Ernst Gombrich, "The Renaissance Concept of Artistic Progress and its Consequences", in his collected essays, *Norm and Form* (London, 1966), p. 9.

12. *Ibid.,* pp. 9-10.

13. On the emancipation and the rise in status of artists during the Renaissance, see Rudolf and Margaret Wittkower, *Born under Saturn* (London, 1963), pp. 31-40; Frederick Antal, *Florentine Painting and its Social Background* (New York, 1948), pp. 274-283, 374-378.

14. In Moscow during the thirteenth and fourteenth centuries, for example, clerical icon painters were even in the majority (see M. N. Tikhomirov, *Srednevekovaia Moskva v XIV-XV vekakh* [Moscow, 1957], p. 77); during this same period icon painters were comparatively well paid, perhaps because of the considerable expenditures on materials their labours entailed. See V.N. Lazarev, "Drevnerusskie Khudozhniki i Metody ikh Raboty", in *Drevnerusskoe Iskusstvo, XV-nachala XVI v.* (Moscow, 1963), p. 8.

15. The growth of Muscovy's population during this period created an increased demand for icons which laymen undertook to fulfill; see H.P. Gerhard, *Die Welt der Ikonen*, 3rd ed. (Recklinghausen, 1970), p. 179.

16. On Makarii's relationship to the visual arts, N.E. Andreev, "Mitropolit Makarii kak Deiatel" Religioznogo Iskusstva", *Seminarium Kondakovianum*, 7 (1935), pp. 227-44, is indispensable.

17. *Stoglav*, p. 153

18. K.N. Serbina, *Ocherki iz Sotsial'no-ekonomicheskoi Istorii Russkogo Goroda* (Moscow-Leningrad, 1951), p. 152.

19. N.P. Kondakov, *The Russian Ikon*, trans. by E.H. Minns (Oxford, 1927), p. 141.

20. Vladimirov, in fact, cites all the chapters of the *Stoglav* pertaining to icon painting by their proper numbers (see "Poslanie..", p. 25).

21. *Ibid.*, pp. 24,28.

22. *Ibid.*, p. 33.

23. See for example, L.A. Uspenskii, "Iskusstvo XVII veka. Rassloenie i Otkhod ot Tserkovnogo Obraza", *Vestnik Russkogo Zapadno-evropeiskogo Patriarshego Ekzarkata* (1971), nos. 73-74, p. 57; Iu. N. Dmitriev, "Teoriia Iskusstva i Vzgliady na Iskusstvo v Pis'mennosti Drevnei Rusi", *Trudy Otdela Drevnerusskoi Literatury*, 9 (1953), pp. 109-110.

24. The "Slovo k Liubotshchatel'nomu Ikonnago Pisaniia" (here-after, "Slovo...") is printed in *Vestnik Obshchestva Drevnerusskago Iskusstva*, nos. 1-3 (1874), "Materialy", pp. 22-24.

25. "Slovo...", p. 24, note. Filimonov based his assessment on phraseological similarities between the closing lines of the "Slovo..." and an inscription on one of Ushakov's icons.

26. A. Nikol'skii, "Slovo k Liubotshchatel'nomu Ikonnago Pisaniia", *Vestnik Arkheologii i Istorii*, 20 (1911), pp. 68-69.

27. N.P. Kondakov, *Russkaia Ikona*, Vol. 3 (Prague, 1931), p. 50, n.2.

28. Iu. N. Dmitriev, *Trudy Otdela Drevnerusskoi Literatury*, 9 (1953), pp. 99.

29. V. M. Puzikau "Novyia Materyialy ab Dzeinasti Simeona Polatskaga", *Vestsi Akademii Navuk Belaruskau SSR, Seriia Gramadskikh Navuk*, no. 4 (1957), pp. 72-73.

30. See Iu. A. Lebedeva, *Drevnerusskoe Iskusstvo X-XVII vekon (Moscow, 1962), p. 233;* V.G. Briusova, *Freski Iaroslavlia XVII-nachala XVIII veka* (Moscow, 1969), p. 13; T. A. Anan'eva, *Simon Ushakov* (Leningrad, 1971), p. 14. Anan'eva's work is the most recent Soviet study of Ushakov.

31. L.N. Maikov, *Ocherki iz Istorii Russkoi Literatury XVII i XVIII stoletii* (St. Petersburg, 1889), p. 143.

32. *Ibid.*

33. "Slovo...", p. 22

34. T. A. Anan'eva, *Simon Ushakov*, p. 14, points out the lack of correspondence between theory and practice in Ushakov's work.

35. Uppsala. Universitet Bibliotek. Mss. "Slav. 61", s.v. "fantazya".

36. Erwin Panofsky, *Idea: A Concept in Art Theory*, trans, by J.J.S. Peake (New York, 1968), p. 48.

37. It is curious that Karion Istomin, the editor of the posthumous second edition of Simeon's treatise, was careful to delete all mention of "fantazia". See A. Nikol'skii, *Vestnik Arkheologii i Istorii*, 10 (1911), pp. 70-77.

38. "Slovo...", p. 22.

39. It was, of course, a commonplace of Western art theory to argue on the basis of Pliny and one or two other texts that painting was a liberal art (see P.O. Kristeller, "The Modern System of the Arts", in *Renaissance Thought*, II: *Paper on Humanism and the Arts* [New York, 1965], esp. 170, 181-182). On the Renaissance notion of painting as a liberal art, see Rudolf Wittkower, *The Artist and the Liberal Arts* (London, 1952), esp. pp. 6-9. This same idea also recurs in seventeenth century art literature, e.g., G.J. Vossius, *De Quatuor Artibus Popularibus*, 1650, where the argument that painting is a liberal art is made both by Vossius and Franciscus Junius, who wrote the preface (see Allan Ellenius, *De Arte Pingendi. Latin Art Literature in Seventeenth-Century Sweden and its International Background* [Uppsala-Stockholm, 1960], pp. 56, 58. This superlative pioneeiring study has never received the attention it deserves).

40. "Slovo...", p. 22: "Ibo obrazy sut' zhivot pamiati, pamiat' pozhivshikh, vremen svidetel'stvo, veshchanie dobrodetel'ei, iz'iavlenie kreposti, mertyvkh vozhivlenie, khvaly i slavy bezsmertie, zhivykh k podrazhaniiu vozbuzhdenie, deistvu vospomi-nanie; obrazy tvoriat, otstoiashchaia predstoiati i v razlichnykh sushchaia mestekh v edino pred' iavliatisia vremia".

41. John Damascene, *Pro Imaginibus Sacris Orationes Tres*, III, 23; English translation by C.A. Mango, *The Art of the Byzantine Empire, 312-1453* (Englewood Cliffs, N.J.: 1972), p. 172.

42. On the Renaissance analysis of painting by analogy to other liberal arts, see R. W. Lee, *Ut Pictura Poesis: The Humanistic Theory of Painting* (New York, 1967); J. Spenser, "Ut Rhetorica Pictura. A Study in the Quattrocento Theory of Painting", *Journal of the Warburg and Courtald Institutes*, 20 (1957), pp. 25-44; Allan Ellenius, *De Arte Pingendi. Latin Art Literature in Seventeenth-Century Sweden and its International Background*, pp. 24-25, 28, 56.

43. SIMEON POLOTSKII:
Ibo obrazy sut' *zhivot pamiati,* pamiat' pozhivshikh, *vremen svidetel'stvo...*
"Slovo...", p. 22.
CICERO:
Historia vero *testis temporum,* lux veritatis, *vita memoriae...* Cicero, *De Oratore,* II,
9, 36.
44. On the place of rhetoric in the Kievan Academy and Simeon's rhetorical studies in
the Jesuit college in Vilnius, see D. Zhukov and L. Pushkarev, *Russkie Pisateli XVII
veka* (Moscow, 1972), pp. 204, 210.
45. Julius Ceaser Bulengerus, *De pictura, statuaria, plastice: libri duo* (Lyons, 1627), p.
7: "Ea est vita memoriae, lux vitae, testis temporum, nuncia virtutis, mortuorum ab
morte restitutio, famae, gloriaeque immortalitas, vivorum propagatio; quae facit,
ut absentes praesto sint, et variis, dissitisque locis uno tempore repraesententur".
The use of Bulengerus typifies Simeon's reliance on second rate scholarly sources.
Bulengerus' treatise had not been well received; Carlo Roberto Dati, for example,
had spoken of it as [un confuso e piccolo repertorio] (see Antonio Minto, *Le vite dei
Pittori antichi di Carlo Roberto Dati e gli Studi erudito-antiquari nel Seicento*
[Florence, 1953], p. 29). This discovery of Simeon's use of Bulengerus also permits
us to ascribe another contemporary art theoretical document to him. The "Charter
of the Three Most Holy Patriarchs" (*Gramota Sviateishikh Triekh Patriarkh*)
appeared over the signatures of the Russian, the Antiochene, and the Alexandrian
Patriarchs, who presided at the Moscow church council of 1667 (see *Izvestiia Imp.
Arkeologicheskago Obshchestva,* T.5, vyp. 5 [St. Petersburg, 1865], cols. 320-325).
This document reechoed Simeon and Vladimirov in their demand that painting be
accorded a high status and further stipulated that painters should be closely
supervised to prevent the production, of unsuitable works of sacred art. In the
course of the argument, reference is made to the ancient Roman family of the Fabii,
whose cognomen was Pictor; the famous remark which Plutarch ascribes to
Simonides-that painting is mute poetry and poetry is painting that speaks-is also
cited (see Plutarch, *De Gloria Atheniensium,* 3, 346, F. ff.). Both of these references
appear in Bulengerus immediately after his rhetorical definition of painting (see
Julius Caesar Bulengerus, *De Pictura, Statuaria, Plastice: Libri Duo,* p. 7).
Furthermore, the "Charter" appeared at approximately the same time as Simeon's
own treatise, *Slovo k Liubotshchatel'nomu Ikonnago Pisaniia,* i.e., 1668 (See *Izvestiia
Imp. Arkeologicheskago Obshchestva* T.5, vyp. 5, col. 325). The conclusion is
unavoidable that Simeon Polotskii drafted the "Charter" for the signatures of the
three patriarchs. Iu. D. Dmitriev's attempt to dispute his authorship (*Trudy Otdela
Drevnerusskoi Literatury,* 9 (1953), p. 99) no longer holds up under scrutiny.
Simeon's citation of Simonides' famous dictum again illustrates his willingness to
pursue the analysis of painting by analogy to other liberal arts.
46. Arnaldo Momigliano, *Secondo Contributo alla Storia degli Studi Classici* (Rome,
1960), p. 421.

BYZANCE APRÈS BYZANCE: LUKE THE CYPRIOT, METROPOLITAN OF HUNGRO-WALLACHIA*

Gary Vikan

Because of her unusual wealth and her uniquely independent status within the Ottoman world, Romania was to assume, after the fall of Constantinople, the role of protector and patron of the Orthodox Church.[1] Her Voevods, who were the only lay Christian rulers left within the old Empire, were to become leaders in reviving and perpetuating the cultural and political heritage of Byzantium. Perhaps nothing is more evocative of the vitality of their leadership than the famous painted churches of Bucovina. There was, however, another major facet to Romania's post-Byzantine cultural revival which has gone substantially unrecognized. Beginning around 1580, and continuing through the middle of the seventeenth century, the Romanian principality of Wallachia fostered a major revival in the production of *deluxe* Greek manuscripts. Today there is hardly an important library or monastery without at least one of these distinctive service books-many of which are richly illustrated, all of which are delicately ornamented and elegantly transcribed in a large, regular minuscule. This article is devoted to the leading personality behind the revival, Luke the Cypriot, Metropolitan of Hungro-Wallachia.

Luke's Career

The identity of Luke the Cypriot may be reconstructed on the basis of Greek and Slavonic archival documents, more than two dozen manuscripts by his hand,[2] and the following short notice included in a

chronicle of the Wallachian Voevods (from 1602 to 1618) composed by
Matthew, Metropolitan of Myra:[3]

> Luke, the most holy Metropolitan being of Hungro-Wallach-
> ia, good and faithful man, having a heart not filled with pain,
> from childhood having turned to the monastic mode of life,
> and highly skilled in calligraphy. He drew his origins from
> Cyprus.

That Luke was a Cypriot is certain, not only from the foregoing
notice, but also from the fact that in many of his colophons he signs as
Kypriou (fig. 1).[4] Yet, it is equally certain that Luke spent most of his
life in Wallachia; indeed, his presence there is documented from 1583
until his death in 1629.[5] Although no firm evidence may be cited, it has
been generally supposed that Luke was among the many Greeks who
emigrated to Romania when the Turks captured Cyprus in 1571.[6] Since
he lived until 1629, Luke could hardly have been more than a young
man at that time.

Luke initially settled in Buzău (ca. 110 km northeast of Bucharest),
and over a period of years was primarily responsible for the creation of
the nearby monastery of Izvorani.[7] The first documentation of Luke as
bishop of Buzău, a post vacant from February, 1581, is a charter issued
by Voevod Petru Cercel and dated September 10, 1583 (or 4?), naming
the "very honest and very saintly Archbishop, Luke of Buzău."[8] Before
that, Luke signs at the rank of deacon in the colophon of a Joseph
Romance (fig. 1), and as *hieromonachos* in a Psalter on Athos dated
June 11, 1583.[9] From that year until 1601, Luke's tenure as bishop is
reflected in more than a half dozen manuscript colophons, as well as in
a series of archival documents relating his ecclesiastical, juridical, and
diplomatic activities.[10]

A charter issued in late 1603 by Voevod Radu Şerban identifies
Luke the Cypriot as Metropolitan of Hungro-Wallachia, the highest
post in the Wallachian Orthodox Church, vacant since August 1602.[11]
Luke's activities as metropolitan, which necessarily drew him to the
capital city Tîrgovişte (ca. 80 km northwest of Bucharest), are recorded
in a series of documents extending from 1603 until his death and burial
in the Izvorani Monastery in 1629.[12] Perhaps the most dramatic
moment in his tenure came in September, 1615, when during the

temporary absence from the Wallachian throne of Luke's patron, Voevod Radu Mihnea, an unsuccessful effort was made to remove him from his ecclesiastical chair.[13]

The attack, launched by Patriarchs Timotheos II of Constantinople and Theophanos of Jerusalem, was based on allegations that Luke had neglected his responsibilities-primarily financial-to the Ecumenical Church. He immediately made reparations, however, and remained in his post.

For nearly half a century Luke the Cypriot, an immigrant Greek, enjoyed extraordinary influence and prestige in Romania. While Bishop of Buzău he was a confidant of the powerful Voevod Michael the Brave (1593-1601), Romanian hero who drove out the Turks and united, for the first time, the principalities of Wallachia, Moldavia, and Transylvania.[14] Luke was dispatched by Voevod Michael on several diplomatic missions, the most important of which was a 1597 visit to Moscow, where he conferred with Tsar Feodor Ivanovich and Boris Godunov.[15]

As Metropolitan, Luke was the dominnt figure in the thriving Wallachian Orthodox Church and enjoyed the continuing protection and patronage of the highly cultivated, westernizing Voevod, Radu Mihnea, who ruled intermittently from 1601 to 1623.[16] Luke was closely acquainted with Anastasios Crîmca, Moldavian Metropolitan, who was also a renowned manuscript illuminator, and with the famous Calvinist Patriarch Cyril Lukaris;[17] among his friends was another important scribe and ecclesiastic, Matthew, Metropolitan of Myra, from 1609 *Hegoumenos* of the Dealu Monastery near Tîrgovişte, and the chief chronicler of the Wallachian court. Moreover, Luke was apparently the author of at least one panegyric, extant in a Paris manuscript of 1592.[18]

Luke as Scribe, Illuminator, and Teacher

Despite his high ecclesiastical rank and considerable diplomatic achievement, Luke is remembered in Matthew's chronicle, quoted above, specifically because he was "highly skilled in calligraphy"; indeed, Anthimios of Adrianople, the future patriarch, wrote in a dedicatory notice "... that he (Luke) has surpassed, in our time, all others in the art of calligraphy."[19] The twenty-eight manuscripts listed in note 2, certainly only a portion of his *oeuvre*,[20] testify to the high sophistication and unfailing quality of his production. Luke seems never to have lessened his output, even as Metropolitan and after having reached an advanced age[21] – his dated works span more than forty-five years. Moreover, it is clear from his generous use of gold, ornament, and illustration, his large, ornate script, and his preference for Lectionaries, Liturgies, and Psalters, that Luke's scribal career was primarily devoted to the production of *deluxe* service books for presentation to important monasteries and churches;[22] furthermore, three of his manuscripts may be associated with Wallachian Voevods, while a fourth seems to have been a gift to Tzar Feodor Ivanovich.[23]

In an important article in the *Byzantinische Zeitschrift* of 1958,[24] Linos Politis identified Luke the Cypriot as one of the most skilled, productive, and influential post-Byzantine practitioners of a tradition of ornate and highly-refined "liturgical" calligraphy traceable back at least three centuries to a Palaeologan scribal school centered in the famous Hodegon Monastery in Constantinople. Significantly, the colophon of Luke's earliest dateable manuscript (fig. 1) begins with the phrase characteristic of that tradition: *Theou to doron...* (cf. fig. 2).[25] Moreover, several of Luke's manuscripts-especialy those from early in his career-show remarkable parallels with Hodegon school products in their carmine ornament, and in their overall script style and page layout (cf. figs. 3 and 4).[26]

Over the decades, Luke's script style remained more or less constant (cf. figs. 5 [ca. 1580] and 6 [1616]);[27] letter forms are large, round, and elegant, becoming, with time, only slightly freer and more expressive.[27] Luke's ornament, on the other hand, periodically took new directions, while all the time retaining formulae and various elegant mannerisms that unmistakeably betray their authorship (cf. *omicrons*, figs. 5 and 6). For example, early in his career Luke prefered a traditional repertoire of carmine decoration (figs. 3,5 [ca. 1580]), with fretwork fillet for initials and interlace headpieces. Such motifs were common among Hodegon manuscripts two centuries earlier, but show as well a continuous tradition from the early Middle Byzantine period down to the seventeenth century.[29] Also evident early, and conspicuous right up to the end of his career, are Slavonic interlace headpieces, in gold and colors, that conform closely to contemporary printed books and manuscript illumination of the region (cf. figs. 7 [1594] and 8)[30] Unlike his contemporary, Matthew Metropolitan of Myra, however, Luke only rarely employed traditional Middle Byzantine "flower-petal" motifs (as in fig. 6),[31] although like Matthew, he was much influenced, especially later in his career, by western engravings as adapted and popularized locally, in Slavonic printed books.[32] Indeed, there are instances where Luke appears to have been making direct, visual "quotations"; figure 9 is a headpiece from a Luke Lectionary date 1627, while figure 10 is a headpiece in a Slavonic Gospels printed by Deacon Coresi in Brasov, Transylvania, in 1581.[33]

Much as Luke the Cypriot's career as a scribe and as an illuminator may be traced over decades, so also may his impact as a teacher.[34] Certainly, Matthew of Myra's manuscripts betray his influence, while several other important and prolific scribes (-illuminators-illustrators) of the period-and of the decades after Luke's death-describe themselves as his "studênts," and clearly emulate him (and Matthew) in both their calligraphy and their ornament. For example, among his most skilled and prolific students was Anthimios, *Hieromonachos* from Ianina,[35] who in a Liturgy dated 1635 (fig. 12) seems to be quoting directly from a Liturgy by Luke dedicated in 1616 (fig. 11).[36]

Luke as Miniaturist

Luke's development as a scribe, an illuminator, and as a teacher over his forty-five year career deserves and will receive more detailed treatment elsewhere-but in any case, its scope and basic outline is already substantially in focus. What is less clear, and what will now be considered in some detail, is Luke's identity as a book painter.

Although several scholars have described Luke as both scribe and illustrator, none has actually isolated or defined his miniature style.[37] This is especially difficult, since among the manuscripts listed in note 2, there are those showing miniatures in quite different styles, including Italo-Byzantine, Moscovite, Cretan, Slavonic, and the style (in fact, the hand) of Anastasios Grîmca. Indeed, the key to Luke's identity as a book painter lies in two closely interrelated manuscripts: an illustrated Joseph Romance in a private American collection (figs.1,3,5,14,16,18,21,

23) signed by Luke *Theou to doron kai diakonou ponos* (fig. 1) sometime before 1583, when he became a bishop, and a closely related, though unsigned, illustrated *Joasaph and Barlaam* in Athens (figs. 13, 15).[38] Although known among iconographers of Byzantine art for some time,[39] these two books, the earliest to survive from Luke's career, remained more or less unknown to students of calligraphy and post-Byzantine art until quite recently.[40]

In fact, the elegantly transcribed Joseph Romance consists of two short, legendary texts - the so-called *Life of Joseph,* carrying a spurious attribution to St. Ephraem, and the anonymous *Romance of Joseph and Aseneth.*[41] Its importance for this discussion, however, lies in its cycle of eighty water color miniature paintings. The unsigned Athens *Joasaph and Barlaam,* by contrast, is a long and undistinguished codex written in an irregular cursive by an unknown hand, but includes a cycle of twenty-three water color miniatures on fourteen scattered, though integral folios. Each miniature is accompanied by a detailed caption written in a large, sophisticated minuscule, to which are occasionally added ornamental carmine initials and tailpieces (fig. 13).[42] Significantly, all three decorative elements-miniature, script, and ornament-appearing on the fourteen folios are stylistically paralleled by their counterparts in the Joseph Romance. The calligraphy is in the simple, early style of Luke; it is a bit less ornate than the Joseph codex script (cf. fig. 3) of the early 1580s, which in turn is less decorative and expressive than that of the Baltimore Lectionary (Walters Art Gall., cod. W535) signed by Luke in 1594.[43]

There is much to connect the Athens miniatures with those of the Joseph manuscript. Both codices are illustrated with one-column narrative scenes rendered in water colors and directly integrated into the relevant text. Expressively gesticulating figures with large extended hands and long sketchy fingers (figs. 13, 14) inhabit atmospheric mountainous landscapes shaded from dark greenish brown in the foreground to pale, watery blue at the horizon (figs. 15,3).[44] Exact counterparts may be found for two ubiquitous floral forms (figs. 15,21)-namely a long-stemmed, double-pod flower, and thick drooping leaves sprouting from the soil-as well as for the characteristic fleshy head type with large, expressive eyes, low brow, wispy beard, and protruding chin (figs. 13, 14). Both cycles betray an aversion to interior settings, showing instead figures floating before complex, three-dimensional backdrops, often inhabited by miniature buildings shown in exterior view (figs. 3, 13). Finally, both miniature cycles show Italianate accoutrements, a westerner's sensitivity to three-dimensional space, and are ornamented from the same vocabulary of simple carmine interlace.

The physical link between the Joasaph and Joseph codices is further assured by the fact that they share a common provenance. That is, the same youthful hand that added extensive doodling to the beginning of the Joseph manuscript rendered closely comparable motifs on fly-leaves of the Joasaph codex.[45] And, more significantly, the same eighteenth-century(?) scribe who added Matthew of Myra's note (quoted above) to the last page of the Joseph Romance added similar notes at the end of the Athens manuscript, and there signed his name as Nicholas. And finally, it is noteworthy that these two manuscripts are nearly identical in folio and text-block dimensions.[46]

The Athens codex poses a basic question: could such a modest, sporadic decorative program added to a manuscript already finished by a mediocre scribe have called for the independent participation of three individual, highly accomplished craftsmen a scribe, a rubricator, and an illuminator and precisely the same three in precisely the same relationship that is evident in the Joseph codex? No, it is much more likely that a single artist, Luke the Cypriot, did all aspects of the occasional embellishment to the Athens *Joasaph and Barlaam* ,and fully produced the Joseph Romance. Significantly, these two miniature cycles are unique among those in manuscripts by Luke's hand in that they show a close physical and contentual link between image and text-a bond suggesting that scribe and illuminator were one and the same. Moreover, the stylistic development of the calligraphy from the Joasaph to the Joseph, an evolution toward greater technical felicity and expressiveness, is precisely paralleled by the corresponding evolution in the figure style.[47] It thus seems reasonable if not necessary to suppose that the *Joasaph and Barlaam* and the Joseph Romance represent the earliest phase of Luke's career (necessarily pre-1583) when, before his reputation as a scribe had been fully established, he acted as his own illuminator.

Luke's Early Patronage

Before looking backward, beyond the Joasaph and Joseph manuscripts toward Luke's artistic roots, it will be worthwhile to pursue the story of the more elaborate of these two early manuscripts a bit further, for it sheds considerable light on this artist's early career, and on his initial status in Wallachia.[48]

The Joseph manuscript is unique among those signed by Luke in that it is non-liturgical in function and, by comparison, almost secular in content. Yet, its program of illustration is by far the most extensive of the group, surpassing even that of the lavishly-decorated Baltimore Lectionary, which was likely an official gift of Voevod Michael the Brave to Tzar Feodor Ivanovich. Together, these facts suggest a high-placed, secular patron. From the preceding discussion of Luke's life it is clear that the production of the codex, wherein Luke signs as deacon, must antedate his elevation to bishop in 1583. And in the absence of evidence to the contrary it is reasonable to suppose that Luke was then, as he would be for the next fifty years, residing in Wallachia. Who may this patron have been?

Although explicit indicators are lacking, there is an impressive body of circumstantial evidence to suggest that Luke's Joseph Romance was commissioned by the ruling Wallachian family of Mircea, whose members in the early 1580s included the young Voevod Mihnea II, his mother Catherine, and his grandmother Despina.[49] The family's history of generous artistic patronage is long and impressive. Mihnea's recently deceased father Alexander II (d. 1577) had commissioned the Sucevița Gospels (cod. gr. 23),[50] which include a series of more than three hundred narrative scenes closely allied to Paris *graecus* 74, as well as a set of dedication portraits.[51] At the same time he added finely-worked gilt covers to a number of Middle Byzantine manuscripts, including a twelfth-century Gospel book which was re-dedicated to the Monastery of St. Catherine at Mount Sinai.[52] Moreover, he was apparently temporary owner of the famous Rockefeller-McCormick New Testament,[53] and was patron of the Chapel of John the Baptist at Mount Sinai.[54] All of this is not surprising, since Alexander was the grandson of Petru Rareș and great grandson of Stephan cel Mare, the two Voevods primarily responsible for the frescoed churches of Bucovina.[55] His mother Despina had been generous in stocking monastic libraries,[56] his wife Catherine was a cultured Levantine from a wealthy Pera family, his son Mihnea was himself destined to become a generous donor,[57] while his grandson Radu became, in the early 1600s, the closest and most enduring patron of Luke the Cypriot. Does it not seem likely that it was through this highly cultured, "hellenisized" family that Luke gained his introduction into the artistic patronage of Wallachia?[58] It was, after all, during the reign of Voevod Alexander (1568-1577) that Luke most likely emigrated to Romania.

Several lines of compelling corroborative evidence emerge from a careful examination of the manuscript itself. The most significant is the presence of folio 59 verso (fig. 16) of what is very likely the autograph signature of Voevod Radu Mihnea *IO (ANNES) RADOUL BOEBOD I (A)*,[59] grandson of Alexander, son of Mihnea II, friend and patron of Luke, and prince of Wallachia from 1601. Moreover, two notes transcribed in an eighteenth-century hand on the final fly-leaf suggest that this Joseph codex was, even long after its production, linked to that royal family.

First, there is an excerpt pertaining to Luke from the chronicle "... concerning Radul, son of Mihnea...,"[60] and below it is repeated the colophon of a (lost) Lectionary produced in 1609 by Luke for Voevod Radu.[61]

Incongruous iconographic elements of the *Life of Joseph* and *Joseph and Aseneth* cycles further suggest a princely patron-namely, episodes nos. 47, 55, A1, and A29, all of which include hieratic representations of frontally-enthroned royal figures, and in each case the configuration diverges precisely in that respect from either (or both) the implication of the narrative or the iconographic tradition as attested in other illustrated manuscripts of the text.[62] Moreover, the Joseph and the Aseneth cycles are marked by unusual attention to princely attire, and in the case of Aseneth, it at times conflicts with the requirements of her ascetic conversion.[63]

The Joseph story may even have had, in the early 1580s, specific significance for the Mircea family. Alexander II and Mihnea II were both, like Joseph, kings who had been forced from their homeland-the former was exiled to Rhodes and Palestine, and the latter to Tripoli.[64] As Joseph gained kingship only through the favour of a powerful heathen, so also Alexander and Mihnea gained the throne only through the favor of the Sultan.[65]   Alexander's wife Catherine mirrors Aseneth insofar as she was born into a Catholic family (Salveresso of Pera) and had turned to Orthodoxy.[66] And finally, in the early 1580s, when the Joseph manuscript was almost certainly produced, Mihnea II was, like Joseph, a young ruler painfully separated from his father (d. 1577). It may even be suggested that this manuscript, with its emphasis on youthful royalty and courtship, was commissioned for Mihnea's marriage in June 1582, when he would have been seventeen, precisely Joseph's age as the story of his life begins.[67] Mihnea's portrait in the Suceviţa Gospels (fig. 17) bears at least general comparison with the enthroned figure of Joseph at the head of the Aseneth romance (fig. 18), which, significantly, stands directly opposite Voevod Radu's signature.[68] One may only speculate as to what more specific dedicatory text or representation may have occupied the lost folios which originally faced the headpieces to the two texts.

Luke's Background

One final question remains to complete this brief survey of Luke, Metropolitan of Hungro-Wallachia-namely, what background, artistically, did he bring with him to Romania, and where did he acquire it? This issue is more complex than it at first appears, since his two surviving picture cycles - those for Joseph and Joasaph — are in each case closely modeled on earlier prototypes, and thus it is only by careful comparison with these prototypes (or with what we can surmise of them) that their stylistic impact may be "purged", and Luke's unique contribution, and artistic identity, properly identified.[69]

Consider first the Athens Joasaph. Sirarpie Der Nersessian has demonstrated that while its archetype was almost certainly a product of the eleventh century, its immediate model was just as certainly Palaeologan-in fact, a manuscript extremely close to, though demonstrably not identical with, Bibliothèque Nationale codex 1128, of the fourteenth century.[70] A comparison of the Athens and Paris miniatures (figs. 13, 19)[71] reveals those elements of the latter which are faithful to its model, and those elements which are personal additions. Clearly, the general narrative configuration is faithfully repeated, even in details of conflation; poses, garments, and gestures are virtually the

same, as is the positioning of individual figures and of textually
motivated architectural motifs. Yet, the sixteenth-century illuminator
has introduced several basic modifications. Most significantly, he has
added painterly mountain peaks and airy blue landscapes behind his
figural compositions, thus creating for them a sense of three-dimensional space completely unanticipated in the Paris miniatures.
Likewise, he has reinterpreted what were already stereometrically
constructed architectural motifs according to a linear perspective
system thoroughly un-Byzantine in its volumetric rigor, and in several
instances, has interjected specifically Italianate motifs.[72] And, in a
similar vein, he has added a new, soft corporeality to what in his model
were likely emaciated, Middle Byzantine figures; yet (as in the Joseph
codex) he has failed to integrate these three individual "naturalizing"
tendencies into a plausible three-dimensional whole. Finally, he has
introduced greater emphasis and elegance to hand gestures, and has
translated a subdued chromatic program of gouache earth tones into
sharply contrasting, tertiary water colors.

Like the *Joasaph and Barlaam,* the Joseph Romance likely derives
from an eleventh-century archetype, and again, almost certainly by
way of a Palaeologan prototype-but in this case, a finer manuscript in a
more unmistakably Palaeologan, Kariye Djami -like style.[73] And
although nothing comparable to Paris 1128 in this instance survives,
the dependency is unmistakable, especially in bodily proportions, and
in the fold patterns of garments. Thus, the Jacob illustrated in our
figure 14 is typically late Byzantine in the volumetric inflation of his
torso; expanding from a narrow pedestal of small, closely-spaced feet,
his ballooning thighs and abdomen taper above through withered
shoulders toward an elongated, conical neck, to which his head is
attached at a strangely inorganic angle (cf. figs. 14 and 20).[74] Likewise
Palaeologan is Jacob's facial type, with his high cheekbones, and
long thin beard, which expressively draws out the mournful arch of his
mouth, and the shaded, sunken V-form of his cheeks.[75] Finally,
numerous distinctly Palaeologan mannerisms may be recognized
among the garments in this manuscript, including a general tendency
to draw the mantle thickly around the lower back, the addition of a
stiff, extended zig-zag dart of cloth over the shoulder, and, most
significantly, the inclusion of a thick, mushroom-shape fold beneath

the thigh.[76] In a few cases, this latter form is extended through a series of heavy ripples into an autonomous dart of cloth, an expressive motif which is among the most characteristic mannerisms of Palaeologan drapery style (figs. 21, 22).[77] Late Byzantine also are the stereometrically designed boxes and cubes that fill the background of many miniatures – which again, find some of their closest parallels among the mosaics of the Kariye Djami.[78] There, as in the Joseph cycle, thin-walled rectilinear forms are set askew to the foreground plane, retreating diagonally in what appears to be exaggerated two-point perspective (cf. figs. 23 and 24).[79] Yet, in the absence of a single horizon line, adjacent cubes are tilted at precipitous angles toward widely varying points, and structures which should be rendered as though seen from below appear in bird's eye view. In both cycles figurative compositions are flanked by angular, vertical blocks, often bearing deep, shaded portals which enhance their volumetric effect.[80] And, in several instances, Luke has clearly misunderstood the shading and delineation of such a three-dimensional portal in his model.

Indeed, that such unmistakably Palaeologan details of architecture and drapery derive primarily from the cycle's lost model, and not from the illuminator's training, is clear from the fact that they are virtually absent from the Joasaph manuscript. Rather it is by stripping away the lost model's impact that one arrives at what is essentially the illuminator's trademark — namely (as in the Joasaph), atmospheric landscapes with soft, painterly mountains, expressively gesticulating figures with large, extended hands and long sketchy fingers, long-stemmed, double-pod flowers, fleshy heads with expressive eyes, low brows, and wispy beards, and various Italianate architectural motifs with, especially, views up into colonnaded porticos (fig. 23).

Once "stripped" and so characterized, Luke's style may be scrutinized, and indeed, his is a highly distinctive mélange of East and West which is without parallel in sixteenth-century Romania. Comparisons are forthcoming neither from Wallachian nor Moldavian fresco, icon or manuscript painting, nor, more significantly, from among the many other codices transcribed by Luke or his students.[81] Furthermore, I have been unable to trace parallels in the contemporary painting of Serbia, Bulgaria, Russia, Athos or Sinai, nor in the style of Theophanes the Cretan and his many followers. Rather, this Joseph

Romance, along with its related Joasaph in Athens, should, on account of their distinctive amalgamation of Byzantine and Latin influences, be recognized as among the long and eclectic series of Greek codices illuminated in Italo-or Franco-Byzantine style. Unknown in the Middle Byzantine period, such cycles become increasingly common from the fourteenth to seventeenth centuries, and represent a gradual and ultimately diametric shift in the flow of artistic influence, which hitherto had been primarily from East to West.[82] Because they arise from the chance fusion of often widely disparate aesthetic outlooks, motifs, techniques, and models, these images show far greater stylistic autonomy than do their counterparts produced within a closed eastern or western tradition.[83]

Where, for Luke, might this fusion have taken place? Of course, one possible location would be Venice, where the Greek colony-and the Confraternity of San Giorgio dei Greci-was, during the second half of the sixteenth century, at the peak of its cultural activity; Luke may easily have enjoyed a stop-over there between the Turkish conquest of Cyprus in 1571 and the early 1580s, when it is certain that he was in Romania.[84] Several lines of evidence, however, militate against this hypothesis. Neither the Joseph nor the Joasaph miniatures show specific stylistic ties to contemporary Greek artists working in Venice, including Michael Damaskinos, a Cretan immigrant whose style was preponderant in the Greek colony from 1574 to 1582, or George Klotzas, who wrote and illuminated well-known book of emperors in 1590.[85] The Italianate component in the painting of these Venetians is specifically sixteenth-century and Mannerist (Correggio, Bassano) while that of Luke reflects a much more general, Early Renaissance aesthetic.[86] Moreover, there is no evidence that Luke was ever in Venice, nor, more significantly, is there any evidence that the Hodegon Monastery style of calligraphy was ever practiced there.

Cyprus, on the other hand, is a much more likely alternative; not only was it Luke's birthplace, it was, until 1571, a colony of Venice. Moreover, Linos Politis has shown that the calligraphic style and colophon formula perpetuated and developed by Luke were practiced in Cyprus by Ambrosios, *Hegoumenos* of the Monastery of St. Andrew (Nicosia), precisely during the years (the 1560s) when Luke would have received his monastic craft training (fig. 25).[87] Finally, the existence of a strong Italo-Byzantine school of painting is witnessed on Cyprus by, among others, the *Akathistos Hymnos* fresco cycle in the Latin Chapel of St. John Lampadhistis, and by the frescoes of *Panayia tis Podithou*, near Galata.[88] Drapery mannerisms, architectural motifs, and landscape vistas of both cycles offer suggestive comparisons for the Joseph and Joasaph miniatures.[89] Also suggestively similar are the sixteenth-century icons of the *dodecaorton* series in the Monastery of St. Neophytos, Paphos.[90] For example, the panel with the Meeting of Joachim and Anna (fig. 26)[91] provides several striking parallels for Luke's miniatures, including a view into an Italianate colonnaded portico (cf. especially, fig. 21), emphatic hand gestures and long fingers (cf. especially, fig. 13), accentuated facial expressions (cf. fig. 23), and the very distinctive di-pod flower (cf. figs. 15, 21). Indeed, such comparisons are so striking that it may eventually be possible to determine where on Cyprus Luke received his initial training. This, however, will have to await a more detailed study.

NOTES

* This article is dedicated to the memory of Linos Politis who, more than anyone, discovered Luke the Cypriot, and on several occasions generously shared his discoveries-and some of his immense knowledge of Greek scribes and calligraphy – with me.

Substantially drawn from Chapter VII of my unpublished dissertation ("Illustrated Manuscripts of Pseudo-Ephraem's *Life of Joseph* and the *Romance of Joseph and Aseneth*," [Princeton, 1976] 485 ff.), this article is a *prolegomenon* to a monographic treatment of Luke the Cypriot's manuscript production. My research on Romanian manuscript illumination has been generously supported by the International Research and Exchanges Board (1974-1975), and the American Council of Learned Societies (1977).

The most important recent studies devoted all or in part to Luke the Cypriot are: G. Cront, "Le chypriote Luca, évêque et métropolite en Valachie (1583-1629), *Praktika tou protou diethnous Kyprologikou Synedriou*, 3 (Nicosia, 1973), 45 ff.; L. Politis, "Un centre de calligraphie dans les principautés danubiennes au XVIIe siècle. Lucas Buzău et son cercle," *Dixième Congrès International des Bibliophiles, Athènes 30 septembre - 6 octobre 1977* (Athens, 1979), 1 ff.; and O. Gratziou, *Die dekorierten Handschriften des Schreibers Matthaios von Myra (1596-1624)*, Sonderheft der Zeitschrift *Mnemon*, 1 (Athens 1982), *passim*.

For the relevant primary sources on Luke the Cypriot, see notes 2, 3.

1. See N. Iorga, *Byzance après Byzance*, rev. ed. (Bucharest, 1971), *passim;* and S. Runciman, *The Great Church in Captivity* (Cambridge, 1968), chap. 10.

2. The Greek documents appear in E. de Hurmuzaki, *Documente privitoare la istoria*

Românilor: XIV, documente greceşti privitoare la istoria Românilor, N. Iorga, pt. 1: 1320-1716 (Bucharest, 1915); the Slavonic documents were published by the Romanian Academy during the 1950s in the series *Documente privind istoria României,* beginning with *Veacul XVI: B. Ţara românească, vol. V. (1581-1590)* (Bucharest, 1952). The evidence has been reviewed and organized by N. Şerbănescu in "Mitropoliţii Ungrovlahiei", *Biserica Orthodoxă,* 77 (1959), 768 ff.

Luke's Manuscripts:

Athens, Byz. Mus., cod. 203

----, Nat. Lib., cods. 755, 836

----, Senate Lib., cod. 11

Baltimore, Walters Art. Gall., cod. W535

Constantinople, Pat. Lib. (lost)

Durham, N.C., Duke Univ. Lib., cod. gr. 39

Jerusalem, Treasury, cod. 2

Leningrad, IAR, cod. 189

Meteora, Barlaam, cods. 34, 78

----, Metamorphosis, cods. 624, 654y

Mount Athos, Dionysiou, cod. 429

----, Iviron, cods. 1385, 1423m,

----- (*Akathistos Hymnos*)

----, Lavra, cods., H148, W140

----, Panteleimon, cod. 426

----, St. Paul Skiti, cod. 806

----, Simonpetras (lost)

Mount Sinai, cods. 1480, (Gospels)

Naxos, Koimesis, cod. 1

Paris, Bibl. Nat., cod. gr. 100A

Princeton, Univ. Lib., cod. 13

San Francisco, Greeley Coll.

3. E. Legrand, *Bibliothèque grecque vulgaire* (Paris,1881), 231 ff.

4. Figure 1: San Francisco, Greeley Coll., fol. 108r: "The gift of God and the labor of Luke of Cyprus, having written in love" (Vikan, 1976, fig. 210).

5. Şerbănescu, 1959, *passim.*

6. See especially A. Camariano-Cioran, "Contributions aux relations rumano-chypriote," *Revue des études sud-est européennes,* 15 (1977), 493 ff.

7. See I. Ionascu, *Mănăstirea Izvorani (Buzău) ctitoria episcopului Luca (1583-1604)* (Buzău, 1936).

8. Şerbănescu, 1959, 769.

9. Mount Athos, St. Paul Skiti, cod. 806. See Kourilds, "Kodikes tes meas sketes tou hagiou Paulou," *Theologia,* 21 (1950), 522.

10. Şerbănescu, 1959, 769 f.

11. Şerbănescu, 1959, 770.

12. Şerbănescu, 1959, 770 ff.

13. Şerbănescu, 1959, 770f.; and É. Legrand, *Recueil de documents grecs concernant les relations du patriarcat de Jérusalem avec la Roumanie (1569-1728)* (Paris, 1895), 2 ff.

14. N. Iorga, *A History of Roumania* (London, 1925) chap. 9; Şerbănescu, 1959, 770; and Camariano-Cioran, 1977, 493 ff.

15. See P. Constantinescu-Iaşi, *Relaţiile culturale rumînoruse din trecut* (Bucharest, 1954), 89.

16. See Iorga, 1971, 151, 164.

17. Şerbănescu, 1959, 771. See, respectively, G. Popescu-Vîlcea, *Anastasie Crimca* (Bucharest, 1972); and Runciman, 1968, chap. 8. In the Sinai Gospels cited in note 2 above, the text and initials are by Luke, while the headpieces and Evangelist portraits are by Crîmca.

18. See Olga Gratziou's excellent 1982 monograph on the manuscripts of Matthew of Myra (esp. 99 ff.). Among her many well-documented and well-reasoned conclusions is that Luke and Matthew were not, despite their parallel careers and close physical proximity at Tîrgovişte, as close as I (1976, 489) and Linos Politis (1979, 4) had thought – that Matthew was neither Luke's student nor direct collaborator.

   For the panegyric (Paris, Bibl. Nat., cod.,supp. gr. 407, fols.158-176["orations, no 6"] see H. Omont, *Manuscrits grecs de la Bibliothèque Nationale* (Paris, 1888), 259; and K. Krumbacher, *Geschichte der byzantinischen Literatur,* 2nd ed. (Munich, 1897), 176n.

19. See Politis, 1977, 4.

20. M. Vogel and V. Gardthausen, *Die griechischen Schreiber des Mittelalters und der Renaissance* (Leipzig, 1909), 266, lists just two manuscripts by Luke the Cypriot; in my 1976 dissertation (620 ff.) sixteen are listed.

21. Of the manuscripts listed in note 2, three (Iviron 1423m; Jerusalem, Treasury 2; and Meteora, Metamorphosis 654y′) are dated 1616, while one (Meteora, Barlaam 34) is dateable to 1616/17. By that time Luke would likely have been close to sixty years old.

22. As were the manuscripts of Matthew,Metropolitan of Myra (see Gratziou, 1982, 111 f.).

23. See Vikan, 1976, 531, note 24, 620 ff., nos. 9 and 11, and the discussion of Luke's illustrated Joseph Romance, below.

24. "Eine Schreiberschule in Kloster *ton Hodegon*," *Byzantinische Zeitschrift,* 51 (1958), 17 ff. 261 ff. (esp. 282 f.).

25. Politis. 1979, 2 (and Politis, 1958,18 ff.). Figure 2: Moscow, State Hist. Mus., cod. Syn. gr. 429, fol. 34v: "The Gift of God" (G. Proxorov, "A Codicological Analysis of the Illuminated *Akathistos* to the Virgin," *Dumbarton Oaks Papers,* 26 [1972], 241, fig. 2). Joasaph, active from the second half of the fourteenth into the early years of the fifteenth century, was the leading scribe of the Hodegon scriptorium tradition (Politis, 1958, 17 ff.).

26. Figure 3: San Francisco, Greeley Coll., fol. 22v (Vikan, 1976, fig. 33). Figure 4: Leningrad, Lib. of Acad. of Science, cod. 2 (liturgical roll) (Proxorov, 1972, 243,

fig. 6). Proxorov attributes this voll and Synodal gr. 429 (preceding note) to the hand of Joasaph.

27. Figure 5: San Francisco, Greeley Coll., fol. 1r (Vikan, 1976, fig. 215). Figure 6: Mount Athos, Iviron, cod. 1423m, fol. 1r (S. Pelekanidis, P. Christou, C. Tsioumis, and S. Kadas, *The Treasures of Mount Athos,* 2 [Athens, 1975], pl. 196).

28. Politis, 1977, 3.

29. See K. Weitzmann, *Die byzantinische Buchmalerei des 9. und 10. Jahrhunderts* (Berlin, 1935), fig. 487; and D. Harlfinger, *Specimina griechischer Kopisten der Renaissance* (Berlin, 1974), pls. 25, 60.

30. Figure 7: Baltimore, Walters Art Gall., cod. W535, fol. 9r (cf. Gratziou, 1982, 26, note 34). Figure 8: Zagreb, Académie yougoslave des sciences et beaux-arts, cod. IIIa, 47, fol. 166r (theological manuscript by Vladislav the Grammarian, dated 1469; S. Radojčić, *Stare srpske minijature* [Belgrade, 1950], color pl. F).

31. Gratziou, 1982, 126 f.

32. Gratziou, 1982, *passim* (esp. 128 ff.).

33. Figure 9: Durham, N.C., Duke Univ. Lib., cod. gr. 39, fol. 1r (Sotheby and Co., *Gatalogue of Western and Öriental Manuscripts and Miniatures* [London, Dec. 12, 1966], lot 199). Figure 10: I. Bianu, N. Hodoş, *Bibliografia românésca veche 1508-1830, 1: 1508-1716* (Bucharest, 1903), no. 29.

34. See Politis, 1977, 4 ff.; and Gratziou, 1982, 98 f.

35. Identifiable in about two dozen manuscripts executed between 1630 and 1648 (Politis, 1972, 10; Gratziou, 1982, 10 f.). In Naxos, Koimesis, cod. 1 (fol. 173r), Anthimios identifies himself as "...student of lord Luke of Hungro-Wallachia."

36. Figure 11: Mount Athos, Iviron, cod. 1423m, fol. 24r (Pelekanidis, Christou, Tsioumis, and Kadas, 1975, pl. 197). Figure 12: Mount Athos, Iviron, cod. 526m, fol. 28r (Pelekanidis, Christou, Tsioumis, and Kadas, 1975, pl. 388).

37. See N. Iorga, "La figuration des evangélistes dans l'art roumain et l'école cypriote-valaque," *Buletinul comisiunii monumentelor istorice,* 26 (1933), 2; and M. Beza, *Byzantine Art in Romania* (London, 1940), no. 41.

38. For the Joseph manuscript, see Vikan, 1976 *passim* (esp. 607 ff.). For the *Joasaph and Barlaam,* see S. Der Nersessian, *L' Illustration du roman de Barlaam et Joasaph* (Paris, 1937), *passim*; and Vikan, 1976, 620.

39. S. Der Nersessian published the Joasaph picture cycle in 1937 (see preceding note), and O. Pächt partially published the Joseph cycle in 1954 ("An Unknown Cycle of Illustrations of the Life of Joseph," *Cahiers archéologiques,* 7 [1954], 35 ff.).

40. See Politis, 1977, 393.

41. Vikan, 1976, chap. II.

42. Figure 13: Athens, Senate Lib., cod. 11, fol. 52r (Der Nersessian, 1937, fig. 378).

43. Politis, 1979, 3.

44. Figure 14: San Francisco, Greeley Coll., fol. 20v (Vikan, 1976, 490, fig. 28). Figure 15: Athens, Senate Lib., cod. 11, fol. 149r (Der Nersessian, 1937, fig. 389).

45. Compare folios 1r, v, 2r, 433v of the Athens codex with flyleaf IIr, v of the Joseph Romance.

46. Compare folios 431v, 432r of the Athens codex with flyleaf Vv of the Joseph Romance.
47. In the Athens codex colors are often added excessively and unevenly, and figures are poorly integrated into their settings. The Joseph codex, on the other hand, betrays greater skill and economy in use of wash, greater variety of pose and action, and a more logical integration of the figure into his surroundings. Its drapery is less thickly painted, and only rarely includes the heavy, convoluted hems found in the Athens manuscript; likewise, its architecture is less painstakingly rendered. As with the script, the general effect is one of greater skill and ease with the medium – less attention to detail is coupled with greater over-all expressiveness.
48. Vikan, 1976, 493 ff. Because of the shared provenance of these two books, much of what can be deduced from the Joseph may well apply to the Joasaph.
49. See A.-D. Xénopol, *Histoire des Romains* (Paris, 1896), I, 316 ff.
50. The Gospels is now in the Museum of Art in Bucharest.
51. See S. Der Nersessian "Two Slavonic Parallels of the Greek Tetraevangelia: Paris 74," *Art Bulletin*, 9 (1927), 226 ff.
52. See Beza, 1940, no. 35. Alexander's father, Mircea III, added similar covers to the famous Dionysiou Lectionary, cod. gr. 587. See K. Weitzmann, "An Imperial Lectionary in the Monastery of Dionysiu on Mount Athos: Its Origins and its Wanderings," *Revue des études sud-est européennes*, 7 (1969), 248 ff.
53. See D. Riddle, *The Rockefeller McCormick New Testament: II, the Text* (Chicago, 1932), 15 ff.
54. M. Beza, *The Romanian Church* (London, 1943), chap. 3.
55. See Xénopol, 1896, 316.
56. See Iorga, 1971, 137.
57. See C. Giurescu, *Istoria Romanilor* (Bucharest, 1943), II, 223 ff., 233 f.
58. According to N. Iorga (*Histoire de Roumains* [Bucharest, 1940], V. 4, chap. 1), Alexander was the first major channel for the absorption of the Greek influence in Romania.
59. Figure 16: San Francisco, Greeley Coll., fol. 59v (Vikan, 1976, fig. 219). The upper "signature" is apparently a later, naive copy of that below. Compare Radu's signature as given on an official document dated December 1, 1621 in the State Archives of Bucharest (T. Ionescu-Nișcov and M. Soveja, *Acte de cancelarie domnească* [Bucharest, 1974], no. IV). For other samples of his signature, see *Documente privind istoria României, XVII: B. Țara românească, III (1616-1621)* (Bucharest, 1951), nos. 522, 550; and *...IV (1621-1625)* (Bucharest, 1954), no 34. For contrasting signatures of contemporary Voevods, see *...Introducere, II* (Bucharest, 1956), figs. 43, 47, 49-51.
60. This is a paraphrase of the chronicle's actual title, which does not specifically mention Radu or Mihnea II (see Iorga, 1898-1899, 3). The change in emphasis was certainly intentional.
61. For a translation, see Vikan, 1976, appendix I.
62. Vikan, 1976, 495.

63. That this manuscript is virtually unique, within Joseph iconography, in portraying Joseph subservintly bowing on one Knee as he meets his father (episode no. 75; Vikan, 1976, fig. 110) further suggests the influence of specific court customs and hierarchies. A princely patron is also suggested by the transcription, on the blank folios at the back of the codex, of a 1535 treaty between King Francis I of France and the Sultan Suliman the Great. For details, see Vikan, 1976, appendix I.

64. See Iorga, 1940, V, 4, chap. 1; and Iorga, 1971, 139.

65. See Xénopol, 1896, 320 ff.

66. See Giurescu, 1943, 223 ff.

67. See Giurescu, 1943, 233, 227.

68. Figure 17: N. Iorga, *Portretele domnilor romani* (Sibiu, 1930), pls. 68a-c. Figure 18: San Francisco, Greeley Coll., fol. 60r (Vikan, 1976, fig. 113).

69. For detailed analyses of Luke's specific dependencies on (now lost) models for each of his two picture cycles, see Der Nersessian, 1937, *passim*; and Vikan, 1976, *passim*.

70. Der Nersessian, 1937, preface, 59, 87. See also the exhibition catalogue, *Byzance et la France médiévale* (Paris, 1958), no. 86.

71. Figure 19: Paris, Bibl. Nat., cod. gr. 1128, fol. 24r (Der Nersessian, 1937, fig. 200).

72. Compare Der Nersessian, 1937, figs. 385, 386.

73. Vikan, 1976, *passim* (esp. 506 ff.).

74. Figure 20: Kariye Djami (P. Underwood, *The Kariye Djami* [New York, 1966], II, pl. 141).

75. Compare Underwood, 1966, II pls. 48, 122, 296.

76. See Vikan, 1976, figs. 5, 24, 27, 84, 107. Compare Underwood, 1966, II, pl. 143; W. Hatch, *Greek and Syrian Miniatures in Jerusalem* (Cambridge, Mass., 1931), pl. LXII; and H. Omont, *Miniatures des plus anciens manuscrits grecs de la Bibliothèque Nationale du VIe au XIVe siècle*, 2nd ed. (Paris 1929), pl. CXXVI.

77. Figure 21: San Francisco, Greeley Coll., fol. 35r (Vikan. 1976, fig. 58). Figure 22: Kariye Djami (Underwood, 1966, II, pl. 85).

78. Vikan, 1976, 509ff.

79. Figure 23: San Francisco, Greeley Coll., fol. 21r (Vikan, 1976, fig. 29). Figure 24: Kariye Djami (Underwood, 1966, II, pl. 90).

80. Compare Underwood, 1966, II, pls. 148, 159, 203.

81. See Vikan, 1976, 523 ff.

82. See, for example, T. Velmans "Le Parisinus grecus 135 et quelques autres peintures de style gothique dans les manuscrits grecs à l'époque des Paléologues," *Cahiers archéologiques,* 17 (1967), 209 ff.; T. Velmans, "Deux manuscrits enlumines inedits et les influences réciproques entre Byzance et l'Italie au XIVe siècle," *Cahiers archéologiques,* 20 (1970), 207 ff.; A. Luttrell, "Frederigo da Venezia's Commentary on the Apocalypse: 1393/94," *Journal of The Walters Art Gallery,* 27/28 (1964/1965), 57 ff. The most thoroughly documented post-Byzantine example of western influence is the absorption of Lucas Cranach Apocalypse iconography by Athonite fresco painters; see L. Heydenreich, "Der Apocalypsen-Zyklus im

Athosgebiet und seine Beziehungen zur deutschen Bibelillustraten der Reformation," *Zeitschrift für Kunstgeschichte,* 8 (1939) 1 ff. And see, for Matthew of Myra, Gratziou, 1982, *passim.*

83. It is interesting to compare the wide variation in Italian influence among the icons produced in Venice between 1574 and 1582 by the Cretan painter Michael Damaskinos. See M. Chatzidakis, *Icônes de Saint-Georges des Grecs et de la collection de l'Institut* (Venice, 1962), 51 ff. (esp. nos 41 and 46).

84. See Chatzidakis, 1962, 45 ff. See also D. Geanakopolos, *Byzantine East and Latin West: Two Worlds of Christendom in the Middle Ages and Renaissance* (Oxford, 1966), chap. 4. Ties between Venice and Wallachia were close during the fourth quarter of the sixteenth century; Mihnea II's aunt lived in Murano, and his son Radu was sent to school in Padua.

85. See Chatzidakis, 1962, 51 ff., 74 f., nos. 27-49; 50-53.

86. Compare, for example, the stylized atmospheric landscapes of the Bible of Borso d' Este, produced in northern Italy soon after the mid-fifteenth century (M. Salmi, *La miniatura Italiana* [Milan, 1955], pls. LII-LV).

87. Figure 25: Paris, Bibl. Nat., cod. gr. 872, fol. 1r (Politis, 1958, fig. 26).

88. For the former, see A. Stylianou, "An Italo-Byzantine Series of Wall-Paintings in the Church of St. John Lampadhistis, Kalopanayiotis, Cyprus," *Akten des XI. Internationalen Byzantinistenkongress, München 1958* (Munich, 1960), 595 ff., pls. LXXIV-LXXXI; G. Sotiriou, *Ta Byzantina mnemeia tes Kyprou* (Athens, 1935), pls. 17, 108a, 109b; and A. Papageorghiou, *Masterpieces of the Byzantine Art of Cyprus* (Nicosia, 1965), pl. XXXV.

For the latter, see A. and I. Stylianou "He mone Podythou para ten Galatan", *Kypriakai spoudai,* 18 (1954), 49 ff., pls. 1-24; and Papageorghiou, 1965, pls. XXXVI-XL. The *terminus post quem* for the cycle is an inscription dated 1502. See also A. Stylianou, "Some Wall-Paintings of the Second Half of the 15th Century in Cyprus," *Actes du XIIe congrès international d'études byzantine, Ochride 10-16 septembre 1961* (Belgrade, 1964), III, 363 f.

89. These comparisons apply especially to the earlier Athens Joasaph cycle. Compare the striding poses, thick convoluted drapery (covering the feet), the deep, coulisselike landscapes, the preference for superimposed vertical cubes topped with crenellations, and for flanking architectural forms receding toward a central vanishing point, the emphasis on delicate hand gestures, and the general soft corporeality of the figures.

90. See *Byzantine Icons of Cyprus* (Athens, 1976), nos. 53-56.

91. Figure 26: *Byzantine Icons,* 1976, no. 54.

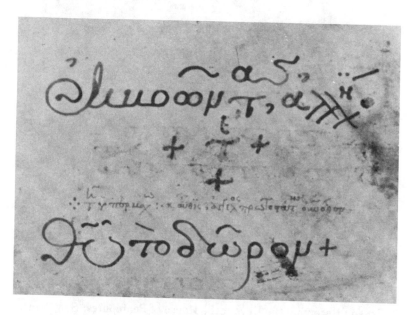

1. Scribal Colophon: San Francisco, Greeley Coll., *Life of Joseph/Romance of Joseph and Aseneth*, fol. 108r (Luke the Cypriot, ca. 1580)

2. Scribal Colophon: Moscow, State Hist. Mus., cod. Syn. gr. 429, fol. 34v (Joasaph of the Hodegon Monastery[?], later 14th c.)

3. Joseph Receiving the Keys to the House of Pentephres: San Francisco, Greeley Coll., *Life of Joseph/Romance of Joseph and Aseneth*, fol. 22v (Luke the Cypriot, ca. 1580)

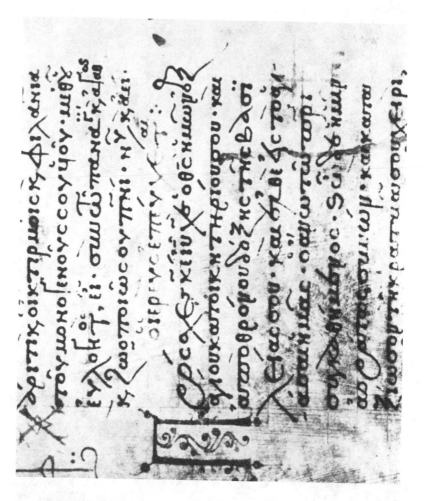

4. Liturgical Roll: Leningrad, Lib. of Acad. of Science, cod. 2
(Joasaph of the Hodegon Monastery[?], later 14th c.)

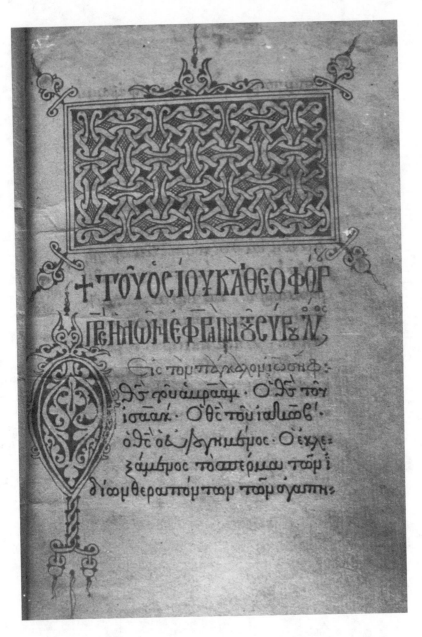

5. Headpiece: San Francisco, Greeley Coll., *Life of Joseph/Romance of Joseph and Asenth*, fol. 1r (Luke the Cypriot, ca. 1580)

6. Headpiece: Mount Athos, Iviron, cod. 1423m, fol. 1r (Luke the Cypriot, 1616)

7. Headpiece: Baltimore, Walters Art Gall., cod. W535, fol. 9r
(Luke the Cypriot, 1594)

8. Headpiece: Zagreb, Academie yougoslave des sciences et beaux-
arts, cod. IIIa, 47, fol. 166r (Vladislav the Grammarian, 1469)

9. Headpiece: Durham, N. C., Duke Univ. Lib., cod. xxx, fol. xxx (Luke the Cypriot, 1623)

ПОꙊченїе нзьранаѡстоеу

10. Headpiece (printed): Slavonic Gospels of Deacon Coresi (Brasov, 1581)

11. Headpiece: Mount Athos, Iviron, cod. 1423m, fol. 24r (Luke the Cypriot, 1616)

12. Headpiece: Mount Athos, Iviron, cod. 523m, fol. 28r (Anthimios
Hieromonachos, 1635)

13. Bariaam Demands to See Joasaph: Athens, Senate Lib., cod. 11, fol. 52r (Luke the Cyrpiot, ca. 1580.

14. Jocob's Lament: San Francisco, Greeley Coll., *Life of Joseph/Romance of Joseph and Aseneth*, fol. 20v (Luke the Cyrpiot, ca. 1580)

15. The Parable of the Kind for One Year: Athens, Senate Lib., cod. 11, fol. 149r (Luke the Cypriot, ca. 1580)

16. Signature of Voevod Radu Mihnea: San Francisco, Greeley Coll., *Life of Joseph/Romance of Joseph and Aseneth*, fol. 59v (1601–1623)

17. Voevod Mihnea II: Bucharest, Museum of Art, Sucevita Gospels,
    cod. 23 (before 1577)

18. Headpiece with Joseph: San Francisco, Greeley Coll., *Life of Joseph/Romance of Joseph and Aseneth*, fol. 60r (Luke the Cypriot, ca. 1580)

19. Barlaam Demands to See Joasaph: Paris, Bibl. Nat., cod. gr. 1128, fol. 24r (14th c.)

20. Christ Healing (detail): Istanbul, Kariye Djami (early 14th c.)

21. Angel Appears to Joseph in Prison: San Francisco, Greeley Coll.,
Life of Joseph in Prison: San Francisco, Greeley Coll., *Life of
Joseph/Romance of Joseph and Aseneth*, fol. 35r (Luke the
Cypriot, ca. 1580)

23. Joseph is Taken to Egypt: San Francisco, Greeley Coll., *Life
of Joseph/Romance of Joseph and Aseneth*, fol. 21r (Luke the
Cypriot, ca. 1580)

22. Annunciation to St. Anne (detail): Istanbul, Karlye Djami (early 14th c.)

24. The Virgin Caressed by Her Parents (detail): Istanbul, Karlye
Djami (early 14th c.)

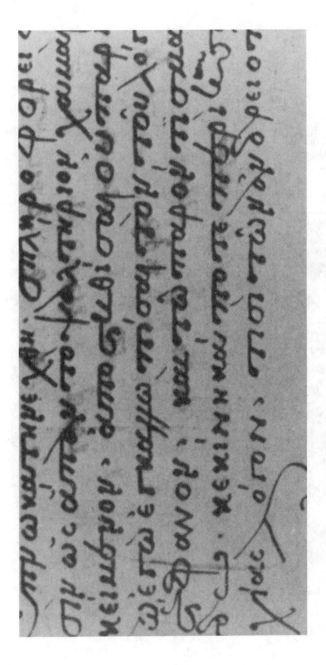

25. Script: Paris, Bibl. Nat., cod. gr. 872, fol. 1r (Ambrosios Hegoumenos, 1560s)

26. The Meeting of Joachim and Anna: Paphos, Monastery of St. Neophytos (16th c.)

IMPERIAL CLAIMS IN THE ROMANIAN PRINCIPALITIES FROM THE FOURTEENTH TO THE SEVENTEENTH CENTURIES NEW CONTRIBUTIONS*

Dimitri Nastase

I have already studied and written about the problem of the imperial idea in the Romanian Principalities in terms of the general claims of the Byzantine Heritage as much as analysed some of its specific areas, of which the ideological area is basic.[1] But in order to provide a correct solution to this problem and clarify all its implications, we first need to know that the imperial idea was born in the Romanian lands long before the fall of Constantinople (1453). This is what I will attempt to show in the first section of this paper. Taking as a starting point the findings of section I, section II will follow the evolution of the imperial idea in the Romanian area after 1453, until the inauguration of the Phanariot's rule, in the beginning of the 18th century. Finally, my conclusions will present the new elements brought to light by this research as well as some of the perspectives thereby opened.

Various written testimonies – chronicles, inscriptions, notes on manuscripts, letters, dedications, etc. – grant to the Romanian princes (as much to Wallachian as to Moldavian ones) the imperial rank.[2] The terms used for this purpose are those of *car'* in the Slavonic documents, βασιλεὺς - even βασιλεὺς καὶ αὐτοκράτωρ - in those written in Greek, and *împărat* (= emperor) in Romanian, as well as their derivatives.[3]

It is however true that these terms never appear in the *intitulatio* of the charters of these princes. In effect, in the preambles of their official acts (written for a long time mainly in Slavonic), the Romanian princes – of Wallachia as well as Moldavia – bear the title of voivode, or often enough of grand voivode, and that of *domn* (<*dominus*, cf. in medieval Latin *domnus*), in Slavonic *gospodin* or *gospodar'*, which would be translated as "prince", keeping in mind its broader sense of "sovereign", or of "lord", which this word also conveys. These titles are accompanied by the abbreviated vocable *Iω (Iôan)*, a title-name rather borrowed from the Bulgarian tsars, which precedes the names of the princes, and also – very often in Wallachia, and exceptionally in Moldavia – by the qualifying term autocrate, in Slavonic *samodăržav-nyi* (with some variants); in the 17th and 18th centuries, this attribute will be expressed in Romanian by several formulas, mainly by that of *singur stăpînitor* (i.e. approximately "sole sovereign" or "sole ruler").[4]

The text itself, however, among the most important of these charters supports the veracity of the above imperial testimonies, either directly, making the aforementioned princes declare that they govern an empire, or indirectly, using some formulas, sometimes veiled, which have the same purpose: to put in evidence the imperial rank of these princes or the imperial character of their sovereign power.[5]

To these titles, formulas and statements, a lot of testimonies bearing an imperial character (even if often secret, concealed), correspond systematically, in parallel and concording series, i.e. testimonies belonging to heraldry, literature, codicology and art.[6] We shall return to this matter below, but it must be noted here that it is exactly these concordances which convinces us that the terms of *car'* and *basileus*, as well as their derivatives, preserve their imperial value when applied to the Romanian princes. Besides, it must be stressed that in general and from the most remote examples that have come down to us, these terms are translated in romanian by *împărat* (= emperor) and its derivatives.[7]

But some of these imperial pieces of evidence – titles included – go back before 1453, or pertain to the same period, which precedes the disappearance of the Byzantine state. Let us discuss the examples we have recorded from the written sources.

In their most solemn "chrysobulls", the Wallachian princes often state that they govern an empire.[8] This statement can be read in a long series of charters, of which the oldest we know is dated to 1464.[9] Even more often, in the same or in similar charters, these voivodes who appear proud to head an empire, also refer to the "emperors and princes before us", even to the "sovereigns, that is to say the emperors, our predecessors".[10] By citing David, prophet as well as "emperor" *(car')*, they still declare there their aspiration to be worthy continuators of the "ancient emperors and princes".[11]

Currently in use from the second half of the 15th century, this declaration, joined to the reference to "the work of David, prophet and emperor", exists already in a donation charter, granted in c. 1400 by the voivode Mircea the Elder (1386-1418) to his foundation of the Cozia monastery, in Lesser Wallachia: in this document, the voivode declares his aspiration to act as successor "of the ancient emperors and princes who have directed the wordly things in benefactions, peacefully,...".[12] But this is not the first of Mircea's charters to have contained it.

Later documents frequently refer to donations made by the same voivode to the Mount Athos monastery of Koutloumous.[13] But offering in 1398 a village to this very monastery, the Wallachian boyar Aldea had already used in his grant the same wording with some differences, yet very suggestive, which prove, in my opinion, that he had borrowed it from a princely document, lost to us: the "emperors and princes" he mentions are not ancient any more and the precise verb, *poslědstvovati,* does not appear.[14] This means that Sire Aldea did not pretend to succeed these monarchs, but intended only to follow their example. Similarly, he abstains from invoking "David, the prophet and emperor". By all the evidence we have here an adaptation of the prince's formula to the status of a nobleman, imitating at his own level the example of his sovereign. This example has to be a donation of Mircea to Koutloumous, thus being somewhat prior to that of Aldea, dated to 21 November 1398.

On the other hand, the example Aldea affirms to follow is that of the "emperors and princes", however omitting the adjective "ancient"! It thus results that in his act this expression refers to the same sovereigns of his country. For this Wallachian boyar of the end of the 14th century, these are, therefore, not only princes, but also emperors. The Wallachian voivodes themselves will further on confirm my explanation of Aldea's reference. Indeed, repeating Mircea's formula insistently, these voivodes will sometimes evoke "those who where, before us, emperors and princes in Wallachia".[15]

But to find the starting point of the ambitious statement of Mircea the Elder, we must go back, to the reign of Vladislav I (called also Vlaicu, 1364 – c. 1377). It is, indeed, inspired by the act of a "new foundation" granted in 1371-2 by this voivode to Koutloumous monastery. In this document, the entire restoration of this monastery, begun at the expense of his father, Nicholas-Alexander of Wallachia (1352-1364), continued and completed by Vlaicu, was equated to the works of the "emperors and princes", benefactors of the Holy Mountain.

Nevertheless, the illustrious hegoumen of Koutloumous, Chariton, as well as the Patriarch of Constantinople, first refused to grant an imperial character for this restoration, and Chariton tried to mention it only as a "princely" work. But at the insistence of the voivode, favoured by certain historical circumstances, they were eventually obliged to accept the formula of the "emperors and princes", i.e. to equate him as well as his father, not only to the princes, but also, and mainly, to the founding emperors on the Holy Mountain.[16]

This assimilation was not an empty word. Truly, the Athonite monastic community, pan-Orthodox and multi-national, was a living symbol of the Christian imperial oecoumene. Within this framework, the convents founded or assisted by various rulers placed them on different levels of the medieval hierarchy of sovereigns.[17] It is thus clear why Vlaicu insisted to obtain that his new foundation of Koutloumous be registered on the "emperors and princes" level, a formula reconciling the actual status of the Wallachian voivodes with the imperial rank, and securing so the fact that the Byzantine Church was obliged to acknowledge them, in the Athonite code, as continuators of the great emperors who had accorded Mount Athos its symbolic value.

This explanation concords with a gift that Vlaicu gave to the Great Lavra's monastery, and which in my opinion exactly "represents" this imperial continuity in the most suitable place and in a visual form, whose power of persuasion was warranted by its sacred character. It is an icon of great dimensions, portraying the founder of the illustrious monastery (and traditionally of the Athonite community), St.

Athanasius. But on the silver-covered margins of this icon, instead of representations depicting the emperors who helped and sustained Athanasius, there appear the portraits of Vlaicu and of his spouse.[18] Naturally – and significantly –, the titles accompanying these effigies imitate carefully the Byzantine imperial *intitulatio:*

a) † ΙΩΑΝΝΗΣ ΒΛΑΝΤΙΣΛΑΒΟΣ ΜΕΓΑΣ ΒΟΕΒΟΔΑΣ ΕΝ Χ(ΡΙΣΤ)Ω ΤΩ Θ(Ε)Ω ΠΙΣΤ(Ο)Σ ΑΥΘ(ΕΝ)Τ(ΗΣ) ΚΕ ΑΥΤΟΚΡΑΤΩΡ ΠΑΣΗΣ ΟΥΓΚΡΟΒΛΑΧΙΑΣ
b) † ΑΝΝΑ ΕΥΣΕΒΕΣΤΑΤΗ ΜΕΓΑΛΗ ΒΟΕΒΟΔΙΣΑ ΕΝ Χ(ΡΙΣΤ)Ω ΤΩ Θ(Ε)Ω ΠΙΣΤΗ ΚΕ ΑΥΤΟΚΡΑΤΟΡΙΣΑ ΠΑΣΗΣ ΟΥΓΚΡΟΒΛΑΧΙΑΣ.[19]

The Romanian voivode intended to portray himself in the icon as a new Nicephorus Phocas!

But the beginning of the Wallachian assistance (and the Romanian in general) to the Holy Mountain is traced back to Vlaicu's father, Nicholas Alexander. Furthermore, according to the metropolitan and hagiographer of the second half of the 14th century, Theophanes of Peritheorion, Gregory the Sinaite had been in correspondence with "the emperors of the world" ("τοὺς βασιλεῖς τῆς γῆς"[20]): in fact, these are the principal Orthodox rulers of South-Eastern Europe, among whom we find Nicholas Alexander of Wallachia in a really imperial company. Indeed, in the text of Theophanes the other "emperors of the world" are Andronicus III Palaeologus, Stephen Dušan of Serbia and John Alexander of Bulgaria.[21]

The testimonies examined until now cast new light to the sovereign status of the Wallachian princes before 1453 and force us to take into account any other document which could possibly be considered connected with this evidence. Such is the case of the title of king, by which some of these princes are mentioned, even if it is mostly attested in western sources, for which this title was more familiar than those they bore in reality.

I have not been able to verify a mention by N. Iorga, asserting that "dans un acte de 1350, Etienne Douchane parle d'Alexandre [i.e. Nicholas Alexander], prince de Valachie, comme du «roi de nos voisins, les Tatars noirs»".[22] But soon after, Vlaicu would have been acclaimed as *kral'* (= king) in Vidin, then occupied by him.[23] As a matter of fact, Catholic hagiographic texts referring to the same occupation, mention him as king.[24] Even in the first years of the 17th century, the chronicler Pietro Luccari from Ragusa will speak of "Vulaico Rè di Valachia".[25]

On the other hand, the memory of Vladislav I – Vlaicu has been preserved in the folklore of the southern Slavs.[26] It is even possible that Cornaro's *Erotokritos* recalls him as king and as emperor. Indeed, in this celebrated poem, the father of the fair Aretousa, Herakles, sometimes entitled king (Ρῆγας) and sometimes emperor (Βασιλέας) of Athens, is warring with a ruler of Wallachia who bears the same titles and is called Vladistratos (Βλαντίστρατος, Βλαδίστρατος). In this name, we can easily recognise that of Vladislav, with the ending grecisised.[27] The two enemies are still "great emperors" ("Βασιλίοι μεγάλοι").[28]

Although Vlaicu kept the west Bulgarian mini-empire of Vidin only for about six months, his brother and successor, Radu I (c. 1377 – c. 1383), will be called prince or, in a variant form, king of Bulgaria, in the chronicle of the Gatari brothers.[29] We reach thus the period of the son of Radu I, Mircea the Elder, who was linked in the above mentioned documents to the "emperors and princes". And, not long ago, a sign on a coin of Mircea appearing next to his effigy, has been interpreted as an abbreviation of the word *car'*.[30] Besides, the Ottoman chronicler Kemal-Pasha-Zade (Ibn-i Kemal) (d. 1535) characterised the same prince as "the king of kings of the Christian countries of his time".[31] But what is a king of kings if not an emperor?[32]

Let us also say something about the Wallachian "imperial monasteries".

As P.Ş. Năsturel observed, the Wallachian monasteries of Tismana and Govora are qualified as imperial, the first by the prince of Wallachia, Vlad the Monk (1481-1495), in 1491, the other by his son and successor, Radu the Great (1495-1508), in two charters, in 1497 and 1500.[33]

To these examples many others can be added, concerning both Danubian Principalities. However, here I shall retain still only those Wallachian cases of the Vişina, Corbii de Piatră and Cotmeana monasteries, which the Wallachian prince, Neagoe Basarab (1512-

1521), honours by the same epithet.[34]

In the first of his aforementioned charters, Radu the Great insists on the antiquity of the monastery of Govora, which he considers as founded by his ancestors. In fact, we do not know the exact date of its foundation. It could have been founded c. 1440 by the Wallachian prince Vlad Dracul,[35] or by Radu I, during the later's rule (c. 1377 – c. 1383).[36] But later on, in the 16th century, other voivodes state in their charters that Govora and its domain had existed "from the time the Romanian Land exists", or "from the beginning of our Romanian Land".[37] At the same period, again in Wallachian princely charters, identical affirmations concern Tismana.[38] On the one hand, the last of the above acts which refer to Govora belongs to the charters where their donors state that they rule an empire and follow the ancient emperors and princes – in this case by assisting the imperial monastery of Govora. On the other hand, the other mentioned monasteries are all actually very old foundations made by Wallachian princes: they go back to the 14th century, except Corbii de Piatră which is even older (end of 13th century). Moreover, recently the initial appearance of this convent with rupestral church has been associated justly with the beginnings of Wallachia.[39] It thus results that "the ancient emperors and princes", whose example the Wallachian voivodes of the second half of the 15th century and 16th century follow by helping the "imperial" monasteries founded "since the beginning" of Wallachia, are their own "ancestors", the voivodes who were founders of these monasteries. It is precisely for this reason that their foundations were "imperial". In this light, the testimony of the Wallachian "imperial monasteries" corroborates the preceding results of our investigation, according to which the imperial claims of the Wallachian princes go back to the 14th century. Besides, these testimonies seem to associate the beginnings of these claims with the birth of the Wallachian state.

Two of these imperial convents, Tismana and Cotmeana, will mainly allow us to approach a heraldic evidence which systematically corresponds to the written testimonies already mentioned. It is the symbol – essentially imperial – of the two-headed eagle, which we find at Tismana in the shape of a metallic simandron, as well as at Cotmeana in the votive mural portrait of Mircea the Elder with his son Michel, on the Mircea's breeches.

It is true that this appearance in the shape of a double-headed eagle simandron, dates only from 1840.[40] But it was made on the order of the hieromonachus Stephen, the author of a *Vita* of Nicodemus, the co-founder (with Radu I) of the monastery, and which was well versed both in the traditions and in the ancient charters of Tismana, which he cites in his hagiography.[41] Moreover, this two-headed eagle of Tismana holds rings in both beaks, that remind us on the one hand certain rather old Byzantine imperial eagles and, on the other, of the ring that the heraldic bird of the Wallachian coat-of-arms holds sometimes.[42] Concerning Mircea's portrait of Cotmeana, it actually is a late repainting, which in fact reproduces the original, painted during the prince's own times, inclusive of the detail of the two-headed eagle.[43]

According to an opinion generally accepted until recently, the two-headed eagle is an element alien to the Romanian heraldry, which appears only sporadically and in an unrelated sequence in this heraldry, from the reign of Mircea the Elder.[44]

Indeed, we have seen that the two-headed eagle appears on the breach-hose of Mircea, in his votive portrait of Cotmeana. It is in the same place (on his knees) that it appears in his votive portrait in the main church of the monastery of Cozia, his most important religious foundation and his burial place. Moreover, another two-headed eagle is carved in relief on the external archivolt of a window of the same church, built c. 1368 (fig. 1).[45]

R. Theodorescu took over and developed an older hypothesis according to which Mircea the Elder adopted more or less temporarily the two-headed eagle as "despotic" emblem, corresponding to the title of despot of the land of Dobrotić, which he assumed in two documents, following the conquest of this region, lying between Danube and the Black Sea.[46] Though at Cozia (and perhaps at Cotmeana) the two-headed eagle appeared also on the garb of Mircea's son, Michael, who succeeded him.[47] Moreover, *jupan* Stan, who was collaterally related to Mircea (most probably his brother), has a seal with a two-headed eagle in 1421, after the death of Mircea and about thirty years after what R. Theodorescu calls the "despotic moment" of this prince.[48] We would say thus in a manner of conclusion to these observations, that during the period considered, the two-headed eagle appears as an emblem of the ruling Wallachian family, represented in our case by Mircea the Elder, his son and successor Michael I, and his parent, probably his only known brother, the *jupan* Stan.

But to have a correct idea concerning the two-headed eagle of the Wallachian princes, we must take into account the fact that Mircea in his turn had inherited it. That is so because the oldest example that I have traced out about it goes back, to the rule of Nicholas Alexander (1352-1364), one of the "emperors of the world". Indeed, as I try to show in a study still in manuscript, in the portraits of Cozia and Cotmeana Mircea's garb does nothing more than repeat that of his great-uncle Nicholas Alexander, the two-headed eagles included, exactly as it has been reproduced in a late document.[49]

In turn, this discovery throws new light on the gilted silver belt-trimmings, appearing in the shape of two-headed eagles, in a treasure found in 1959 in the Wallachian village Olteni.[50] Studying these two-headed eagles, D.V. Rosetti relates them with those of Mircea at Cozia and with others, from the south of the Danube, all of which however are previous to Mircea's reign and rather close to the reign of Nicholas Alexander.[51]

But the belt trimmings of Olteni force us to consider also the decoration of another belt, i.e. that worn by the founder voivode buried in the sepulchre of the Wallachian princes, namely the church of St. Nicholas at Argeş. This voivode is identified with Vladislav I,[52] or, more probably, with Radu I.[53] His belt of cloth is decorated with a repeated motive embroidered with golden threads and pearls, enclosed in lozenges.[54]

R. Theodorescu believes that this motive is just a geometric design, not connected to the two-headed eagle.[55] But other scholars have seen it as stylised two-headed eagles.[56] Moreover, N. Constantinescu has observed that the decoration of this belt is actually a transposition of metal trimmings of a leather belt.[57] This should make us think of the contemporary trimmings of the Olteni treasure. In another respect, we shall later encounter the two-headed eagle in the Romanian lands under aspects that will make it recognisable with difficulty. The stylised decoration of the Argeş belt could thus presage this tendency. It is chiefly for this reason that I retained here this testimony, even if not everybody agrees, and despite the fact that my demonstration can actually dispense with it.[58]

Taken separately, the invoked testimonies – those written on the one hand, and the heraldic on the other – may seem inconclusive. But what must be taken into consideration is the perfect concordance of the two series. Here is indeed the relevant table.

Nicholas Alexander, one of the "emperors of the world"	Nicholas Alexander, two-headed eagles
Vladislav I, "emperor and prince"	Vladislav I or Radu I, possibly two-headed eagles
Mircea the Elder: "emperor and prince"; "king of kings"; possibly "tsar" on his coins	Mircea the Elder, his son Michael I and the *jupan* Stan, two-headed eagles
Cotmeana, "imperial monastery"	Cotmeana, two-headed eagles
Tismana, "imperial monastery"	Tismana, two-headed eagle

Thus confronted, the two kinds of evidence cross-check and clarify each other reciprocally with only one possible conslusion:

The above titles bear an imperial meaning and the corresponding two-headed eagles appear with their import as an imperial heraldic symbol.

Moving now to Moldavia, in the period of interest, we encounter only once a formula reminding that of "ancient emperors and princes" of the Wallachian charters (and evoking David, too). Indeed, in 1384 in a charter to the "Dominican Friars" of the church of St. John the Baptist in the town of Siret, the voivode of Moldavia, Peter I Muşat (c. 1374 – c. 1392), states that he follows "sanctorum regum et principum exemplo qui suis muneribus et donariis cultum et servitium devinum ampliaverunt et multipliciter augmentaverunt, sicut *David et alii reges et principes,* qui tam in veteri testamento, *quam in novo fuerunt sibi similes".*[59] As it appears, the emperors and princes of the Greek and Slavonic documents that we have examined, are transposed here in the wording of the Latin Bible, where David is only king. But the latter can only be Christian rulers, a fact worth keeping in mind. On this occasion we must also note, that in the beginning of the 17th century, P. Luccari – the one who referred to Vlaicu of Wallachia as king – stated in his chronicle that the emperor of the Greeks had conferred the title of king of Bogdan I (c. 1360 – c. 1365), who was the first independent prince of Moldavia.[60]

A few decades after Peter I, an epitrachilion made after 1425 on the order of the Moldavian prince Alexander the Good (1399 or 1400-1432), presents him assuming the title of αὐτοκράτωρ πάσης Μολδοβλαχίας καὶ παραθαλασ(σ)ίας, in an "inscription grecque dont – according to N. Iorga – le style politique même est celui des empereurs".[61] Besides, the court-chronicle of Stephen the Great (1457-1504), the most important prince of Moldavia, accorded globally the title of *Moldavstii carie* ("The Moldavian emperors"), in addition to that of voivodes, to the rulers of that country, beginning precisely with Alexander the Good.[62]

The justification of this imperial title is revealed to us by the manuscript *codices* containing the Moldavian chronicles written in Slavonic, and particularly by one of these chronicles, compiled about 1512 and entitled *Khrystianstii carie* ("The Christian emperors").[63]

This text starts with a list of the eastern emperors from Constantine the Great to Manuel II Palaeologus (1391-1425), the somewhat older contemporary of Alexander the Good. An account of the Ottoman progress in the Balkans follows. This narrative first opposes symbolically the Ottoman penetration in Europe to the "beginning" of Moldavia, and then, the fall and death of the Balkan rulers, to the long reign of Alexander the Good. We stress that the latter is the only Moldavian prince mentioned by the compiler, except his own prince, Bogdan II (1504-1517) and voivode Dragoş (1352-1354, or 1359 – c. 1361), the "founder" of the "Moldavian land".

Alexander the Good is the prince during whose reign the Ottoman expansion reached the Moldavian border and this symbolic language aims to suggest that by divine will "the Moldavian land" was destined from its "beginning" to repel the invaders and that its princes are the heirs of all the Orthodox rulers of the states conquered by or submitted to the Turks.[64]

This "succession" includes also the emperors of Constantinople as is indicated by the fact that for the Moldavian literati the last Byzantine emperor was not Constantine XI (or XII, d. 1453), but Manuel II (d. 1425).[65] We know that in 1424 Manuel II was forced to accept the suzerainty of the sultan Murat II and to pay tribute.[66] Precisely then, under Alexander the Good, the long confrontation between Moldavia and the Turks began.[67]

But in principle the victory against the Infidel was ideologically conditioned by the strict observance of the true faith, i.e. Orthodoxy. This preoccupation with respect to Orthodoxy explains the existence of numerous anti-Latin "treatises" along with the chronicles in the same Moldavian manuscripts.[68] Indeed, John VIII, successor of Manuel II, was the Unionist basileus who prepared and accepted the Florence Union (1439).[69] Finally, Constantine XI (XII) was also a pro-unionist and a union of the Churches was proclaimed again, in Hagia Sophia in 1452, just before the final siege of the capital, by Mehmet II.

These are the principal reasons why the Moldavians considered that the last two (real) Byzantine emperors had forfeited the imperial dignity, for which the Moldavian literati felt justified to transmit it after Manuel II to their own princes. Thus in the vision of those literati, the "Moldavian emperors" of their chronicles only succeed the "Christian emperors" of the chronicle with this title.

These results of my research could give us a key to explain also the testimonies examined above referring to the imperial rank of the Wallachian princes.

A century before Moldavia – that is, during the "imperial and princely" reign of Mircea the Elder – Wallachia already possessed a historical text which has a striking analogy with the Moldavian chronicle of "the Christian emperors". It is a chronicle from the beginning of the 15th century recounting the Ottoman progress from 1296 to 1413 and "at the same time illustrating the fall of the Balkan peoples under the Turkish domination".[70] This chronicle gives the Ottoman victories over the Bulgarians and Serbs the significance of God's castigation. Quite the contrary, the same text directs the divine favour on Wallachia and especially on Mircea the Elder.[71]

But in this chronicle, written before the fall of Constantinople, Wallachia shares this favour with the Byzantine capital. In effect, the Wallachian successes against the Turks are there symbolically associated with the miraculous outcome of the long blockade by which Bayazit I besieged Constantinople without success from 1394 to 1402.

It must be stressed that according to the symbolic code of the chronicle, this association is not related to the Byzantine state but only to its capital "protected by God". To explain this distinction it is enough to say that the chronicle under discussion adopts a determined anti-Latin stance.[72] In general, this attitude did not characterize the emperors, partisans on the union with Rome, but the Byzantine clergy and was elevated to the level of a political conception by the "Orthodox opposition" of Byzantium, organised and directed by the supreme leaders of this clergy.[73] It is from the point of view of this opposition that our chronicle sees Constantinople, which maintains itself in divine favour as capital of Orthodoxy and seat of the Oecumenical Patriarch, as a "Holy City".[74]

The progress of the Ottoman Turks in the Balkans coincides with a crumbling process of the states in that area. This process drew the remnants of the Byzantine empire as well as Serbia (after the death of tsar Dušan, in 1355) and Bulgaria, transforming them into a multitude of unstable principalities, an easy prey for the Moslem conqueror.[75] Moreover, efforts to reunite the South Slavonic states, or, at least, to establish on their ruins the hegemony of some dynast, did exist. I shall mention here those partially successful that happened in Serbia by the Mrnjaević brothers – the kral Vukašin and the despot Uglješa – and then by the prince Lazar Khrebljanović.[76]

It must also be noted that, in spite of the breaking-up of the Balkan empires, various princes ruling over their ruins continued to flaunt the imperial title. Such is the case of the two rival half brothers, the Bulgarian tsars John Šišman (1371-1393) and John Stracimir (1365-1396), the first ruling at Tirnovo, the other at Vidin.[77] Neither did the imperial idea die in Serbia with tsar Dušan, but there it also adapted, so to speak, to the crumbling of his state. Thus his son and successor Uroš IV (1355-1371), although he ruled only in name, nevertheless retained the title of tsar, while Dušan's half brother, Symeon, whose rule was reduced to Thessaly only, did not hesitate to call himself "basileus and autocrator of the Romans and Serbs and of all the Albanians".[78] On the other hand, G. Ostrogorsky has shown the imperial pretentions of the Serbian "despot and autocrator" of Serres, Uglješa (d. 1371).[79] The opinion that their power has an imperial character will be found again with other Serbian dynasts. The most important among them was the "great prince" Lazar (d. 1389), as is his title in a contemporary text which affirms at the same time that he kept the *sceptrum* of the "Serbian *empire*".[80]

Uglješa as well as Lazar, played realy important roles against the Ottoman invader. The attempts they directed would nevertheless end in disasters, where they lost their lives, the first in 1371, in the battle of Maritsa, and the other 18 years later, in the battle of Kossovo Polje.

In the meantime, on the other side of the natural barrier of the Danube, the Romanian principalities of Wallachia and Moldavia witnessed rapid development.[81] This impetus and their protected geographical position would secure them an increasingly important role in the framework of the policy of coalitions among the Orthodox princes, promoted by the Patriarchate of Constantinople.

The first of the Romanian princes who supported this policy was Nicholas Alexander of Wallachia, and it is under such circumstances that the patriarche Callistus I elevated in 1359 his Church to a metropolis.[82]

As D.A. Zakythinos has observed, in that time, "Byzance restant une unité idéale, une pléiade de principautés semblent avoir partagé la gestion du pouvoir".[83] This subtle remark can be applied to the policy patronized by the Oecumenical Patriarchate. Indeed, it seems that in the supreme effort to unite the Orthodox princes in the face of the Turkish threat, but also in view of the "Latin" menace, the "political Orthodoxy" comes to a sort of theoretical reconstitution of "the Christian empire", under the collegial government of the "emperors", more or less in coalition, who rule over its various fragments. This is what the anti-unionist Metropolitan Theophanes of Peritheorion means when he admits the existence of several "emperors of the world", amongst them the Romanian prince Nicholas Alexander!

The rise of Wallachia continued under Vladislav I and Radu I and reached a climax under Mircea the Elder, after 1396. During the blockade of Constantinople by Bayazit (1394-1402) the voevode won several victories against the Turks (in 1394 or 1395, 1397, 1400).[84]

In 1399 or 1400 he had also a very important success in his policy of assembling the Romanian lands.[85] At that time Mircea succeeded in deposing the Moldavian voivode Iuga (1398-1399/1400) and in setting up in his place a prince according to his own interest, Alexander, nicknamed later "the Good" (1399/1400-1432). Starting with this moment, and probably until the end of Mircea's reign, Moldavia will remain in a dependent condition to the Wallachian voivode.[86]

This authority should make Mircea a particulary important factor in the eyes of the Oecumenical Patriarchate, separated from the Moldavian princes by a long conflict.[87] And indeed, it is not by chance that it was Alexander the Good who, in 1401, put an end to this crisis which had lasted for fifteen years.[88]

It is just during this period of efflorescence that the testimonies examined above put Mircea the Elder among the "emperors and princes". Truly, we have seen that it is around 1400 that he bestowed to Cozia monastery the charter containing this formula which he already employed shortly before 21 November 1398.[89]

But it was the consequences of the battle of Angora (1402) that carried Mircea to the peak of his power. In the years following this battle the friendship and alliance of the Wallachian prince began to be sought, not only by the Serbian despot Stephen Lazarović and by the king of Hungary, Sigismund of Luxemburg, but even by various emirs and Turkish notables, as well as by pretenders to Bayazit's throne. It is during this period of crisis and breaking up of the Ottoman empire that, thanks to his skilful policy, Mircea became for a short period the arbiter of affairs in the Balkans.[90]

Therefore it is not surprising that later Ottoman chroniclers consider him "the king of kings of the Christian countries of his time";[91] or, according to Leunclavius, "among the Christians, the mightiest prince and the most valiant".[92]

But the bellicose policy and the ferocity of sultan Musa (1411-1413), whom Mircea helped to conquer the throne, put up a strong reaction. Thus Musa soon yielded to his brother Mehmet I, called for assistance and supported by Manuel II.[93] As it is known, in keeping good relations with Byzantium, Mehmet I (1413-1421) took advantage to reestablish the unity of the Ottoman Empire and consolidate its might. As early as 1414, he directed his agressiveness against Wallachia by sending an expedition which devastated the country.[94] Isolated, it seems, by the unstability of his Hungarian and Polish allies, in 1415, Mircea paid tribute to the Turks for the first time.[95] This did not hinder him to foment troubles in the Balkans by sending his troops to support revolts.[96] But in 1417, Mehmet I organized a big campaign of repression against Wallachia. Defeated, the voivode had to accept not only to pay tribute, but also to give to the sultan members of his family as hostages, and troops in case of war.[97] Early in 1418, Mircea the Elder died.

Under the short reign (1418-1420) of his son Michael I – an

adolescent – the Turks once more laid Wallachia waste, and annexed Dobrudja.[98] With this last territorial enlargement, the Ottoman Empire reached the Moldavian frontier and in 1420 its troops besieged Cetatea Albă, a stronghold and key maritime harbour of that country. But the long confrontation of the second Romanian state with the Turks was only beginning.

Attaining independence towards 1360, Moldavia soon extended its frontiers, from the Eastern Carpathians, northward and eastward, where they became fixed on the Dniestr river, and southward, reaching the Black Sea.

The first stage of this progress coincides with the reign of Peter I Muşat (c. 1374 – c. 1392). The new territories gained by this prince included in the North "the land of Sepenic".[99] It is even possible that the Moldavian voivodes before Peter I claimed or even tried to occupy this region.[100] But what is of interest here is that Sepenic belonged to the Little-Russian principality of Galič, which Louis I of Anjou, king of both Hungary and Poland, had occupied, entrusting it c. 1372 to Wladislaw of Oppeln. In my opinion, the aims of the Moldavian princes over Galician territories go back to this period and particularly to this incident. A few years later, Peter I Muşat lent an important sum of money to the king of Poland, Wladislaw Jagellon, who accepted to pledge the city of Galič and the surrounding country to him.[101]

But from the 13th century the prince of Galič, Daniel Romanović (d. 1264), had received from the Pope the title of king and even before that, the king of Hungary, Andrew II (1206-1235), was calling himself also *Galiciae Lodomeriaquae rex.* Moreover, the chronicle of that same Daniel Romanović, styled *car'* his father and predecessor, Roman Mstislavić.[102] Furthermore, in its Galician version, the old Russian chronicle *(Povest' vremennykh let)* is entitled *Letopisec' Ruskikh carei.*[103] This compells us to remember the *Moldavstii carie* of the older Moldavian *letopisec* (= chronicle in Romanian).[104] We are thus entitled to think that the Moldavian voivodes challenged the kings of Poland and Hungary for the right of succession to the Galician "Kings" and "Tsars", and that is it to them that the declaration about 1384, of Peter I Muşat alluded when he stated that he follows the "example of the saintly kings and princes" who resembled David, in the New Testament.[105] As for the title of *Moldavstii carie,* one would think that it *also* alluded to the same claim. This is at least what makes us believe, on the one hand, in the striking similarity with the title of ancient Russian-Galician chronicle, and, on the other, in the fact that during the time when their chronicle was written and expanded, the Moldavian voivodes lay claim insistently, even by force of arms, to the region of Pocutia, that is the part of the ancient kingdom of Galicia on the borderland of their country.[106] This is how this region first became a Moldavian possession during the rule of Alexander the Good who according to the same chronicle was the first of the "Moldavian emperors".

We also know, and it is a support in the same direction, that Peter I Muşat could impose his authority on the Metropolitan of Galić as far as to make him consecrate two Moldavian bishops, of whom one, Joseph, a relative of the prince, was entrusted with the direction of the Moldavian Metropolitanate, in spite of the opposition of the Patriarchate of Constantinople.

This is how a conflict between Moldavia and the Great Church was born, a conflict which will continue under the following voivodes and will last for about fifteen years, until 1401, when the Patriarchate accepted Joseph as Metropolitan.[107] In my view, the solution of the conflict was fostered, as I pointed out above, by the influence Mircea the Elder of Wallachia had over the new prince of Moldavia, but mainly by the need that Constantinople, being besieged by the Turks, had of both Wallachia and Moldavia.

Judging by the few documents we have, we can consider that nothing disturbed the relations between Alexander the Good and the Byzantine Church, based on the reconciliation of 1401. On the contrary, the contacts seem to have been very friendly. At least this may be inferred, among others, by a charter of Alexander, dated to 16 September 1408, in which, in addition to the usual stereotype maledictions of the penal clause, we also have those of the Oecumenical Patriarch, a detail most unusual.[108]

Beginning under the circumstances described above, the reign of Alexander the Good will be the longest any Moldavian ruler had attained until then. His prosperous and rather peaceful government, along with stability brought notable progress to Moldavia, which played a most important role in central and eastern Europe.[109]

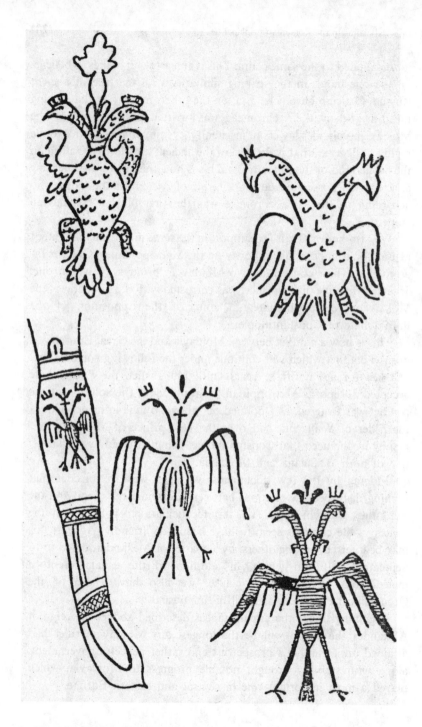

1. Two–headed eagles from foundations or portraits of Mircea the
Elder (After P. Chihaia)

2. A Wallachian coat of arms of Matthew Basarab (Govora code 1640)

The recovery of its might, enabled the Ottoman Empire not long afterwards to turn also against Byzantium. This new wave of aggression began with the accession of Murat II (1421), who in 1422 came to lay siege to Constantinople. Although the sultan was not successful in conquering the city, the basileus had to pay tribute once again.[110]

As early as 1423, John VIII left Constantinople in quest for help in Italy and Hungary. Following the death of his father (1425) he openly took the lead of the Unionist party and after negotiations which would last out until 1439, the union would be proclaimed in Florence on 6 July of the same year.

I called to mind these well known facts only to emphasise the analogy with the events of the previous Ottoman expansion, concluded at the battle of Angora. With the difference – among others – that now historical fate gave Moldavia the dangerous privilege to be in the first row of the Orthodox states fighting against the Turks.

Since the march of events resulting in this situation is identical to that registered in the manner I indicated by the "chronicle of the Christian emperors", we can conclude that the title of "Moldavian emperors" expressed a real claim based on the justifications that this chronicle acquaints us with, and that this title, at least up to a certain point, was accepted by the Church of Byzantium.

The death of Alexander the Good was followed by a period of struggles for the throne and in 1456 Moldavia paid tribute to the Turks for the first time.[111]

Three years earlier, Mehmet II had conquered Constantinople, thus putting an end to the Byzantine state, and was destined to install there the power of the sultans for almost five centuries.

In the following years the Turks liquidated the last precarious possessions still in power of various of Byzantine and south Slavic dynasties: in 1459 Moravian Serbia, in 1460 the Despotate of the Morea and in 1461 the Empire of Trebizond.

Now, it is in the same period that the Wallachian princes started adding systematicaly to the old reference to "ancient emperors and princes" the statement that they ruled an empire. Indeed, it is in 1464 that we have encountered for the first time a Wallachian charter bearing this statement, and this practice will only multiply later.[112] At the same time, the chronicles of Moldavia attribute to Stephen the Great (1457-1504), and then to the Moldavian princes of the 16th century, the title of *car'*, in addition to their usual titles.[113] Lastly, in sufficient other cases, from the second half of the 15th century to the 17th, in Wallachia as well as in Moldavia those last titles are supplemented by the imperial title and by other formulas of imperial character, in addition by those already mentioned.[114]

A key contribution for the explanation of these titles and formulas is provided by iconographic evidence.[115]

This imperial iconographic language is the counterpart of the narrative sources.

Like the "chronicle of the Christian emperors", the chronicles of Stephen the Great and of the Moldavian princes of the 16th century are integrated in manuscript *codices,* in which they are written symbolically in continuation of universal chronographies. Thus the history of the "Moldavian emperors" is presented as extending the history of the Byzantine emperors.[116]

In spite of the loss of the Slavonic chronicles of Wallachia, we must surmise that they circulated integrated in *codices* organised in the same way, and attributing the same imperial succession to the Wallachian princes.[117]

In very precise and complete expressions, these pretentions are also formulated in another code, particularly appropriate to this occasion: the Heraldic code. Indeed, in the coat of arms and in the emblems of the Romanian princes we shall find again after 1453 various symbols bearing an imperial character, especially one which is already familiar to us before this date: the two-headed eagle.

A double-headed eagle of great dimensions is represented on an embroidery donated by Neagoe Basarab of Wallachia in 1515/1516 to the Great Lavra of Athos, where it still stands.[118] The same emblem reappears in the votive portrait of Neagoe, in the church of the monastery of Argeş.[119] Let us also note that on the long dress of the voivode, the large two-headed eagle is placed on the same level with that on the western style hose of Mircea the Elder, but in a such way as to show only half of it.[120]

The garb of Neagoe in this portrait is in fact that of a Byzantine emperor.[121] As for the conventual church of Argeş – which, right or wrong, is the most celebrated monument of ancient Romanian architecture – it had been rebuilt anew, along with the whole monastery, by Neagoe Basarab.[122] To stress the importance he gave, Neagoe did not content himself to state in a chrysobull he conferred to the monastery on that occasion, that he rules an empire and also to put there all the other formulas, imperial in character, which we know: he repeated this act in the votive inscription which he set well exposed on the west façade of the church, next to its main gate.[123]

After Neagoe Basarab, and till the last decade of the 16th century, the Wallachian princes seem not to have used anymore the two-headed eagle. At least there is no testimony to allow us to suppose the contrary.

But this does not mean that the two-headed eagle was forgotten in Wallachia. We have seen that it was probably in 1526 that the portrait of Neagoe Basarab was painted in the conventual church of Argeş. In 1542/1543 the mural portraits of Mircea the Elder and his son Michael were painted in the new and elegant church of the monastic hospital of Cozia, both decorated with double-headed eagles.[124] In 1563 the Neagoe's portrait of Argeş was copied, its half two-headed eagle included, in the narthex of the important church of the Snagov monastery.[125]

At the Iviron monastery at Athos, there survives an icon of a somewhat later date, with a portrait of a youth with a long dress, strewn with two-headed eagles. This youth is Radu Mihnea, who would reign alternately in Wallachia and Moldavia. He was the illegitimate son of the Wallachian prince, Mihnea II, with Vişa, who used to sign as princess Vişa.[126] His father converted to Islam in 1591, and Radu is said to have been intrusted to the monks of Iviron so as avoid the same fate. But N. Iorga observed that this scheme aimed only at preparing the dynastic access of the child to the throne which his father was obliged to vacate on account of his change of faith.[127] Apparently his portrait with the two-headed eagles must be understood in the same light, but it gives too an imperial sense to this wish for heritage.

At the same time, Stephen the Deaf (1591-1592), the ephemeral voivode, who referred to his predecessors as "emperors and princes in Wallachia", used a "bizarre sceau à aigle bicéphale portant une couronne royale".[128]

The 16th century ended with Michael the Brave's epic. This Wallachian prince (1593-1601) succeeded to get rid of the Ottoman yoke and unite – albeit only for a brief moment (1599-1600) – the lands inhabited by Romanians, under his sceptre.

The first act of this union was the conquest of Transylvania, which Michael effected in October 1599. But on August 28 of that year, the Wallachian voivode, while carefully preparing his Transylvanian campaign, conferred to the Athonite monastery of Simonopetra a very solemn chrysobull confirming an important donation he had already made to this monastery.[129] On the head of this act, instead of Wallachia's coat of arms, there is a floral ornament which in fact is a stylised two-headed eagle, hidden under this decorative appearance.[130] To throw light on its meaning, Michael stated in a charter, that he "held with *imperial* glory his father's throne", and in another charter he referred to "the emperors who were before us".[131] On later occasion it was about the "empire" (i.e. reign as emperor) of Michael.[132]

Shortly after Michael the Brave, Radu Mihnea reigned several times between 1601 and 1626, sometimes in Wallachia, other times in Moldavia, establishing in fact his hegemony on both principalities.[132]a And if we give credence to the Moldavian chronicler Miron Costin (1633-1691), the wish expressed at Iviron had been accomplished at least in part. Indeed, according to Miron Costin, the reign of Radu Mihnea – whom he calls "the Great" – resembled that of an emperor and not of a prince.[133] And it is not by chance that in his praise of Radu Mihnea, after the above statement, the Moldavian chronicler cites in connection with him "The Life of Alexander the Great" of Plutarch and refers to the merits "of the emperors and the princes".[134]

A few years after the death of Radu Mihnea (1626), the throne of Wallachia was occupied by Matthew Basarab (1632-1654). Starting with his reign, the Wallachian princes regularly used the two-headed eagle, but its presence has escaped modern historians, because of its cryptic representation. This strange two-headed eagle, crested in general by an imperial crown, is partly covered by the official coat of arms and by a characteristic system of scrolls organised in baroque pseudo-cartouch (fig. 2).[135] Under this disguise, the two-headed eagle would thenceforth be revived systematically until the end of the period", during which this camouflage would sometimes be altered in new variants.[136]

Nevertheless, to remain within our defined chronological limits, some regular two-headed eagles of the second half of the 17th century and beginning of 18th century from Wallachia were previously known to scholars, namely those of the voivodes Mihnea III Radu (1658-1659), Şerban Cantacuzenus (1678-1688), Constantin Brancovan (1688-1714), Stephen Cantacuzenus (1714-1715/6). Adding to the specimens already known our disguised two-headed eagles, we obtain *a perfect continuity* of the use the Wallachian princes made of this sign, from Matthew Basarab (1632-1654) to the end of autochthonous reigns (1716).[137]

In Moldavia, two-headed eagles appear in the 15th century – perhaps already before the fall of Constantinople –, as heraldic decorative motifs in princely residences.[138] But it is from the second half of the 16th century that the two-headed eagle becomes more familiar to the Moldavians as a symbol of their princes. Its use reached its climax in Moldavia during the reigns of Basil Lupu (1634-1653) and of his son Stephen Lupu (1659-1661).[139] Thereafter, it will continue to appear more or less regularly. It will be the last autochtonous Moldavian prince before the Phanariots, the learned Demeter Cantemir (1710-1711) who seems to have introduced in his official seal the concealed two-headed eagle, as in the case of Wallachia.[140]

A correlation of all these two-headed eagles with the other examined testimonies sufficiently proves that following the fall of Constantinople, as well as before, the two-headed eagles of the Romanian princes constituted the heraldic expression of their imperial concept. It is precisely the need to conceal the imperial claim it contains which explains why the voivodes of Wallachia and Moldavia had been constrained to camouflage their two-headed eagles. Also its other possible particular meanings – ecclesiastical, family, etc. – do not preclude the other fundamental meaning, the imperial, but on the contrary they protect it by producing an alibi. We can thus state that the two-headed eagle of the Romanian princes has in general a *crypto-imperial character.*

*

A historical concept which we owe particularly to Nicholas Iorga, prolongs Byzantine life long after 1453, up to the Hellenic Revolution of 1821. This conception is now currently named with the suggestive title of "Byzantium after Byzantium", which the great historian gave to its synthesis that he published in 1935.[141]

Iorga ascribes a very important place to Wallachia and Moldavia in this survival and confers to a certain category of Romanian princes the heritage of the Byzantine emperors. But, according to him, this inheritance was limited to the cultural and ecclesiastical areas and this claim would start only towards the middle of the 16th century. Until that date, the Romanian princes would have ruled their countries with a specific sovereign conception, say, voivodal, which would have been far from aiming at the imperial title.[142]

It is only after they had been forced to recognize the authority of the sultan and to frequent his capital that these princes could be acquainted with the imperial tradition of Byzantium and, entering in solid attachments – of family and interests – with the Greek circles of Constantinople, became "byzantinized" too.[143] It is in this train of circumstances, which appeared in the 16th century, that they would have acquired a sovereign quality which their predecessors, elevated to the throne by the will of the boyars and of the "land", presumably did not possess: that of "basileis", in the limited meaning indicated above.[144]

According to this theory by Iorga, the old voivodal conception of sovereignty was not destined to disappear because of these changes. On the contrary, in his writings it will play, for the later periods, an extremely important role: that of a term specifically and genuinely Romanian, opposed to the new imperial conception which would affect the behaviour of only certain princes, mostly of non-Romanian extraction, and who would keep up to the end the seal of its origin and foreign ties.[145] On the other hand, Iorga was of the opinion, as all Romanian historians, that the princes of Wallachia and Moldavia never pretended to bear the same imperial title.[146]

But the testimonies we presented – and which could be still furthered – seem to put us in front of a phenomenon which started long before "Byzantium *after* Byzantium", a historical concept which is therefore not sufficient to explain it. On the other hand the cultural and ecclesiastical limits in which Iorga placed his concept are overthrown by the fact that some activities which define it proved to have a precise political role, in the service of projects for the liberation from the Ottoman yoke.[147]

Thus, all this seems to give the imperial idea in the Romanian lands new significances and a new chronology, which go beyond "Byzance après Byzance".

So, as we have seen, it is in the second half of the 14th century that we can register imperial claims manifested by the Romanian princes.[148] These pretentions are tightly connected with the anti-Ottoman coalitions and resistance and are based on the idea of the imperial-Orthodox and south-Slavic legacies. But, primary in their ideology, we also find the anti-Latin factor, corresponding to a contest against the catholic kings of Hungary and Poland. These claims never had an official character. Nevertheless, they were expressed as early as that time, above all by adding to the princely title an imperial one, of a restrained but persistent use, and by adopting corresponding emblems, among which the two-headed eagle had the first place.

After the fall of Byzantium and of all other Christian States south of the Danube, the only remaining Orthodox rulers liable to take arms against the Turks were the voivodes of Wallachia and Moldavia. In giving their armed actions a sense of providential mission, these rulers were advancing the idea of a leadership of imperial rank, which they had already assumed while claiming an imperial Byzantine succession in its broadest oecumenical sense.[149]

Even when they eventually had to accept the burdensome suzerainty of the sultan, they never renounced the imperial character of their standing. However, the new set-up required some adjustments which, when in operation would give the concept a typical *crypto-imperial* character, manifest throughout the duration of the Ottoman domination.[150]

In spite of the steady worsening of this domination, the Romanian principalities succeeded in preserving an internal autonomy and their princes were always looked upon by their subjects as real sovereigns, namely "God-anointed" sovereigns. Moreover, it was this crypto-imperial policy which acted as a link between the Moldo-Wallachian rulers and the Greek circles of Constantinople. Actually, although paradoxically, it is after their subjection to the Turks that these princes could better advance their imperial status in their dealings with the authorized representatives of the Byzantine surviving vestiges.[151]

It is only now that the imperial concept of the Romanian princes joins the beginning of what Iorga called "Byzantium after Byzantium". Thus, what the great historian has defined as a starting point, was in fact a tardy phase of a long and complex process covering very broad grounds.

Naturally, such considerations are bound to raise a set of totally different data to the problem of Byzantine survival, and the light cast into the matter by Iorga suffers a substantial change of quality in the examination of the phenomena brought to attention by him, for the period he studied.

In effect, it was then that came into existence the phenomenon which I shall tentatively call "the Christian Crypto-empire" under Ottoman domination, a real *imperium in imperio*.[152] This very particular state structure, whose groundworks had been laid before to the fall of Constantinople, was to be operational until 1821. It took advantage in the first place of the autonomy of the Danubian Principalities, where the Romanian dominant class ruled, as well as of the favorable conditions to the Greeks who would subsequently live in the Phanar, in having succeeded beneficial relations with the Sublime Porte.[153] Moreover, it took advantage of other "local autonomies", among them that of Mount Athos, which projected a prestigious status as a symbol of the Christian Oecumenical Empire.[154]

It is ascertained that the imperial concept of which the Romanian princes considered themselves the bearers, had to become a real status through a series of intermediate stages. The first stage meant to unite the whole of the Romanian territories under one single sceptre, and thus create a solid base for a liberation offensive in the Balkans. It is consequently natural that, from the beginning, a conflict for hegemony in the Romanian area was to occur between the voivodes of Wallachia and those of Moldavia, and that their imperial title carried, in the first place, the quality of exclusive leadership in this area. In fact, for centuries one can note the development of such a conflict, which could be described as *the medieval phase of the Romanian people's fight for national unity*.[155] It is within this aspect that one should consider the sustained efforts of the voivodes of these two lands to impose their authority upon each other. This same reason explains the voivodes' efforts to extend their authority over Transylvania, and to this end they employed the Orthodox Church, which advanced and supported inside the Romanian population of this country the idea of their being its real sovereigns, in their capacity of "Orthodox Emperors".[156]

From this point of view, the action of Michael the Brave appears no longer as an isolated instance, but as the most important attempt of a Romanian prince to realize through military action the *traditional* projects of the imperial idea we study, of gathering under one sceptre all Romanian territories. On the other hand, it incited the Balkan peoples in getting prepared for subsequent liberation movements coveted for a long time. This is the reason why, in 1600, the year when he accomplished the ephemeric unity of Romanian lands, Michael was expected to launch a massive offensive against the Turks that would end in his own proclamation as Emperor of Constantinople.[157]

As it appears, the opposition in the Romanian lands of a "voivodal idea" to an "imperial idea" is only an apparent one, both ideas being just two aspects of the same problem. Of course, this reasoning is valid not only in relation to Michael the Brave's politics. Actually, as already stated, the great merit of his exploits was that of achieving the first step – and the only one which promised a great future – of a broader programme which, along with its alternatives and progressive stages, had always been adopted by the Romanian princes in general. Thus, from the standpoint of their programme and conception of their sovereign powers, these princes could not be classified according to their origin and background, since both "autochtonous" and "foreign" shared the same imperial claims.

*

Evidently, the imperial idea that I have examined here concerns primarily the historian researching the Romanian past. It has been noted that the behaviour of the one or the another voivode was the particular expression of a general and *sui generis* imperial concept, which could set them within a suitable context. It is this very concept which can produce a fundamental appraisal, in fact the simplest, clearest and most logical way of explaining all the imperial elements of

Romanian history, from the Middle Age until the Modern time.

It so happens that such elements can be found in abundance. I have already so far examined in my work several instances in the light of the aforementioned concept; considerably more elements can be added, whose intrinsic imperial value no one could contest, and which might belong to such diverse fields as iconography, legislation, heraldry and folklore.[158]

But I must especially insist on the fact that, in spite of the unavoidable "local realities" of various political trends which divided the Romanian territories, the imperial ideology of the voivodes had always considered these territories as one single national entity, a large "Romanian land" covering the Romanian ethnical and historical area as a whole, supported in its accomplishment's efforts by a stable, permanent ideological programme.

But the same concept also concerns the history of late Byzantine period and its neo-Hellenic continuation during the "Turcocratia". In fact, the imperial idea of the Romanian voivodes was essentially founded upon an ideology typically Byzantine. As such, this idea helps bring to surface some hitherto unknown or less familiar details relating to the final phasis of Byzantium. Among others, it is worth mentioning the part played then by Mount Athos and the Patriarchate of Constantinople through their representatives – metropolitans and other Greek clergymen – in the Orthodox countries.[159] During the following period, the concept which I have termed 'crypto-imperial' continued to grant the Oecumenical Patriarchate a key political position, which is the proof of a close Greek-Romanian collaboration, whose Greek side naturally belongs to Greek history. And this is an almost totally unexplored area.

What is left to be done may well be a broadening of research on the crypto-imperial Greek activities in many Hellenic areas. It should be reminded that, if the Romanian provinces were the most important Christian autonomous areas of the Ottoman system, they were not the only ones: Let us only mention such religious-territorial formations as those on Mount Athos; or the self-government of the famous region of Mane.

It goes without saying that the survival of the "Christian Empire" proposes an ideological and political status also valid for other

Christian peoples of the Balkans, even of the Ottoman state itself. It remains to establish to what extent and with what consequences we can attach to this survival the vestiges which these peoples were able to safeguard out of their national and religious existence and, in the first place, their own "local autonomies", of which the most important was the south-Slav autonomy of Montenegro.

From the point of view of Turkish history, no less, these phenomena bring forth new and considerable problems, such as those of the lengths to which the Ottoman system would go in tolerating – even exploiting – the existence among its Christian subjects of such forms of "imperial life", in its aspects implying the acceptance of this system.[160]

Thus, as in many of my other studies relating to the problems discussed here, my enquiry ends with perspectives that should be further explored within the frame of a modern and complex programme. No doubt, such a research would cast new light on more than one aspect either unknown or not known enough, of the historical areas with which this research is concerned.[161]

NOTES

* I would like to extend my thanks to those who contributed to the realization of my study's English version, and especially Mircea Ciulli and Alexis Savvides.

1. Especially, D. Nastase, *Ideea imperială în ţările române. Geneza şi evoluţia ei în raport cu vechea artă românească (secolele XIV - XVI)*, Athens 1972 (Fondation Européenne Dragan, 9); *id., L'héritage impérial byzantin dans l'art et l'histoire des pays roumains*, Milan 1976 (hereafter, Nastase, *L'héritage); id.,* "L'idée impériale dans les pays roumains et «le crypto-empire chrétien» sous la domination ottomane. Etat et importance du problème", *Σύμμεικτα* 4 (1981), 201-250 (hereafter, Nastase, "L'idée impériale"); *id.,* "La survie de «l'empire des chrétiens» sous la domination ottomane. Aspects idéologiques du problème", *Da Roma alla Terza Roma*. Studi – III. 21 aprile 1983, 459-471.

2. See Petre Ş. Năsturel, "Considérations sur l'idée impériale chez les Roumains", *Byzantina* 5 (1973), 395-413; cf. D. Nastase, "La survie de «l'empire des chrétiens»...", *passim,* and my studies cited there, n. 7; cf. also *infra.*

3. For the equivalence *car'* = *împărat* = emperor in the Romanian case, see D. Nastase, "La survie...", 461 and n. 14.

4. On the titles of the Romanian princes, particularly E. Vîrtosu, *Titulatura domnilor şi asocierea la domnie în Ţara Românească şi Moldova pînă în secolul al XVI-lea,* Bucharest 1960; previously, I. Bogdan, "Originea voevodatului la Români",

Analele Academiei Române, Memoriile secțiunii istorice, seria II, 25 (1902),
191-207; reprinted in *id., Scrieri alese* (selection of his studies edited by G.
Mihaila), Bucharest 1968, 165-179.

5. Cf. *supra,* n. 2. As I shall show elsewhere, the testimonies on the imperial rank of
the Romanian princes are more numerous than the examples published until
now, inclusive of this study.

6. See D. Nastase, "Ideea imperială în țările române...", 6 ff.; *id., L'héritage,* 5-13,
17-18, 21-22, 28-29, 34-35; cf. *id.,* "L'idée impériale", 232-234, 243-244.

7. *Supra* and n. 3.

8. "... I strove [in other places "I was eager"] not only to rule this empire *(sie carstvo
ispraviti* or *okărmiti),...".* Cf. D. Nastase, *Ideea imperială...,* 13; cf. also P.Ș.
Năsturel, *op.cit.,* 399, n. 9.

9. D. Nastase, "La survie de l' empire...", 458 and n. 18. There I have isolated in the
published documents more than thirty examples from 1464 until the end of the
16th century.

10. See, among others: *Documenta Romaniae Historica, B. Țara Românească,*
Bucharest 1966-(hereafter, DRH, B.), I, no. 298 (1500, Radu the Great); DRH,
B., II, nos. 189 (1519, Neagoe Basarab), 242 (1525, Radu de la Afumați); DRH,
B., III, nos.181 (1534-1535), 187 (1534), 194 (1535), 195 (1535), all four from Vlad
Vintilă.

11. Cf. P.Ș. Năsturel. *op. cit.,* 402. See, for example: DRH, B., I, nos, 151 (1475,
Laiotă Basarab), 220 (1489, Vlad the Monk), 290 (1499, Radu the Great); DRH,
B., II, no. 242, (1525, Radu de la Afumați); DRH, B., III, nos. 80 (1529, Moses),
96 (1530, Vlad the Drowned), 195 (1535, Vlad Vintilă); DRH, B., IV., nos. 39
(1537), 71 (1539), 74 (1539), 119 (1542), all four from Radu Paisius; *Documente
privind istoria României, Veacul XVI, B. Țara Românească,* Bucharest 1951-
(hereafter, DIR, XVI, B.), III, nos. 375 (1569), 435 (1570),both from Alexander
Mircea; DIR, XVI, B., V, nos. 224 (1585), 283 (1586), 299 (1587), all three from
Mihnea II.

12. *revnuja poslědstvovati drevniim carem'i gospodam eže zemnaa v blagodětelstvě,
mirně, prěprovodišja...* DRH, B., I., no, 20. p. 48.

13. DRH, B., I, no. 151 (1475/1476, Basarab Laiotă); DRH, B., II, nos. 105
(1512/1513), 130 (1514), both from Neagoe Basarab. Cf. P.Ș. Năsturel, "Aperçu
critique des rapports de la Valachie et du Mont Athos des origines au début du
XVIe siècle", *Revue des études Sud-Est Européennes* 2/1-2 (1964), 97, 99-100; cf.
also D. Nastase, "le Mont Athos et la politique du patriarcat de Constantinople,
de 1355 à 1375", Σύμμεικτα 3 (1979), 150, n. 3.

14. The act of Aldea, more recently in DRH, B., I, no. 19. For the date, see T.
Bodogae, *Ajutoarele românești la mânăstirile din sfântul Munte Athos,* Sibiu 1940,
176; and, especially, P.Ș. Năsturel, "Legăturile țărilor romane cu Muntele Athos
pînă la sfîrșitul veaculul al XV-lea", *Mitropolia Olteniei* 10/11-12 (1958), 750.

15. This specification shall be made several times by Mihnea II (in 1587: DIR, XVI,
B., V, nos. 288, 290, 291) and repeated by his ephemeral successor, Stephen the

Deaf (1591-1592), DIR, XVI, B., VI, no. 61.

16. On all these question, see D. Nastase, *op. cit.* (*supra*, n. 13) 148-152; *id.*, "La signification cachée des documents athonites", *XVI. Internationaler Byzantinistenkongress, Akten* 11/2 (*Jahrbuch der Österreichischen Byzantinistik* 32/2), Vienna 1981, 260-262, 264.

17. See D. Nastase, "Les débuts de la communauté oecuménique du Mont Athos", Σύμμεικτα 6 (1985), 251-314; *id.*, "Le patronage du Mont Athos au XIIIᵉ siècle", *Cyrillomethodianum* 7 (1983), 71-87; cf. the studies cited in the previous note ("Le Mont Athos et la politique du patriarcat...", 174; "La signification cachée...", 259 ff.).

18. On this icon, see P. Năsturel, "Aux origines des relations roumano-athonites. L' icone de Saint Athanase de Lavra du voïvode Vladislav", *Actes du VI ᶜCongrès international des études byzantines, Paris 1948*, II, Paris 1951, 307-314.

19. The transcription, *ibid.*, 308.

20. P.Ş. Năsturel drew my attention to the fact that this formula is borrowed from psalm 2.2 («βασιλεῖς τῆς γῆς»).

21. «Καὶ τοὺς βασιλεῖς τῆς γῆς, ᾿Ανδρόνικον λέγω καὶ τὸν ᾿Αλέξανδρον, Στέπανον καὶ ᾿Αλέξανδρον...». François Halkin, "Deux vies de S. Maxime le Kausokalybe ermite au Mont Athos (XIVᵉ siècle)", *Analecta Bollandiana* 54 (1936) |(=*id.*, *Saints moines de l' Orient*, London, Var. Repr., 1973, XI), 90 and n. 3; cf. also Tit Simedrea, "Viața mînastireasca în Țara Românească înainte de anul 1370", *Biserica Ortodoxa Română* 80/7-8 (1962), 679-680; R. Theodorescu, *Bizanț, Balcani, Occident la începuturile culturii medievale românești*, Bucharest 1974, 202. The first Alexander is the Bulgarian tsar Ivan Alexander; the second is, most certainly, the Wallachian voivode [Nicholas-] Alexander (often cited only with this name). Theophanes affirms in the same place (F. Halkin, *op.cit.*, 90, 11. 13-18) that in Parorea, the celebrated monastic center, founded and managed by Gregory the Sinaite, there were people from Constantinople and Byzantine provinces, and also from Bulgaria, Serbia and from the regions beyond the Danube («καὶ τὰ πέρα ῎Ιστρου», *loc. cit.*, 11. 14-15), i.e. Wallachia (cf. Tit Simedrea, *loc. cit.*, 670): as the first three sovereigns mentioned above correspond to Byzantium, Serbia and Bulgaria, there remains for the second Alexander only Wallachia from "beyond the Istros". Cf. John VI Cantacuzenus (ed. Bonn, I, 465), «τοὺς πέραν ῎Ιστρου Γέτας», who are the Romanians (see *Fontes Historiae Daco-Romanae*, vol. III, ed. A. Elian - N.-S. Tanasoca, Bucharest 1975, 484 485, II); cf. also Critobulus of Imbros, ed. V. Grecu, Bucharest 1963, 61, 11. 10-11 («...τούς πέραν τοῦ ῎Ιστρου Γέτας»).

22. N. Iorga, *Histoire des Roumains et de la romanité orientale*, III, Bucharest 1937, 206 and n. 2, with a reference to "Maïkov, chez Hasdeu, *Ist. critică*, p. 99". At this date Nicholas-Alexander played already a leading role, and was probably associated to the throne of his father Basarab I (± 1310-1352).

23. See N. Iorga, *Istoria popoarelor balcanice în epoca modernă*, Vălenii-de-Munte 1913, 8; *id.*, *Histoire des Etats balcaniques jusqu' à 1924*, Paris 1925, 39; *id.*,

Relations entre les Serbes et les Roumains, Bucharest 1922, 19.

24. "... *regem Bozorad scismaticum... dictus enim rex...*", etc. "Chronicon observantis provinciae Bosnae Argentinae ordinis s. Francisci Seraphici", *Starine,* vol. XXII, Zagreb 1890, 11. Cf. I. Dujčev, "Il francescanesimo in Bulgaria nei secoli XIII e XIV", republished in *id., Medioevo bizantino-slavo,* I, Rome 1965, 420.

25. Giacomo di Pietro Lvccari, *Copioso ristretto degli Annali di Ravsa, libri quattro,* In Venetia 1605, 47. *Apud* A. Armbruster, *La romanité des Roumains,* Bucharest 1977, 138 and n. 30.

26. See A. Balotă, "«Radu Voïvode», dans l'épique sud-slave", *Revue des études Sud-Est Européennes* 5/1-2 (1967), 204-205, 211-219.

27. See V. Cornaros, Ἐρωτόκριτος (critical edition S. Alexiou), Athens 1980, chapter 4, *passim.* Cf. the modifications in the South Slavic ballads of the names of the Wallachian voivodes Radu and Vladislav I himself, where they are sometimes called Radosav and Vlatko (see A. Balotă, *op. cit.,* 211). For the similarity of the name of Vladistratos and those of Vlad and Vladislav of many Romanian princes, see: V. Grecu, "Erotocritul lui Cornaro în literatura românească", *Dacoromania* 1 (1920-1921), 70; S. Alexiou, Introduction of his cited ed. of Cornaros, n. 99 (p. οη΄). For the opinion that Cornaro's Wallachia is the Romanian principality of this name, see: N.G. Politis, "'Ο Ἐρωτόκριτος", Λαογραφία 1 (1909), 53; V. Grecu, *op. cit.,* 70-71; S. Alexiou *op. cit., pp.* π΄ -πα΄.

28. Ἐρωτόκριτος, ed. cit., chapter 4, 1. 868 (p. 294).

29. Cf. Maria Holban, "Peut-il être question d' une seconde occupation roumaine de Vidin, par Radu Ier...?", *Revue des études Sud-Est Européennes* 18/3 (1980), 457, n. 11; cf. also S. Iosipescu, *Balica, Dobrotiță, Ioancu,* Bucharest 1985, 161.

30. After the fashion of the abbreviations "of the Bulgarian coins of that period of Alexander and Michael (1331-1355) or of Alexander (1355-1371)". Elena Isăcescu, "Monedele atribuite lui Nicolae Redwitz", *Studii și cercetări numismatice* 7 (1980), 105.

31. I cite after the Romanian translation of Mustafa Ali Mehmet, *Istoria Turcilor,* Bucharest 1976, 126, where this passage, unpublished, is rendered after "the manuscript no. 3078 of the Library of Nuruosmaniye mosque in Istanbul". Cf. *infra.*

32. Cf. Daniel, *2, 37-38,* saying to Nebuchadnezzar: "O king, *art* a king of kings: for the God of heaven hath given thee a kingdom [in Greek βασιλείαν], power and strength, and glory. And wheresoever the children of men dwell, the beasts of the field and the fowls of the heaven hath be given into thine hand, and hath made three ruler over them all". Cf. also the French Bible: "O roi, tu es le roi des rois, car le Dieu des cieux t'a donné *l'empire,...*".

33. DRH., B., I., nos 228 (1491), 273 (1497), 303 (1500). Cf. P.Ș. Năsturel, "Considérations sur l'idée impériale...", 412-413 (Additifs, III).

34. DRH, B., II, nos. 97 (Vișina, incertain date, "[1512-1521]"), 153 (Corbii de Piatră, 1517), 173 (Cotmeana, 1518).

35. N. Stoicescu, *Bibliografia localităților și monumentelor feudale din România,* I

- *Ţara Românească*, vol. 1, 346; P. Chihaia, "Date noi despre începuturile mănăstirii Govora", *Studii şi cercetări de istoria artei, seria artă plastică*, 13/2 (1966), 247-253.

36. G. Ionescu, "Mănăstirea Govora şi egumenia lui Meletie Macedoneanul", (I), *Buletinul Monumentelor Istorice* 40/2 (1971), 20 and n. 3, with reference also to another study by the same author, study which has been inaccesible to me.

37. Vlad-Vintilă, in 1533, DRH, B., III., no. 170; Mircea the Shepherd, in 1551, DIR, XVI, B., III, no. 3.

38. Charters from: Mircea the Shepherd (in 1547), DRH, B., IV., no. 232; Alexander II Mircea (in 1569), DIR, XVI, B., III, no. 351. Cf. P. Chihaia, *De la "Negru Vodă" la Neagoe Basarab*, Bucharest 1976, p. 114.

39. Carmen Laura Dumitrescu, "Chronique et monument témoin. Une hypothèse à propos d'une église rupestre à deux absides en Valachie", *Buletinul Bibliotecii Române*, vol. XI (XV) - serie noua, Freiburg (Germany), 1984, 15-54.

40. E. Lăzărescu, "Nicodim de la Tismana şi rolul său în cultura veche românească", I (pînă la 1385), *Romanoslavica* II (1963), 239, n. 8; cf. Rada Teodoru, *Mănăstirea Tismana*, 2nd ed., Bucharest 1968, 32. A photograph, *ibid.*, fig. 12.

41. Cf. E. Lăzărescu, *op. cit.*, 241 and the list of these acts drawn up by the author, *ibid.*, annex II, p. 280. We should notice that the simander was wrought by a monk of Tismana. R. Teodoru, *op. cit.*, 34.

42. Cf. D. Cernovodeanu, *Ştiinţa şi arta heraldică în România*, Bucharest 1977, 56-57.

43. Lia Bătrîna and A. Bătrîna, "Date noi cu privire la evoluţia bisericii fostei mănăstiri Cotmeana", *Revista muzeelor şi monumentelor. Monumente istorice şi de artă*, 44/1 (1975), 18 and fig. 12, 13.

44. See. P.P. Panaitescu, "L'aigle byzantine sur les vêtements des princes roumains du Moyen Age", *Académie Roumaine. Bulletin de la section historique*, 17 (1930), 64-67; R. Theodorescu, "Despre un însemn sculptat şi pictat de la Cozia (1n jurul "despotiei" lui Mircea cel Bătrîn)", *Studii şi cercetări de istoria artei, seria artă plastică*, 16/2 (1969), 191-208; abridged French version: "Autour de la "despoteia" de Mircea l' Ancien",*Actes du XIVe Congrès international des études byzantines, Bucarest 1971*, II, Bucharest 1975, 625-635.

45. In 1858, the writer Alexander Pelimon saw in the ambo of the same church, "above a stone seat", yet another two-headed eagle, "engraved in a stone found in the mountains". A. Pelimon, *Impresiuni de călătorie în România*, ed. Dalila-Lucia Aramă, Bucharest 1984, 69-70.

46. R. Theodorescu, "Despre un însemn...", 197-199; *id.* "Autour de la "despoteia"...", 627-628. The two acts, of 1390 and 1391, where Mircea titles himself "terrarum Dobrodicii despotus", in Hurmuzaki-Densuşianu, *Documente privitoare la istoria Românilor*, I, 2, Bucharest 1890, 322, 334-335. On this subject, previously, D. Onciul, *Mircea cel Bătrân*, republished in *id.*, *Scrieri istorice* (critical ed. A. Sacerdoţeanu), II, Bucharest 1968, 247.

47. R. Theodorescu, "Despre un însemn...", 192-193, 205-208; *id.*, "Autour de la "despoteia"...", 625-626, 634, 635; cf., L. Bătrîna, A. Bătrîna, *op. cit.*, 18.

48. R. Theodorescu, "Despre un însemn...", 206-208 and fig. 5; *id.*, "Autour...", 634-635 and fig. 4.

49. Cf., for the time being, D. Nastase, "L' aigle bicéphale dissimulée dans les armoiries des pays roumains", *Roma Costantinopoli Mosca. Da Roma alla Terza Roma.* Studi - I. Seminario 21 Aprile 1981, 373.

50. D.V. Rosetti, "Tezaurul de podoabe medievale din Olteni (Teleorman) și elementele lor byzantine", *Buletinul Monumentelor Istorice* 41/4 (1972), 3 and fig. 18.

51. Cf. *ibid.*, 7-8 and notes 25-29, 46.

52. More recently, N. Constantinescu, "Curtea domnească din Argeș, probleme de geneză și evoluție", *Buletinul Monumentelor Istorice* 40/3 (1971), 18; *id., Vladislav I, 1364-1377,* Bucharest 1979, 156-157.

53. Carmen Laura Dumitrescu, "Le voïvode donateur de la fresque de Saint-Nico-lae-Domnesc (Argeș) et le problème de sa domination sur Vidin au XIVe siècle", *Revue des études Sud-Est Européennes* 17/3 (1979), 556.

54. *Curtea domnească din Argeș (= Buletinul Comisiunii Monumentelor Istorice* 10-16, 1917-1923), Bucharest 1923, fig. 52,55 and pl. X; N. Constantinescu, *Curtea de Argeș (1200-1400). Asupra începuturilor Țării Românești,* Bucharest 1984, fig. 50.

55. "Despre un însemn...", 196, n. 21.

56. P. Chihaia, "Observații asupra portretelor lui Mircea cel Bătrîn și doamnei Mara, de la Brădet", *Studii și cercetări de istoria artei* 7/1 (1960), 254, n. 3; recently, S.Iosipescu, *Balica, Dobrotiță, Ioancu,* Bucharest 1985,168.Without stating it categorically, N. Constantinescu, *op. cit.*, 116, envisages the possibility that this motif could be a stylised two-headed eagle, and even a crowned one.

57. *Ibid.*, 115-117.

58. According to P. Chihaia, *Din cetățile de scaun ale Țării Românești,* Bucharest 1974, "the winged bird" on a ring found in the excavations of the church of "Sânicoară" (14th century) of Curtea de Arges "was probably a two-headed eagle".

59. This document is preserved in a later 16th - early 17th century copy. Recent edition, DRH, A. *Moldova,* I, Bucharest 1975, no. 1, Latin text with Romanian translation and commentary. The cited extract, p. 1.

60. Luccari's chronicle (cit. *supra,* n. 25), p. 105. *Apud* V. Spinei, *Moldova în secolele XI-XIV,* Bucharest 1982, 320.

61. N. Iorga, *Histoire des Etats balcaniques jusqu' à 1924,* 47. The inscription goes with "le portrait du prince, sous un chapeau pareil à celui du Paléologue contemporain" [i.e. the emperor John VIII] (*loc. cit.*). Published by *id.*, "Patrahirul lui Alexandru-cel-Bun. Cel dintâi chip de domn român", *Analele Academiei Române. Memoriile secț. istorice.* Seria II, 35 (1913), 344.

62. *Cronicele slavo-romîne din sec. XV-XVI* publicate de Ion Bogdan. Ediție revăzută și completată de P.P. Panaitescu, Bucharest 1959, 6, 1. 12. This formula

constitutes the very title of the chronicle, the real narrative part of which began o»ly with Alexander the Good. For its translation as 'the Moldavian emperors' see D. Nastase, "Unité et continuité dans le contenu de recueils "manuscrits" dits «miscellanées», *Cyrillomethodianum* 5 (1981), 24 and n. 29 (p. 41- 42); cf. *id.*, "La survie de l' empire des chrétiens sous la domination ottomane...", 461.

63. I. Bogdan, *Cronice inedite atingătoare de istoria Românilor,* adunate şi publicate cu traduceri şi adnotaţiuni de, Bucharest 1895, 91-96 the only complete edition of this text).

64. For this intepretation of the Moldavian chronicle of the "Christian emperors" see the commentary by D. Nastase, "Unité et continuité... ", 27 ff.

65. Cf. *ibid.*, 24 and n. 18.

66. See G. Ostrogorsky, "Byzance, Etat tributaire de l'Empire turc", in his collection of studies *Zur byzantinischen Geschichte,* Darmstadt 1973, 244.

67. Cf. D. Nastase, *op. cit.,* 29.

68. Cf. *ibid.*, 30, 32.

69. Cf. *infra.*

70. Published by I. Bogdan, "Ein Beitrag zur bulgarischen und serbischen Geschichtschreibung", *Archiv für slavische Philologie* 13 (1891), text in middle Bulgarian, 526-535, with a Latin translation by V. Jagić, 536-543. The fragment I cited is extracted from the introductory study of Bogdan, *ibid.*, 491.

This acount has been considered as an original Bulgarian work until recently. In fact it is a partial translation, made in Wallachia (in my opinion at the monastery of Tismana) of a lost Byzantine chronicle. I attributed the original to the notary of the Patriarchate of Constantinople, John Chortasmenus (c. 1370 - c.1436/7). D. Nastase, "Une chronique byzantine perdue et sa version slavo-roumaine (la Chronique de Tismana, 1411-1413)", I, *Cyrillomethodianum* 4 (1977), 100-171. Cf. H. Hunger, *Die hochsprachliche profane Literatur de Byzantiner,* I, Munich 1978, 428 and notes 186, 186b. I proposed to call the existing Slavonic fragment "The Byzantin-Romanian chronicle of the Ottoman expansion" and, more briefly, "The Tismana Chronicle" (D. Nastase, *op. cit.*, 143).

71. D. Nastase, *op. cit., passim.*

72. Cf. *ibid.*, 109 ff., 124-125.

73. Cf. *ibid.*, 125 and n. 84.

74. It is thus called thrice in the chronicle. I Bogdan, *op. cit.*, 533-534.

75. On the subject of this fragmentation see, in general, D.A. Zakythinos, "Etats-Sociétés-Cultures. En guise d'introduction", in *Art et société à Byzance sous les Paléologues,* Venise 1971 (= *id.,Byzance: Etat- Société-Economie,* London, Var. Repr., 1973, XII), 1-12; cf. D. Nastase, "Le Mont Athos et la politique du patriarcat de Constantinople...", 121 and n. 3. On Serbia, especially the book of Rade Mihaljčić, *Kraj Srpskog carstva* (with a French summary), Belgrade 1975.

76. Particularly R. Mihaljčić, *op. cit., passim.*

77. Cf. the title of "Very pious and very high Tsar and Autocrat of the Bulgarian and the Greeks" of John Stracimir, in fact a modest prince with an apanage. For this

title, see *Bdinski Zbornik...*, Facsimile edition, with a presentation by I. Dujčev, London, Var. Repr., 1972, f. 242.

78. A. Solovjev, V. Mošin, *Grčke povelje srpskih vladara (Diplomata Graeca regum et imperatorum Serviae)*, Belgrade 1936 (=London, Var. Repr., 1974), no. XXXIV, 11. 101-103.

79. G. Ostrogorsky, *Serska oblast posle Dušanove smrti*, Belgrade 1965, chapter IV, particularly p. 81-82. (Republished in *id.*, *Sabrana dela*, IV, *Vizantija i Sloveni*, Belgrade 1970, with indication of pages of the 1965 edition).

80. Dj. Trifunović, "Žitije svetog patrijarha Jefrema od episkopa Marka", *Beogradski Universitet, Anali Filološkog Fakulteta* 7 (1967), 71.

81. On this subject one may consult any manual of Romanian history. Most recently, C.C. Giurescu, D.C. Giurescu, *Istoria Românilor*, I, Bucharest 1975, 261-274, and especially II, Bucharest 1976, 22- 49, 66-111, 381 ff. In English, a compendium by D.C. Giurescu, *Illustrated History of the Romanian People*, Bucharest 1981, see 130 ff.

82. F. Miklosich - J. Müller, *Acta et Diplomata Graeca Medii Aevi sacra et profana*, I, Vienna 1860, no. 171.

83. D.A. Zakythinos, *op. cit.*, 9.

84. Cf. D. Nastase, «Une chronique byzantine perdue...», 114 ff., 164; cf. also C.C. Giurescu, D.C. Giurescu, *op. cit.*, 11, 71-75, 78.

85. For which, P.P. Panaitescu, *Mircea cel Batrân*, Bucharest 1945, 188, 346. For the efforts towards this goal by Romanian princes in general, see Nastase, *L'héritage, passim; id.*, «L' idée impériale», 238 ff.

86. P.P. Panaitescu, *op. cit.*, 281· S. Papacostea, «Aux débuts de l'Etat moldave. Considérations en marge d'une nouvelle source», *Revue roumaine d'histoire* 12/1 (1973), 148-149.

87. Cf. *infra* and n. 107.

88. On this conflict, caused by the foundation of the Moldavian Metropolitan See and terminated in 1401, see especially V. Laurent, «Aux origines de l' Eglise de Moldavie. Le métropolite Jérémie et l'évêque Joseph», *Revue des études byzantines* 5 (1947) 158-170. On the evolution of the crisis and on its solution, see now D. Nastase, «Les débuts de l'Eglise moldave et le siège de Constantinople par Bajazet Ier», *Σύμμεικτα* 7 (1987) 205-213 Cf. *infra*.

89. See *supra* and nn. 12,14.

90. On tne period of Mircea the Elder's apogee, see P.P. Panaitescu, *op. cit.*, 292-341.

91. See *supra* and n. 31.

92. Leunclavius, *Historia musulmana Turcorum de monumentis ipsorum excriptae libri XVIII*, Frankfurt 1591, col. 418.

93. Cf. L. Bréhier, *Vie et mort de Byzance*, Paris 1969, 391 (with more older bibliography in the notes). On the military operations undertaken by Musa against Byzantium and on his end, see J.W. Barker, *Manuel II Palaeologus (1391-1425)*, New Brunswick New Jersey 1969, 284-288. For the role of Mircea the Elder in the accession of Musa to the throne, see P.P. Panaitescu, *op. cit.*, 308-317.

94. See the Turkish chroniclers Urudj, Asîk-Paša-Zadé, etc., in Romanian translation, in *Cronici turcești privind țările române. Extrase,* vol. I, întocmit de Mihail Guboglu și Mustafa Mehmet, Bucharest 1966, *passim.*

95. *Cf. Istoria Rominiei,* II, Bucharest 1962, 382-383 (authors of the chapter, B. Câmpina, D. Mioc.)

96. Cf. Ducas, ed. V. Grecu, Bucharest 1958, 155-157.

97. See P.P. Panaitescu, *op. cit.,* 341-344; cf. C.C. Giurescu, D.C. Giurescu, *op. cit.,* II, 81-82.

98. *Istoria Rominiei* cit., II, 385-386 (authors of the chapter, B. Câmpina, N. Stoicescu). It is even possible that Dobrudja had been annexed by the Turks since 1417. See: Ș. Ștefănescu, in I. Barnea, Ș. Ștefănescu, *Din istoria Dobrogei,* III, Bucharest 1971, 374; C.C. Giurescu, D.C. Giurescu, *op. cit.,* 386-387.

99. *Istoria Rominiei* cit., II, 355 (author of the chapter, C. Cihodaru); cf. V. Spinei. *Moldova în secolele XI-XIII,* 293, 321.

100. V. Spinei, *op. cit.,* 321, cf. 293-294.

101. The document, M. Costăchescu, *Documentele moldovenești înainte de Ștefan cel Mare,* II, Iași 1932, 605-606; cf. *ibid.,* 603-604. On this loan, particularly O. Iliescu, «Le prêt accordé en 1388 par Pierre Mușat à Ladislas Jagellon», *Revue Roumaine d' Histoire* 12/1 (1973), 123-138.

102. See W. Wodoff, «Remarques sur la valeur du terme 'tsar' appliqué aux princes russes avant le milieu du XVe siècle», *Oxford Slavonic Papers,* N.S., (1978), 14 (no. 25).

103. *Ibid.,* (no. 30) and n. 75.

104. Cf. *supra.*

105. *Supra and n. 59.*

106. Cf. O. Iliescu, *op. cit.,* 135-138.

107. Cf. *supra* and n. 88.

108. M. Costăchescu, *op. cit.,* I, 61. See the elucidations brought by P.Ș. Năsturel (who draws attention to this pecularity), «Un témoignage byzantin sur la métropole de Roman (Moldavie)», *Revue des études roumaines* 15 (1975), 201-202 and n. 1 (p. 202).

109. On Alexander the Good, apart from the obsolete monograph by E. Picot and G. Bengescu, *Alexandre le Bon, prince de Moldavie,* Vienna 1882, see: P.P. Panaitescu, *Alexandru cel Bun. La cinci sute de ani de la moartea lui,* Bucharest 1932; E. Diaconescu, *Alexandru cel Bun,* Bucharest 1968; recently, the monograph by C. Cihodaru, *Alexandru cel Bun (23 aprilie 1399 - 1 ianuarie 1432),* Iași 1984, and the French compendium by the same, *Alexandre le Bon, prince de Moldavie (av. 1400-1432),* Bucharest 1984.

110. At the beginning of 1424. Cf. *supra* and n. 66.

111. The decision to pay this tribute in DRH, A., II, no. 58.

112. See *supra* and n. 9.

113. See P.Ș. Năsturel, "Considérations sur l' idée impériale...", 404-405; of my studies already cited, cf. particularly "L' idée impériale", *passim.* The chronicles

in Slavonic of Wallachia have not been preserved.

114. See P.S. Nasturel, *op. cit.* D. Nastase, «Βοεβόδας Ούγγροβλαχίας καί αύτοκράτωρ Ρωμαίων». Remarques sur une inscription insolite", *Byzantinisch-neugriechische Jahrbücher* 22 (offprint, Athens 1976), 1-16.

115. See *id.* "Unité et continuité..." (*supra* n. 62), 35-36. On the imperial symbolism in the ancient Romanian ecclesiastical iconography - and art, in general,-see my studies "Ideea imperială în țările române...", 6 ff.; *L' héritage*, 2-15, 17-18, 21-22, 28-29, 34-35.

116. See D. Nastase, "Unité et continuité...", 22 ff.

117. *Ibid.*, 33-35.

118. This unpublished embroidery was recently discovered by P.Ș. Năsturel, who kindly allowed me to utilize his precious finding.

119. The portrait of Neagoe (d. 1521) in the conventual church of Argeș was painted possibly during his lifetime, but most probably in 1526, on the order of the voivode Radu de la Afumați. See P. Chihaia, *Din cetățile de scaun ale Tarii Românești*, 142-143; cf. Carmen Laura Dumitrescu, *Pictura murală din Țara Românească în veacul al XVI-lea*, Bucharest 1978, 14-15, 68-70.

120. Cf. Corina Nicolescu, *Istoria costumului de curte în țările române. Secolele XIV-XVIII*, Bucharest 1970, 235 (no. 98).

121. *Ibid.*, 123 ff., 235-236.

122. See E. Lăzărescu, *Biserica mănăstirii Argeșului*, Bucharest 1967 (with bibliography).

123. See P.Ș. Năsturel, "Învățăturile lui Neagoe Basarab în lumina pisaniilor de pe Biserica Mănăstirii de la Argeș", *Mitropolia Olteniei* 12/1-2 (1960), 20; cf. G. Mihăilă, in *Literatura română veche (1402-1647)* (ed. G. Mihăilă and D. Zamfirescu), I, Bucharest 1969, 155.

124. R., Theodorescu, "Despre un însemn...", 191-193 and fig. 3, 4; *id.*, "Autour de la despoteia...", 625 and fig. 3; cf. P. Chihaia, "Observații asupra portretelor lui Mircea cel Bătrîn și doamnei Mara de la Brădet", *loc. cit.* (*supra*, n. 56). On the date, see C.L. Dumitrescu, *op. cit.*, 16.

125. *Ibid.*, 18, 57. Reproductions in: N. Iorga, *Domnii români după portrete și fresce contemporane*, Sibiu 1930, pl. 36; P. Chihaia, *De la "Negru Vodă" la Neagoe Basarab. Interferențe literar-artistice în cultura românească a evului de mijloc*, Bucharest 1976, fig. 10.

126. N. Iorga, "Noi descoperiri privitoare la istoria Românilor", *Analele Academiei Române. Memoriile secțiunii istorice*. Seria III, 19 (1937-1938), 189-198; A. Xyngopoulos, "Portraits inédits de deux voïvodes valaques", *Actes du XIVᵉ Congrès international des études byzantines, Bucarest 1971*, II, 647-649 and fig. 1. Cf. A. Pippidi, *Tradiția politică bizantină în țările române în secolele XVI-XVIII*, Bucharest 1983, 192 and n. 235.

In my communications "Roumains romains et Grecs romains", *Da Roma alla Terza Roma*. Studi-II. 21 Aprile 1982, 399, n. 52, and "La survie de l'empire des chrétiens...", 463, n. 25, I wrote that this Radu was the son of Mihnea II and his wife Neaga. I proceed here to a necessary rectification.

The portraits of Mihnea II - crowned, with a cross in his right hand - and of Radu (although without two-headed eagles) appear also in the mural painting of the catholicon of Iviron. See T. Bodogae, *Ajutoarele românești...* cit. (*supra*,n. 14), 142. A color reproduction in V. Cândea, C. Simionescu, *Mont Athos. Présences roumaines,* Bucharest 1979, p. no number.

127. N. Iorga, *Histoire des Roumains...* cit. (*supra,* n. 22), V. Bucharest 1940, 299.

128. *Ibid.,* 306 and n. 5.

129. On this original act, unpublished and till recently unknown, see D. Nastase, "Les documents roumains des archives du couvent athonite de Simonopetra. Présentation préliminaire", Σύμμεικτα 5 (1983), 373-388. A later Greek translation in DRH, B., XI, no. 339.

130. "Une aigle bicéphale déguisée sur un chrysobulle inédit de Michel le Brave (1599)". (In manuscript; will be published shortly).

131. DRH, B., XI., nos. 274, 292.

132. V. Cărăbiș, "Urme de cultură veche", *Mitropolia Olteniei* 1970/5-6, 483 (information from P.Ș. Năsturel).

132a See Ș. Andreescu, "Radu Mihnea Corvin, domn al Moldovei și Țării Românești", I-II (with Frence summary), *Revista de istorie* 39/1,2 (1986), 12-30, 119-136.

133. *"Domnia Radului vodă celui Mare împărăției nu domniei sămănătoare..."*. Miron Costin, *Opere* (critical ed. by P.P. Panaitescu), Bucharest 1958, 89, 11. 2-3.

134. *Loc. cit.,* 11. 5-11.

135. D. Nastase, "L' aigle bicéphale dissimulée dans les armoiries des pays roumains", 358 ff.

136. *Ibid.,* 358-361, 366 ff.

137. See *loc. cit.*, 358-361. To the cited examples, it should be added a coat of arms of Gregory I Ghica (1660-1664; 1672-1673) with a two-headed eagle, hidden in the manner I described. This coat of arms overhang the lapidary votive inscription, dated 1661, of the church of Dragoslavele, a foundation of this voivode. A photograph of this inscription in N. Ghika-Budești, *Evoluția arhitecturii în Muntenia și în Oltenia,* IV, Bucharest 1936 (= *Buletinul Comisiunii Monumentelor Istorice* 29/fasc. 87-90, 1936), fig. 913.

138. See: M.D. Matei-Em. Emandi, "O casă de orășean din secolul al XV-lea de la Suceava", *Studii și cercetări de istorie veche și arheologie* 28/4 (1977), 570-571, 573-574 and fig. 7/2; Rica Popescu, "Cahle și plăci decorative la curtea domnească din Vaslui", *Revista muzeelor și monumentelor. Monumente istorice și de artă* 47/2 (1978), 68-69 and fig. 7. Two-headed eagles adorn also the embroidered funerary portrait of the wife of Stephen the Great, Maria of Mangop (d. 1477), who called herself Assanina and Palaeologina. Reproductions of the veil and the detail on one of its eagles in N. Iorga, *Les arts mineurs en Roumanie,* II, Bucharest 1936, plates 73, 74.

139. See D. Nastase, *op. cit.,* 362-364.

140. *Ibid.,* 365 and notes 43-45. This seal was used also on an unpublished document of Dimitrie Cantemir, of 2 March 1711. This act is now in the archives of the Zaïmis family in Athens. Microfilm at the Center for Neohellenic Research of the Hellenic National Research Foundation, Athens.

141. N. Iorga, *Byzance après Byzance.* Continuation de l' Histoire de la vie byzantine [subtitle very characteristic], Bucharest 1935; reprinted Bucharest 1971, with a *Postface* by V. Cândea. Cf. my analysis of the works of Iorga pertaining to this conception, and the related bibliography, Nastase, "L'idée impériale", 201 ff.

142. Cf. Nastase, *op. cit.,* 204-205 and n. 1 (p. 205).

143. N. Iorga, *Byzance après Byzance* (1971), 139-142; *id., Histoire des Roumains...* cit., V, Book IV, chapter I, characteristically entitled "Un commencement d' influence grecque". On the survival of a Byzantine patrimony in the framework of the Ottoman state and society, see Sp. Vryonis Jr., "Byzantium and Islam, Seven-Seventeenth Century", *East European Quarterly* 2/3 (1968) (= *id., Byzantium: its internal history and relations with the Muslim World,* London, Var. Repr., 1971, IX), 205-240 (III. "The Turkish Period", 230-240); *id.,* "The Byzantine Legacy and Ottoman Forms", *Dumbarton Oaks Papers* 33-34 (1969-1970), 251-308.

144. *Byzance après Byzance, ed. cit.,* 141-142.

145. Cf. Nastase, *op. cit.* 203-206.

146. *Loc. cit.,* 204-205; cf. *id.,*" «Βοεβόδας Οὐγγροβλαχίας καὶ αὐτοκράτωρ ῾Ρωμαίων...» „ 12-14; cf. also *id.,* "La survie de «l'empire des chrétiens»...", 455-457.

147. On this subject, see: V. Cândea, "Semnificaţia politică a unui act de cultură feudală", *Studii. Revistă de istorie* 16/3 (1963), 651-671; French version, *id.,* "Les Bibles grecque et roumaine de 1687-1688 et les visées impériales de Şerban Cantacuzène", *Balkan Studies* 10/2 (1969), 351-376; *id., Stolnicul între contemporani,* Bucharest 1971, 113-115; M. Neagoe, *Neagoe Basarab,* Bucharest 1971, 93 ff.; P.Ş. Năsturel, "Considérations sur l'idée impériale...", 408 and 413, additif V.

148. On the general evolution of the imperial idea in the Romanian lands which I present hereafter, see further details in my "L' idée impériale", 234 ff.

149. Cf. *id., L'héritage,* 13-14.

150. Cf. *id.,* "L'idée impériale", 236 and n. 2.

151. See *id., L'héritage,* 16-17.

152. On this expression, see A. Randa, "Le Sud-Est Européen partie intégrante de l' l' Europe", *Revue des études roumaines* 7-8 (1961) (= *Actes du premier cycle des journées d'études roumaines,* [Paris] 24-26 janvier 1959), 135.

153. Cf. Nastase, *L' héritage,* 16-17, 25-26; *id.,* "L' idée impériale", 236, 237.

154. "Les autonomies locales" is the title of chapter III of *Byzance après Byzance.* On the imperial symbolic value of Mount Athos, *supra,* and n. 17.

155. Cf.: D. Nastase, "Ideea imperială în ţările române...", 21; *id.* L' héritage, 20; *id.,* "L'idée impériale", 238-239.

156. *Id.*, L'héritage 15; *id.*, "L'idée impériale", 239.
157. See A. Mesrobeanu, "Contribuție la istoria catolicismului în Moldova", *Cercetări istorice* 4/2 (1928), 86-87.
158. A summary of these elements in Nastase, "L'idée impériale", 243-246.
159. *Id.*, "Le Mont Athos et la politique du patriarcat de Constantinople..."; cf. *id.*, "Une chronique byzantine perdue...", 160 ff.
160. On the perspectives that the results of my researches presented above reveal for the understanding of the elements bearing an imperial character in the history of various European states - from Venice to Spain and England, via pre-imperial Russia and Serbia - see, briefly, Nastase, "L'idée impériale", 248-250; cf. *id.*, "Unité et continuité...", 36 ff.
161. The contributions and the informations, linked to Mount Athos, of P.Ş. Nasturel mentioned in this study, should now be reported to his book *Le Mont Athos et les Roumains. Recherches sur leurs relations du milieu du XIV*e *siècle à 1654*, Rome 1986.

RUSSIAN POLICY IN CONSTANTINOPLE AND MOUNT ATHOS IN THE NINETEENTH CENTURY

Theofanis G. Stavrou

> Russia from eternity has been ordained to illumine Asia and to unite all Slavs. There will be a union of all Slav races with Armenia, Syria, Arabia, and Ethiopia and they will all praise God in Hagia Sophia.[1]

This mid-nineteenth century statement by the controversial Russian hierarch and leader of the First Russian Ecclesiastical Mission to Jerusalem, Archimandrite, later Bishop, Porfirii Uspenskii, anticipated by a quarter of a century pronouncements of leading Panslavs and especially the well-known statement by Dostoevsky that sooner or later Constantinople should become Russian. It is a relevant point of reference for the main objective of this paper, for it is a reminder of a cultural policy which the Russians pursued with considerable success during the course of the nineteenth century in the area usually referred to as the Orthodox East (*Pravoslavnyi Vostok*). It is an aspect of Russian policy in the region which has not received the attention it deserves. In fact it has all too hastily been dismissed as, at best, constituting romantically exaggerated visions of Panslavs and other nineteenth-century conservative national publicists. The accomplishment of such policy aside, investigating it properly could reveal important realities about Russia and the Near East and, more significantly, it could shed light on the perceptions of these realities by all parties concerned. In the final analysis, Russia's involvement and policy in the Orthodox East, it could be argued, provided the tsarist regime with the opportunity to assume a philosophical as well as political stance. For while presumably concerned with geographic realities in the region, intellectually as well as diplomatically this stance also constituted part of Russia's philosophical struggle with the West. It is no accident that several conservative thinkers during the second half of the nineteenth century in expounding their philosophical positions regarding Russia and Europe frequently invoked the weight of the Orthodox East or of Byzantinism.[2]

Constantinople and Mount Athos, the two geographic locations suggested by the organizers of this colloquium are convenient (important to be sure) political and cultural symbols for Russia's policy in the Orthodox East. Despite the decline of the Ottoman Empire, Constantinople retained considerable prestige as political, diplomatic and religious center throughout the century and Mount Athos was after all the center of Eastern Orthodox monasticism venerated by Orthodox believers ever since its founding in the tenth century. In the nineteenth century the scene on the Holy Mountain became increasingly complex as the Russian contingency on Athos grew in numbers and power. Russian presence on Athos reflected Russia's growing diplomatic presence in Constantinople. Indeed the "City" served as a sort of barometer of Russia's involvement in the Eastern Mediterranean and a transmitter of policies and instructions. What this paper proposes to do, however, is to outline some of the most important manifestations of Russian cultural policy in the Orthodox East, a policy frequently influenced from Constantinople as much as from St. Petersburg depending on the Russian representatives in the region. This presentation may also be viewed as a contribution toward understanding the culmination of a Russian policy which decidedly reversed an old tradition of cultural interaction in l.c. Which the Orthodox East presumed itself to be the contributing agent and Russia the receiver. During the nineteenth century, the empire of the tsars became indisputably the active contributor leaving its indelible political and cultural mark on the Orthodox East.

I like to refer to this neglected aspect of Russian involvement in the Orthodox East as "cultural diplomacy" which sought to supplement conventional Russian diplomacy at a time when the latter could not act aggressively in the Near East thanks to pressures from some European powers, especially Great Britain. My assessment of the situation is that Russian interests and policy in the Near East remained constant throughout the nineteenth century and one could argue that they remained central to imperial ambitions, despite deviations elsewhere such as Central Asia or the Far East. Articles in the Russian press at the beginning of the twentieth century underscored this constancy of Russian interests in the Near East. And as an article in *Novoe Vremia* (1901) put it: "What we want is the good of Slavdom and the entrance to the Black Sea: no Port Arthur, no Shan-hai Kwan, no Pei-ho can take [the] place of the Bosphorus".[3] I am not suggesting that Russian foreign policy irresponsibly pursued or even advocated the dismemberment of the Ottoman Empire as a solution to the Eastern Question. If anything, for ideological and practical reasons Russian policy on the whole was a conservative one, the Russophobia of European powers notwithstanding. But Russia insisted, indeed perceived itself as maintaining and expanding spheres of influence in the Near East or the Levant. To this end ideological and political objectives often converged and the Russian government was willing to make use of any cultural channels regardless of whether they were strictly speaking under the jurisdiction of the ministry of Foreign Affairs or its Asiatic Department.

Understandably, central to Russia's cultural diplomacy in the Orthodox East was "Orthodoxy" itself, an ingredient of long standing, providing a sense of community and agencies of contact between Orthodox groups -- Greek, Arab and Slavic, most of them under the jurisdiction of the Eastern Patriarchates. In a spiritual and cultural sense, this affinity or communion continues to our day. But in a political and ideological sense, Orthodoxy in the area felt the impact of the rise of nationalism or more precisely began to experience the emergence of the primacy of national identity over the religious one. Thus the Orthodox Arabs and the Bulgarians, to use only two outstanding and pertinent examples, began to think of themselves primarily as Arabs and Bulgarians rather than Orthodox owing allegiance to the Eastern patriarchs and their Greek cultural heritage. Meaningful as their common religious heritage was, during the nineteenth century, they all used it for nationalistic objectives with serious and irreversible repercussions for the unity of the Orthodox Commonwealth. Ironically, the process of this disintegration began in the 1830s when, following political independence, the modern Greek state claimed and acquired ecclesiastical "autocephalicity" from the Ecumenical Patriarchate.[4] The seriousness of this precedent was appreciated later in the century in the wake of nationalism among the other Balkan states, many of which demanded ecclesiastical autonomy even before acquiring political independence. In short, Orthodoxy no longer provided a common "political" bond. Instead it served to proliferate areas of conflict. This conflict was symbolized best in the struggle between Panhellenism and Panslavism, two conflicting ideologies and policies even though both were sustained by a great dose of Orthodox passion. As the modern Greek state began its efforts to fulfill the Great Idea by expanding its political frontiers, it inevitably clashed with Slavic aspirations. It is at this juncture of these two emerging rivalries by the Greeks and the Panslavs, both of whom invoked their own version of Byzantinism or Panbyzantinism that Russian policy in the area takes on meaning. For part of Russia's cultural policy developed as an expression of Panslavism, despite the misgivings with which the Russian government frequently received the latter.[5]

The first systematic attempt by the Russian government to supplement its diplomacy with the use of cultural channels occurred in 1841, soon after the signing of the London Convention for the Pacification of the Levant which, among other things, allowed the Treaty of Unkiar Iskelessi, and the exaggerated implications about Russian advantages in the Ottoman Empire to lapse. It was a realistic appraisal of the Eastern Question by the Russian Foreign Minister Nesselrode who did not want to aggravate the situation further by moves such as the one that led to Unkiar Iskelessi. He decided instead to dispatch an ecclesiastic, a "mysterious pilgrim" as he later came to be known, who would survey the situation in the Orthodox East and then write a report to be used for future action in the area. The responsibility for this mission fell on Konstantin Aleksandrovich, later Porfirii Uspenskii (1804-85), a graduate of St. Petersburg Ecclesiastical Academy (1825-29), an early Panslav and an avid student of

Eastern Orthodoxy, to which he dedicated his life. Made an Archimandrite in 1834 and after holding several posts as a teacher of theology, he was sent to Vienna in 1840 to be in charge of the Russian legation's church there. He was recalled a year and a half later and dispatched by Nesselrode to the Near East. He was selected on the basis of his knowledge of modern Greek and because of experience he gained while in the Austrian Empire of dealing with "foreign coreligionists".[6]

To understand the significance of Porfirii's mission to the Orthodox East, one should keep in mind the general political, religious, and economic rivalry which characterized the relations of the Great Powers in the Levant in general and in Syria and Palestine in particular during the forties of the last century. One should also keep in mind that after the 1839-40 Turko-Egyptian crisis, a sort of attempt at cultural imperialism replaced, in appearance at least, the old rivalry of the European powers. This cultural imperialism found expression in the establishment of the Anglo-Prussian Bishopric in Jerusalem (1841) and the revival of the Latin Patriarchate of Jerusalem in 1847. The establishment of the Russian Ecclesiastical Mission in Jerusalem the following year, then, should come as no surprise. As is known, the Catholics were expedient tools for French policy, the Protestants for the British and other Protestant nations, and naturally enough the Orthodox for the Russians. In connection with this, Porfirii's appointment by Nesselrode to investigate the Orthodox East takes on meaning as it formed part of the general diplomacy of Russia in the area. And even though Porfirii was never completely taken into the confidence of the Foreign Office, partly because of personality problems and partly because of clashes between the Holy Synod and the Foreign Office over broader questions about policy in the Orthodox East and Jerusalem, the Porfirii mission was as much political as it was religious and in the general context of Russia's Near Eastern policy for the rest of the century the results were far-reaching.

This is not the place to recount in detail Porfirii's first trip to the East which led to the founding of the First Russian Ecclesiastical Mission in Jerusalem. We are concerned here with his interest in the fate of Orthodoxy, as well as the use he suggested of making of the same. Most of his recommendations were not listened to by the

Foreign Office, but they nevertheless presaged future policy in the area.

For good reasons, the Foreign Office was very concerned about the reaction to the Porfirii mission and they tried to keep it secret. When accidentally the secrecy was uncloaked even before Porfirii left St. Petersburg, his instructions still stated that he was to perform faithfully and inconspicuously the duties of a pilgrim and definitely not to reveal to anybody that he was sent there by the Russian government. Although he was not supposed to commit himself in any way, he was to try to win the trust of the Eastern clergy and try to discover their real demands. Also he should evaluate the aims and attitudes of the Catholics, Armenians, and Protestants. He should especially try to gain the trust of the Arab clergy.

For purposes of this paper, Porfirii's first mission was significant because of the way he became involved in the affairs of the Eastern Churches, especially the Jerusalem Patriarchate, an involvement which led to an acrimonious alienation from the Greeks. The subject over which Porfirii and the Greek clergy became alienated from the start was the Orthodox Arabs of the Jerusalem Patriarchate. The Greek-dominated Brotherhood of the Holy Sepulcher, he maintained, exploited the Arabs whom Porfirii gradually came to identify with the Balkan Slavs, especially the Bulgarians whose cultural and political revival and independence he favored. The friction between the Greeks and Porfirii was further complicated by the fact that the latter was not a diplomat in any sense of the word,[7] but in fact was capable of uncontrollable outbursts presenting the Greeks in quite unfavorable colors, corrupt and unfit for their jobs. Unfortunately, some of the accusations were true, but many of them were the result of his excited imagination. But even those accusations which were true were often grossly exaggerated.[8]

Unconsciously in the beginning, but deliberately later on, Porfirii was responsible for inspiring an ethnic consciousness among the Arabs, leading to a special type of Arab nationalism striving for ecclesiastical independence from the Greeks. As his dislike and disgust for the Greek clergy increased through the years, Porfirii became convinced that the Greeks no longer could be considered spiritual leaders of the Orthodox world and he tried to exert influence in various crises over the election of the Eastern patriarchs. He also attempted to alienate the Alexandrine Patriarch from the Ecumenical Patriarchate and to bring the former as well as the Ethiopian Church under the aegis of the Russian Church.[9]

His impressions of the state of Orthodoxy in Syria and Palestine as well as the criticism of the Greek clergy, found expression not only in his diary but also in two memoranda which he submitted through the Russian Ambassador in Constantinople, Titov.[10] According to Porfirii, the Jerusalem Church was in danger of internal corruption and outside pressures. He felt that the Greek clergy, who also lacked theological education, were unable to counter the non-Orthodox missionary activity which was winning to its side the Arab Orthodox population. As in the case of his observations in the Austrian Empire, he was concerned most with the threat stemming from the French-protected Uniates.[11] He cites several cases of Orthodox families who were tempted into Uniatism through disillusionment with the Greek hierarchs or by the offer of French protection. The Anglicans under their newly appointed bishop were gradually wooing the Arab Orthodox from the splendor of the Orthodox service for more simple forms of worship and some of them inclined towards Protestantism.

In the same report, Porfirii made the following recommendations with regard to Russian action in the area. He first of all suggested a series of reforms in the Palestine Patriarchate but more importantly he suggested that a permanent Russian representation, an ecclesiastical mission under a bishop, be established in Jerusalem. Among other things, this establishment would stir the conscience of the Greek hierarchy. The mission would also endeavor to treat the Arabs with all respect, protect them from Turkish authorities, run a school for the education of native children and distribute Russian alms. He also suggested that Russian clergymen should study Arabic and translate Russian books and distribute them to people in Syria, Palestine and Egypt. Russia should establish philanthropic centers which would enable Russian clergy to win the confidence of the natives.

Thus, whereas he was asked to provide only information, Porfirii conceived it his duty to provide a plan of action and proceeded to win the support of influential people for his schemes. The details of his plans and Porfirii's behavior alientated many people both in the Ministry of Foreign Affairs and the Holy Synod. But he must have made an impression in certain circles, for in response to the establishment of the Anglo-Prussian Bishopric in Jerusalem as well as the reestablishment of the Latin Patriarchate in the same city, the Russians also decided to establish an ecclesiastical mission. Much to the surprise of many, the mission was to be headed by none other than Porfirii himself, who, however, was not promoted to the rank of bishop.

Despite the limitations set upon him by the Ministry of Foreign Affairs as was the case in 1843, Porfirii during his six-year stay in Jerusalem as head of the Mission[12] was in a position to espouse the Arab cause with fanaticism and, much to the frustration of the Greeks, he supported Arab clergy from funds of the Mission and also was instrumental in naming priests for several desolate Arab pastorates. He did inspire an ethnic consciousness in the Arabs, both clergy and laity, who loved him dearly. Even though he did not see many of his plans materialize, he left a basis of future policy. As a matter of fact, the second Russian Mission in Jerusalem (March 2, 1857) as well as the celebrated Russian Palestine Society (May 21, 1882) adopted and indeed perfected Porfirii's plans for action in Palestine and the Orthodox East.

The areas of conflict between Porfirii and the Greeks increased as the former traveled extensively throughout the Orthodox East. His travels in Egypt, Mount Sinai and especially Mount Athos, brought him increasingly under the constant suspicion of the Greeks. His habit of removing manuscripts from the monasteries caused many monks to refuse him access to the libraries, a refusal which irritated Porfirii to no end.[13] He wrote to the Russian Consul in Thessaloniki, Mustoksidi, requesting a special letter to the Greek monks to allow him access to the libraries.[14] While alienating and alienated by the Greeks, Porfirii became friendlier to the Slavic groups of monks who lived on Mount Athos and he was especially impressed by the Bulgarians who not only offered him excellent hospitality but who also opened the archives to the satisfaction of his curiosity. He was also impressed by their virtues and devotion to Russia and requested Mustoksidi to champion the venerable fathers in a dispute which went on between the monks and the inhabitants of the village of Ierissos and to help them as much as possible at the Turkish Tribunal in Salonica. He felt that through the

Bulgarians his reputation on Mount Athos would grow and thus accomplish the task which had been assigned to him in St. Petersburg. At Mount Athos, Porfirii's imagination about the future of Orthodoxy and Slavdom must have caught fire and needless to say reinforced his conviction that, as in Jerusalem, the Balkan Christians including the monks of Mount Athos were stifled by Greek ecclesiastical and cultural domination. And so gradually there crystallized in his mind a combined plan which would lead to the political and cultural liberation of the Orthodox Christians from the Turks and Greeks. Returning from Mount Athos to Constantinople, he noted in his diary, "A Turkish steamer brought me to Constantinople, the future Russian-Slav capital". And further in his diary he noted that he was in Hagia Sophia whose cupola approaches the sky and under which the Slavs and Russians will worship God.[15]

One must conclude that despite the controversy over the personality of Porfirii and his behavior in the East, his activity in the area made a tremendous impact on his messianic ideas and also he initiated a policy which the Russian Foreign Office in varying degrees kept under its watch until 1914. As Professor Kapterev put it, he opened a new era in the relations between Russia and the Jerusalem Patriarchate and hence the entire Orthodox East.[16] In this respect, Porfirii justifiably deserves the title of precursor of Russian ecclesiastical and cultural policy in the Near East in the nineteenth century.

The Porfirii Mission came to an end with the outbreak of the Crimean War. Elsewhere, I have suggested that the heads of the various ecclesiastical missions in Jerusalem contributed significantly to the outbreak of the Crimean War because of the exaggerated reports they sent home concerning religious and political involvement in the Holy Land. Porfirii shared fully in this collective responsibility and his behavior caused the Foreign Ministry, the Holy Synod and the Russian Ambassador in Constantinople grave concern. Still, the existence of the Mission proved its potential usefulness and its reopening in 1857 soon after the signing of the Treaty of Paris attests to that. The Treaty of Paris put severe restrictions of Russian action in the Levant. It even deprived Russia of the unique privilege it had enjoyed since 1774 of making representations on behalf of the Orthodox in the Ottoman Empire. It stood to reason that a cultural policy incorporating some of the ideas put forth by Porfirii in the 1840s would now make sense. Furthermore, there developed a growing awareness in Russia about the Christian East heightened partly by the Crimean confrontation but chiefly as a result of Russian travel and pilgrimages to the Holy Places. Russian travel accounts of the Christian East increased in popularity and contributed to this awareness. Thus between the Treaty of Paris and the outbreak of the 1877-78 Russo-Turkish War, Russian cultural diplomacy in the region expanded itself and took new dimensions.

As far as the Mission itself was concerned, its policy under its successive leaders Cyril Naumov, Leonid Kavelin and especially Antonin Kapustin deepened Russian involvement in local affairs.[17] With the status of its leader elevated to that of bishop, the Mission proceeded to acquire property, build churches and hostels for pilgrims and embark upon an educational policy for the Arab Orthodox as well as participate in archeological and other scholarly ventures in Jerusalem and the surrounding area. And as Russian clergymen and statesmen came to appreciate the opportunities afforded them through this cultural penetration of the region, they also realized how serious and obstructive to this penetration the traditional domineering position of the Greek element in the Christian East could be. Consequently, with some exceptions Russian policy during this period was by and large anti-Greek. It continued to manifest itself, of course, in Jerusalem, but it also surfaced on Sinai where among other things the issue over the fate of the *Codex Sinaiticus* became a matter of considerable concern.[18] It also began to develop on Mount Athos which until the middle of the century was relatively free of Greco-Russian rivalry and of course it rattled the Orthodox world over the issue of the creation of the Bulgarian Exarchate. It is important to keep in mind that during this period Russia was represented in Constantinople by the Ambassador N. P. Ignatiev, an ardent Panslav, who sought to advance Russian interests through precisely these cultural channels which he attempted to politicize. Admittedly, Ignatiev, too, irritated the Foreign Office with his excessive involvement but he demonstrated a matchless talent for instigating and for manipulating crises. And whereas in the beginning he complained that church matters hindered him, he soon realized that they provided a leverage he could not afford to ignore. From Constantinople he tried to influence matters under the jurisdiction of the four Patriarchates.

The interrelationship of these varied questions is best reflected in the correspondence of Ignatiev with the head of the Russian Ecclesiastical Mission in Jerusalem, Antonin Kapustin. Thus writing on March 4, 1870, he urged the latter:

> Accelerate your activities in Jerusalem; do your work thoughtfully and we shall win. If you do not have money, it is, of course, sad, but neither do they give me any money [for this purpose]; this however, in no way does it prevent me from pursuing my objectives relentlessly and continuously, putting my trust in nobody's help, because our own people in the North [he refers to the Russian Foreign Office] want only their peace and quiet, not being enamored with the Eastern problem.[19]

A year earlier on March 30, 1873, referring to the Ecumenical Patriarch Anthimos he confided: "I can secretly announce to you that Anthimos will be dethroned on Sunday and Joachim will succeed him". He is referring to Joachim II who later turned over to the Russians the Monastery of St. Panteleimon on Mount Athos, about which more later. And in July of the same year writes: "We have broken the back of Anthimos but through shrewdness he is holding on to a thread. I hope that we will be through [with this problem] in a few days".[20] Jumping to a problem affecting the Patriachate of Alexandria, he informed Kapustin: "We cannot take care of the affair of the church of Alexandria... Do not ask. It is worse when you are dealing with people of the cloth than with lay people... Neilos, despite his machinations did not 'manage' things in Egypt and we are forced to accept his being pushed away". (March 14, September 12, 1869)[21]. As far as the Jerusalem Patriarch Cyril was concerned, who found himself in difficulties with the other Greek Patriarchs because he did not join them in denouncing the creation of the Bulgarian Exarchate, Ignatiev asked his Jerusalem contact to inform Cyril that if "Sometimes the Embassy's policy saddens him it is simply to make him realize that without our help or consent he cannot possibly succeed in the future. Greeks are such people. It is possible to be their friends but this should not prevent you from keeping a stone in your belt. Is it not so?"[22] And with regard to the Sinai question he congratulated himself that he worked hard for the pacification of the rivalries between the contestants there. In connection with the same monastery - Sinai - he wrote, "It is necessary to get from the [leaders of the] Monastery of Sinai a certified document stating that the precious manuscript [the famous *Codex Sinaiticus*, taken by Tischendorf and presented to Alexander II] was sent by them as a gift to the Emperor. In exhange for it we could give 3-4 medallions of different orders, perhaps even ten to twelve thousand rubles". (March 8, 1868) In another letter he wrote: "I have the medallions with me but I do not intend to send them. I enjoy being obstructive otherwise you cannot succeed when you deal with obstinate people". (March 14, 1869) [23]

It is clear, however, that of major concern to Ignatiev were the repercussions over the Bulgarian Exarchate and its impact on the Jerusalem Patriarchate. In a letter on January 13, 1873 he conveyed his feelings in this way:

> The Bulgarian and Jerusalem question have caused me much grief and concern. This is especially true of the latter [the Jerusalem Question]. Until today I cannot understand how the whole Monastery [the Brotherhood of the Holy Sepulcher] managed to slip through our fingers. I anticipate that when the revolutionaries and troublemakers [the Brotherhood] rob the Jerusalem Treasury... they will then turn toward us begging for the abrogation of the confiscation by Russia of the [Jerusalem Patriarchate's] property in Bessarabia. I am anxiously awaiting for this moment in order to propose to the Holy Fathers the acceptance of certain preliminary conditions which will facilitate our position in Jerusalem by frustrating the imagination of the Greeks.[24]

Nothing illustrates Ignatiev's perception of the Greek presence in the Holy Land and his determination to put an end to that than a letter dated January 13, 1873.

> Because the Greeks insist that the Holy Places in Palestine are Greek property, it is imperative that we demonstrate to them that it is not to their advantage to apply racism to Jerusalem.

I have therefore written confidently to the Serbian Metropolitan and our own Georgian Exarch to search and find in their archives proof of claims by the Serbs and the Georgians on the Holy Places. I beg you warmly to help me in my research referring to the definition of equal rights of all the Orthodox nationalities over the Holy Places of Palestine and the absence of evidence concerning exclusive control by the Greeks. Whatever help you give me in connection with this I shall accept with gratitude and I will utilize it in time profitably... Remember that in this matter, I have a special method.[25]

And two months later in a telegram he urged: "Support as much as possible the Arabs; as far as the [Greek] monastery is concerned, do not defend it without my special order and do not transfer any money to them". And concerning the education of the Arabs he wrote:

I agree with you about the usefulness of the Arab gymnasium. I wrote that it is necessary to appropriate ten to twelve thousand rubles each year from the proceeds of the Holy Sepulcher properties presently under our control for the support of the Arabs; I am waiting for permission from Petersburg. (February 3, 1873)[26]

Needless to say, not everybody shared Ignatiev's extreme views about the Greeks and Hellenism. In fact Antonin Kapustin with whom he carried on his correspondence was in many ways the antithesis of Ignatiev's personality and was concerned about the strains under which Russian policy put the Greek hierarchy. But there was little choice in the matter especially as the Jerusalem Mission came increasingly under the control of the Foreign Ministry and especially under Ignatiev's influence. Ignatiev's activity among the Arab Orthodox through the Mission corresponded to the activities of the Slavonic Benevolent Committees in the Balkan Peninsula, including Mount Athos, among the Slavs. In both cases success of Russia's policy could be accomplished at considerable cost to Greek cultural and political hegemony. It was a complex policy which became even more so by the Balkan crises of the 1870s when the Russians discovered that encouraging nationalism in the Balkans and the Levant did not always serve Russian national interests. Frequently in fact such policy was counterproductive. But in the presence of growing European pressure against Russian overt diplomatic activities in the Near East following the Congress of Berlin (1878), ecclesiastical and other cultural channels could still be useful if handled efficiently and with more finesse than hitherto had been the case.

Russian cultural policy in the Near East reached its high point with the creation of the Orthodox Palestine Society in 1882 which also overshadowed the work of the Russian Ecclesiastical Mission in Jerusalem. For the sake of brevity, and since I have discussed the origins, organization and activities of the Society elsewhere, a brief report may suffice for our present purpose.[27]

The Orthodox Palestine Society, after 1889 known as the Imperial Orthodox Palestine Society, came into existence as a response to developments both inside and outside Russia. Nearly half a century of Russian religious, scholarly and philanthropic activity in the Orthodox East created an atmosphere of genuine interest in the region by a large section of Russian society from the Imperial family to the most humble peasants. Scholarly societies and the growth of Byzantine studies in the country encouraged inquiry into Russia's connection with the Orthodox East.[28] Add to that the flowering of Russian messianism reflected in the works of professional writers, publicists and conservative political activists (M. Katkov, F. Dostoevsky, N. Danilevsky, K. Leontiev, K. Pobedonostsev, not to mention N. P. Ignatiev), and which messianism referred to Constantinople and the East as constituting an indispensable cornerstone for Russia's political future and the atmosphere could not have been more ideal for the creation of the Palestine Society. But there were outside factocrs which made its founding desirable. Almost all Western countries, including the United States were represented in the Holy Land by active Palestine organizations or societies[29]. The founders of the Russian Palestine Society, especially its first secretary V. N. Khitrovo, had studied carefully this form of Western presence in the Eastern Mediterranean.

Thus the idea of a Russian Palestine Society was not difficult to sell to the Emperor or for that matter to the Ministry of Foreign Affairs.

The announced purpose of the Society enjoyed wide approval from the start. According to its constitution, it was:

...founded exclusively for scientific and charitable purposes for the attainment of which it endeavors: a) to collect, elaborate on and propagate in Russia news about the Holy Places of the East, b) to render assistance to Orthodox pilgrims to these places, and c) to found schools, hospitals, hostels and simultaneously render material aid to the native citizens, to churches, monasteries and clergy.

The Society performed admirably in all these fields despite inevitable problems resulting from excessive interference by the Ministry of Foreign Affairs and by several Panslavs who frequently sought to dominate and exploit the Society's prestigious accomplishments. It should be indicated that even though Constantinople remained the center of Russian high diplomatic representation from 1882 to 1914, Russian presence in the Orthodox East during the same period, from the Eastern Mediterranean to Mount Athos, including Constantinople, was often assessed in terms of the Society's activities and the energy of its representatives.

What then were its accomplishments: In the field of scholarship, scholars are certainly well-acquainted with the sixty-three volume project, the *Pravoslavnyi Palestinskii Sbornik (Orthodox Palestine Collection)* which is a landmark in Palestinology and Byzantology and a rich source for the study of Russian and Near Eastern culture. The same can be said about the Society's journal the *Soobshcheniia Imperatorskago Pravoslavnago Palestinskago Obshchestva (Bulletin of the Imperial Orthodox Palestine Society)* published from 1885 to 1925. Both of these publications engaged some of the leading Russian scholars on the Orthodox East. Equally important were the Society's popular publications which fell under the following categories: *Palestinskii Paterik (Palestine Patrologia), Chteniia o Sviatoi Zemle (Readings about the Holy Places), Besedy o Sviatoi Zemle (Sermons About the Holy Places),* and *Palestinskie Listki (Palestine Leaflets).*

Thousands of these inexpensive publications found their way into many households throughout the Russian Empire. There was, to be sure, a great deal of propagandistic publication mostly in the form of monographs about the mission of the Society and the future of Russia in the Orthodox East. This was especially true in the 1890s when the

Society's publication committee came under the influence of Panslavs, but it survived this trend and by and large the Society remained faithful to its scholarly objectives thanks to the initiative of such scholars as I.I. Sokolov and A.A. Dmitrievskii who dominated the scene at the turn of the century.[31]

Turning to the Society's activities concerning Russian pilgrims to Jerusalem and other places of the East, accomplishments were phenomenal. Thanks to Society efforts traveling costs were reduced to a fraction of what they were earlier, and in the Holy Land the Society built hostels, refectories, cisterns and other facilities totally lacking before. When the Society came into existence in 1882 approximately two thousand pilgrims visited the Holy Land annually.[32] By the outbreak of the First World War fifteen thousand Russians visited Jerusalem annually, a large majority being there on Easter Sunday. As Sir Harry Luke observed, "In pre-war days the Russian pilgrims constituted one of the most characteristic elements in Jerusalem life".[33] I should point out, however, that the scene was not drastically different in other Holy Places of the East, especially in Constantinople and on Mount Athos which most pilgrims included on their itineraries.

Disturbing as Russian activity in these two fields may have been to those who began to view the new phase of Russian presence in the East with misgivings, it was somehow tolerable, even justifiable. But the critics or antagonists of the Society, ranging from the local Greek hierarchy to representatives of foreign powers, reacted with alarm and hostility when the Society sought to fulfill its third objective: support of the native Orthodox population in the area. The latter was supported through the building of schools, hospitals, churches and through direct financial aid to native Arab prelates who gradually became less and less dependent on their Greek hierarchs. In the beginning, the Society's educational activity centered in Jerusalem. But as the polemics between Panslav and Panhellenists took a turn for the worse in the 1890s, and as individuals with Panslav proclivities dominated the Society's Council, hostility of the Greeks toward the Society increased also. As a result, in 1895 the Society transferred most of its educational activities to Syria, where the Patriarchate of Antioch extended it a warm welcome.

The transfer of Society activity to Syria crystallized the issues on which the Greeks viewed the Society with suspicion. In addition to building schools in the area, the Society supported the native Arab prelates against their Greek hierarchs with the result that the new Antioch Patriarchs, Meletios (1899) and Gregorios (1906), both of them Arabs, who ascended the Patriarchal throne thanks to Russian support through the Society. And through such cooperation with the Arabs, the Society increased its number of schools so that by the outbreak of World War I there were over one hundred schools supported by the Society in Syria and Palestine. So visible was the Russian presence in the region that many observers pondering on the fate of the Ottoman Empire intimated that "the most likely heir-apparent to the Sultan in Palestine was Nicholas II".[34]

As indicated earlier, Russian presence in Palestine radiated influence throughout the Orthodox East. Before concluding, I should say a few words about Russian policy on the Holy Mountain, thus justifying, partly at least, the title of this paper. In one respect Russian policy on Mount Athos after the Crimean War was similar to that in the Holy Land where it sought to reduce the influence of the Greeks by supporting the Arabs. On Mount Athos, the same policy objectives were pursued by supporting non-Greek monastic groups, especially Russian. The aggressive architect of this policy in both cases was the Russian Ambassador in Constantinople, N.P. Ignatiev, who during his tenure there visited Athos several times. The strategy was simple: increase the number of Russians in the sketes and monasteries where until the Crimean War the Russians either coexisted with Greek monks or lived under Greek administrative control; claim their right to first participate in and ultimately rule the places where their numbers were equal to or exceeded that of the Greeks; raise the status of Russian and other Slavic *kellia* to sketes and of sketes to monasteries. Having accomplished this they could be represented on the Governing Council of the Holy Mountain where their opinions would be voiced and where in collaboration with representatives of other non-Greek monasteries they could exert pressure on the Greeks and gradually reduce their power on the Mountain and beyond. The classical example of this takeover was the monastery of St. Panteleimon, also known as the Rossikon—the Russian. Before the Crimean War the few Russian monks were inundated by the Greeks. By 1869 the number of the Russian monks equalled that of the Greeks, by 1875 it passed to Russian control, and by the end of the century it surpassed the latter dramatically (1100 to 17). Many of the reasons which account for the growth of Russian presence in the Eastern Mediterranean account for this phenomenal growth on Mount Athos: scholarly interests, pilgrimages (including some high ranking visitors), and direct financial aid. There were two other factors. Athos was under the jurisdiction of the Ecumenical Patriarch residing in Constantinople and the Russian Ambassador there exercised great pressure on the Greek Patriarch to ask his coreligionists on Mount Athos to accept the increasing demands of the Russians in their attempts to emerge autonomous on the Mountain. The example of St. Panteleimon was repeated in other Russian establishments and even attempted at the monasteries of Koutloumousiou and of Iviron.[35] You may recall Ignatiev's correspondence with Kapustin on the subject of pressuring the Ecumenical Patriarch: "Secretly, I can announce to you that Anthimos will be dethroned and Joachim will succeed him". Ignatiev was happy with his accomplishments there: "On Mount Athos... I have been crowned with complete success. Not only Father Makarios is an hegoumen but all the monasteries in their turn are seeking after our good will".[36] In a rather comical statement he also informed Kapustin that when on a recent visit to Mount Athos, he anticipated opposition from the Greeks who tried to marshal the support of the British and German Consuls, he took with him to counter this move "the German and the American Ambassadors".[37] Thus by the outbreak of the First World War Russian possession of establishments on Mount Athos valued at fifty million rubles, consisted of one of the major twenty monasteries; two of the twelve sketes; thirty-one of the 204 cells dependent on the major monasteries and several huts *(kalyvas), kathismata* and *hesychastiria.* Numerically, out of a total population of nearly eight thousand the Russians were second only to the Greeks–1914 as opposed to 5331. More meaningful perhaps is the fact that whereas the Greeks constituted approximately 66 percent of the population of Mount Athos and the Russians only 24 percent, by counting the Roumanians (5 percent), the Bulgarians (3 percent), the Serbs (1 percent) and the Georgians (0.2 percent), they could offer sizable opposition to the Greeks especially when the Russians enjoyed the moral and financial support of their Ambassador in Constantinople, their Consul in Salonica and the Holy Synod in St. Petersburg.[38] Understandably, the Slavic groups had their differences as did the Russian group, internally threatened by the rise of independent, schismatic groups,[39] but the general impression of the Russian presence on Mount Athos was such that European observers viewed it as a veritable base which could be used for political and military objectives in the Aegean and on the Balkan Peninsula.

Statistically, it seems, the Greeks exaggerated the fears of a Russian takeover of the Holy Mountain. But Russian policy or attempts to influence the political status of the Mountain in 1912 when as a result of the Balkan Wars the Athos Peninsula was no longer under Turkish rule, did not help to allay Greek fears. The Greeks naturally had taken it for granted that the Mountain would be incorporated within the Greek state and they celebrated the event accordingly on Mount Athos. But their celebration was dampened by the news from London that Russia insisted that the Holy Mountain should not be part of the territories to be apportioned to victorious Balkan states. It should, instead, form politically and ecclesiastically an autonomous republic with the Ecumenical Patriarch as President, and continue under the existing system but with its territory as neutral. After considerable inquiries and debates during which the Russians discovered that they were not necessarily supported in this by other Balkan states represented on Mount Athos, the Russians put forth a plan that the Athos Peninsula should be neutral territory under the ecclesiastical jurisdiction of the Ecumenical Patriarchate and the protection of all Orthodox states. The proposals did not materialize, but they are indicative of Russian policy attempts to expand their sphere of influence in the area, a policy which prompted a British visitor to volunteer the metaphor that the two mountains, Athos and Golgotha, would support the axle around which Russian Eastern policy would revolve.[40]

The metaphor seems farfetched, even a bit unbalanced, and in view of what happened in 1917 irrelevant. But this whole phenomenon of Russian policy in Constantinople, Mount Athos, Syria and Palestine and by extension to the whole Orthodox East from the Crimean to the outbreak of the First World War does make some sense if it is viewed in the context of the objectives and expectations articulated during the First World War when the Entente Powers planned the future of Ottoman territories in a post-war settlement. Despite setbacks experienced by all Russian establishments in the Near East during the war, the latter also provided an opportunity for the possible fulfillment of some of the traditional Russian policy objectives in the area. This was especially evident in 1915 when Russian diplomacy faced success and the Russian Foreign Minister Sazonov extracted the consent of the Allies about Russia's claim to Constantinople and the Straits. In the summer of the following year Russia was also promised part of northeastern Asia Minor.[41]

The clamor for Constantinople, before the catastrophic deepening of the War, was not limited to politicians. It electrified a good many nationalist and Panslav or Neoslav groups reviving the old dream of Russian dominance in Constantinople. Such books as P. Kudriatsev's *Rossia i Tsargrad (Russia and Constantinople)* (Moscow, 1914) repeated ideas discussed by Tyutchev and Dostoevsky in the nineteenth century, as did S. Durylin's *Grad Sofii, Tsargrad i Sviataia Sofiia (The City of [St.] Sophia, Constantinople and St. Sophia)* (Moscow, 1915).

Sazonov also discussed Russian interests in Palestine with the Allies. He pointed out that Russia claimed no special rights or privileges "but merely wished to preserve the position she had attained in Palestine under Turkish rule, and, first and foremost, required that her pilgrims should be freely admitted to the Holy Land whatever regime might be established there". Sazonov reasoned that Russian interests could be best served through the channels and the prestige generated by the Palestine Society. And since according to the Secret Agreements Russia was to occupy Constantinople, he felt that here was no need for political control of Palestine.[42]

It should also be pointed out that while these negotiations were going on, Russian ecclesiastical authorities were discussing their plans for action in the Orthodox East in the event of Allied victory. To some ecclesiastics at any rate, it seemed that the Russian dream to absorb Mount Athos, the Ecumenical Patriarchate, and consequently, the entire Orthodox East was reaching fulfillment. One of the witnesses to these deliberations, the well-known Metropolitan Antonii Khrapovitskii furnishes the following description of the situation:

In the spring of 1915 the problem of Russia taking over the rule of Constantinople seemed likely to be realized in a few weeks. The Synod was asked for its opinion concerning the Church of Constantinople, and I was summoned from Kharkov to attend a private meeting on this matter. For over half an hour I tried to convince them that Constantinople should be returned to the Greeks and that the Byzantine Empire should be reconstituted, and Russia to take the Holy Land and a wide zone from Jaffa to the Southern Caucasus.[43]

Khrapovitskii's political acumen aside, his testimony underlines the convergence of Russian ecclesiastical and political objectives in the Orthodox East in pursuit of which a variety of cultural channels were used to supplement conventional diplomacy and *vice versa*. It also underscores the inevitable rivalry between Panslavs and Panhellenists which continued unabeted from just before the Crimean War to the First World War and beyond.

By way of conclusion, I would like to suggest that this whole involvement of Russia in the East in the nineteenth century provides an excellent case study of cultural diplomacy some aspects of which have been profitably employed by the Soviet Union in the same region. Finally, it also attests to the persistence of certain cultural realities, which, despite their having undergone profound changes, almost transformation, still bear the mark of their Byzantine or Eastern Orthodox origins with strong symbolic significance for the heirs of that tradition, be they Greeks or Slavs. As Alexandros Papadiamantis, the Saint of Greek letters or the Greek Dostoevsky as some would call him, put it (on the occasion of celebrating the 900th anniversary of the Great Lavra on Mount Athos in 1889) "The torrent which has descended upon us from the North has brought with it besides rubles, and political 'objectives', certain customs and ideas going all the way back to genuine Byzantine traditions."[44]

NOTES

1. Porfirii Uspenskii, *Kniga bytiia moego. Dnevniki i avtobiograficheskiia zapiski*, vol. III (St. Petersburg, 1869), p. 588 Afterward cited as *Kniga.*

2. During the last two decades, several goods monographs on Russian conservative

thinkers have shed considerable light on this question. The best overall account on the subject remains Edward G. Thaden, *Conservative Nationalism in Nineteenth-Century Russia* (Seattle: University of Washington Press, 1964), especially pp. 73-101; 164-82.

3. *Novoe Vremia,* April 1901, as quoted in Edgar Alexander, "Russian Messianism and the Middle East", in Ernest Jackh (ed.), *Background of the Middle East* (Ithaca, 1952), p. 138.

4. The literature on this topic is vast, especially in Greek. In English the best treatment is Charles A. Frazee, *The Orthodox Church and Independent Greece 1821-1852* (Cambridge University Press, 1969). See also Steven Runciman, *The Orthodox Churches and the Secular State* (Auckland University Press; Oxford University Press, 1971), pp. 68-69.

5. The role of Panslavism as a factor in Russian foreign policy has been exaggerated. The fact does remain, however, that it was an ever present irritant in the relations between Greeks and Slavs especially during the decades following the Crimean War. As for the Russian government, it soon discovered that it could exploit Panslavism when it suited political objectives. The Russian Foreign Office did not hesitate to make scapegoats out of Panslav adventurists.

6. Porfirii Uspenskii, *Materialy dlia biografiia Porfiriia Uspenskago,* vol. I (St. Petersburg, 1910), p. 8. Afterward cited as *Materialy.*

7. The best source for the study of Porfirii's personality, his dealings with the Greeks, as well as his general policy in the East is his own eight-volume published diary *Kniga bytiia moego. Dnevniki i avtobiograficheskiia zapiski* (St. Petersburg, 1894-1902). Understandably, there is quite a range of opinion about the personality and behavior of Porfirii as reflected in commentaries by contemporaries. See, for example, J. A. Finn, *Stirring Times 1853-1856,* Vol. I (London, 1878), p. 81.

8. Porfirri, *Kniga,* I (1894), p. 335, 373, 420; II (1895), p. 255 ff.

9. The efforts of Porfirii to bring the Ethiopian Church within the sphere of influence of the Russian church presaged future Russian action in the same direction during the second half of the nineteenth century. For this exotic enterprise, consult Czestaw Jesman, *The Russians in Ethiopia, An Essay in Futility* (London, 1958); Le Vicomte Jean Robert Constantin, *L' Archimandrite Paisi et l' Ataman Achinoff. Un Expedition Religieuse en Abyssine* (Paris, 1891); and Porfirii's illuminating work, *Aleksandriskaia Patriarkhia,* Kh. M. Loparev (ed.., vol. I (St. Petersburh, 1898), pp. 386-410.

10. Porfirii, *Materialy,* I, pp. 59-60.

11. Porfirii, *Kniga,* I, p. 271, 676; II, p. 74.

12. The outbreak of the Crimean War terminated his activities as head of the Mission, although he was to return to the area after the war presumably chiefly for scholarly reasons.

13. The reputation of Porfirii as a manuscript snatcher became proverbial. He is usually the first person that comes to mind when Greek scholars discuss the question of the disappearance of Greek manuscripts in the nineteenth century.

14. The Porfirii archives, presently housed in the Archives of the Academy of Sciences in Leningrad, reflect his scholarly interests in the Orthodox East. See Fond 118, No. 50, 11. 219-220 1/2.

15. Fond 118, No. 12, 1. 3 1/2.

16. Nikolai E. Kapterev, *Snosheniia Ierusalimskikh Patriarkhov s russkim pravitelstvom s poloviny XVI do serediny XIX stoletiia* (St. Petersburg, 1895-98), p. 808.

17. For a discussion of the Second Russian Mission in Jerusalem and the relevant bibliography see Theofanis George Stavrou, *Russian Interests in Palestine, 1882-1914. A Study of Religious and Educational Enterprise* (Thessaloniki, 1963), pp. 40-55.

18. See the fascinating account by Ihor Ševčenko, "New Documents on Constantine Tischendorf and the Codex Sinaiticus", *Scriptorium*, XVIII, 1 (Brussels, 1964), 55-80.

19. Meletios Metaxakis, *To Agion Oros kai i Rosiki Politiki en Anatoli* (Athens, 1913), p. 68. A series of documents dealing with Russian intrigues in the Orthodox East in the nineteenth century, which were originally published by Gregorios Papamichael in the journal of the Alexandria Patriarchate *Nea Sion* (1909) and later as a separate booklet under the title *Apokalypseis peri Rosikis Politikis en ti Orthodoxo Anatoli* (Alexandria, 1910). Metaxakis utilized the latter.

20. Metaxakis, *op. cit.*, p. 68; Papamichael, *op. cit.*, pp. 11-12.

21. Metaxakis, *op. cit.*, p. 68.

22. *Ibid.*

23. Metaxakis, *op. cit.*, p. 71.

24. *Ibid.*, Papamichael, *op. cit.*, 16.

25. Metaxakis, *op. cit.*, p. 72.

26. *Ibid*; Papamichael, *op. cit.*, p. 18ff.

27. I am referring to my study *Russian Interests in Palestine, 1882-1914,* already mentioned above. See also Derek Hopwood, *The Russian Presence in Syria and Palestine 1843-1914* (Oxford: Clarendon Press, 1969) which goes over the same material; and the brief account prepared by the Russian Ecclesiastical Mission in Jerusalem, *The Russian Presence in Palestine 1843-1970* (Jerusalem, 1970).

28. Stavrou, *op. cit.*, pp. 57-79.

29. *Ibid.*, pp. 62-63.

30. *Ustav Pravoslavnago Palestinskago obshchestva* (St. Petersburg, 1882), article one.

31. Stavrou, *op. cit.*, p. 208.

32. *Ibid.*, p. 209. A mark of the Society's success in this field can be seen in the growing number of travel accounts about the Christian East during the second half of the nineteenth century as compared with earlier periods. For a comparative picture of Russian travelers to the East, see the recently published bibliography on the subject by Theofanis G. Stavrou and Peter R. Weisensel, *Russian Travelers to the Christian East from the Twelfth to the Twentieth Century* (Columbus, Ohio: Slavica Publishers, Inc., 1986).

33. Sir Harry Luke, *An Eastern Chequerboard* (London, 1934), p. 196.

34. *Ibid.*, p. 282.

35. Papamichael, *op. cit.*, p. 88. For the manipulation of the so-called Georgian question, connected with the Monastery of Iviron, by the Russian representatives in the Near East, consult the thoroughly documented study by Antonios-Aemilios N. Tahiaou, *To Georgianikon zitima, 1868-1918. Symvoli eis tin istorian tis Rosikis Politikis en Agio Orei* (Thessaloniki, 1962).

36. Papamichael, *op. cit.*, pp. 86-87.

37. *Ibid.*, p. 87.

38. This was the inevitable consequence of a policy which alarmed the Greeks during the last quarter of the nineteenth century. The best evidence of this concern is to be found in a report submitted in 1887 by the Consul General of Greece in Thessaloniki, G. S. Dokos, to the Deputy Minister of Foreign Affairs Stefanos Dragoumis. Besides statistical information, the report concentrates on the activities of the Russians who sought to change the demographic physiognomy of the Holy Mountain. This extraordinary report consisting of 98 manuscript pages is located in the Historical Archive of the Greek Ministry of Foreign Affairs (AYE-/KY/1187/aak/φ.θ'). It was discovered by Professor Konstantinos K. Papoulidis who kindly made it available to me and gave me permission to mention it in this article. Presently, we are considering the possibility of publishing the entire report in a forthcoming issue of the *Modern Greek Studies Yearbook.*

It should also be pointed out that the successors to Ignatiev as Russian representatives in Constantinople from 1878 to 1918 (Lobanov-Rostovsky, Novikov, Nelidov, Zinoviev and Charicov) all of them became involved in ecclesiastical matters, especially those which had political consequences such as the Georgian Question on Mount Athos. They also were supportive of the scholarly and cultural activities of the Russian Archeological Institute in Constantinople under the able leadership of Feodor Uspenskii. For the activities of the Institute see the recent doctoral dissertation of Konstantinos K. Papoulidis, *To Rosiko Arhaiologiko Institouto Konstantinoupoleos, 1894-1914,* submitted to the Department of Theology, the Aristotelian University of Thessaloniki, 1984.

39. The most noticeable of these schismatic groups was the one connected with the name of A. K. Bulatovich and usually referred to by the common name of *Onomatolatrai* in Greek or *Imiabozhniki* in Russian. The movement started with Bulatovich in the Caucasus in 1907 and then moved to Mount Athos where, by 1912 it had made a tremendous impact among the Slavic, especially Russian communities on Mount Athos. In essence, the movement was hesychastic and received its name from invoking the name of Jesus repeatedly as indispensable for prayer, meditation and salvation. After considerable controversy, the movement went back to Russia with Bulatovich in 1913. Bulatovich died during the revolutionary period but the movement was again brought to western Europe by Orthodox theologians who left Russia after the revolution. See the useful study by Konstantinos A. Papoulidis, *Oi Rosoi Onomatolatrai tou Agiou Orous* (Thessaloniki, 1977), which also contains a rich bibliography on the subject.

40. *Ibid.*, p. 93.
41. Serge Sazonov, *Fateful Years, 1909-1916* (New York, 1928), pp. 257-58.
42. *Ibid.*, pp. 258-61.
43. Antonii Khrapovitskii, *Slovar k Tvoreniiam Dostoevskago* (Sofia, 1921), pp. 172-73.
44. *Ephimeris* (5.7.1889).

THE BYZANTINE LEGACY
IN EASTERN EUROPE
IN THE TWENTIETH CENTURY

THE BYZANTINE LEGACY
IN THE MODERN GREEK WORLD:
THE MEGALI IDEA

Richard Clogg

Shortly after the conclusion of the Crimean War which, for Greece, was a time both of intense national exaltation and of national humiliation, the economist Nassau Senior, a shrewd observer of the Ottoman and Greek worlds, recorded the following remarks of an Athenian Greek, a literary man whom he named simply as Zeta. "Do not think that we consider this corner of Greece as our country, or Athens as our capital, or the Parthenon as our national temple. The Parthenon belongs to an age and to a religion with which we have no sympathy. Our country is the vast territory of which Greek is the language, and the faith of the Orthodox Greek church is the religion. Our capital is Constantinople; our national temple is Santa Sophia, for nine hundred years the glory of Christendom. As long as that temple, that capital, and that territory are profaned and oppressed by Mussulmans, Greece would be disgraced if she were tranquil"[1]. This is as good a short definition as one could want of the *Megali Idea*, the Great Idea of uniting within the bounds of a single state all the areas of substantial Greek population in the Near East. This dream was to dominate the foreign relations and, indeed, to a large degree, the domestic politics of the Greek state during the first century or so of its independent existence. Moreover, as another acute observer of nineteenth century Greek society, Charles Tuckerman, the first United States minister in Greece, was to note, the *Megali Idea* was not a notion espoused by a small coterie of nationalist fanatics. Rather it permeated all classes of society[2]. The *Megali Idea* was not merely the dominant ideology of the nascent Greek state, it was in effect the *only* ideology.

The classic definition of the *Megali Idea* and, indeed, its first formulation at an official level was made in the course of a debate in the Constituent Assembly convened in 1844. This had been called together to promulgate the first constitution of independent Greece, in the wake of the pronunciamento of 3 September 1843 that had obliged the Bavarian King Otto finally to concede the constitution that had been provided for in the settlement by which Greece had emerged into theoretically independent statehood in the early 1830s. The speech was made by Ioannis Kolettis, himself, significantly, a Hellenised Vlach, who had acquired his early political experience as a doctor at the court of Tepedelenli Ali Pasa. It was delivered in the course of discussion as to whether a privileged status should be accorded to the *autochthons*, the natives of the lands that constituted the rump Greece that emerged from the protracted struggle for independence and which contained within its borders scarcely a third of the Greeks hitherto under Ottoman rule. For a considerable antagonism had developed during the first decade of Otto's reign between the *autochthons* and the *heterochthons*, the incomers from the lands still under Ottoman rule, whose frequently superior education and greater political experience had enabled them to acquire a disproportionate number of offices of state. One veteran of the war of independence, Yannis Makriyannis, had contemptuously dismissed these carpet-baggers as "the scum of Constantinople and of Europe[3]", who enjoyed fat ministerial salaries while the widows and orphans of the heroes of 1821 were reduced to begging for their daily bread in the streets of Athens. Kolettis, not suprisingly, perhaps, in view of his own background, was a staunch opponent of the granting of a special status to the *autochthons*. He regarded the members of the Constituent Assembly as "plenipotentiaries of the nation who had come together to reach decisions not merely about the fate of Greece, but of the Greek race"[4]. Some uncertainty still surrounds his precise words, but according to one widely quoted passage he declared that "the Greek kingdom is not the whole of Greece, but only a part, the smallest and poorest part. An *autochthon* is not only someone who lives within this kingdom, but also one who lives in Jannina, in Salonica, in Serres, in Adrianople, in Constantinople, in Trebizond, in Crete, in Samos and in any land associated with Greek history or the Greek race... The struggle did not begin in 1821; it began the day after the fall of Constantinople; the fighters were not simply those of 1821; the fighters were and are those who have continued the struggle against the crescent for 400 years"[5]. It is perhaps worth observing here that in 1840 Athens is estimated to have had a population of some 26,000, while the Greek population of Constantinople at that time was almost five times larger at 120,000[6].

Although it appears that Kolettis was the first to use the term *Megali Idea* with its modern meaning, similar sentiments had, of course, been expressed earlier. Neophytos Doukas, for instance, had declared in 1811 that "when I pronounce the sweet name of the Hellenes I do not mean only those few inhabiting the lands of ancient Greece, but simply the whole area in which the modern tongue of the Greeks is spoken...', 'Such', he maintained with the characteristic exaggeration of the romantic nationalist, 'are almost all those living between the Pruth and Nile Rivers'[7].

Moreover, Rigas Velestinlis, the proto-martyr of the struggle for Greek independence, although he never employed the term *Megali Idea*, essentially adumbrated a secularised version of it. He it was who was put to death by the Ottoman authorities in the fortress of Belgrade in the summer of 1798 in the wake of an abortive effort, in the words of an Austrian police inquiry, 'die Freyheit überall zu predigen und... die ganze Halbinsel mit Gewalt vom türkischen Joche zu befreyen'[8]. He advocated the re-establishment of what was essentially a restored Byzantine Empire, with republican institutions on the French model being substituted for the authority of a divinely ordained Emperor. As part of his revolutionary portfolio he had printed a map of "Ellas", in which the boundaries of Hellenism were set wide indeed and which did not fall all that far short of a Greek world extending from the Pruth to the Nile. He also elaborated a detailed constitution for this revived Greek Empire, "The New Political Constitution of the Inhabitants of Rumeli, Asia Minor, the Archipelago and the Danubian Principalities" (*Nea Politiki Dioikisis ton Katoikon tis Roumelis, tis Mikras Asias, ton Mesogeion Nison kai tis Vlakhobogdanias*). This provided for a complex hierarchy of representative institutions, with ultimate sovereignty residing in the people. According to article seven, 'the sovereign people comprise all the inhabitants of this Empire, without distinction of religion and speech, Greeks, Bulgarians, Albanians, Wallachians, Armenians, Turks and every other kind of race'[9]. Yet, elsewhere, he makes it clear that the official language of this Greek Republic (*Elliniki Dimokratia*) was to be the 'simple Greek tongue' (article 53), while Greek was to be the mandatory language of instruction (Declaration of the Rights of Man, article 22). Anyone who spoke either modern or ancient Greek ('even were he to live in the Antipodes') was to be both a Greek and a citizen. It has sometimes been suggested that Rigas was an early proponent of federalism among the Balkan peoples but his constitution very much envisaged a unitary state dominated by an elite that was Greek by culture if not necessarily by ethnic origin. Rigas' insistence that his proposed new Empire should be linguistically and culturally Greek, although not ethnically exclusive, is again a reflection of Byzantine practice. It is not surprising that his appeal to the non-Greek peoples of the Ottoman Empire should have been limited[10], just as efforts to create a pan-Balkan coalition against the Ottomans at the time of the outbreak of the Greek struggle for independence were likewise doomed to failure.

The views of the *megaloideates* (or proponents of the *Megali Idea*, a neologism introduced into the Greek language in 1886)[11] are sufficiently well known not to need rehearsal in any great detail here. Instead, I want to focus on a rather less well explored aspect of the *Megali Idea*, namely perceptions of the Great Idea at a popular level among the largely unlettered mass of the Greek people during the *Tourkokratia*, or period of Turkish rule, and after. At the outset I should enter the caveat that trying to penetrate the 'unspoken assumptions' of any society is a hazardous enterprise at the best of times, the more so in a society where literacy was limited. Nonetheless there exists a considerable corpus of evidence that demonstrates widespread credence, and not only among the unlettered, in a whole host of messianic and prophetic beliefs forecasting the ultimate liberation, as a result of Divine intervention, of the Greeks from the Hagaren yoke of the Ottomans and the restoration of 'their Race of Princes to the throne and possession of Constantinople'[12]. Prophetic and apocalyptic beliefs were, of course, widely disseminated during the

Byzantine Empire. It was generally believed, for instance, in the declining years of the Empire, that the end of the world would coincide with the end of the seventh millenium since Creation, which, in turn, was calculated as the year 1492. Such beliefs helped to enhance the spirit of fatalism with which many of the inhabitants of the pitiful rump of the Empire that remained awaited the end.

After the fall of Constantinople a whole corpus of legends and prophecies about the future resurrection of the Empire came into existence. There was the legend of the *Marmaromenos Vasilias,* of the Emperor turned into Marble. According to this, Constantine XI Palaiologos bravely fought alongside his troops in the defence of 'The City' until at last his horse was killed under him and he fell to the ground. A Turkish soldier, with sword in hand, was poised to cut him down when suddenly an angel of the Lord came down from heaven, seized the Emperor and took him to cave deep beneath the earth near the Khrysoporta, one of the gates of Constantinople. There he lay, turned into marble, awaiting the day when the angel would return to rouse him. Once re-awakened, and equipped with his old sword, the Emperor would expel the Turks from the Greek lands as far as the *Kokkini Milia* (Golden Apple Tree), the reputed birthplace of the Turks[13]. Then there were the miraculous fishes of the monastery of the Zoodokhos Pigi at Balikli, near the Silivri Kapi in the land walls of Constantinople. As the Turks were finally encircling 'The City', a monk was frying seven fish. He had fried them on one side and was about to turn them over when he was told that the Turks had taken 'The City'. 'The Turks will never take the City', he declared. 'I'll believe it when these fried fish come to life again'. Whereupon they leapt from the pan into a well, where they remain until the Greeks once again take 'The City'[14]. Another tradition recorded that when the Turkish invaders burst in upon the final liturgy in Aghia Sophia, the priest gathered up the chalice and fled through a door, which immediately closed upon him. Despite all their efforts the Turks were unable to break down the wall. For it was the will of God for the wall to open and for the priest to emerge to complete the liturgy in Aghia Sophia only when the Greeks would regain 'The City'[15].

The last liturgy in Aghia Sophia was also recalled in the most famous of the laments associated with the downfall of Constantinople.

This was the ballad known as The Taking of the City (*To parsimo tis Polis*). As the Liturgy was being chanted in the presence of the Emperor and of the Patriarch, an archangelic voice commanded that the Cherubic hymm cease and that the priests gather up the holy vessels 'for it was the will of God that the City should fall to the Turks'. It commanded that word be sent to *Frangia*, or the West, for three ships to come, one to take the cross, one the Gospel and one the Holy Altar: 'lest the (Turkish) dogs take it from us, and foul it'. The ballad concluded with the famous couplet:

> Hush, Virgin Lady, do not weep too many tears, Again with the passing of the years, in time, again they will be yours

(A number of rescensions of the text give as the final refrain 'again they will be ours' or 'ours once more''. Such an ending, of course, gives a more specifically nationalistic colouring to the ballad but makes no sense in the context). The marxist historian Yannis Kordatos has questioned the antiquity of this threnody but the reason that he advanced, namely that in the 15th century the Palaiologoi were despised as Latinizers is unconvincing[16].

One of the most widely disseminated of the prophecies concerned the *xanthon genos*, the fair haired race of liberators from the north, who were widely interpreted to be the Russians. George Wheler, travelling in the Greek lands towards the end of the 17th century, noted that:

> of all the Christian princes none was feared as greatly as the Grand Tsar of Muscovy, for he can easily mobilise great armies and enter the domains of the Grand Seigneur: but that which gives him the greatest advantage over the others is that he is the only Monarch of the Greek religion, and that undoubtedly the Greeks would be delighted to come under his domination, and that they would declare themselves in his favour if they saw him enter Turkey with a powerful army. Also I have heard several Greeks, among others sieur Manno Mannea, merchant of the city of Arta, a man of spirit and knowledge for this country say that there was a Prophet amongst them who foretold that the Empire of the Turk would be destroyed by a Chrysogenos Nation, that is

to say blonde, which can refer only to the Muscovites who are almost all blondes[17].

At much the same time Thomas Smith likewise recorded that 'a certain Prophecy, of no small Authority, runs in the minds of all the People, and has gained great credit and belief among them, that their Empire shall be ruined by a Northern Nation, which has white and yellowish Hair. The Interpretation is as various as their Fancy. Some fix this character on the Moscovites; and the poor *Greeks* flatter themselves that they are to be their Deliverers... Others look upon the Sweeds as the persons describ'd in the Prophecy'[18]. Paul Rycaut, the well-informed British consul in Smyrna between 1667 and 1677, reported that 'the *Greeks* have also an inclination to the *Moscovite* beyond any other Christian Prince, as being of their Rites and Religion, terming him their Emperor and Protector, from whom, according to the ancient Prophesies and modern Predictions, they expect delivery and freedom to their Church'[19].

Prophecies as to the downfall of the Ottoman Empire were current as early as the 16th century[20] and the legend of the *xanthon genos* appears to have enjoyed a wide currency throughout the period of the *Tourkokratia*, and was particularly in vogue during the course of the recurrent Russo-Turkish wars. It was certainly current on the eve of the Greek War of Independence. The Reverend Robert Walsh, chaplain to the British Embassy at Constantinople at the time of the outbreak of the struggle, for instance, noted that among the prophecies circulating among the Greeks was one to the effect that' "a race with yellow hair, along with their coadjutors, should overthrow Ishmael". All this, and more, a monk of the sacred Mount, Athos, put together, and solemnly proclaimed that it was predicted in Holy Writ that the Greeks should soon be liberated by the aid of the Russians'[21].

Among the most widely disseminated of the oracles during the period of the *Tourkokratia*, and one that was of explicit Byzantine origin, were those attributed to the Byzantine Emperor Leo the Wise. A graphic illustration of the credence attached to these is confirmed in an entry in the diary of Ioannis Pringos, a native of Zagora who had prospered mightily as a merchant in the great commercial centre of

Amsterdam during the eighteenth century. In the entry for 22 July 1771 he wrote that:

> Now should the prophecies of Leo the Wise be fulfilled, where he says 'Two eagles shall devour the snake'. These are the two insignia, or flags, of the Russian Empire- the double-headed eagle, the insignia of the Roman (Byzantine) Empire, and the snake is the Turk, who has wrapped himself around a corpse, that is to say the Empire of the Romans (Byzantines). Here Leo says, as they have interpreted, that the Turk shall remain for 320 years in the City (Constantinople). And it is 317 years from 1454 (sic) when they took The City until now, 1771. The Lord during these years has made it possible for them (the Russians) to throw the Turk out of Greece and out of Europe.

Later in the same entry he stated that the Turks in Constantinople had become fearful that the time had come for the fulfilment of the prophecies of the *seyids*, the descendants of the prophet, when they read that the Turks would be expelled to the *Kokkini Milia*, 'that is to say as far as the vault of heaven'[22]. The oracles of Leo the Wise circulated not only by word of mouth at this time but also in printed form. A section, for instance, of the fourth volume of a six volume History of Byzantium published in Venice in 1767 by Spyridon Papadopoulos was given over to Leo's *khrismoi*[23]. Moreover, a collection of prophecies about Constantinople, the 'New Rome', dedicated, significantly, to Alexei Mikhailovitch, the tsar of Russia, had been published a century or so before Papadopoulos' compilation. This was put together by Paisios Ligaridis, the metropolitan of Gaza and entitled *Khrismologion Konstantinoupoleos neas Romis, parokhimenon, enestos kai mellon, ek diaphoron syngrapheon syllekhthen kai synarmosthen para tou panierotatou kai sophotatou mitropolitou Gazis kyriou Paisou...* and published in Venice in 1656[24].

It is somewhat ironic that Pringos frequently should have been held up by historians as the very epitome of the progressive bourgeois merchant chafing under the arbitrariness of the Ottoman system of government and anxious to emancipate Greece from the Ottoman incubus so as to institute a state of law in which the opportunities for profit would be maximised[25]. Pringos was certainly interested in the maximisation of profit but was far from being the radical minded progressive it is sometimes argued. His thought world, indeed, as the passage quoted above indicates, remained quintessentially Byzantine. He placed no credence in dynamic action by the Greeks themselves to rid them of the yoke of the 'impious Hagaren', the 'bloodthirsty wolf, this insatiable animal' that was destroying Greece with an insufferable burden of impositions and taxes. Rather he trusted that God would impart to the 'Christian Kings', and more particularly to the tsars, a desire to overthrow the Ottoman yoke.

A more ambiguous case, which well illustrates the degree to which traditional and modern modes of thought could co-exist in the same person, is that of a Vlach from Metsovo, Nikolaos Zarzoulis (Nicolae Cercel). Zarzoulis studied for seven years in Western Europe, acquiring a sound knowledge of Latin, French and Italian. After directing the *Athoniada Skholi* on Mount Athos for a time in succession to Evgenios Voulgaris, he moved to Moldavia to undertake the direction of the Princely Academy until his death in 1772. He found nothing incongruent in translating works by Christian Wolff on arithmetic, geography and trigonometry, the experimental physics of the Newtonian Pieter van Musschenbrock and, indeed, a section of Newton's *Elements* and in compiling, in 1767, a *Brief Interpretation of the Oracles of Leo the Wise concerning the Resurrection of Constantinople*[26]. Moreover, further evidence of his attachment to the prophecies, if such were needed, is afforded by Kaisarios Dapontes' assertion that Zarzoulis did not put his name to the *Brief Interpretation* for fear of attracting Ottoman reprisals[27].

Pringos' hopes in the early 1770s for the imminent regeneration of Greece appear to have been widely shared although it is seldom that we are vouchsafed so explicit a reference as this to the apocalyptic beliefs that constituted so important an element in the collective mentality of the Greeks during the *Tourkokratia*. And, indeed, at the time that he was writing Leo the Wise's prophecy had a certain plausibility for, since 1768, Russia had been locked in a protracted war with the Ottoman Empire which was only resolved by the Treaty of Küçük Kaynarca of 1774. When peace came, however, without bringing any noticeable alleviation of the lot of the Orthodox populations of the

Empire, let alone the expulsion of the Turks to the *Kokkini Milia*, some Greeks abandoned hope that the Greek empire would ever be restored. The chronicler, Athanasios Komninos Ypsilantis, for instance, averred that by the time that the war had ended, there had been no resurrection of the 'Empire of the Romans' despite 'the prophecies of so many astronomers and wise and holy men' and the passing of 320 years since the Fall of Constantinople and the emergence of a grave Russian threat to the Ottoman Empire. It was clear, therefore, that the Lord had taken it upon himself to nullify the prophecies rather than to permit the rule of the unworthy. This he had done on account of the 'unrepentant immorality' and 'incorrigible pride' of the Emperors of Byzantium. 'The enslaved Jews would not have been liberated by the Lord if, sitting by the waters of Babylon, they had not wept, remembering Sion. If, therefore, in the time appointed by the prophecies, and after so many and splendid victories of the Muscovites against the Ottomans and if, at such an opportunity, the Romans (Greeks) were not liberated, then it will be very difficult for the resurrection of the Greek Empire to take place, for a prophecy to this effect by some or other seer does not survive'[28].

A contemporary of Athanasios Komninos Ypsilantis, Kaisarios Dapontes, shared Ypsilantis' pessimistic view that the Greeks could never hope for the resurrection of the 'Empire of the Romaioi'. Although it was written in the prophecies that the Empire would be revived three hundred and twenty years after the fall of Constantinople, during the six years of the Russo-Turkish war the Russians had approached and encircled 'The City', they had laid siege to it so as to take it, but they never did succeed in taking it. For this reason liberation would not in future be possible whatever means the Russians employed, or with whatever forces they brought down to the Crimea. 'Because even if it was assured in the oracles, God (and may God forgive me for daring to say so) forced by our sins, prevented and forestalled it, and it did not happen when it should have happened. He preferred to nullify the words of such wise and holy men and astrologers rather than that Emperors should reign who, in truth, are unworthy of this life. How, then, from now henceforth, is there a way for there to be a resurrection of the Roman Empire, when there is no further assurance, prophecy or oracle remaining? Neither Greeks nor

Russians will reign again in the City until the end of time'[29]. Dapontes expressed himself in agreement with the early eighteenth century divine, Anastasios Gordios, who, in his treatise 'About Mohammed and against the Latins' (*Peri tou Moameth kai kata Latinon*) averred that 'there will not be another Christian kingdom after the passing of the Turks', adding that the prophecies were 'untimely fantasies, the imaginings of men devoid of divine inspiration', which could not come true even if written by certain holy men. Among these last he included Saint John the Divine, whose Apocalypse had been interpreted as signifying that the Empire of the Turks would last for 130 years and would perish with the end of the world[30].

There were others who, like Gordios, poured scorn on the message enshrined in the prophecies. One such was Matthaios, a 17th century metropolitan of Myra, the author of a long history of 'Oungrovlakhia' in rhyming couplets, one passage in which reads:

We hope for the fair haired races to deliver us,
To come from Moscow, to deliver us.
We trust in the oracles, in the false prophecies,
And we waste our time in such vanities
We place our hope in the north wind
To take the snare of the Turk from upon us[31].

But while there is evidence that some, such as Athanasios Komninos Ypsilantis and Kaisarios Dapontes, in their bitter disappointment at the discouraging outcome for the Orthodox *pliroma* of the Russo-Turkish war of 1768-1774, regarded the prophecies as having been annulled as an indication of divine retribution for the manifest failings of the emperors of Byzantium, and that others, such as Anastasios Gordios and Matthaios of Myra, simply placed no credence in the corpus of prophetic beliefs, there seems little evidence of any general weakening in the attachment of the great mass of the Greek people to the prophecies during the decades before the outbreak of the Greek war of independence. Richard Chandler, the antiquarian who travelled extensively in the Greek lands on behalf of the Society of Dilettanti, recorded that, during the first year of his residence in the Levant (1764), a rumour had been current to the effect that a cross of shining light had been seen at Constantinople 'pendant in the air' over

Aghia Sophia. The Turks had been 'in consternation at the prodigy, and had endeavoured in vain to dissipate the vapour'. For the sign had been interpreted 'to portend the exaltation of the Christians above the Mohametans'.'By such arts as these are the wretched Greeks preserved from despondency, roused to expectation, and consoled beneath the yoke of bondage'[32]. Not all prophetic beliefs, it should be noted, forcast an eventual Greek triumph over the Hagaren yoke and the re-taking of 'The City'. In prophecies appended by the monk Dionysios of Phourna to an eighteenth century chronicle, he foretells that the annihilation of the entire world through fire would take place in 1772, followed a year later by the fearful Day of Judgement of the Second Coming of Christ. These apocalyptic events would be preceded in 1765 by a fearful war throughout all the world, followed in 1766 by the laying waste of Constantinople and, in 1767, by the sinking into the sea of England[33].

It was during the course of the 18th century that what appear to have been the most widely circulated prophetic works, those attributed to Agathangelos came into existence. These had purportedly been written in Sicily in 1279 and printed in Milan in 1555. They were, however, forgeries compiled towards the middle of the eighteenth century by the archimandrite Theoklitos Polyeidis, a native of Adrianople, who, for some years towards the middle of the century, was the priest of the Greek church in Tokay in Hungary and later (c. 1774) founded the Orthodox church established for the Greek mercantile community in Leipzig. His sojourn in the west doubtless explains the garbled references to the Kingdoms of Europe and, in particular, to Germany and its heretical religion with which the text is littered. Whereas the prophecy as to the overthrow of the Turkish yoke in 'The City' attributed to Leo the Wise is quite explicit, there is not much in the prophecies of Agathangelos to give comfort to the Greeks save for vague references to the discomfiture of the Hagarens and exhortations to Russia to awaken from her slumbers. The following is a characteristic example:

> The Fearful Century approaches the Golden Twelfth Number; afterwards milk and honey shall flow for ever. The storms abate, and for a full fifty years Peace reigns. Truth

triumphs. And the Heavens vouchsafe True Glory. The Orthodox faith is raised up, and it leaps from East to West, so as to be blessed. The Barbarians tremble, and all, fearful, flee rapidly, abandoning the Capital of the World. Then the Lord is blessed. And mankind beholds His Almighty works. May this be and thus it is. Amen.

The very vagueness and ambiguity of the *Optasia tou Agathangelou*, indeed, may have contributed to its popularity, for much, indeed almost anything, could thereby be read into the text[34]. Such, indeed, was the popularity of the prophecies of Agathangelos that it has been suggested that Rigas Velestinlis, whose revolutionary aspirations were explicitly influenced by the example of the French Revolution, saw in the almost universal subscription to the prophecies a useful adjunct to his advocacy of an armed uprising as the essential precondition for the overthrow of the Ottoman yoke and that he therefore undertook the printing of an edition of the prophecies of Agathangelos. Such an edition, whether or not printed under Rigas' auspices, was certainly printed in Vienna between 1791 and 1796 and appears to have been the first printed version[35], the prophecies hitherto having circulated widely in manuscript both before and after this time. The next printed version was published, significantly, during the War of Independence. As Ioannis Philimon, a contemporary historian of the war, informs us certain clever men, knowing the esteem in which Agathangelos' prophecies announcing 'the certain salvation of Greece from the Turks' were held by the people, arranged for its reprinting in Mesolonghi in 1824[36].

Certainly, we know that all kinds of apocalyptic beliefs and rumours were circulating at the time of the outbreak of the war of independence[37]. Indeed, a number of protagonists in the war on the Greek side record how they and the Greek people as a whole had been nurtured on the prophecies. Theodoros Kolokotronis, for instance, the former klephtic leader, recorded that the prophecies, with the *psaltirion*, the *okhtoikhos* and the *minaion*, formed the staple of his childhood reading. Another, Photakos Khrysanthopoulos, recalled in his memoirs that the Greek *raya* studied the prophecies of Agathangelos 'and found much nourishment and consolation therein'[38]. Vahit

Passa, the Ottoman governor of Chios, attributed the revolt in part to the fact that the Greeks had for long been persuaded and nurtured 'by certain very old and mythical prophecies of theirs... that the time for the liberation of the Greek nation (*Yunan milleti*)... had arrived[39]. A remarkable and rare testimony to the way in which Greeks not only subscribed to these apocalyptic beliefs but, for time to time, actually, proceeded to act on them is contained in a despatch of Francis Werry, the Levant Company's consul in Smyrna, and dated 2 June 1821, some three months after the outbreak of hostilities on the mainland. In this he reported that:

> ... This day, the festival of the Greek St. Constantine, the founder of Constantinople, has cost the lives of 16 Greeks shot in the Bazar, so very fanatic are these deluded people. They yesterday openly congratulated each other (the lower orders) on the approach of the morrow, as the day appointed by heaven to liberate them from the Ottoman yoke and to restore their Race of Princes to the throne and possession of Constantinople. The Turks who entered on their fast of Ramazan yesterday heard this, and began their fast in the evening with human sacrifices and I fear much it will be followed up...[40].

Moreover, even after the emergence of the independent Greek state, faith in the prophecies remained substantially undiminished. It is recorded, for instance, that there was a widely based belief, based on a reading of Agathangelos, throughout the new Kingdom that 1840 would see the complete regeneration of Greece: 'The formulas remained imprecise and enveloped in smoke-screens like those of Python, and they gave flight to imaginations. Some saw in it the regime of the Ionian Islands extended to all of Greece; the others, the Napists... interpreted in more grandiose terms... Greece, reunited to the Turkish empire under the government of a Greek, that is to say Orthodox, prince, for example, one of the sons of Tsar Nicholas'[41]. A few years later a Church of England divine, Dean Church, during the course of a visit to Athens in 1847 encountered a 'good deal of vapouring about war with Turkey, and approaching marriages and christenings were to be celebrated in Santa Sophia...'[42].

Inevitably, particular credence appears to have attached to prophetic beliefs at times of national crisis and exaltation. One such period was the time of the Balkan wars of 1912-13. It is recorded, for instance, that, at the battle of Sarantaporon in October 1912, Greek *evzones* witnessed 'with their very eyes' the *megalomartyrs*, Saints George and Dimitrios, mounted on horseback and moving ahead of the Greek forces and inducing blindness in their enemies[43]. The conjunction of Greece's startling successes during the Balkan wars, as a consequence of which the country's land area increased by almost 70 per cent, and her population from approximately 2,800,000 to 4,800,000, with the accession to the throne of a king with the emotive name of Constantine in March 1913, following the assassination of his father George I, led to a renewed outburst of apocalyptic fervour. It is recorded that, at the funeral of King George on 28 March 1913, the metropolitan of Athens, in the course of his funeral peroration, recalled the legend of the last liturgy held in Aghia Sophia, and its promise of a restoration of the Christian empire and addressed the new king in the following terms: 'Thou bearest the name of Constantine and art the heir of Constantine the Eleventh, the last Emperor of Constantinople'[44]. Another source recounts that 'an alleged mediaeval prophecy' to the effect that the 'City' of Constantinople would be wrested from the Turks and again become Greek when a King Constantine, wedded to a Queen Sophia, sat on the throne of Hellas, enjoyed a considerable vogue during the Balkan wars. It was widely, although in the event erroneously, expected that the new king would adopt the style of Constantine XII to indicate that he was the direct successor of the last emperor of Byzantium, Constantine XI Palaiologos. It was moreover, reported that, in advance of his coronation, the new king wrote after his name the initial B in imitation of Byzantine practice[45].

A few years later, Compton Mackenzie, the novelist who worked for British intelligence in Greece during the First World War, recorded a cafe conversation with a stranger in 1915. His interlocutor, a committed Venizelist, claimed that for the royalists the *Megali Idea* was nothing, for they did not want a greater Greece in which they would be swallowed up: 'What is Cavalla if we may win Smyrna and perhaps even *I Poli*?'[46] Likewise, Arnold Toynbee encountered among the

Greeks of the kingdom, during the critical summer of 1921 when the fortunes of the Greek armies in Asia Minor hung in the balance, expectations that, in the hundredth year after the beginning of the war of independence, the Great Idea would be fulfilled. 'Crudely coloured broadsheets of their King riding over the corpse of the Turkish dragon through the Golden Gate, with his namesake the last East Roman Emperor riding at his side, were passed from hand to hand, and the children were repeating doggerel prophecies'...[47].

Once Greece had achieved independent statehood in the early 1830s, even if this independence was substantially qualified in practice, the Greeks had before them other options than credence in the corpus of prophetic beliefs in securing the idela of the *Megali Idea*, which of their essence implied that the resurrection of the Byzantine Empire would come about as a result of divine intervention rather than human endeavour. Greece, as that noted scholar journalist William Miller once observed, might have the dimensions of a Switzerland but she also had 'the appetite of Russia'[48] and there were always noisy advocates of a military solution to the achievement of her irredentist ambitions. Among these were the eighty six officers who, on May Day 1894, wrecked the offices and printing presses of the newspaper *Acropolis* because the paper had expressed reservations about the army, the race and the *Megali Idea*. In a speech before the subsequent court-martial of the officers involved, it was argued for the defence that the officers, were 'the sword-wielding guardians of the *Megali Idea*, its most valuable military proponents. They have sworn by its bloodstained and martyred flag, because they have sworn (allegiance) to the Motherland. Motherland without *Megali Idea* cannot endure'[49].

Yet, whenever the Greek state and militant nationalists attempted to accomplish the *Megali Idea* through military means, as in 1854-57, 1885 and 1896-7 and in the various uprisings, to a greater or lesser degree inspired and encouraged by the government of the kingdom, in areas of the Greek lands under Ottoman rule, as in Thessaly in 1841 and 1854, in Epirus and Macedonia in 1853, and in the periodic revolts in favour of *enosis* with the Kingdom which shook the island of Crete in 1833, 1841, 1858, 1868-9, 1877-8, 1888-9 and 1896-7, the results were generally humiliating. Between 1854 and 1857, for instance, an Anglo-French occupation of the Piraeus was imposed to prevent

Greece from exploiting the discomfiture of the Ottoman Empire during the Crimean War. In 1885, Theodoros Deliyannis' mobilisation at the time of the Eastern Rumelian crisis was countered by a Great Power blockade, while in 1897, Greece's lightning defeat in the Greek-Turkish war of that year, resulted in the establishment of the International Financial Commission. The only actual accessions of territory to the Greek state during the course of the 19th century, the cession of the Ionian Islands in 1864 by Great Britain and of Thessaly and the Arta region of Epirus in 1881 by the Ottoman Porte, came about, not through military action, but rather through the mediation of the Great Powers. Only when Greece had digested the lessons of 1854-57, 1885 and 1896-7, namely that she could not hope to go it alone against the still not inconsiderable power of the Ottoman Empire, and allied herself in 1912-1913 with her Balkan neighbours in an albeit fragile and temporary alliance, was she able to add, and then very considerably, to her territories by military means.

While subscription to the ultimate end of the *Megali Idea* was well nigh universal in 19th and early 20th century Greece, there were always Greeks who criticised their country for, in effect, trying to run before she could walk. Alexandros Mavrokordatos, for instance, drew up in 1848 a memorandum that has been described as 'a masterful indictment of extreme irredentism and a persuasive presentation of the moderate stand'[50]. In this, he declared his opposition to sporadic border raids and to the establishment of secret societies with the purpose of forwarding irredentist aims. He held that the creation of the autocephalous Church of Greece and the breaking of historic ties with the Ecumenical Patriarchate in Constantinople, together with the exclusion of *heterochthons* from government service in the Kingdom, had unneccesarily alienated many Ottoman Greeks, relations with whom had been adversely affected by the failure to negotiate a commercial treaty with the Ottoman Empire. This, in turn, had led to Ottoman commercial reprisals. The internal chaos that characterised Greece had resulted in her being completely incapable of exploiting the Mehmet Ali crisis of 1840-41 to her own advantage. Moreover, the fledgling Greek state had not been able to demonstrate to the Ottoman Greeks that self-government had proved any more enlightened or efficient than Ottoman rule. In fact, the Greeks of the kingdom had been voting with their feet by emigrating in substantial numbers from the kingdom to the Ottoman Empire from the earliest years of the Greek state, a largely one-way traffic that was to continue throughout the 19th century. A.W. Kinglake reported such migrations as early as 1835, which seemed to him to show that, on balance, the Greeks preferred 'groaning under the Turkish yoke' to the honour of 'being the only true source of legitimate power in their own land'[51]. It is significant that, in 1859, for instance, there were some four and half thousand subjects of the Greek kingdom resident in Smyrna alone, more than the entire population at that time of Piraeus, the port of the Greek capital[52]. Mavrokordatos' first priority was the development of trade, the improvement of communications and the betterment of education. In effect he was arguing for political power to be wielded by the bureaucracy and the mercantile classes rather than by the traditional military class that customarily took the lead in irredentist agitation[53].

Moreover, in parallel with sporadic, government inspired revolts in Greek inhabited parts of the Ottoman Empire and a generalised bellicosity at times of particular crisis for the Ottoman Empire, strenuous efforts, particularly during the second half of the century were made to propagate by peaceful means the gospel of Hellenism among Orthodox populations substantial numbers of whom, in both European and Asiatic Turkey, were not Greek speaking. A substantial proportion of the Greeks of Asia Minor (including a significant minority of the Greek population of the Ottoman capital) were Turkish speaking. These Turcophone Greeks were known as *karamanlides* (Turkish *karamanlilar*), their written language as *karamanlidika* (Turkish *karamanlica*)[54]. There is little evidence that any substantial number of these Turcophone Greeks thought themselves to be Greek, or identified to any significant degree with the kingdom of Greece during the early part of the nineteenth century, or even during the latter half of the century, despite the vigorous efforts of schoolteachers, many of them of Anatolian origin, and trained at the University of Athens, one of the very few centres of higher education in the Greek world. Much of this educational and cultural propaganda was carried out, or sponsored by, societies known as *syllogoi*. Some of these were funded from official and private sources in the kingdom, others by well-to-do Ottoman Greeks or members of the wider Greek *diaspora*.

There were some twenty such *syllogoi* in Constantinople alone at the time of Congress of Berlin of 1878, the most important being the Greek Literary Society of Constantinople (*O en Konstantinoupolei Ellinikos Philologikos Syllogos*), which was responsible for some two hundred schools throughout the Empire[55]. Particularly active among the Greek populations of Asia Minor was the *Syllogos ton Mikrasiaton i Anatoli*. Founded in 1891,with the support of Greek banks, the University and municipality of Athens, and enjoying subsidies from the Greek state, the basic objective of *I Anatoli* was the education of young Greeks from Asia Minor, either in the university of Athens or in Greek theological colleges, or in one of the Greek schools and colleges of Constantinople and Smyrna. It was intended that the beneficiaries of these scholarships should then return to engage in the 're-hellenization' of their communities[56]. The resources of the Greek state, such as they were, were also harnessed to the cause of re-hellenization. In a circular letter of 22 May 1871, addressed by the Ministry of Foreign Affairs to the consuls of the Greek East, the prime minister of the day, Alexandros Koumoundouros, emphasized that the first duty of consular officials in their jurisdiction was to establish primary schools, with more advanced schools being set up wherever practical, and teachers educated in the kingdom being employed in the more important centres. The circular also called for the establishment of libraries, reading rooms and clubs[57].

These efforts at 're-hellenization' met with little challenge from the Ottoman authorities: in the words of Charles Tuckerman, the first American minister in Athens, the stream of the University of Athens was allowed to meander more or less unimpeded through the Greek provinces of Turkey, giving 'to no small portion of them all the intellectual freshness and growth they possess'[58]. Tuckerman astutely pointed out that, in addition to patriotic zeal, there was a further powerful incentive for Athens graduates to take up teaching appointments in the Turkish provinces, namely the chronic lack of employment opportunities in the kingdom. Abdolonyme Ubicini, in the mid-nineteenth century, wrote of Greek teachers within the Ottoman Empire 'haranguing from their professorial seats against the government, and openly making their lectures the vehicle of sedition'. In a number of Greek schools in the capital he had come across portraits of the Emperor of Russia opposite those of Christ[59].

After they had emerged, during the later 19th century, as the patrons of the Bulgarians, the great rivals of the Greeks in Macedonia, a rapid and general disenchantment with the Russians as potential liberators set in. In the early years of the present century, an elderly Greek, indeed, informed William Miller that Russia's reverses in the Russo-Japanese war were a divine judgement on the way in which the Greeks had been treated by the Russians[60]. It would appear that the Crimean War was the last occasion during which there was extensive faith in the Russians as the *xanthon genos*, the future liberators of Greece. Ottoman tolerance of this great outpouring of Greek educational and cultural propaganda is illustrated by the fact that it was only after disturbances at the Great School of the Nation (*Megali tou Genous Skholi*) at Kuruçeşme in 1849 that the Porte was to prohibit Greek nationals from teaching in any part of the Empire. This prohibition does not, however, seem to have been very vigorously enforced and subsequent measures such as the censorship of Greek books printed outside the confines of the Empire proved difficult to enforce. It was only in 1894 that the teaching of Turkish was made compulsory in all the schools of the Empire.

For all the energy put into the efforts at 're-hellenization' they appear to have met with relatively little success. One careful Greek observer, indeed, could write in the early 1890s that, among the Turkish speaking Anatolian Greeks of the interior of Asia Minor, there was not the least idea of Greece, of Athens, or of the Parthenon[61]. Not only did these educational endeavours meet with relatively little success in inculcating an awareness of Greek among the turcophone *karamanlides* but they proved incapable of stemming the transition from Greek to Turkish that occurred during the nineteenth century in a number of communities where the Greek language, albeit in a pronounced dialect, had survived[62]. One reason for the relative failure of these efforts at re-hellenization was the insistence of these teachers, nurtured in the University of Athens, at the very fount of Hellenism, on promoting extreme forms of the *katharevousa*, or purified, form of the language then fashionable in the kingdom. Georges Perrot, a French traveller in Asia Minor, noted that in the wake of the Athenian newspapers, books and schoolteachers despatched to the depths of

Anatolia, there arrived 'le pédantisme et le purisme'. For the idiosyncracies of local dialect had been substituted 'cette gauche et plate contrefaçon du grec ancien qui est maintenant de mode à Athènes'[63] Only in the first decade of the present century does it appear that the linguistic ideas of the champions of the demotic form of the Greek language penetrated the interior of Asia Minor[64].

Clearly, however, the Hellenic propaganda emanating from the kingdom had some impact, particularly in the sea ports of Asiatic Turkey where, in any case, there were almost always large concentrations of citizens of the kingdom who acted as a nationalist leaven among the Ottoman Greek population. There are many examples of nationalist manifestations on the part of Ottoman Greeks during the later nineteenth and early twentieth centuries which seem to have attracted few, if any, resprisals on the part of the Ottoman authorities. During the period of the Crimean War, for instance, a period of intense national exaltation and expectation among the Greeks, Madame de Steindl, the wife of the Austro-Hungarian consul-general in Smyrna, illuminated her house-apparently the finest in Smyrna-to celebrate the capture of Sebastopol, a move she thought politic in one of the major towns of the Ottoman Empire. She was fearful, however, that the Greeks were going to pull it down. 'During the whole war', she wrote, 'our Greeks were threatening an insurrection. None of them disguised their Russian sympathies'[65]. Pericles Triandaphyllidis, a schoolmaster from Pontos who had studied at the University of Athens, recorded a speech delivered to a Greek audience in Trebizond in 1865 to celebrate the accession of King George I of the Hellenes. It concluded with the stirring peroration: 'Come sovereign, the peoples of the East await you... and like... the Greek Alexander, implant civilization in barbarized Asia ...Long Live King George I of the Hellenes! Long Live the Greek Nation! Long Live the Protecting Powers!'[66] It is recorded that, at the time of the Greek-Turkish war of 1897, Greek clerks and employees left Constantinople for Greece, to fight under Greek colours, and then returned unmolested[67]. One British resident in Constantinople, Lady Dorina Neave, shortly after the outbreak of hostilities in the war of 1897, embarked on a Messageries Maritimes steamship in the Ottoman capital, bound for Smyrna. After sailing, the captain told Lady Neave that the ship was to make a detour to

Bandirma, a town on the sea of Marmara with a large Greek population, to pick up recruits for the Greek army. From there the ship was to sail first to Athens and only then to Smyrna[68].

When hundreds of Greeks, apparently Greek nationals, who had abandoned Mersin on the outbreak of the 1897 hostilities, began to flock back, the Ottoman authorities sought to require them to sign a document renouncing Greek nationality. The British consulate in the town afforded consular protection to those who refused and upheld the contention of the Greek minister to the Porte that, since the documents had been signed under duress, they had no validity[69]. In the aftermath of the Goudi coup of 1909, as Eleftherios Venizelos bent his efforts towards strengthening the country's armed forces, he could count on the open support of wealthy members of the Greek communities of Asia Minor. One British traveller, for instance, reported that rich Greeks in Samsun had subscribed the very substantial sum of £12000 for the re-equipping of the Greek navy, 'hoping dimly for the reconstitution of the Greek Empire with Constantinople for its capital'. While sitting in a Samsun café in 1911, he was openly approached by a boy with a collecting box who asked for a contribution in aid of the Hellenic navy. '"No, Monsieur", he added with Greek adroitness, finding me without hostility, "for the navy of all the Hellenic peoples"'[70]. It was reported, perhaps with some exaggeration, for its author was a noted Turcophil that at the time of the Balkan wars 'every Greek café in Pera shouted its song of triumph'[71]. As early as 1866, Namik Kemal, the Young Ottoman ideologue, complained of the impertinence of the Greeks of Constantinople who sang songs in their cafés which had 'as leitmotiv the extermination of the Turks'.[72]

The Greeks were essentially faced with two basic options in seeking to achieve the *Megali Idea* in the nineteenth century, the military option and a process of gradual infiltration from within so that they might hope to achieve some kind of dyarchy or condominium with the Ottomans in the governance of the Near East or, to use that evocative Greek phrase, '*i kath'imas Anatoli*' (our East). Variations on this last theme were espoused in the early years of the present century by Ion Dragoumis and Athanasios Souliotis-Nicolaidis. Souliotis-Nicolaidis, for instance, hoped that, just as once captive Greece had subdued her fierce Roman conqueror, so Greek civilization in modern times would dominate the East 'in all domains, commerce, industry, culture, sciences'[73]. But these notions of some kind of Eastern Federation between the Greeks and the Ottomans never amounted to anything more than matters for debate among intellectuals and Greece was, in the end, to choose the military option in seeking to implement the *Megali Idea*. Her successes during the Balkan wars lent credence to the widespread expectation that Greece would be able to regain many of the territories that had once composed the Byzantine Empire, and, in particular, Constantinople. In the initial stages of her entanglement in Asia Minor, in the aftermath of the First War and with the signing of the Treaty of Sèvres in 1920, it looked as though the Greece of the 'Two Continents and of the Five Seas' was truly within her grasp. The Greek landings in Asia Minor, in May 1919, however, were to act as the catalyst for a revived Turkish nationalism and with the *catastrophe*, as it is known in Greece, the defeat of the Greek forces at the hands of the Turkish nationalists, the age old dream of the *Megali Idea* was shattered. As a result of the ensuing exchange of populations, the boundaries of Hellenism, with the notable exception of Cyprus, became broadly contiguous with those of the Greek state. The *Megali Idea*, save to a handful of fanatics, was no more[74].

NOTES

1. Nassau W. Senior, *A journal kept in Turkey and Greece in the autumn of 1857 and the beginning of 1858* (London 1859) 358.
2. Charles K. Tuckerman, *The Greeks of today* (New York 1878) 120.
3. Yannis Makriyannis, *Apomnimonevmata* (Athens 1947) ii, 93, cited in John Anthony Petropulos, *Politics and statecraft in the kingdom of Greece 1833-1843* (Princeton 1968) 488. It is instructive to compare the anti-heterochthon sentiment of the early years of the independent state with the parallel nativist reaction on the part of the indigenous population against the massive refugee influx consequent on the Exchange of Populations with Turkey of 1923-24. Among other epithets, the refugees were derisively called '*giaourtovaptismenoi*', or baptised in yoghurt, a reference to the frequent use of yoghourt in Anatolian cuisine, George Mavrogordatos, *Stillborn republic: social coalitions and party strategies in Greece, 1922-1936* (Berkeley 1983) 194.
4. K. Th. Dimaras, *Tis megalis taftis ideas* (Athens 1970) 8.
5. Epaminondas Kyriakidis, *Istoria tou synkhronou Ellinismou 1832-1892* (Athens 1892) i 501, cited in Gerasimos Augustinos, *Consciousness and history: nationalist*

critics of Greek society 1897-1914 (New York 1977) 14.

6. Th. Veremis, 'Kratos kai ethnos stin Ellada: 1821-1912' in D.G. Tsaousis, ed., *Ellinismos-Ellinikotita. Ideologikoi kai viomatikoi axones tis neoellinikis koinonias* (Athens 1983) 63.

7. Neophytos Doukas cited in K. Th. Dimaras, 'I ideologiki ypodomi tou neou ellinikou kratous. I klironomia ton perasmenon, oi nees pragmatikotites, oi nees anagkes' in *Istoria tou Ellinikou ethnous*, xiii, *Neoteros Ellinismos apo 1833 os 1881* (Athens 1977) 458.

8. Emile Legrand, *Documents inédits concernant Rhigas Velestinlis...* (Paris 1892) 70.

9. For a partial English translation of Rigas' Constitution, Declaration of the Rights of Man and Revolutionary Proclamation, see Richard Clogg, *The movement for Greek independence 1770-1821: a collection of documents* (London 1976) 150-63.

10. Cf. A. Elian, 'Sur la circulation manuscrite des écrits politiques de Rhigas en Moldavie', *Revue Roumaine d' Histoire*, i (1962) 491.

11. Together with *megaloideatismos* ('Great Ideaism') (1894), Dimaras, op. cit., 22.

12. See below p. 266.

13. N. G. Politis, *Meletai peri tou viou kai tis glossis tou ellinikou laou. Paradoseis* (Athens 1904) i 22.

14. Ibid., i 21.

15. Ibid., i 23 and ii 678.

16. Yannis Kordatos, *I koinoniki simasia tis ellinikis epanastaseos* (reprinted Athens 1973) 55. On the 'laographic' significance of this ballad and its variants, see Michael Herzfeld, *Ours once more. Folklore, ideology, and the making of modern Greece* (Austin 1982) 130ff.

17. George Wheler and Jacob Spon, *A journey into Greece...*, (London 1682) 38, quoted in L.S. Stavrianos, *Balkan federation. A history of the movement towards Balkan unity in modern times* (Hamden, Conn., 1964) 7.

18. Quoted in F.W. Hasluck, 'The Crypto-Christians of Trebizond' in *Christianity and Islam under the Sultans* (Oxford 1929) 471.

19. Paul Rycaut, *The history of the present state of the Ottoman Empire...* (London 1682) 176.

20. *Stephan Gerlachs des aelteren Tage-Buch der... an die Ottomannische Pforte zu Constantinopel abgefertigten und durch David Ungnad... vollbrachter Gesandtschafft* (Frankfurt 1674) 102.

21. Robert Walsh, *A residence at Constantinople, during a period including the commencement, progress and termination of the Greek and Turkish revolutions* (London 1836) i 80. A variant of the prophecy appears to have existed among the Orthodox peasantry of southern Syria, who, in the early nineteenth century, believed that the hour was approaching when 'the Yellow King' *(al-malik al-asfar)* 'would take upon himself their and Syria's deliverance from the Muslim yoke', J.L. Burckhardt, *Travels in Syria and the Holy Land* (London 1822) 40, cited in Robert M. Haddad, *Syrian Christians in Muslim society. An interpretation* (Princeton 1970) 84. For millenarian ideas among the South Slavs see Traian Stoianovich, 'Les

structures millénaristes sud-slaves aux xviie et xviiie siècles', *Actes du Premier Congrès International des Etudes Balkaniques et Sud-Est Européenes*, iii (Sofia 1969) 809-19.

22. N.P. Andriotis, 'To khroniko tou Amsterdam', *Nea Estia*, x (1931) 914.

23. *Vivlos khroniki periekhousa tin istorian tis Vyzantidos metaphrastheisa... eis to koinon imeteron idioma, para Ioannou Stanou... kai epimelos diorthotheisa para... Spyridonos Papadopoulou...* (Venice 1767) iv, 470-87. On the oracles of Leo the Wise, see Emile Legrand, ed., *Les oracles de Léon le Sage* (Paris 1875) 7-50; Cyril Mango, 'The legend of Leo the Wise', *Zbornik Radova Vizantoloski Institut*, vi (1960) 59-93, Borje Knös, 'Les oracles de Leon le Sage (d' après un livre d' oracles byzantins récemment decouvert)', *Aphieroma sti mnimi Manoli Triandaphyllidi* (Athens 1960) 155-88; and A. Kominis, 'Paratiriseis eis tous khrismous Leontos tou Sophou', *Epetiris Etaireias Vyzantinon Spoudon*, xxx (1960) 398-412.

24. Cited in N.A. Veis, 'Peri tou istorimenou khrismologiou tis Kratikis Vivliothikis tou Verolinou (Codex Graecus fol. 62-297) kai tou thrylou tou "Marmaromenou Vasilia"', *Byzantinisch-Neugriechische Jahrbücher*, xiii (1937) 203-44 1st. Veis' article is richly informative on the subject of messianic beliefs during the *Tourkokratia*.

25. See, eg. L.S. Stavrianos, 'Antecedents to the Balkan revolutions of the nineteenth century' *Journal of Modern History*, xxix (1957) 342; Yannis Kordatos, *Rigas Pheraios kai i valkaniki omospondia* (reprinted Athens 1974) 28.

26. *Ermineia peri anastaseos Konstantinoupoleos syntomon eis tous khrismous Leontos tou Sophou.*

27. On Zarzoulis see Kh. S. Tsogas, 'Nikolaos Zarzoulis o ek Metsovou', in I.E. Anastasiou and A.G. Geromikhalou, eds., *Mnimi 1821* (Thessaloniki 1971) 129-42 and Ariadna Camariano-Cioran, *Les Academies Princières de Bucharest et de Jassy et leurs professeurs* (Thessaloniki 1974) 599-604.

28. Athanasios Komninos Ypsilantis, *Ekklisiastikon kai politikon ton eis dodeka vivlion... itoi ta meta tin Alosin (1453-1780)*, ed. G. Aphthonidis (Constantinople 1870) 534.

29. Kaisarios Dapontes, *Istorikos katalogos andron episimon (1700-1784)* in K.N. Sathas, ed., *Mesaioniki Vivliothiki*, iii (Venice 1872) 119-20. Cf. P.M. Kontoyiannis, *Oi Ellines kata ton proton epi Aikaterinis B. Rossotourkikon polemon 1768-1774* (Athens 1903) 375-77.

30. Asterios Argyriou, *Sur Mahomet et contre les Latins. Une oeuvre inédite d' Anastasios Gordios, religieux et professeur grec (xviie-xviiie siècles)* (thesis Strasbourg 1967) 81-2, 74, 34, quoted in A. Vakalopoulos, *Istoria tou Neou Ellinismou, iv (Tourkokratia) 1669-1812: I oikonomiki anodos kai o photismos tou genous* (Thessaloniki 1973) 317. See also Asterios Argyriou, *Les exégèses grecques de l' Apocalypse à l' epoque turque 1453-1821, esquisse d' une histoire des courants idéologiques au sein du peuple grec asservi* (Thessaloniki 1982).

31. Matthaios Myreon, 'Etera istoria ton kata tin Oungrovlakhian telesthenton', in Emile Legrand, *Bibliothèque grecque vulgaire* (Paris 1881) ii 314, cited in Veis, op., cit., 244 kth.

32. Richard Chandler, *Travels in Greece* (Oxford 1776) 137-8.

33. D.M. Sarros, 'Palaiographikos eranos', *O en Konstantinoupolei Ellinikos Philologikos Syllogos*, xxxiii (1914) 83.

34. The passage from Agathangelos is cited in Alexis Politis, 'I prosgrafomeni ston Riga proti ekdosi tou Agathangelou. To mono gnosto antitypo', *O Eranistis*, vii (1969) 192. On the prophecies of Agathangelos see Evlogios Kourilas Lavriotis, 'Theoklitos o Polyeidis kai to lefkoma aftou en Germania (ex anekdotou kodikos). O philellinismos ton Germanon', *Thrakika*, iii (1932) 84-149; iv (1933) 128-99; v (1934) 69-162 and Damianos Doikou, 'O Agathangelos os prophitikon apokalyptikon ergon kai to minyma tou' in I.E. Anastasiou and A.G. Geromikhalou, eds., *Mnimi 1821. Afieroma eis tin ethnikin palingenesian epi ti 150 epeteio* (Thessaloniki 1971) 95-126. Agathangelismos is still not wholly dead in the Greek world and it is recorded that in the aftermath of the Turkish invasion of Cyprus in 1974 some Greek Cypriots believed that the *graphomena* of Agathangelos foretold the liberation of their *khamenes patrides*, I.S. Yiannakou, *Folk-tale and its contribution to the survival of Hellenism during the Turkish period*, University of Birmingham MA thesis 1977, 75-6. See also Triandaphyllos S. Sklavenitis, 'Khrismologiko eikonographimeno monophyllo ton arkhon tou 18ou aiona', *Mnimon*, vii (1978-9) 46-59.

35. Politis, op. cit., 173-7.

36. Ioannis Philimon, *Dokimion istorikon peri tis Philikis Etairias* (Nafplion 1834) 67-8, cited in Politis, op. cit., 175.

37. Dennis Skiotis has argued, surely correctly, that it is within 'this context of a powerful millenarian tradition, further stimulated by the extraordinary political ferment occurring in Europe as a result of the Revolutionary and Napoleonic wars, that we should seek to understand and explain the Revolution of 1821' *'To Romaiko-* Greek consciousness under Ottoman rule', paper delivered at the Princeton Millet Conference June 1978.

38. Theodoros Kolokotronis, *Apomnimonevmata*, ed. T. Vournas (Athens n.d.) 70 and Photakos Khrysanthopoulos, *Apomnimonevmata peri tis Ellinikis epanastaseos* (Athens 1899) i, 35.

39. *Apomnimonevmata politika tou Vahid Pasa, presveos en Parisiois to 1802, Reis efendi to 1808, kai topotiritou tis Khiou to 1822. Ek anekdotou Tourkikou idiokheirographou eleftheros metaphrasthenta kai simeiosesi synodefthenta ypo D.E.D.* (Ermoupolis 1861) 52.

40. Richard Clogg, 'Smyrna in 1821: documents from the Levant Company archives in the Public Record Office', *Mikrasiatika Khronika*, xv (1972) 325-6.

41. Edouard Driault and Michel Lhéritier, *Histoire diplomatique de la Grèce de 1821 à nos jours* (Paris 1925-6) ii, 185-7, quoted in Petropulos, op. cit., 346.

42. Mary C. Church, ed., *Life and letters of Dean Church* (London 1897) 98.

43. A. Adamantiou, *I vyzantini Thessaloniki* (Athens 1914) 49ff, cited in Veis, op. cit., 244 iz. When Halley's Comet flashed across the skies in 1910 it was thought to point towards Macedonia and to be a portent of war, A.J.B. Wace and M.S.

Thompson, *The nomads of the Balkans. An account of life and customs among the Vlachs of northern Pindus* (London 1914) 13.

44. Reginald Rankin, *The inner history of the Balkan War* (London 1914) 386.

45. Lucy M.J. Garnett, *Greece of the Hellenes* (London 1914) 49-50. The prophecy relating to a restoration of the empire when a King Constantine was married to a Sophia was already in circulation by the 1890s, R.A.H. Bickford-Smith, *Greece under King George* (London 1893) 333-4.

46. Compton Mackenzie, *First Athenian memories* (London 1930) 52.

47. Arnold Toynbee, *The Western question in Greece and Turkey. A study in the contact of civilisations* (London 1922) 243. In July 1918 each Greek migrant in the United States was asked to donate one day's wages for the redemption of Smyrna and Constantinople, Theodore Saloutos, *The Greeks in the United States* (Cambridge, Mass. 1964) 172.

48. William Miller, *Greek life in town and country* (London 1905) 44.

49. Nikolaos Levidis, *Agorefsis enopion tou b diarkous stratodikeiou ti 24i Septem. 1894 etous, kata tin dikin ton 86 axiomatikon katigorithenton epi phthora tis ephimeridos Akropoleos, 1894*, quoted in Mario Vitti, *I ideologiki leitourgia tis Ellinikis ithographias 1850, 1855, 1870, 1880, 1883, 1896, 1936, 1943* (Athens 1974) 84.

50. Petropulos, op. cit., 510.

51. A.W. Kinglake, *Eothen, or traces of travel brought home from the East* (London 1844) 74. M.A. Ubicini, *Letters on Turkey* (London 1856) ii 18 recorded that between 1834 and 1836 some 60,000 Greeks had left the liberated areas to migrate to the Ottoman lands. Ubicini was told that 'in the Christian villages of Turkey we find a greater amount of prosperity and comfort than in those of Greece', quoted in L.S. Stavrianos, *The Balkans since 1453* (New York 1959) 296.

52. G.K. Typaldos, *Anatolikai epistolai. Smyrni, Aigyptos, Palaistin* (Athens 1859) 2.

53. Petropulos, op. cit., 510-11.

54. On these *karamanli* Christians, see, *inter alia*, Richard Clogg, 'Anadolu Hiristiyan karindaşlarimiz: the Turkish speaking Greeks of Asia Minor' to be published in the proceedings of the 1985 University of Melbourne conference on Hellenism and Neo-Hellenism: Problems of Identity.

55. Cf. Tatiana Stavrou, *O en Konstantinoupolei Ellinikos Philologikos Syllogos: to ypourgeion tou Alytrotou Ellinismou* (Athens 1967) passim. There is a useful outline of the history of the Constantinople Literary Society in the introduction to Paul Moraux, *Bibliothèque de la Société Turque d' Histoire. Catalogue des manuscrits grecs (Fonds du Syllogos)*, Türk Tarih Kurumu Yayinlarindan, xii seri no. 4 (Ankara 1964). See also S.I. Papadopoulos, 'Eisagogi stin istoria ton Ellinikon philekpaideftikon syllogon tis Othomanikis aftokratorias kata ton 19on kai 20on aiona' *Parnassos*, 2nd series, iv (1962) 247-58; Kyriaki Mamoni, 'Les associations pour la propagation de l' instruction grecque à Constantinople (1861-1922)', *Balkan Studies*, xvi (1975) 103-12 and Eleni Belia, 'I drastiriotis tou en Athinais Syllogou pros Diadosin ton Ellinikon Grammaton yper tou ellinismou tis Thrakis', *Athina*, lxxix (1974-1975) 85-94.

56. See eg., N.E. Milioris, 'O syllogos ton Mikrasiaton i "Anatoli"', *Mikrasiatika Khronika*, xii (1964) 348; Kyriaki Mamoni, 'To arkheio tou Mikrasiatikou syllogou "Anatoli"', *Mnimosyni*, vii (1978-1979) 123-50 and Matoula Kouroupou, 'Vivliographia entypon ton mikrasiatikon idrymaton kai syllogon 1846-1922', *Deltio Kentrou Mikrasiatikon Spoudon*, iii (1982) 149-83.

57. *O en Athinais pros Diadosin ton Ellinikon Grammaton Syllogos. Ekthesis ton pepragmenon apo tis systaseos aftou mekhri toude 17 April 1869-31 Dekemvriou 1871*, 122-31.

58. Charles K. Tuckerman, *The Greeks of today* (New York 1878) 155.

59. H.A. Ubicini, *Letters on Turkey* (London 1856) ii, 194-5.

60. Miller, op. cit., 46-7.

61. Ioakheim Valavanis, *Mikrasiatika* (Athens 1891) 2, 7.

62. There is Little evidence to indicate that the efforts of these educational missionaries resulted, as has been suggested, in Greek being revived in the remotest villages in Anatolia, Veremis, op. cit., 64. Still less is there evidence that fanatical nationalists were numbered among the turcophone Greeks of Asia Minor, Konstantinos Tsoukalas, *Exartisi kai anaparagogi. O koinonikos rolos ton ekpaideftikon mikhanismon stin Ellada (1830-1922)* (Athens 1977) 287.

63. Georges Perrot, *Souvenirs d' un voyage en Asie Mineure* (Paris 1864) 383-4. For an example of the problems occasioned by the insistence on the teaching of archaic forms of Greek among the bulgarophones of Macedonia, see a letter of Stratis Doukas, dated 1972, in Mesimvrinos, *I prodomeni glossa* (Athens 1974) 335-7. I am grateful to Dr Stathis Gauntlett of the University of Melbourne for this last reference.

64. Kh. Vaianou, 'O protos malliaros sto esoteriko tis Mikrasias', *Deltio tou Ekpaideftikou Omilou*, v (1915) 234-7.

65. Nassau Senior, op. cit., 209.

66. Periklis Triandaphyllidis, *I en Ponto Elliniki phyli, itoi ta Pontika* (Athens 1866) 17.

67. Aubrey Herbert, *Ben Kendim. A record of Eastern travel* (London nd) 273.

68. Dorina Neave, *Romance of the Bosphorus* (London nd) 96.

69. A.F. Townshend, *A military consul in Turkey. The experiences and impressions of a British representative in Asia Minor* (London 1910) 102.

70. W.J. Childs, *Across Asia Minor on foot* (Edinburgh 1917) 13.

71. Herbert, op. cit., 273.

72. 'Bir Mülâhaza', Tasvir-i Efkàr (1 October 1866), cited in Şerif Mardin, *The Genesis of Young Ottoman thought. A study in the modernization of Turkish political ideas* (Princeton 1962) 27.

73. A.J. Panayotopoulos, 'The "Great Idea" and the vision of Eastern Federation; a propos of the views of I. Dragoumis and A. Souliotis-Nicolaidis', *Balkan Studies*, xxi (1980) 335. See also Athanasios Souliotis-Nikolaidis, *Organosis Konstantinoupoleos*, ed., Thanos Veremis and Katerina Boura (Athens 1984).

74. The serious deterioration in relations between Greece and Turkey in recent years has led to a revival of suggestions in some quarters in Turkey that the Greeks still

hanker after the *Megali Idea.* In January 1975, for instance, the commander of the Turkish Second Army Corps was quoted in the Greek press as saying that 'the Greeks can never become friends to the Turks, unless they abandon the "Great Idea"', *Günaydin,* 25 January 1975, quoted in Khristos Z. Sazanidis, *Oi Ellinotourkikes skheseis stin pentaetia 1973-1978* (Thessaloniki 1979) i 444. It is interesting to note that Konstantinos Karamanlis, when prime minister, in the course of his drive for accelerated membership for Greece of the European Community, referred to Greek accession as the new *Megali Idea* of the Greeks, *Apologismos tis kyvernitikis drastiriotitos 1974-1977* (Athens 1977) 10.

RELATIONS BETWEEN CHURCH AND STATE IN CONTEMPORARY ROMANIA: ORTHODOXY, NATIONALISM, AND COMMUNISM

Stephen Fischer-Galati

Romanian historians have claimed, at least since the beginning of the twentieth century, that the Byzantine legacy in Eastern Europe has been most manifest in Moldavia and Wallachia and, by extension, in the history of Romania as a whole. In turn, Romanian political leaders–and particularly ruling princes, monarchs, and even communist heads of state–have made similar claims in their own behalf. "Byzantine" to them is not the equivalent of "devious" or "Levantine" but a legitimizing–perhaps the legitimizing–factor for the conduct of political affairs in a manner compatible with the Byzantine tradition and legacy of which they claim to be the executors.[1]

The elements of the Byzantine legacy and, for that matter, the entire nature thereof have, of course, been carefully selected and defined to suit the evolution of the history of the Romanians. The imperial tradition, the specific relations between church and state, the institutional framework were emphasized with reference to pre-nineteenth century Romanian history. The downplaying of the imperial tradition and the identification of Byzantine emperors as forerunners of modern Balkan nationalism became a necessity in explaining the history of the Romanians in the nineteenth and early twentieth centuries. Attribution to the emperors and patriarchs of enlightened political attitudes, albeit within the framework of the national interest, became more prevalent during the interwar years. De-Byzantinization was inevitable in the early years of the postwar Communist people's democracy especially since the arrogation of the Byzantine legacy by Stalin precluded similar action by leaders unidentifiable with the Romanian and/or the Byzantine historical legacies, such as Ana Pauker and her so-called Moscovite associates in Romania. However, after Stalin's death and the ensuing struggle for power not only in the Soviet Union but also in Romania, the anti-Moscovite, Romanian, faction of the Romanian Communist Party sought legitimacy first by claiming a "democratic" Romanian historic legacy and, after 1965, the totality of that legacy which nowadays is clearly and expressly identified with the Byzantine. It is fair to say that the present leader of Romania, Nicolae Ceauşescu, regards himself as the legitimate successor of the Dacian chieftain Burebista, of Justinian, of Basil Bulgarochthonous, of medieval Romanian princes and, in the last analysis, as the reincarnation of what a successful, modern, Byzantine emperor should be.[2]

It is indeed noteworthy that in recent years a renaissance in Byzantine studies has been recorded in Romania. Nicolae Iorga's *Byzance après Byzance,* -the original attempt at identification of the Byzantine legacy with the history of Romania–has been republished, with proper addenda and corrigenda, twice since 1970 and that other works, designed to equate the Byzantine tradition with the present order in Romania, are continuously published at a time when the cult of personality of President Ceauşescu has reached heights unsurpassed since Byzantine times.[3]

The various writings on "Byzantium and the Romanian Lands", regard the Byzantine legacy in Romania as the corner-stone of "defense of the national interest". In foreign affairs, it is characterized by "tenacious" resistance to external enemies (historically, against the Ottoman Turks) and, internally, by the consolidation and centralization of the power of the state for the defense of the interests of the people against both foreign and domestic enemies. The coincidence between the utterances of Romanian political leaders and propagandists and the writings of historians and other members of the intellectual and spiritual communities is by no means accidental. The election and instalation of President Ceauşescu to the Honorary Presidency of the Romanian Academy in July 1985 and the homilies and hosannas accompanying that event delivered, inter alia, by the Romanian Patriarch and upper clergy, provide the immediate framework for assessing the relations between chureh and state in contemporary, neo-Byzantine, Romania.

In its efforts to minimize the fundamental incompatibility between religion and atheism in general and between Orthodoxy and communism in Romania, in particular, the Romanian Patriarchate has expressed the official position of the Orthodox Church in recent issues of its journal *Biserica Ortodoxă Română* as follows:

"As the unifying force of the Romanian people the Romanian Orthodox Church, from its origins, has made common cause with the faithful in good times as well as in bad. By sharing the aspirations and achievements of the people the Romanian Orthodox Church has proven itself, throughout history, to be the mainstay of the people's legitimate rights. Wholly integrated in the people's life the Church has supported its quest for the attainment of the new man and the new society under the conditions prevailing after 23 August 1944. In supporting all actions designed to improve the people's well being, the Church continues to faithfully serve the people and shows that its road in none other than that of the people.[4]

President Ceaușescu's appreciation of the contribution of religious organizations to the construction of Romania is well known. This fact makes the servants of the Church and its faithful to, in turn, show the same devotion and the same traditional loyalty toward the fulfilment of their tasks and manifest endless love for and confidence in the leader of the Romanian people in all aspects of his activity.

In serving the people, who are urged to serve their country, the Church serves God".[5]

Such carefully phrased statements have led students of church and state relationships in contemporary Romania to widely different interpretations of the role of the Church in influencing the evolution of "Romania's road to communism" as devised by Nicolae Ceaușescu. Supporters of collaboration have emphasized the compatibility between the Church's historic attitudes toward the state–characterized by the Byzantine legacy of a "symphony" between secular and spiritual powers - and its long-standing commitment to nationalism, which has now become the theoretical "raison d' être" of the Ceaușescu regime.

They have also pointed out the state's need to view the Orthodox Church as a primary vehicle for the preservation of the national spirit and for persuading the faithful that the communists are the executors of Romania's historic legacy and that orthodoxy and communism can coexist during the construction, and even after the attainment, of the Romanian communist fatherland.[6]

Opponents of collaboration, in turn, are emphasizing the fundamental ideological and spiritual incompatibility between orthodoxy and communism, between church-supported historic Romanian nationalism and communist nationalism, between the social teachings of the church and communist practices, and condemn the Patriarchate for not using its spiritual influence with the overwhelmingly faithful and anti-communist masses in a manner comparable to that of the Catholic Church in Poland.[7]

There are merits to both arguments no matter how simple and seemingly contradictory they may appear to be. The issues, however, the somewhat more complex and less easy to define.

A few are self-evident. Thus, there can be little doubt that the present regime in Romania is trying to legitimize itself through the historic experience of the Romanian people rather than through Marxist-Leninist ideology. The history of the Romanian people is officially characterized as one of continuing struggle for the maintenance of a national identity, for political independence, and for social progress and equality - equated with communism. This historic struggle is assumed to be nearing completion under the leadership of the Romanian Communist Party and, specifically, that of President Ceauşescu "the greatest Romanian of all times".[8] Why then, may one ask, is there any need in this "Age of Ceauşescu" to recognize the historic role of the Orthodox Church in the struggle for independence, for the maintenance of a national identity, and even for social progress? The essential answer is simple: Because the overwhelming majority of the Romanian people rejects the claimed historic and political legitimacy of the Romanian communist regime and of Nicolae Ceauşescu. Whether the Romanians recognize the historic importance of the Orthodox Church as professed by nationalist communists or by other, pre-communist, Romanian nationalists is uncertain. What is certain, however, is that their orthodoxy is the repository of their hopes for spiritual and political salvation and that the Church has historically been the intermediary between the people and God. In fact, the political and social roles ascribed to the Orthodox Church by politicians, ideologues, intellectuals, and demagogues since the beginnings of political discourse in the various component parts of the Romanian state – in the eighteenth century – are by necessity, and by choice, idealized or denigrated depending on the ambitions, interests, or ideologies of individual writers or orators.[9]

Our skepticism is based on two separate considerations. The first is related to the misuse of history by Romanian nationalists and, the second, to the presumption that the Romanian Orthodox Church was a unitary body that unified the totality of the Romanian people's historic aspirations at least until 1944 (as assumed, of course, by anti-communists) if not to the "Age of Ceauşescu".

The historical myths, propounded and expounded by all subscribers to the theory that the history of the nations of Eastern Europe is a function of the triumph of nationalism over imperialism, would make us believe that the only concern of all Romanians at all times was the liberation of the people from foreign domination and oppression with a view to re-establishing the original, free, ancestral land of the Romanians–that of the Dacians of the age of Burebista and Decebalus. Moreover, throughout the course of Romanian history from Burebista to the monarchs of the late nineteenth and early twentieth centuries or to the dictators of the last half-century, the Romanians fought a "people's war" for national independence and social progress. Prior to the establishment of the unitary Romanian state in 1918, the leaders of these struggles were the ruling princes in the case of Wallachia and Moldavia, the intellectuals in the case of the Transylvanian Romanians and, of course, progressive patriotic nationalists–reformers of revolutionaries– from all strata of society. After 1918 the task of preserving the integrity of the Greater Romanian state was assumed by all political, intellectual, and spiritual leaders all, in their own way, defenders if not promoters of the historic legacy. The dismemberment, albeit temporary, of Greater Romania in 1940 was reversed by the valiant military effort of the Romanian people during World War II[10]

At this juncture, however, the historic fairy tale desintegrates as separate variants emerge. The official one expounded by Nicolae

Ceauşescu states that in August 1944 the Romanian Communist Party led the Romanian people in an armed uprising against Nazi Germany which, in turn, resulted in the restoration of Greater Romania and the attainment of the people's ultimate goal, communism.[11] An alternate version is that military action against Nazi Germany was decided on by the ruling monarch, King Michael I, supported by the traditionally democratic political organizations. These forces, however, were unable to attain the ultimate people's goal of a bourgeois democratic society in an independent Romania because of Romania's occupation by the Red Army and the ensuing installation by Stalin of a communist dictatorship.[12] A third variation, one propagated by the right wing Iron Guard, is essentially the same as the second except for its claiming that the historic goal of the Romanians was not bourgeois democracy but national Christian populism.[13] It is in the context of these readings of the history of the Romanians that the historic significance of the Orthodox Church must be analyzed.

The nationalist interpretation of the history of the Romanians is flawed in several major respects. First, it is absurd to argue that the primary purpose of the Romanians has been, throughout their history, the reestablishment of the unitary, national, state of their Dacian ancestors and making the supreme sacrifice in battle for the attainment of that goal. Second, it is equally absurd to argue that the ultimate socio-political goal of the Romanians was the establishment of a national-socialist order of the right or of the left or, for that matter, of a bourgeois democratic one. Finally, it is as erroneous to ascribe a decisive role to the Orthodox Church in promoting the attainment of the presumed ultimate goals of the Romanians as it is to exponents of other ideologies, doctrines, or dogmas.

This is not to deny the fact that nationalism was a significant factor in legitimizing political action resulting in the establishment of the Romanian national state or that the Orthodox Church played a significant role in Romanian political and social life over the centuries. It is, however, to suggest that the establishment of the Romanian national state was ultimately determined by the action of the European powers and that the role of the Orthodox Church in Romanian political and social life was markedly different from what it has been assumed or claimed to have been.

The history of the Romanians is ultimately the history of an enserfed peasantry and a small feudal aristocracy, occasionally native but mostly, if not foreign, at least subject to external pressures or to foreign suzerains.[14] In the core areas of the Romanian national state of the nineteenth century, in Wallachia and Moldavia, the dominant political forces were, internally, the Romanian boyars and lesser aristocracy and, externally, the Ottoman Turks, the Phanariot Greeks, the Russians, and the Austrians. In Transylvania, the third major component of the Greater Romanian state established in 1918, the political power was shared by the dominant Magyar feudal magnates, the German Saxon bourgeoisie, the Habsburg political establishment and, to a lesser degree, by the Romanian bourgeoisie and clergy. The common denominator of all political forces was the securing of their conflicting, or at least contradictory, positions by using the masses for their own purposes without, however, addressing the ultimate question of genuine political and socio-economic emancipation of the peasantry and corollary land reform. The upper hierarchy of the Orthodox Church was always politically active and, as a rule, supportive of the ruling establishments. In fact, in Wallachia and Moldavia the metropolitans and bishops were generally members of the upper aristocracy, and, as such, expressly identified with the ruling class, while in Transylvania they sought accommodation with the Habsburg monarchy in the common opposition to the prerogatives claimed and exercised by the Magyar and Saxon elites.[15] The political and social attitudes and actions of the upper clergy were thus determined by specific "objective conditions" which affected their rights, interests, and privileges. Inasmuch as the objective conditions invariably involved foreigners and external forces of a different religion and/or nationality it is fair to say that the upper clergy legitimized political and/or military action against enemies of the Christian faith such as the Ottoman Turks, Tatars, and Jews, against enemies of Romanian Orthodoxy such as Catholics and Protestants as well as Orthodox coreligionaries, such as Phanariot Greeks, when they were acting on behalf of the Turks or in a manner inimical to the interests of the Romanian Orthodox establishment, and even against fellow Romanians who compromised with the Catholic Church, such as the Uniates of Transylvania. It is also fair to say that if originally the upper

Orthodox hierarchy in Wallachia and Moldavia exerted its power by sanctifying actions against enemies of the faith and of Romanian Orthodoxy, it was at the forefront in identifying coreligionaries by nationality when Orthodox Greeks and Orthodox Russians sought to gain ascendancy over the political life of Wallachia and Moldavia in the eighteenth and nineteenth centuries. In that manner, then, the upper church hierarchy became closely identified with the national interest and with nationalism. This identification, however, was limited and often at variance with the political and social doctrines of the upper hierarchy of Transylvania and of the rural clergy and secular nationalist leaders in all Romanian-inhabited provinces.

The Orthodox establishment in Wallachia and Moldavia invariably espoused conservative causes designed to retain political power in the hands of the landed aristocracy. It favored union with Transylvania and other Romanian-inhabited provinces but only on condition that the political and religious leaders of Wallachia and Moldavia–the components of the Old Romanian Kingdom of the late nineteenth century–be also the leaders of a united Romania and, respectively, of the Romanian Orthodox Patriarchate. It had little use for the Romanian middle class and its political aspirations and paid only lip service to the peasantry's demands for land. In fact, it was supportive of the "neo-serfdom" which characterized the socio-economic and political structure of the Old Kingdom prior to World War I. As such it was largely disassociated from the village and from the rural intelligentsia–teachers and village priests–who favored abolition of all forms of agricultural servitude and distribution of land held by secular as well as religious estate owners to the peasantry. It was also suspicious of the Orthodox Church of Transylvania whose leaders, both spiritual and lay, were of peasant or middle class origin and who sought to secure socio-economic and legal equality for Romanian peasants working on estates owned by Magyar landlords. Of course,it regarded the Uniates as heretics and modernizers. It did, however, identify itself with the nationalist anti-Magyar and, to a lesser extent, anti-Saxon positions of the leaders of the Transylvanian Orthodox Church primarily because the irreconcilability of the nationalisms of the non-Romanian and of the Romanian populations of Transylvania seemed to augur well for the establishment of Greater Orthodox Romania.[16]

The essential differences between the political and socio-economic positions of the conservative, nationalist Romanian Orthodox establishment of the Old Kingdom, of the nationalist but progressive Romanian Orthodox leaders of Transylvania, and of the nationalist, but populist, rural intelligentsia and of the land hungry, and in a primitive sense, nationalist masses could be reconciled only superficially through advocacy and sanctification of a war of national liberation and integration of all Romanian-inhabited provinces into the unitary, historic, Greater Orthodox Romanian state. After 1918, however, the Orthodox church and orthodoxy itself faced serious crises and alterations corresponding to the crises of the new state.[17]

These crises ultimately focussed on the legitimacy, external and internal, of Greater Romania and its rulers. The territorial acquisitions at the end of World War I were contested by Communist Russia and revisionist Hungary and Bulgaria. The monopoly of power assumed by the Bucharest political establishment was challenged by the representatives of Romanians from the newly incorporated provinces, especially Transylvania. The attempted resolution of these conflicts by the Bucharest power elite through promotion of xenophobic nationalism directed primarily against the Russian Bolsheviks and Hungarian revionists, as well as their presumed agents the Jews and Hungarians of Romania, tended to placate the opposition during the years of relative prosperity antedating the Great Depression. It facilitated, however, the evolution of political ideologies and practices that were to challenge both the secular and religious establishments in the 1930s. Most dangerous in this respect was the virulently anti-Semitic Christian populism of the Legion of the Archangel Michael, the spiritual and political forerunner of the totalitarian Iron Guard.[18]

Originally an organization of Christian students and intellectuals of Moldavia directed against Jews and communists, the Legion gradually expanded its activities throughout Romania by appealing to the empoverished peasantry, to the restless youth, to nationalist intellectuals, to the exploited urban proletariat all in the name of a spiritual orthodox revival and political Christian crusade against the Jews and the presumably Judaized elements of the ruling elite.[19] The leaders of the Legion and of its political arm, the Iron Guard, were students and intellectuals of peasant origin, many enrolled in or graduated from orthodox theological seminaries, often sons of village priests, who enjoyed the support of much of the lower Romanian orthodox clergy. The national orthodox Christian crusade engendered by the legionaries sought a new social Christian order through the elimination of all Jewish and Judaized influences in Romanian life, partial redistribution of the national wealth, primarily through expropriation of Jewish property, and, ultimately, creation of a national Christian orthodox state. Although it threatened the stability of the ruling elite and of the upper church hierarchy, the legionary movement helped to enhance the power of the Orthodox Church as a whole since the monarchy sought the support of the Patriarch in combatting the challenge posed by radical Christian populism. By the late thirties King Carol II, supported by the then Patriarch of the Romanian Orthodox Church and Prime Minister, Miron Cristea, adopted much of the political theology of the legionaries.[20] The triumph of external revisionism, resulting in the temporary territorial dismemberment of Greater Romania through actions by the Soviet Union, Hungary, and Bulgaria, enhanced the power of the legionaries and, by extension, that of the Romanian Orthodox Church, as the National Legionary Christian Romanian state was formally established in October 1940 under the leadership of Marshal Ion Antonescu.[21] This event marked the zenith of the power of the Orthodox Church in Romanian history, of a church committed to the implementation of a Romanian Christian crusade against the historic enemies of Romanianism and Romanian Orthodoxy-the Russian Bolsheviks, the Hungarian revisionists, and their accomplices, the Jews.

The crusade failed, however, not because of lack of fervor on the part of Romanian combattants but because of military and political factors beyond the control of its leaders and supporters. However, as a phoenix, orthodoxy, if not immediately the Orthodox Church, rose from the ashes.

The return of northern Transylvania to Romania and the incorporation of the Uniate Church into the Romanian Orthodox, while welcomed by the Orthodox Church, did not compensate for the establishment of a Jewish-dominated communist regime in Romania after World War II. The primacy of the prime targets of Romanian nationalism–Jews, communists, and Judeo-Bolshevik Russia–together with the disastrous economic and social conditions prevalent in Romania during the Stalinist period made orthodoxy and the church the principal instruments of tacit resistance to the highly unpopular communist order. Orthodoxy became identified with Romania's cultural values and traditions and fundamental religious practices and rituals–baptisms, weddings, and above all prayer for deliverance from communism–assumed ever greater significance throughout Romania.

Because of conditions specific to the struggle for power between communist factions in Romania, the ethnic Romanian leaders bent on removing the Jewish-dominated, Moscovite, branch of the Romanian Communist Party, gradually assumed the role of continuator of the historic traditions of the Romanian people and, by the early 1960s, even that of executor of the historic legacy and aspirations of the Romanians.[22] In the process, as mentioned previously, the historic role of the Orthodox Church–subject, of course, to interpretations compatible with communist political interests–was recognized and, occasionally, even emphasized. These political maneuvers while leading to an overt revival of nationalist propaganda and manifestations directed, as in the past, primarily against Jews and Hungarians (but not Russians), did not lead to acceptance of communist ideology and practices by the Romanian population nor, for that matter, by a superficially cooperative Romanian Orthodox Church. If anything, national communism, in the process of becoming increasingly more national socialism of the left or, more accurately, left-wing fascism, revived the waning fortunes of the Iron Guardist legionaries and their sympathizers in the diaspora. It is indeed interesting and important to observe that right wing Romanian nationalists are still frequently led by orthodox clergymen, such as the notorious Bishop Valerian Trifa, that the churches of the diaspora are generally supportive of the traditional nationalist, anti-Semitic and anti-communist ideologies of Christian populism, and that compromises with the Bucharest Patriarchate are usually rejected out of hand.[23] But it is also important to note that the Patriarchate, acting on behalf of the Ceaușescu regime, has sought to win over the diaspora through the appointment of priests to several congregations abroad, through dissemination of political propaganda favoring the policies of Nicolae Ceaușescu which are represented as compatible with the interests of the Romanian people and, as such, with those of the Orthodox Church.

Nevertheless, as the Romanian President becomes more and more persuaded that "l' Etat c' est moi" he is bent on doing away with all what to him are relics of the pre-Ceauşescu era. This accounts largely for the razing of historic churches and monasteries, intensification of atheistic propaganda among the young, discouraging of religious activities–even of a ritualistic nature–by members, or prospective members, of the Communist Party.

The actions of the contemporary ruler of Romania are, ultimately, bound to fail if their ultimate purpose is substitution of communism for orthodoxy. Orthodoxy remains the most elemental force for the overwhelming majority of Romanians, whether nationalist or not, for overcoming adversity and for solace in times of trouble. The Romanian proverb *"apa trece, pietrele rǎmîn"* (The water flows but the stones stay behind) remains indicative of the resilience of the faithful. It is as characteristic of Romanian political philosophy as cooperation with the state is of the Romanian Orthodox Church. But we must not forget that the Church also happens to be a believer in Romanian folklore.

NOTES

1. See in particular Nicolae Iorga, *Byzance après Byzance: Continuation de l' histoire de la vie byzantine.* (Bucarest 1934); Mircea Musat and Ion Ardeleanu, *De la statul Geto-Dac la statul român unitar* [From the Getae-Dacian State to the Romanian Unitary State]. (Bucuresti, 1983); Adolf Armbruster, *La romanité des roumains: Histoire d' une idée.* (Bucarest, 1977).
2. *Ibid.* See also illustration.
3. Most important is the series *Etudes byzantines et post-byzantines,* published since 1979 under the auspices of the Romanian Academy of Social and Political Sciences.
4. *Biserica Ortodoxǎ Românǎ,* 101:1-2 (1983), pp. 8-14.
5. *Biserica Ortodoxǎ Românǎ,* 101:7-8 (1983), pp. 457-59.
6. Representative is the very positive assessment by Miranda Villiers, "The Romanian Orthodox Church Today", *Religion in Communist Lands,* 3 (May-June, 1973), pp. 4 ff.
7. Representative of opposing points of view is C. Michael Titus, *In Search of "Cultural Genocide"* (Essex, 1976), *passim.*
8. *Scinteia, passim.*
9. The most learned and objective statements are contained in the works of Keith Hitchens, *The Rumanian National Movement in Transylvania, 1780-1849* (Cambridge, Mass., 1969) and *Orthodoxy and Nationality* (Cambridge, Mass., 1977). See also his

study "The Orthodox Church and State", in Bohdan Bociurkiw and John Strong (eds.), *Religion and Atheism in the USSR and Eastern Europe* (Toronto, 1975), pp. 314-27.

10. See Stephen Fischer-Galati, "Myths in Romanian History", *East European Quarterly*, 15:3 (1981), pp. 324-34.

11. Ilie Ceauşescu (ed.), *War, Revolution, and Society in Romania: The Road to Independence* (Boulder, 1983), *passim*.

12. See especially Vlad Georgescu, *Istoria românilor de la origini pînǎ în zilele noastre* [The History of the Romanians From Its Origins to Our Days] (Los Angeles and Munich, 1984), 271-85.

13. Most informative is the material published in the "Information Bulletin of the Legionary Movement" –published in Spain under the title *Ţara si exilul* (The Fatherland and Exile).

14. See Henry L. Roberts, *Rumania: Political Problems of an Agrarian State* (New Haven, 1951), *passim*; Hugh Seton-Watson, *Eastern Europe Between the Wars, 1918-1941* (Cambridge, England, 1945), *passim*.

15. *Supra*, note 9. See also Stephen Fischer-Galati, "The Romanians in the Habsburg Monarchy, "*Austrian History Yearbook,* 3 (1978), pp. 430-49.

16. Trond Gilberg, "Religion and Nationalism in Romania", in Pedro Ramet (ed.), *Religion and Nationalism in Soviet and East European Politics* (Durham, 1984), 170-76; George R. Ursul, "From Political Freedom to Religious Independence: The Romanian Orthodox Church, 1877-1925", in Stephen Fischer-Galati, Radu R. Florescu, George R. Ursul (eds.), *Romania Between East and West* (Boulder, 1982), pp. 217-44; Stephen Fischer-Galati, "'Autocracy, Orthodoxy, Nationality' in the Twentieth Century: The Case of Romania", *East European Quarterly*, 18:1 (1984), pp. 25-34.

17. *Ibid.*

18. The most authoritative discussions will be found in the works of Eugen Weber, "Rumania", in Hans Rogger and Eugen Weber (eds.), *The European Right: A Historical Profile* (Berkeley and Los Angeles, 1966), pp. 501-74 and of Nicholas M. Nagy-Talavera, *The Green Shirts and the Others: A History of Fascism in Hungary and Rumania* (Stanford, 1970), *passim*.

19. *Ibid.* See also Gerald J. Bobango, *Religion and Politics: Bishop Valerian Trifa and His Times* (Boulder, 1981), *passim*; and Gheorghe Racoveanu, *Miscarea legionarǎ şi biserica* [The Legionary Movement and the Church] (Rome, 1973), *passim*.

20. Georgescu, *op. cit.,* pp. 250 ff.; Lucreţiu Pǎtrǎşcanu, *Sub trei dictaturi* [Under Three Dictatorships] (Bucureşti, 1945). See also Andreas Hillgruber, *Hitler, König Carol und Marschall Antonescu* (Wiesbaden, 1954).

21. *Ibid.*

22. Stephen Fischer-Galati, *Twentieth Century Rumania* (New York, 1970), pp. 128 ff.

23. Bobango, *op. cit.,* pp. 188 ff.; Irving Louis Horowitz et al., "Left Wing Fascism", *Society,* 18:4 (1981), pp. 19 ff.; 30-31; Daniel N. Nelson (ed.), *Romania in the 1980s* (Boulder, 1981).

CONTRIBUTORS

RICHARD CLOGG *King's College London*
DIMITRI E. CONOMOS *University of British Columbia*
ROBERT CROSKEY *Muhlenberg College*
SLOBODAN ĆURČIĆ *Princeton University*
STEPHEN FISCHER–GALATI *University of Colorado, Boulder*
GEORGE P. MAJESKA *University of Maryland, College Park*
JOHN MEYENDORFF *St. Vladimir's Orthodox Theological Seminary*
DECLAN MURPHY *The Kennan Institute for Advanced Russian Studies*
DIMITRI NASTASE *The National Hellenic Research Foundation*
THEOFANIS G. STAVROU *University of Minnesota*
GARY VIKAN *The Walters Art Gallery, Baltimore*
SPEROS VRYONIS JR. *University of California, Los Angeles*